HISTORY OF

TV WESTERNS

1960's & 1970's

By Grahame Stanford

Also by Grahame Stanford

Classic TV Trivia & Tidbits – 1950's to 1970's

Classic TV Trivia & Tidbits – 1950's TV Westerns

Academy Award Winners – A Quick Reference Guide 1928-2013

First Published in Australia in 2017

49 Muru Avenue Winmalee NSW 2777 Australia

ISBN 978-1-5206130-1-7

Contents

Hec Ramsey

Here Come the Brides

The High Chaparral

Hondo

How the West Was Won

The Iron Horse

Klondike

Kung Fu

Lancer

Laredo

The Legend of Jesse James

The Life and Times of Grizzly Adams

Little House on the Prairie

The Loner

A Man Called Shenandoah

The Monroes

Nichols

The Oregon Trail

The Outcasts

Outlaws

Overland Trail

Pistols 'n' Petticoats

The Quest

Rango

The Road West

The Rounders

Sara

Shane

Stagecoach West

Stoney Burke

The Tall Man

Tate

Temple Houston

The Travels of Jaimie McPheeters

Two Faces West

The Virginian

The Westerner

Whiplash

Whispering Smith

The Wide Country

The Wild Wild West

Wrangler

Young Dan'l Boone

Young Maverick

Introduction

Let's start off with a few statistics. In the 1950's there were 81 TV Western series on television. The popularity of Westerns continued into the 1960's where another 47 new Westerns were produced. However, by the 1970's there were only 17 new Westerns.

This eBook covers two decades - 1960's and 1970's. As mentioned above, during this period there were 64 new Westerns produced. Some were fleeting (only lasting one season) and others, such as "The Big Valley", "Daniel Boone", "The High Chaparral", "Little House on the Prairie" and "The Virginian", lasted multiple seasons.

As well as talking about the shows, I have included over 250 biographies of the principal characters.

I hope you enjoy this new book and don't forget if you want to check out the Westerns produced in the 1950's see my ebook "Classic TV Trivia & Tidbits – 1950's TV Westerns".

Grahame Stanford

"Alias Smith and Jones"

Years : 1971 - 1973

Episodes : 50 (3 seasons)

Cast :-

Peter Duel (b. 1940 d. 1971) - Played Hannibal Heyes (alias Joshua Smith)

Ben Murphy (b. 1942) - Played Jed 'Kid' Curry (alias Thaddeus Jones)

Roger Davis (b. 1939) – Played Narrator/Hannibal Heyes (alias Joshua Smith)

Synopsis :-
Story about two outlaw cousins trying to reform.

Trivia & Tidbits :-

"The Show"

- **"Alias Smith and Jones"** premiered on ABC on January 5, 1971 and last aired on January 13, 1973.

- The show ran for three seasons with a total of 50 episodes.
- The series was preceded by a made-for-TV movie called "The Young Country" (1970).
- "Alias Smith" was created by Glen A. Larson and produced by Universal TV and Universal/Public Arts Production.
- The theme music was composed by Billy Goldenberg.
- The series was inspired by the success of the movie "Butch Cassidy and the Sundance Kid" (1969).
- Actor Peter Duel committed suicide on December 31, 1971 and the show only lasted another 17 episodes before cancellation (actor Roger Davis had been brought in to fill the role of "Hannibal Heyes" after Peter's death).

"In Memoriam"

- **Peter Duel** committed suicide on December 31, 1971 (31) in Hollywood, California.

"The Stars"

- **Peter Duel** was born Peter Ellstrom Deuel on February 24, 1940 in Rochester, New York.
- Peter's father was a physician.
- He grew up in Penfield, New York and attended St. Lawrence University in Canton, where he majored in English.

- Peter then moved to New York City and landed a role in a touring production of the comedy "Take Her, She's Mine".
- In 1965, after moving to Hollywood, he was cast as "John Cooper" in the TV series "Gidget". He appeared in 22 episodes from 1965 to 1966.
- Then in 1966, he was cast as "David Willis" in the TV series "Love on a Rooftop" with Judy Carne ("Laugh-In"). He appeared in 30 episodes from 1966 to 1967.
- In 1971, he was cast as "Hannibal Heyes" (alias "Joshua Smith") in the TV series "Alias Smith and Jones". He appeared in 33 episodes from 1971 to 1972.
- Peter was the brother of Pamela Deuel (singer) and Geoffrey Deuel (actor). Geoffrey appeared in the film "Chisum" (1970) opposite the great John Wayne.
- In 1966, he was named the "Most Promising Male Star" in Quigley Publications' "Television Almanac".
- After becoming involved in politics, he campaigned for Democrat Eugene McCarthy in the 1968 presidential election race.
- Peter committed suicide (by gunshot) in December 1971, reportedly after consuming heavy amounts of alcohol.
- His film credits include "Diamond Jim: Skulduggery in Samantha" (1965) (TV), "The Hell With Heroes" (1968), "The Young Country" (1970) (TV) and "The Scarecrow" (1972) (TV).

- Peter's other TV credits include "Channing" (1963), "Combat!" (1964), "The Fugitive" (1965), "Ironside" (1968), "The Virginian" (1968-69) and "The Name of the Game" (1968-71).

- **Benjamin E. Murphy** was born on March 6, 1942 in Jonesboro, Arkansas.
- He grew up in Clarendon Hills, Illinois and was an alumnus of Benet Academy in Lisle, Illinois.
- After attending many colleges he decided to pursue an acting career.
- Ben made his uncredited acting debut in the film "The Graduate" (1967).
- In 1968, he was cast as "Joseph Sample" in the TV series "The Name of the Game". He appeared in 10 episodes from 1968 to 1970.
- Then in 1971, he was cast as "Jed 'Kid' Curry" (alias "Thaddeus Jones") in the TV series "Alias Smith and Jones". He appeared in 50 episodes from 1971 to 1973.
- In 1973, he appeared in the TV series "Griff" with Lorne Greene ("Bonanza").
- In 1976, he was cast as "Sam Casey" in the TV series "Gemini Man". He appeared in 12 episodes.
- In 1983, he appeared in 7 episodes of the TV mini-series "The Winds of War".
- Following this, he was cast as "Patrick Sean Flaherty" in the TV series "Lottery!" He appeared in 17 episodes from 1983 to 1984.
- In 1985, he was cast as "Paul Berrenger" in the TV series "Berrenger's". He appeared in 11 episodes.

- In 1988, he was cast as "Lieutenant Danko" in the TV series "Dirty Dozen: The Series". He appeared in 7 episodes.
- Ben is an avid tennis player and was once top seeded in Southern California.
- He was once apprenticed at the Pasadena Playhouse.
- Ben's other film credits include "Yours, Mine and Ours" (1968), "The Thousand Plane Raid" (1969), "Bridger" (1976) (TV), "Uncommon Valor" (1983) (TV), "Gidget's Summer Reunion" (1985) (TV) and "The Genesis Code" (2010).
- His other TV credits include "It Takes a Thief" (1968), "The Mod Squad" (1970), "Matt Houston" (1983), "The Love Boat" (1979-86), "In the Heat of the Night" (1991) and "Cold Case" (2006).

- **Roger Davis** was born Jon Roger Davis on April 5, 1939 in Louisville, Kentucky.
- He attended both Castle Heights Military Academy in Tennessee and Columbia University in New York.
- Roger made his TV acting debut as "Roger Gibson" in the TV series "The Gallant Men". He appeared in 26 episodes from 1962 to 1963.
- In 1963, he was cast as "Mike" in the TV series "Redigo" (this was the second season of the TV series "Empire", with a name change). He appeared in 10 episodes.

- In 1968, he appeared in the TV series "Dark Shadows". He played four different characters in 128 episodes from 1968 to 1970.
- In 1971, he was the "Narrator" (30 episodes) on the TV series "Alias Smith and Jones". In 1972, following the death of Peter Duel, he took over the role of "Hannibal Heyes". He appeared in 17 episodes before the show was canceled.
- His last acting appearance, to date, was in the film "Beyond the Pale" in 2000.
- Roger has been married four times – Jaclyn Smith (1968-75), Suzanne Irwin (1979-83), Alice LeGette (1985-88) and Donna Jenis (1991-present).
- As a voice artist, he has made over 6,000 commercials for TV and radio.
- Since his acting career, he has become a real estate developer and builder.
- Roger's other film credits include "PT 109" (1963) uncredited, "Ride the Wild Surf" (1964), "The Young Country" (1970)(TV), "House of Dark Shadows" (1970), "River of Gold" (1971)(TV), "Parachute to Paradise" (1972)(TV), "Killer Bees" (1974)(TV), "Flash and the Firecat" (1975), "Ruby" (1977), "The Act" (1984) and "Chameleons" (1989).
- His other TV credits include "Dr. Kildare" (1965), "The Big Valley" (1967), "Bonanza" (1966-71) 2 episodes, "Medical Center" (1971) 2 episodes, "McCloud" (1973), "Ironside" (1974), "The Bionic Woman" (1976), "Aspen" (1977) (mini-series) 3 episodes, "Galactica

1980" (1980) 2 episodes, "Matlock" (1989) and "Night Man" (1998).

"The Americans"

Years : 1961

Episodes : 17 (1 season)

Cast :-

Darryl Hickman (b. 1931) - Played Cpl. Ben Canfield

Richard Davalos (b. 1935 d. 2016) - Played Cpl. Jeff Canfield

John McIntire (b. 1907 d. 1991) - Played Pa Canfield

Synopsis :-
The American Civil War seen through the eyes of brothers on opposite sides of the conflict.

Trivia & Tidbits :-

"The Show"

- **"The Americans"** premiered on NBC on January 23, 1961 and last aired on May 15, 1961.
- The show ran for one season with a total of 17 black and white episodes.

- The series was inspired by James Warner Bellah's 1953 novel "The Valiant Virginians" which was serialized in the Saturday Evening Post as "Tales of the Valorous Virginians" from 1953 to 1954.
- NBC introduced the show as a mid-season replacement for the canceled series "Riverboat".
- In Australia and the U.K. the series was shown under the title of "The Blue and the Grey".
- Some of the writers on the series were John Gay, William D Gordon, Andy Lewis, Carey Wilber and Pat Falken Smith.
- The music was composed by Bernard Herrmann and Hugo Friedhofer.

"In Memoriam"

- **Richard Davalos** died on March 8, 2016 (85) in Burbank, California.
- **John McIntire** died of lung cancer and emphysema on January 30, 1991 (83) in Pasadena, California.

"The Stars"

- **Darryl Gerard Hickman** was born on July 28, 1931 in Hollywood, California.
- He gained fame as a child actor appearing in films such as "The Grapes of Wrath" (1940), "Men of Boys Town" (1941), "The Human Comedy" (1943), "Henry Aldrich, Boy Scout" (1944) and "Rhapsody in Blue" (1945).

- By the time he had reached the age of 21 he had appeared in over 100 motion pictures.
- In 1961, he was cast as "Cpl. Ben Canfield" in the TV series "The Americans". He appeared in 12 episodes.
- In 1983, he voiced the character "Wags" in the TV series "The Biskitts". The series lasted 13 episodes.
- In 1984, he voiced the character "Roadie" in the TV series "Pole Position". The series lasted 13 episodes.
- In 1951, Darryl abandoned Hollywood and joined a monastery, but was back making pictures after twelve months.
- Darryl's younger brother, Dwayne, played the title role of "Dobie Gillis" in the TV series "The Many Loves of Dobie Gillis". They appeared in two films together, "Captain Eddie" (1945) and "The Happy Years" (1950).
- He has been married twice - Pamela Lincoln (1959-82) and presently to Lynda Farmer Hickman. He had two children from his first marriage (his son Justin committed suicide in 1985).
- In 2007, his book titled "The Unconscious Actor: Out of Control, In Full Command" was published.
- Darryl's other film credits include "If I Were King" (1938) uncredited, "The Strange Love of Martha Ivers" (1946), "Submarine Command" (1951), "Southwest Passage" (1954), "Network" (1976) and "Aftermath" (1991) (TV).

- His other TV credits include "The Lone Ranger" (1951-53), "Annie Oakley" (1954), "Perry Mason" (1957), "Whirlybirds" (1957-59), "Gunsmoke" (1959), "The Many Loves of Dobie Gillis" (1959-60), "Disneyland" (1959-63), "Baywatch" (1996) and "The Nanny" (1997-99).

- **Richard Davalos** was born on November 5, 1930 in The Bronx, New York.
- He is of Finnish and Spanish descent.
- In 1953, Richard made his TV acting debut in the TV series "Goodyear Television Playhouse".
- In 1955, he won the "Theatre World Award" for his performance in the Arthur Miller play "A Memory of Two Mondays".
- In 1961, he was cast as "Cpl. Jeff Canfield" in the TV series "The Americans". He appeared in 11 episodes.
- He appears on the album cover of The Smiths' "Strangeways, Here We Come".
- Richard is the father of Elyssa Davalos (actress) and Dominique Davalos (musician).
- His film credits include "East of Eden" (1955), "The Sea Chase" (1955), "All the Young Men" (1960), "Cool Hand Luke" (1967), "The Quest: The Longest Drive" (1976) (TV), "Death Hunt" (1981) and "Ninja Cheerleaders" (2008).
- Richard's other TV credits include "West Point" (1957), "Bonanza" (1960), "Laramie" (1961), "Rawhide" (1965), "Mannix" (1969), "Hawaii Five-O" (1977), "The Fall Guy" (1983) and "Murder, She Wrote" (1990).

- **John Herrick McIntire** was born on June 27, 1907 in Spokane, Washington.
- He grew up in Montana where he learned to raise and ride broncos on the family homestead.
- John was married to fellow actor Jeanette Nolan. They had two children, Tim and Holly, who were also actors. Sadly, Tim passed away at age 41 years in 1986 of heart problems.
- After two years at the University of Southern California and a stint at sea, John chose the entertainment industry as a vocation.
- As a radio announcer, he gained quite a following announcing on the "March of Time" broadcasts.
- In the 1950's, he played in a number of Western films such as "Winchester '73" (1950), "The Far Country" (1954) and "The Tin Star" (1957).
- In 1958, he was cast as "Lt. Dan Muldoon" in the TV series "Naked City". He appeared in 25 episodes from 1958 to 1959.
- In 1960, he was cast as "Christopher Hale" (after Ward Bond had passed away) in the TV series "Wagon Train". He appeared in 151 episodes from 1960 to 1965.
- Then in 1961, he was cast as "Pa Canfield" in the TV series "The Americans". He appeared in 5 episodes.
- In 1967, he was cast as "Clay Grainger" in the TV series "The Virginian" (replacing Charles Bickford). He appeared in 69 episodes from 1967 to 1970.

- Then in 1979, he was cast as "Dutch McHenry" in the TV series "Shirley". He appeared in 8 episodes from 1979 to 1980.
- John's other film credits include "Call Northside 777" (1948), "The Asphalt Jungle" (1950), "Psycho" (1960), "Elmer Gantry" (1960), "Flaming Star" (1960), "Herbie Rides Again" (1974), "Rooster Cogburn" (1975) and "Turner and Hooch" (1989).
- His other TV credits include "Father Knows Best" (1958), "Cimarron City" (1959), "Overland Trail" (1960), "Daniel Boone" (1965), "Dirty Sally" (1974), "Dallas" (1979), "Quincy M.E." (1983) and "St. Elsewhere" (1986).

"Barbary Coast"

Years : 1975 - 1976

Episodes : 13 (1 season) (1 TV Movie)

Cast :-

William Shatner (b. 1931) - Played Jeff Cable

Richard Kiel (b. 1939 d. 2014) - Played Moose Moran

Dave Turner - Played Thumbs

Doug McClure (b. 1935 d. 1995) - Played Cash Conover

Synopsis :-
The story of government agent Jeff Cable and his best pal Cash Conover.

Trivia & Tidbits :-

"The Show"

- **"Barbary Coast"** premiered on ABC on September 8, 1975 and last aired on January 9, 1976.

- The show ran for one season with a total of 13 episodes. The series was preceded by a TV movie that aired on May 4, 1975.
- "Barbary Coast" was inspired by the TV series "The Wild Wild West".
- The series was created by Douglas Heyes and produced by Francy Productions and Paramount Television.
- Filming took place at Paramount Studios in California.
- The theme music was provided by John Andrew Tartaglia.

"In Memoriam"

- **Richard Kiel** died of acute myocardial infarction on September 10, 2014 (74) in Fresno, California.
- **Doug McClure** died of lung cancer on February 5, 1995 (59) in Sherman Oaks, California.

"The Stars"

- **William Alan Shatner** was born on March 22, 1931 in Montreal, Quebec, Canada.
- He was the son of Joseph Shatner, a clothing manufacturer. He has two sisters Joy and Farla.
- William attended McGill University in Montreal, where he studied economics and graduated with a Bachelor of Commerce degree.

- In 1951, he made his film debut in the Canadian movie "The Butler's Night Off".
- After graduating from university in 1952, he became business manager for the Mountain Playhouse in Montreal. He then joined the National Repertory Theatre in Ottawa.
- In 1954, he was cast as "Ranger Bob" in the Canadian "Howdy Doody Show".
- In 1961, he started the recurring role of "Dr. Carl Noyes" on the TV series "Dr. Kildare". He appeared in in 6 episodes from 1961 to 1966.
- In 1965, he was cast as "David Koster" in the TV series "For the People". He appeared in 13 episodes.
- Then in 1966, he was cast in his most famous role as "Captain James T. Kirk" in the TV series "Star Trek". He appeared in 79 episodes from 1966 to 1969.
- In 1973, he provided the voice of "Captain Kirk" in the animated TV series "Star Trek". The series lasted 22 episodes.
- In 1975, he was cast as "Jeff Cable" in the TV series "Barbary Coast". He appeared in 13 episodes and 1 TV movie from 1975 to 1976.
- In 1982, he was cast as "Sgt. T. J. Hooker" in the TV series "T. J. Hooker". He appeared in 90 episodes from 1982 to 1986.
- From 1994 to 1996 he appeared as "Walter H. Bascom" in the TV series "TekWar". The series lasted 18 episodes.
- In 1999, he was the narrator on the TV series "A Twist in the Tale". This lasted 15 episodes.
- In 2004, he was cast as "Denny Crane" in the TV series "The Practice" (5 episodes).

- When the TV series "Boston Legal" was spun-off from "The Practice" he continued his role of "Denny Crane". He appeared in 101 episodes from 2004 to 2008.
- In 2010, he was cast as "Dr. Edison Milford Goodson III" in the TV series "$#*! My Dad Says". He appeared in 18 episodes from 2010 to 2011.
- Bill appeared as "Captain Kirk" in seven "Star Trek" movies from 1979 to 1994. They were :- "Star Trek : The Motion Picture" (1979), "Star Trek II : The Wrath of Khan" (1982), "Star Trek III : The Search for Spock" (1984), "Star Trek 1V : The Voyage Home" (1986), "Star Trek V : The Final Frontier" (1989), "Star Trek V1 : The Undiscovered Country" (1991) and "Star Trek : Generations" (1994).
- He has won one Golden Globe Award (2005 - Best Supporting Actor "Boston Legal") and two Emmy Awards (2004 - Outstanding Guest Actor "The Practice" and 2005 - Outstanding Supporting Actor "Boston Legal").
- Bill has been married four times - Gloria Rand (1956-1969), Marcy Lafferty (1973-1996), Nerine Kidd (1997-1999) and Elizabeth Anderson Martin (2001-present). He has three daughters from his first marriage.
- He has written several "Star Trek" novels including "Spectre (Star Trek)", "Star Trek : Avenger", "The Return (Star Trek)", "Star Trek : Captain's Blood" and "Star Trek Memories".
- Bill's daughter, Lisabeth, was "Miss Golden Globe" in 1985.

- He has a Star on the Hollywood Walk of Fame for his contribution to the television industry.
- Bill began his musical career with the spoken-word 1968 album "The Transformed Man".
- In February 2012, Bill performed in a new one-man show on Broadway called "Shatner's World : We Just Live In It".
- Bill suffers from tinnitus and is involved with the American Tinnitus Association.
- His other film credits include "The Brothers Karamazov" (1958), "Judgment at Nuremberg" (1961), "Flying High II : The Sequel" (1982), "Miss Congeniality" (2000) and "Horrorween" (2011).
- Bill's other TV credits include "Alfred Hitchcock Presents" (1957-60), "Outlaws" (1960), "Naked City" (1962), "The Defenders" (1961-65), "The Big Valley" (1966), "The Virginian" (1965-69), "Mannix" (1973), "Ironside" (1970-74), "The Oregon Trail" (1977), "Columbo" (1976-93), "Cosby" (1997) and "Rookie Blue" (2012).

- **Richard Dawson Kiel** was born on September 13, 1939 in Detroit, Michigan.
- His height and features are the result of a hormonal condition known as acromegaly. Richard stands 7 feet 1.5 inches (217 cm) tall.
- Richard made his uncredited acting debut in a 1960 "Laramie" episode titled "Street of Hate".
- He then guest starred in a number of TV shows including "Klondike" (1960), "The Rifleman" (1961), "Lassie" (1963), "Honey

West" (1966), "The Monkees" (1967) and "The Wild Wild West" (1965-68).

- In 1975, he was cast as "Moose Moran" in the TV series "Barbary Coast". He appeared in 14 episodes from 1975 to 1976.
- In 1977, he was cast as "Jaws" (probably his most famous role) in the James Bond film "The Spy Who Loved Me".
- In 1979, he reprised the role in the James Bond film "Moonraker".
- Then in 1991, he wrote, produced and starred in the film "The Giant of Thunder Mountain".
- In 2003, he provided the voice and likeness of "Jaws" in the video game "007: Everything or Nothing".
- Richard broke into films in the early 1960's with the B-movie "Eegah" (1962).
- He was one of the original choices (the other was Arnold Schwarzenegger) to play "The Incredible Hulk" in the 1977 TV series. He lost out because he wasn't muscular enough.
- In 2002, he penned his autobiography "Making It Big In The Movies".
- Richard suffers from acrophobia (fear of heights).
- His other film credits include "The Phantom" (1961) (TV), "The Nutty Professor" (1963) uncredited, "The Longest Yard" (1974), "Force 10 From Navarone" (1978), "Pale Rider" (1985), "Happy Gilmore" (1996) and "The Engagement Ring" (2013).
- Richard's other TV credits include "Daniel Boone" (1969), "Disneyland" (1970), "The Fall

Guy" (1981), "Superboy" (1989) and "BloodHounds, Inc." (2011).

- **Dave Turner** made his uncredited acting debut in a 1972 episode of the TV series "Sanford and Son"
- Following this he was cast as "Thumbs" in the TV series "Barbary Coast". He appeared in 14 episodes from 1975 to 1976.
- Over the next six years he appeared infrequently as a guest star in such TV series as "That's My Mama" (1975), "What's Happening!!" (1976), "Sanford and Son" (1976-77), "Good Times" (1975-79) and "Quincy M.E." (1981).
- Dave's last known acting appearance was in the TV series "Hill Street Blues" (1983).
- His film credits include "Like Normal People" (1979) (TV) and "Tomorrow's Child" (1982) (TV).

- **Douglas Osborne "Doug" McClure** was born on May 11, 1935 in Glendale, California.
- He was the son of Donald Reed McClure and Clara Clapp.
- Doug was educated at UCLA and made his uncredited acting debut in the film "Friendly Persuasion" (1956), starring Gary Cooper and Dorothy McGuire.
- In 1960, he was cast as Frank 'Flip' Flippen in the TV series "Overland Trail". He appeared in 17 episodes.

- Following this series, he was cast as "Jed Sills" in the TV series "Checkmate". He appeared in 70 episodes from 1960 to 1962.
- In 1962, he was cast as "Trampas" in the TV series "The Virginian". He appeared in 249 episodes from 1962 to 1971.
- Then in 1972, he was cast as "C.R. Grover" in the TV series "Search". He appeared in 23 episodes from 1972 to 1973.
- In 1975, he was cast as "Cash Conover" in the TV series "Barbary Coast". He appeared in 13 episodes from 1975 to 1976.
- In 1987, he was cast as "Kyle X. Applegate" in the TV series "Out of This World". He appeared in 81 episodes from 1987 to 1991.
- Doug was married five times - Faye Brash (1957-61), Barbara Luna (1961-63), Helen Crane (1965-68), Diane Soldani (1970-79) and Diane Furnberg (1979-95). He had two daughters, Tana and Valerie.
- Along with Troy Donahue, he was the inspiration for the "Troy McClure" character in the TV series "The Simpsons".
- Doug made over 500 appearances in films and television.
- His character "Trampas" and James Drury's "The Virginian" were the only two characters to remain with the TV series for the entire run.
- In 1994, he was awarded a Star on the Hollywood Walk of Fame for his contribution to television.
- In the 1970's and 1980's, he appeared in commercials for Hamms Beer.

- In 2014, he was inducted into the Hall of Great Western Performers at the National Cowboy and Western Heritage Museum.
- Doug's other film credits include "South Pacific" (1958), "Gidget" (1959), "The Unforgiven" (1960), "Shenandoah" (1965), "The Land That Time Forgot" (1975), The People That Time Forgot" (1977), "Prime Suspect" (1989) and "Maverick" (1994).
- His other TV credits include "Men of Annapolis" (1957), "Maverick" (1957), "26 Men" (1958-59), "Lawman" (1959), "Chips" (1982), "Magnum, P.I." (1985), "The Fall Guy" (1982-85), "Matlock" (1992) and "Kung Fu: The Legend Continues" (1995).

"The Big Valley"

Years : 1965 - 1969

Episodes : 112 (4 seasons)

Cast :-

Barbara Stanwyck (b. 1907 d. 1990) - Played Victoria Barkley

Richard Long (b. 1927 d. 1974) - Played Jarrod Barkley

Lee Majors (b. 1939) - Played Heath Barkley

Peter Breck (b. 1929 d. 2012) - Played Nick Barkley

Linda Evans (b. 1942) - Played Audra Barkley

Synopsis :-
Stories of a Californian ranching family in the 1870's.

Trivia & Tidbits :-

"The Show"

- **"The Big Valley"** premiered on ABC on September 15, 1965 and last aired on May 19, 1969.
- The show ran for four seasons with a total of 112 episodes.
- The series was created by A.I. Bezzerides and Louis F. Edelman.
- It was loosely based on the Hill Ranch located at the western edge of Calaveras County, near Stockton, California.
- There were five main cast members - Barbara Stanwyck, Richard Long, Lee Majors, Peter Breck and Linda Evans.
- At the start of the series there was another brother, "Eugene", played by Charles Briles, however, he was written out of the show after seven episodes.
- The theme music was composed by George Duning.
- Actor Paul Henreid ("Casablanca") directed a number of episodes.
- Four Star Television (Dick Powell & Co.) produced the series.
- There was a six issue comic book of the series published by Dell Comics from 1966 to 1969.
- "Victoria's" horse was named "Misty Girl" and "Nick" rode "Coco".
- Although the series was set in Stockton (Northern California) it was filmed in Southern California.

"In Memoriam"

- **Barbara Stanwyck** died of congestive heart failure on January 20, 1990 (82) in Santa Monica, California.
- **Richard Long** died of multiple heart attacks on December 21, 1974 (47) in Los Angeles, California.
- **Peter Breck** died of advanced dementia on February 6, 2012 (82) in Vancouver, British Columbia, Canada.

"The Stars"

- **Barbara Stanwyck** was born Ruby Catherine Stevens on July 16, 1907 in Brooklyn, New York.
- She was the fifth child of Catherine Ann McPhee and Byron E. Stevens. Her mother was killed when she was only four years old, and her father abandoned the family. Barbara and her brother, Byron, were brought up in a number of foster homes.
- When Barbara was 14 years old she dropped out of school and got a job wrapping packages in a Brooklyn department store.
- Following this she worked in a Brooklyn telephone office filing cards and then took a job cutting dress patterns for Vogue.
- In 1922 and 1923, she worked as a dancer in the Ziegfeld Follies.
- Then in 1926, she secured a part in the play "The Noose". The play ran for nine months and 197 performances on Broadway.

- Next she played the lead role in the Broadway play "Burlesque".
- In 1927, she made her uncredited screen debut in the film "Broadway Nights". She played a fan dancer.
- Barbara went on to appear in a number of popular films including "The Locked Door" (1929), "Mexicali Rose" (1929), "Ladies of Leisure" (1930), "Baby Face" (1933), "Stella Dallas" (1937), "Union Pacific" (1939), "The Lady Eve" (1941), "Double Indemnity" (1944), "Christmas in Connecticut" (1945) and "Sorry, Wrong Number" (1948).
- In 1956, she made her television debut in an episode ("Sudden Silence") of "The Ford Television Theatre".
- In 1960, Barbara hosted the TV series "The Barbara Stanwyck Show". The series (37 episodes) ran from 1960 to 1961 and she appeared in all but four episodes.
- Then in 1965, she was cast as "Victoria Barkley" in the TV series "The Big Valley". She appeared in 112 episodes from 1965 to 1969.
- In 1985, she was cast as "Constance 'Conny' Colby Patterson" in the TV series "The Colbys" (a spin-off of the popular TV series "Dynasty"). She appeared in 24 episodes from 1985 to 1986.
- Barbara was married twice - Frank Fay (1928-35) and Robert Taylor (1939-52). Both ended in divorce. She had one adopted son, Dion, with Frank Fay.

- In 1944, the government listed her as the highest paid woman in America (income: $400,000).
- She was nominated for four Academy Awards ("Stella Dallas" - 1937; "Ball of Fire" - 1941; "Double Indemnity" - 1944 and "Sorry, Wrong Number" - 1948).
- Barbara was presented with an honorary Academy Award in 1982 by John Travolta.
- She won three Emmy Awards ("The Barbara Stanwyck Show" - 1961; "The Big Valley" - 1966 and "The Thorn Birds" - 1983).
- In 1984, she won a Golden Globe Award for "The Thorn Birds" and in 1986 the "Golden Globes" presented her with their "Cecil B. De Mille Award".
- Barbara was presented with the Screen Actors Guild's "Life Achievement Award" in 1967 and the American Film Institute's "Life Achievement Award" in 1987.
- In 1973, Barbara was inducted into the Hall of Great Western Performers at the National Cowboy and Western Heritage Museum.
- Barbara was listed as No.11 on the American Film Institute's "100 Years of the Greatest Screen Legends".
- Her character "Phyllis Dietrichson" from the film "Double Indemnity" (1944) was ranked No.8 on the American Film Institute's "100 Greatest Screen Heroes and Villains" list.
- Entertainment Weekly voted her 40th on their "Greatest Movie Stars of All Time".
- Barbara has a Star on the Hollywood Walk of Fame for her contribution to Motion Pictures.

- She was a staunch Republican and conservative and in the 1950's was a member of The Motion Picture Alliance for the Preservation of American Ideals.
- Barbara was reported to be a very heavy smoker.
- After she passed away in 1990 her remains were cremated and the ashes scattered in Lone Pine, California.
- Barbara's other film credits include "Annie Oakley" (1935), "Golden Boy" (1939), "Meet John Doe" (1941), "Titanic" (1953), "Cattle Queen of Montana" (1954), "Roustabout" (1964) and "The Letters" (1973) (TV).
- Her other TV credits include "Zane Grey Theatre" (1958-59), "Rawhide" (1962), "The Untouchables" (1962-63), "Wagon Train" (1961-64), "Charlie's Angels" (1980) and "Dynasty" (1985).

- **Richard Long** was born on December 17, 1927 in Chicago, Illinois.
- He was the son of Sherman D. Long, a commercial artist, and Dale McCord Long.
- Richard attended several schools including Waller High School in Chicago, Evanston Township High School and Hollywood High School (senior year) in California.
- He made his acting debut in the 1946 film "Tomorrow Is Forever".
- Following this he appeared as the character "Tom Kettle" in the 1947 film "The Egg and I" starring Fred MacMurray and Claudette Colbert.

- This was the beginning of the "Ma and Pa Kettle" films and following this appeared in three others - "Ma and Pa Kettle" (1949), "Ma and Pa Kettle Go to Town" (1950) and "Ma and Pa Kettle Back on the Farm" (1951).
- Several more film roles followed including "Back at the Front" (1952), "Saskatchewan" (1954), "Cult of the Cobra" (1955), "Fury at Gunsight Pass" (1956) and "Tokyo After Dark" (1959).
- In 1959, he was cast as "Rex Randolph" in the TV series "Bourbon Street Beat". He appeared in 37 episodes from 1959 to 1960.
- Starting in 1959, he played the same character in the TV series "77 Sunset Strip". This lasted 22 episodes and finished in 1962.
- In 1965, he was cast as "Jarrod Barkley" in the TV series "The Big Valley". He appeared in 112 episodes from 1965 to 1969.
- Then in 1970, he was cast as "Professor Everett" in the TV series "Nanny and the Professor". He appeared in 54 episodes from 1970 to 1971.
- In 1973, he appeared as "Ernie Paine" in the TV series "Thicker Than Water". He appeared in 9 episodes and this was to be his last series before he died in 1974.
- Richard was married twice - Suzan Ball (1954-55) and Mara Corday (1957-74). He had three children, Carey, Valerie and Greg, with Ms. Corday.
- His sister, Barbara, was married to actor Marshall Thompson ("Daktari").

- Richard's son, Carey, passed away in 2008 from the same condition his father had - congestive heart failure.
- He served in the United States Army during the Korean War.
- Richard was reported to be a heavy smoker and drinker.
- His remains were cremated and scattered at sea.
- Richard's other film credits include "Follow the Boys" (1963), "The Girl Who Came Gift-Wrapped" (1974) (TV) and "Death Cruise" (1974) (TV).
- His other TV credits include "Hey Jeannie!" (1956), "Wagon Train" (1958), "Sugarfoot" (1959), "Lawman" (1959), "Maverick" (1958-59), "Hawaiian Eye" (1960), "Tales of Wells Fargo" (1962), "Disneyland" (1964) and "Bonanza" (1971).

- **Lee Majors** was born Harvey Lee Yeary on April 23, 1939 in Wyandotte, Michigan.
- His parents were both killed in separate car accidents when he was very young. He was adopted by his uncle and aunt, Harvey and Mildred Yeary.
- The new family moved to Middlesboro, Kentucky where he later attended Middlesboro High School (he was very good football player) and then Eastern Kentucky University in Richmond (he graduated in 1962 with a History and Physical Education Degree).

- After college he moved to Los Angeles, studied acting and changed his name to Lee Majors (a tribute to his childhood hero John Majors).
- In 1964, he made his uncredited acting debut in the film "Strait-Jacket".
- In 1965, he was cast as "Heath Barkley" in the TV series "The Big Valley". He appeared in 112 episodes from 1965 to 1969.
- Then in 1970, he was cast as "Roy Tate" in the TV series "The Virginian". He appeared in 24 episodes from 1970 to 1971.
- In 1971, he was cast as "Jess Brandon" in the TV series "Owen Marshall: Counselor at Law". He appeared in 50 episodes from 1971 to 1974.
- In 1974, he was cast as "Col. Steve Austin" in the hit TV series "The Six Million Dollar Man". He appeared in 99 episodes from 1974 to 1978.
- In 1981, he was cast as "Colt Seavers" in the TV series "The Fall Guy". He appeared in 112 episodes from 1981 to 1986.
- In 1990, he played the character "Pop Scarlet" in the TV series "Tour of Duty" (5 episodes).
- Then in 1992, he played "Herman 'Ski' Jablonski" in the TV series "Raven". He appeared in 20 episodes from 1992 to 1993.
- Following this his next TV series was "Too Much Sun" (2000). He played "Scott Reed" in 6 episodes.
- In 2007, he played the recurring role of "Coach Ross" in the TV series "The Game". He appeared in 6 episodes.

- Lee has been married four times - Thelma Kathleen Robinson (1961-65), Farrah Fawcett (1973-82), Karen Velez (1988-94) and Faith Majors (2002-present).He has one child with Ms. Robinson and three children with Ms. Velez.
- He won the role of "Joe Buck" in the film "Midnight Cowboy" (1965) but had to pass because of his role in "The Big Valley".
- In 1991, Middlesboro High School inducted Lee into their Sports Hall of Fame.
- Lee has a Star on the Hollywood Walk of Fame for his contribution to television.
- He was nominated for a Golden Globe Award in 1977 for his role in "The Six Million Dollar Man".
- Lee made his directorial debut in 1975 in an episode of "The Six Million Dollar Man" entitled "One of Our Running Backs Is Missing".
- In 2003, he had heart bypass surgery.
- Lee has appeared in seven films as "Steve Austin" - "The Six Million Dollar Man" (1973) (TV), "The Six Million Dollar Man : Wine, Women and War" (1973) (TV), The Six Million Dollar Man : Solid Gold Kidnapping" (1973) (TV), "The Return of the Six-Million-Dollar-Man and the Bionic Woman" (1987) (TV), "Bionic Showdown : The Six Million Dollar Man and the Bionic Woman" (1989) (TV), "Bionic Ever After?" (1994) (TV) and "Guys Choice" (2007) (TV).
- His other film credits include "Will Penny" (1968), "The Ballad of Andy Crocker" (1969) (TV), "The Norseman" (1978), "The Cowboy

and the Ballerina" (1984) (TV), "Danger Down Under" (1988) (TV), "Primary Suspect" (2000), "Hell to Pay" (2005) and "The Big Valley" (2012).

- Lee's other TV credits include "Gunsmoke" (1965), "Bracken's World" (1970), "The Bionic Woman" (1976) 5 episodes, "Trauma Center" (1983), "Lonesome Dove: The Series" (1995), "Walker" (1998), "Son of the Beach" (2002), "Weeds" (2008) and "CSI: NY" (2012).

- **Peter Breck** was born Joseph Peter Breck on March 13, 1929 in Rochester, New York.
- At an early age he was sent to live with his grandparents in Haverhill, Massachusetts.
- After his parents were divorced he went back to New York to live with his mother and step-father.
- His father was a jazz musician who worked with such stars as Fats Waller, Bix Beiderbecke, Paul Whiteman and Billie Holiday.
- Peter attended John Marshall High School in Rochester and after he graduated served in the United States Navy.
- Following this, he studied English and drama at the University of Texas in Houston.
- Whilst performing in the 1957 production of "The Man of Destiny", in Washington D.C., he was discovered by Robert Mitchum who cast him in an uncredited role in the film "Thunder Road" (1958).
- In 1959, he was cast as "Clay Culhane" in the TV series "Black Saddle". He appeared in 44 episodes from 1959 to 1960.

- After this series finished he gained a contract with Warner Bros. and guest starred in shows such as "Sugarfoot", "Surfside 6", "Bronco", "77 Sunset Strip" and had a recurring role ("Doc Holliday") in "Maverick".
- Peter eventually left Warners and appeared in such films as "Shock Corridor" (1963), "The Crawling Hand" (1963) and "Hootenanny Hoot" (1963).
- In 1965, he was cast as "Nick Barkley" in the TV series "The Big Valley". He appeared in 112 episodes from 1965 to 1969.
- After "The Big Valley" finished Peter concentrated on theater work in the United States and Canada.
- Peter was married to Diana Bourne for 52 years and they had one child.
- In an earlier life Peter was a club singer in Houston. He put out a CD entitled "Just Kickin' Back With Peter Breck" (all original tunes).
- He was one of only a few actors to appear in the original "Outer Limits" (1963) and also the revival "Outer Limits" (1995).
- His other film credits include "The Beatniks" (1960), "Portrait of a Mobster" (1961), "The Glory Guys" (1965), "Highway 61" (1991), "Decoy" (1995) and "Jiminy Glick in Lalawood" (2004).
- Peter's other TV credits include "The Gray Ghost" (1957), "Tombstone Territory" (1958), "Sea Hunt" (1959), "Lawman" (1962), "Branded" (1965), "The Fall Guy" (1985) and "John Doe" (2002).

- **Linda Evans** was born Linda Evenstad on November 18, 1942 in Hartford, Connecticut.
- She was the second of three daughters to a couple who were professional dancers.
- When she was six months old the family moved to North Hollywood and she later attended Hollywood High School.
- Linda made her acting debut in a 1960 episode ("A Crush on Bentley") of the hit TV series "Bachelor Father" starring John Forsythe.
- Twenty-one years later she would play Forsythe's wife in the TV series "Dynasty".
- Following "Bachelor Father" she appeared in five episodes of "The Adventures of Ozzie & Harriet".
- In 1965, she was cast as "Audra Barkley" in the TV series "The Big Valley". She appeared in 112 episodes from 1965 to 1969.
- In 1976, she was cast as "Marty Shaw" in the TV series "Hunter". She appeared in 13 episodes from 1976 to 1977.
- Then in 1981, she was cast as "Krystle Carrington" in the TV series "Dynasty". She appeared in 209 episodes from 1981 to 1989.
- Linda has been married twice - John Derek (1968-74) and Stan Herman (1975-81). She doesn't have any children.
- After she retired from acting in 1997 she opened the Linda Evans Fitness Centers (15 locations). However, these closed down in 2004 due to her moving to another fitness chain.
- Linda's surname of Evenstad is of Norwegian origin.

- She featured in an ad campaign for Crystal Light beverages during the 1980's.
- Her singing vocals in the film "Beach Blanket Bingo" (1965) were dubbed by Jackie Ward.
- Linda has a Star on the Hollywood Walk of Fame for her contribution to television.
- In 1982, she won a Golden Globe Award for "Best Performance by an Actress in a TV Series - Drama". She tied with Barbara Bel Geddes from "Dallas".
- In 1964, Linda was "Miss Golden Globe".
- From 1982 to 1986, she was voted "Favorite Female Performer" at the People's Choice Awards.
- Linda's other film credits include "Twilight of Honor" (1963), "Those Calloways" (1965), "Female Artillery" (1973) (TV), "Avalanche Express" (1979), "Tom Horn" (1980), "Dazzle" (1995) (TV) and "The Stepsister" (1997) (TV).
- Her other TV credits include "Outlaws" (1962), "The Untouchables" (1962), "Wagon Train" (1965), "McCloud" (1973), "The Rockford Files" (1975), "The Love Boat" (1981-83) and "Glitter" (1984).

"Branded"

Years : 1965 - 1966

Episodes : 48 (2 seasons)

Cast :-

Chuck Connors (b. 1921 d. 1992) - Played Jason McCord

Synopsis :-
A U.S. Army Cavalry captain is drummed out of the service following an unjust accusation of cowardice.

Trivia & Tidbits :-

"The Show"

- **"Branded"** premiered on NBC on January 24, 1965 and last aired on September 4, 1966.
- The show ran for two seasons with a total of 48 episodes.
- The first 13 episodes were filmed in black and white with the remaining 35 episodes in color.
- The series was created by Larry Cohen and co-produced by Mark Goodson-Bill Todman Productions in association with Sentinel Productions Inc.

- The theme music was composed by Dominic Frontiere with lyrics by Alan Alch.
- The show was sponsored by Procter and Gamble.
- Some of the filming locations were Kanab Movie Fort, Kanab, Utah; Kanab Movie Ranch; Red Rock Canyon State Park, California and Paramount Studios.
- "Jason McCord's" horse was named "Domino".
- The series is set in the 1880's.

"In Memoriam"

- **Chuck Connors** died of lung cancer on November 10, 1992 (71) in Los Angeles, California.

"The Star"

- **Chuck Connors** was born Kevin Joseph Aloysius Connors on April 10, 1921 in Brooklyn, New York.
- He was the son of Allan and Marcella Connors, emigrants from the Dominion of Newfoundland. Chuck had one other sister.
- Chuck was a good athlete and gained a scholarship to the private high school Adelphi Academy, where he graduated in 1939.
- Following this he went to the Catholic college Seton Hall University in New Jersey, but only lasted two years before joining the U.S. Army during the Second World War. He was

stationed at Camp Campbell, Kentucky as a tank-warfare instructor.

- After the war, he joined the Boston Celtics basketball team and played center in the 1946/47 season.
- Because his first love was baseball, he left the Celtics early to attend spring training with the Brooklyn Dodgers.
- He played in the minors for a while and then was called up and played one game for the Dodgers in 1949.
- Chuck then had a stint with the Chicago Cubs, but ended up with their Triple-A-farm team, the L.A. Angels, in 1952.
- A casting director saw him at a game and recommended him for a part in the film "Pat and Mike" (1952). He played the "Police Captain".
- For the next six years he played in several movies including "Trouble Along the Way" (1953), "South Sea Woman" (1953), "Dragonfly Squadron" (1954), "The Human Jungle" (1954), "Target Zero" (1955), "Walk the Dark Street" (1956), "Tomahawk Trail" (1957), "Old Yeller" (1957) and "The Big Country" (1958).
- In 1958, he was cast as "Lucas McCain" in the TV series "The Rifleman". He appeared in 168 episodes from 1958 to 1963.
- In 1963, he was cast as "Attorney John Egan" in the TV series "Arrest and Trial". He appeared in 30 episodes from 1963 to 1964.

- Then in 1965, he was cast as "Jason McCord" in the TV series "Branded". He appeared in 48 episodes from 1965 to 1966.
- In 1967, he was cast as "Jim Sinclair" in the TV series "Cowboy in Africa". He appeared in 26 episodes from 1967 to1968.
- Chuck appeared in 3 episodes of the mini-series "Roots" in 1977. He played the character "Tom Moore".
- In 1983, he was cast as "Jeb Hollister" in the TV series "The Yellow Rose". He appeared in 22 episodes from 1983 to 1984.
- In 1987, he appeared in 8 episodes of the TV series "Werewolf". He played "Janos Skorzeny".
- His last acting appearance was in the film "Three Days to Kill" in 1992.
- Chuck was married three times - Elizabeth "Betty" Riddell (1948-1961); Kamata Devi (1963-1972) and Faith Quabius (1977-1980). He had four sons with Ms. Riddell.
- In 1991, he was inducted into the Hall of Great Western Performers at the National Cowboy and Western Heritage Museum.
- He has a Star on the Hollywood Walk of Fame for his contribution to the television industry.
- In 1997, author David Fury published a biography of Chuck titled "Chuck Connors - The Man Behind the Rifle".
- He was a staunch Republican and very good friends with Richard Nixon.
- Chuck is one of only 12 athletes in the history of American professional sports to have played

for both Major League Baseball and the National Basketball Association.

- His other film credits included "The Hired Gun" (1957), "Geronimo" (1962), "Flipper" (1963), "Move Over, Darling" (1963), "Pancho Villa" (1972), "Soylent Green" (1973), "Day of the Assassin" (1979), "Airplane II" (1982), "Maniac Killer" (1987) and "The Gambler Returns : The Luck of the Draw" (1991) (TV) - he played "Lucas McCain".

- Chuck's other TV credits included "Adventures of Superman" (1955), "Frontier" (1956), "Gunsmoke" (1956), "The Silent Service" (1957), "The Restless Gun" (1957), "Zane Grey Theatre" (1958) - he played "Lucas McCain", "Night Gallery" (1972), "Stone" (1980), "The Love Boat" (1983) and "Paradise" (1990).

"Cade's County"

Years : 1971 - 1972

Episodes : 24 (1 season)

Cast :-

Glenn Ford (b. 1916 d. 2006) - Played Sam Cade

Edgar Buchanan (b. 1903 d. 1979) - Played J.J. Jackson

Taylor Lacher (b. 1942 d. 2005) - Played Arlo Pritchard

Peter Ford (b. 1945) - Played Pete

Synopsis :-
Cases of a New Mexico sheriff.

Trivia & Tidbits :-

"The Show"

- **"Cade's County"** premiered on CBS on September 19, 1971 and last aired on April 9, 1972.
- The show ran for one season with a total of 24 episodes.

- The series was produced by 20th Century Fox Television and David Gerber Productions.
- The theme music was composed by Henry Mancini.
- In 1972-73, "Cade's Country" was replaced by the TV series "MASH".

"In Memoriam"

- **Glenn Ford** died of multiple strokes on August 30, 2006 (90) in Beverly Hills, California.
- **Edgar Buchanan** died of a stroke on April 4, 1979 (76) in Palm Desert, California.
- **Taylor Lacher** died on June 21, 2005 (63) in Killen, Alabama.

"The Stars"

- **Glenn Ford** was born Gwyllyn Samuel Newton Ford on May 1, 1916 in Sainte-Christine-d'Auvergne, Quebec, Canada.
- He was the son of Newton Ford, a railway conductor, and Hannah Wood Mitchell.
- Glenn moved to Santa Monica, California, with his family, when he was eight years old and became a U.S. citizen in 1939.
- After graduating from Santa Monica High School he began working in small theatre groups.
- In 1937, he made his acting debut in the film short "Night in Manhattan.

- Several more movie roles followed including "Heaven with a Barbed Wire Fence" (1939), "Convicted Woman" (1940), "Blondie Plays Cupid" (1940), "Texas" (1941), "The Adventures of Martin Eden" (1942), "The Desperadoes" (1943) and "Destroyer" (1943).
- In 1942, he joined the United States Marine Corps Reserve. He was honourably discharged in 1944.
- After the war he resumed his acting career and appeared in such films as "Gilda" (1946), "The Man from Colorado" (1948), "Lust for Gold" (1949), "The Redhead and the Cowboy" (1951), "The Man from the Alamo" (1953), "The Big Heat" (1953), "Backboard Jungle" (1955), "The Fastest Gun Alive" (1956), "The Teahouse of the August Moon" (1956), "3:10 to Yuma" (1957), "The Sheepman" (1958), "The Courtship of Eddie's Father" (1963), "Day of the Evil Gun" (1968) and "Heaven with a Gun" (1969).
- In 1971, he was cast as "Sam Cade" in the TV series "Cade's County". He appeared in 24 episodes from 1971 to 1972.
- In 1975, he was cast as "Rev. Tom Holvak" in the TV series "The Family Holvak". He appeared in 10 episodes.
- In 1976-77, he appeared as "George Caldwell" in the TV mini-series "Once an Eagle".
- Glenn was married four times (all finishing in divorce) - Eleanor Powell (1943-59), Kathryn Hays (1966-69), Cynthia Hayward (1977-84) and Jeanne Baus (1993-94). He had one son, actor Peter Ford, with Ms. Powell.

- In 1978, he was inducted into the Hall of Great Western Performers at the National Cowboy and Western Heritage Museum.
- Glenn has a Star on the Hollywood Walk of Fame for his contribution to Motion Pictures.
- In 1992, France awarded him the French Legion of Honor Medal for his service in the Second World War.
- In 1958, he was voted the No.1 box office attraction.
- He campaigned for Ronald Reagan during the 1984 and 1988 presidential elections.
- Although he never won an Oscar, in 1962 he won a Golden Globe Award for his performance in the film "Pocketful of Miracles" (1961).
- In 1978, he appeared in the film "Superman" as "Clark Kent's" adopted father.
- Glenn's other film credits include "Jubal" (1956), "Torpedo Run" (1958), "Cimarron" (1960), "Santee" (1973), "Midway" (1976), "The Sacketts" (1979) (TV), "Beggarman Thief" (1979) (TV), "Border Shootout" (1990) and "Final Verdict" (1991) (TV).
- His only other TV credit was "Police Story" (1978).

- **Edgar Buchanan** was born Willian Edgar Buchanan on March 20, 1903 in Humansville, Missouri.
- At an early age his family moved to Oregon and after studying at the University of Oregon he decided to study dentistry (following in his father's footsteps).

- He graduated from North Pacific Dental College and practised in Eugene, Oregon from 1929 to 1937.
- Edgar moved his practise to Altadena, California and joined the Pasadena Playhouse.
- He handed over his practise to his wife and decided to become an actor.
- Edgar made his film debut in the movie "My Son Is Guilty" in 1939.
- Several movies followed including "Escape to Glory" (1940), "Arizona" (1940), "Texas" (1941), "Tombstone : The Town Too Tough to Die" (1942), "Buffalo Bill " (1944), "Abilene Town" (1946), "The Black Arrow" (1948), "Cheaper by the Dozen" (1950) and "Rawhide" (1951).
- In 1952, he was cast as "Red Connors" in the TV series "Hopalong Cassidy". He appeared in episodes from 1952 to 1954.
- Then in 1955, he was cast as "Judge Roy Bean" in the TV series of the same name. He appeared in 39 episodes from 1955 to 1956.
- From 1957 to 1961, he played "Doc Dawson" in six episodes of "Tales of Wells Fargo".
- In 1963, he was cast as "Uncle Joe Carson" in the TV series "Petticoat Junction". He appeared in 222 episodes from 1963 to 1970.
- During this time he also played "Uncle Joe" in "Green Acres" (16 episodes) and "Beverly Hillbillies" (3 episodes).
- In 1971, he was cast as "J.J. Jackson" in the TV series "Cade's County", starring Glenn Ford. He appeared in 24 episodes from 1971 to 1972.

- His last acting role was in the film "Benji" in 1974.
- Edgar was married to his wife, Mildred Marguerite Spence (a dentist), from 1928 until his death in 1979.
- During his career he appeared in over 100 films.
- Edgar was one of only three actors to appear in all seven seasons of "Petticoat Junction" (Linda Henning and Frank Cady were the other two).
- He appeared in 13 different films with Glenn Ford.
- Edgar's other film credits include "Shane" (1953), "Destry" (1954), "Wichita" (1955), "The Sheepman" (1958), "King of the Wild Stallions" (1959), "Hound-Dog Man" (1959), "The Comancheros" (1961), "Ride the High Country" (1962), "McLintock" (1963), "The Over-the-Hill Gang" (1969)(TV) and "Yuma" (1971)(TV).
- His other TV credits include "Whirlybirds" (1957), "The Adventures of Jim Bowie" (1958), "Lawman" (1959), "Bronco" (1960), "Wagon Train" (1960), "Maverick" (1958-61) 5 episodes, "The Rifleman" (1958-61) 6 episodes, "Laramie" (1960-62) 4 episodes, "Leave it to Beaver" (1957-63) 3 episodes, "Gunsmoke" (1962-63) 2 episodes and "The Partridge Family" (1972).

- **Taylor Lacher** was born Bluford Taylor Lacher on April 2, 1942 in Ohio, U.S.A.

- In 1971, he made his acting debut as "Arlo Pritchard" in the TV series "Cade's County". He appeared in 24 episodes from 1971 to 1972.
- In 1974, he was cast as "Deputy Hubber Martin" in the TV series "Nakia". He appeared in 14 episodes.
- Taylor's film credits include "Santee" (1973), "Peopletoys" (1974), "Mr. Majestyk" (1974), "Crisis in Sun Valley" (1978) (TV), "The Return of Mod Squad" (1979) (TV), "The Return of Frank Cannon" (1980) (TV), "A Summer to Remember" (1985) (TV), "Deadly Stranger" (1990) and "Cellblock Sisters : Banished Behind Bars" (1995).
- His other TV credits include "Ghost Story" (1972), "The Mod Squad" (1973), "Dusty's Trail" (1973), "Joe Forrester" (1975), "Barnaby Jones" (1977), "Police Story" (1973-78) 5 episodes, "How the West Was Won" (1979), "The Waltons" (1981), "Little House on the Prairie" (1982), "Knight Rider" (1983) and "Dynasty" (1985-86) 3 episodes.

- **Peter Ford** was born Peter Newton Ford on February 5, 1945 in Los Angeles, California.
- He is the son of actor Glenn Ford and actress Eleanor Powell.
- Peter graduated from Chadwick High School, California in 1962 and then received an Associates of Arts degree from Santa Monica College in 1966. In 1968, he graduated from the University of Southern California with a B.A. degree in English.

- Following this he pursued a musical career, eventually releasing a single titled "Blue Ribbons" for Phillips Records.
- He later formed his own band, "The Creations", and performed in San Francisco and Las Vegas.
- In 1963, he made a guest appearance in an episode ("A Thousand Voices") of the TV series "Mr. Novak".
- In 1971, he was cast as "Pete" in the TV series "Cade's County". He appeared in 22 episodes from 1971 to 1972.
- Peter married Lynda Gundersen in 1970 and they have three children.
- Being the son of celebrities afforded Peter many opportunities. He learned swimming from Johnny Weissmuller (Olympian and actor), tennis from Pancho Segura and golf from Ben Hogan.
- Peter was a reserve deputy for the Los Angeles County Sheriff's Department for 22 years. He retired in 1996.
- His film credits include "The Rounders" (1965) uncredited, "Day of the Evil Gun" (1968) uncredited, "The Proud and Damned" (1972) and "Punch and Jody" (1974) (TV)
- Peter's other TV credits include "Cannon" (1974), "Police Story" (1974) and "Barnaby Jones" (1975-76) 2 episodes.

"Cimarron Strip"

Years : 1967 - 1968

Episodes : 23 (1 season)

Cast :-

Stuart Whitman (b. 1928) - Played - Marshal Jim Crown

Percy Herbert (b. 1920 d. 1992) - Played Angus MacGregor

Randy Boone (b. 1942) - Played Francis Wilde

Jill Townsend (b. 1945) - Played Dulcey Coopersmith

Synopsis :-
The story of a marshal keeping the peace around the Oklahoma Panhandle

Trivia & Tidbits :-

"The Show"

- **"Cimarron Strip"** premiered on CBS on September 7, 1967 and last aired on March 7, 1968.

- The show ran for one season with a total of 23 color episodes.
- The series was created by Christopher Knopf and produced in association with The Stuart Whitman Organisation.
- The theme music was composed by Maurice Jarre (he also scored the films "Lawrence of Arabia" and "Doctor Zhivago").
- "Cimarron Strip" was one of only three 90 minute Western series that aired during the 1960's (the other two were "The Virginian" and "Wagon Train").
- Some of the filming locations were the Alabama Hills near Lone Pine, California; Bishop, California; Kanab, Utah; Tucson, Arizona and the CBS Studio Center.
- The show aired opposite ABC's "The Flying Nun", "Batman" and "Bewitched" and NBC's "Daniel Boone" and "Ironside".

"In Memoriam"

- **Percy Herbert** died of a heart attack on December 6, 1992 (72) in Kent, England.

"The Stars"

- **Stuart Maxwell Whitman** was born on February 1, 1928 in San Francisco, California.
- His parents were Cecilia (nee Gold) and Joseph Whitman.

- After attending over 20 schools he graduated high school and spent three years with the Army Corps of Engineers.
- Following his discharge, he attended Los Angeles City College and then the Los Angeles Academy of Dramatic Art.
- Stuart made his first credited acting appearance in an episode ("Silver Blade") of "The Range Rider" in 1952.
- His first credited movie appearance was in the film "The All American" in 1953.
- In 1956, he was cast as "Sergeant Walters" in the TV series "Highway Patrol". He appeared in 13 episodes from 1956 to 1957.
- In 1967, he was cast as "Marshal Jim Crown" in the TV series "Cimarron Strip". He appeared in 23 episodes from 1967 to 1968.
- Then in 1988, he had a recurring role as "Clark Kent's" father, "Jonathan Kent" in the TV series "Superboy". He appeared in 10 episodes from 1988 to 1992.
- In 1990, he had another recurring role, as "Mr. Willis", in the TV series "Knots Landing". He appeared in 5 episodes.
- His last acting appearance, to date, was in the film "The Color of Evening" in 2006.
- Stuart has been married twice – Patricia LaLonde (1952-1966) and Caroline Boubis (1966-1974). He has a total of five children.
- In 1962, he was nominated for a Best Actor "Oscar" for his role in the film "The Mark" (1961).

- In 1988, he was awarded a Star on the Hollywood Walk of Fame for his contribution to Motion Pictures.
- Stuart's other film credits include "Silver Lode" (1954), "7 Men from Now" (1956), "Johnny Trouble" (1957), "Darby's Rangers" (1958), "Ten North Frederick" (1958), "Hound-Dog Man" (1959), "The Comancheros" (1961), "The Longest Day" (1962), "Sands of the Kalahari" (1965), "Run, Cougar, Run" (1972), "The Ransom" (1977), "Cuba Crossing" (1980), "The Treasure of the Amazon" (1985), "Omega Cop" (1990), "Walker Texas Ranger 3 : Deadly Reunion" (1994) and "The President's Man" (2000)(TV).
- His other TV credits include "Navy Log" (1955-56) 3 episodes, "Gunsmoke" (1956), "The Silent Service" (1957), "Harbor Command" (1957), "Bracken's World" (1970), "The Streets of San Francisco" (1973), "Disneyland" (1972-73) 3 episodes, "Cannon" (1975), "Tales of the Unexpected" (1981), "Fantasy Island" (1978-84) 7 episodes, "Matt Houston" (1982-84) 2 episodes, "Simon & Simon" (1982-86) 2 episodes, "Murder, She Wrote" (1984-92) 4 episodes, "Walker" (1994) and "Courthouse" (1995).

- **Percy Herbert** was born on July 31, 1920 in Kent, England.
- He served in the Royal Army Ordnance Corps during the Second World War and spent four years in the Japanese prisoner of war camp Changi.

- Following the war, he gained a scholarship at the Royal Academy of Dramatic Art (helped by Dame Sybil Thorndike).
- After acting in the theatre he made his TV debut in an episode ("The Scarlet Pimpernel") of "BBC Sunday-Night Theatre" in 1951.
- His film debut was in the TV movie "Montserrat" in 1954.
- Several more film roles followed including "The Green Buddha" (1955), "The Cockleshell Heroes" (1955), "The Steel Bayonet" (1957), "The Bridge on the River Kwai" (1957), "Barnacle Bill" (1957), "The Devil's Disciple" (1959), "There Was a Crooked Man" (1960), "The Guns of Navarone" (1961), "Mutiny on the Bounty" (1962), "Carry on Jack" (1963), "Becket" (1964), "Carry on Cowboy" (1966) and "Tobruk" (1967).
- In 1967, he was cast as "Angus MacGregor" in the TV series "Cimarron Strip". He appeared in 23 episodes from 1967 to 1968.
- As well as starring in the film "Bridge on the River Kwai" (1957) he also acted as a technical consultant.
- Percy's other film credits include "Casino Royale" (1967), "Too Late the Hero" (1970), "The Other Reg Varney" (1970)(TV), "The Fiend" (1972), "The Mackintosh Man" (1973), "The Wild Geese" (1978), "The Sea Wolves" (1980) and "The Love Child" (1988).
- His other TV credits include "Glencannon" (1959) 2 episodes, "Kraft Mystery Theater" (1959), "ITV Play of the Week" (1955-59) 3 episodes, "ITV Television Playhouse" (1956-60) 5 episodes, "Danger Man" (1961-65) 2

episodes, "The Saint" (1962-65) 2 episodes, "The Worker" (1965) 6 episodes, "Z Cars" (1965), "The Main Chance" (1970), "Justice" (1971-72) 2 episodes, "Dixon on Dock Green" (1965-74) 3 episodes, "Disneyland" (1963-79) 4 episodes and "Fair Ground!" (1983).

- **Randy Boone (see "The Virginian")**

- **Jill Townsend** was born on January 25, 1945 in Santa Monica, California.
- Her father, Robert Townsend, was a former head of Avis and also wrote the best-selling book "Up the Organisation".
- Jill was brought up in Locust Valley, Long Island and graduated from The Master's School in Dobbs Ferry, New York in 1963.
- Following this she studied acting at the Royal Academy of Dramatic Art in London.
- Jill made her TV debut in an episode ("The Drublegratz Affair") of "The Girl from U.N.C.L.E." in 1967.
- Her movie debut was in the film "The Spirit Is Willing" (1967) where she played three characters.
- In 1967, she was cast as "Dulcey Coopersmith" in the TV series "Cimarron Strip". She appeared in 23 episodes from 1967 to 1968.

- In 1972, she played "Maggie Verver" in the TV mini-series "The Golden Bowl". She appeared in 6 episodes.
- Then in 1975, she was cast as "Elizabeth Warleggan" in the TV series "Poldark". She appeared in 27 episodes from 1975 to 1977.
- Her last acting appearance, to date, was in an episode ("Ship to Spies") of "Scarecrow and Mrs. King" in 1985.
- Jill has been married three times – Tom Sutton (1967-69), Nicol Williamson (1971-77) and Robert Sorel (1993-present). She has a son, Luke, from her marriage to Mr. Williamson.
- After she quit acting, Jill worked as a journalist for the Daily Mail newspaper in London.
- Following this, she returned to the United States and worked as a teacher and then a spiritual counsellor.
- Jill's other film credits include "Sitting Target" (1972), "Alfie Darling" (1976), "The Seven-Per-Cent Solution" (1976) and "The Awakening" (1980).
- Her other TV credits include "The Wild Wild West (1969), "Bonanza" (1969), "The Name of the Game" (1969), "The Virginian" (1969), "Ironside" (1970), "Family Affair" (1970), "The Sweeney" (1975) and "Space: 1999" (1977).

"The Cowboys"

Years : 1974

Episodes : 13 (1 season)

Cast :-

Moses Gunn (b. 1929 d. 1993) - Played Jebediah Nightlinger

Diana Douglas (b. 1923 d. 2015) - Played Annie Anderson

Jim Davis (b. 1909 d. 1981) - Played Marshal Bill Winter

A. Martinez (b. 1948) - Played Cimarron

Robert Carradine (b. 1954) - Played Slim

Clay O'Brien (b. 1961) - Played Weedy

Clint Howard (b. 1959) - Played Steve

Synopsis :-
The adventures of teenage boys in the 1870's New Mexico Territory.

Trivia & Tidbits :-

"The Show"

- **"The Cowboys"** premiered on ABC on February 6, 1974 and last aired on May 8, 1974.
- The show ran for one season with a total of 13 episodes.
- The series was based on the film of the same name starring John Wayne.
- David Dortort, of "Bonanza" fame, produced the show for Warner Bros. Television.
- The theme music was composed by John Williams.

"In Memoriam"

- **Moses Gunn** died of asthma on December 16, 1993 (64) in Guilford, Connecticut.
- **Diana Douglas** died of cancer on July 3, 2015 (92) in Woodland Hills, Los Angeles, California.
- **Jim Davis** died of multiple myeloma on April 26, 1981 (71) in Northridge, California.

"The Stars"

- **Moses Gunn** was born on October 2, 1929 in St. Louis, Missouri.
- He was the son of Mary and George Gunn and the oldest of seven children.

- Moses graduated from Tennessee State University after serving in the United States Army.
- He then went to graduate school at Kansas University and graduated with a master's degree.
- Moses then briefly taught at Grambling College, Louisiana before going to New York to try acting as a career.
- He made his New York stage debut in the off-Broadway production of "The Blacks" (1962).
- Several more plays followed including "A Hand is on the Gate", "Twelfth Night", "I Have a Dream" and "The Poison Tree".
- He made his TV debut in an episode ("The Name of the Game") of "East Side/West Side" in 1964.
- Moses then made his movie debut in the film "Nothing But a Man" in 1964.
- More film roles followed including "Of Mice and Men" (1968)(TV), "WUSA" (1970), "The Great White Hope" (1970), "Wild Rovers" (1971), "Shaft" (1971), "Eagle in a Cage" (1972), "Shaft's Big Score!" (1972) and "The Iceman Cometh" (1973).
- In 1974, he was cast as "Jebediah Nightlinger" in the TV series "The Cowboys". He appeared in 12 episodes.
- In 1977, he played the recurring character "Carl Dixon" in the TV series "Good Times". He appeared in 6 episodes.
- Another recurring role he had was in the TV series "Little House on the Prairie". He played

the character "Joe Kagan" in 5 episodes from 1977 to 1981.

- Then in 1981, he was cast as "Moses Gage" in the TV series "Father Murphy". He appeared in 34 episodes from 1981 to 1983.
- In 1989, he appeared as the "Old Man" in the TV series "A Man Called Hawk". He appeared in 10 episodes.
- His last acting appearance was in an episode ("Three Men and Adena") of "Homicide: Life on the Street" in 1993.
- Moses was married to Gwendolyn Mumma Landes from 1966 until his death in 1993. They had two children.
- In the 1960's, Moses co-founded "The Negro Ensemble Company".
- He won two Obie Awards for his roles in "Titus Andronicus" and "First Breeze of Summer".
- Moses gained a Tony Award nomination as Best Actor in "The Poison Tree".
- He was also nominated for an Emmy Award for his portrayal of "Kintango" in the TV mini-series "Roots" (1977).
- Moses' other film credits include "Amazing Grace" (1974), "Rollerball" (1975), "Remember My Name" (1978), "Ragtime" (1981), "Amityville 11: The Possession" (1982), "The NeverEnding Story" (1984), "Heartbreak Ridge" (1986), "Dixie Lanes" (1988), "Memphis" (1992)(TV) and "No Room for Opal" (1993)(TV).
- His other TV credits include "The F.B.I." (1969), "Hawaii Five-O" (1971), "Kung Fu" (1973), "The Jeffersons" (1975), "Switch"

(1977), "Highway to Heaven" (1985), "Hill Street Blues" (1987), "The Cosby Show" (1989) 2 episodes and "Gabriel's Fire" (1990).

- **Diana Douglas** was born Diana Love Dill on January 22, 1923 in Devonshire, Bermuda.
- She is the daughter of Ruth Neilson and Lieutenant-Colonel Thomas Melville Dill, a former Attorney General of Bermuda. Her brother, Bayard, was a prominent Bermudian lawyer and politician.
- Diana studied acting with Kirk Douglas before the start of the Second World War.
- She made her uncredited acting debut in the film "Keeper of the Flame" in 1942.
- This was followed by a number of movie roles including "Let's Live Again" (1948), "House of Strangers" (1949), "The Whistle at Eaton Falls" (1951), "Storm Over Tibet" (1952), "Monsoon" (1952) and "The Indian Fighter" (1955).
- One of Diana's first appearances on TV was in an episode ("The Rivals") of "Masterpiece Playhouse" in 1950.
- In 1974, she was cast as "Annie Anderson" in the TV series "The Cowboys". She appeared in 12 episodes.
- She had a recurring role as "Martha Evans" on the daytime soap "Days of Our Lives" from 1977 to 1982.
- In 1985, she played the recurring character "Professor Tyler" on the TV series "The Paper Chase". She appeared in 6 episodes from 1985 to 1986.

- Her last acting appearance was in an episode ("Heal Thyself") of "ER" in 2008.
- Diana was married three times – Kirk Douglas (1943-51); Bill Darrid (1956-92) and Donald Albert Webster (2002-15). She had two children, Michael (Academy Award winner) and Joel, with Mr. Douglas.
- In 1999, she released her autobiography titled "In the Wings: A Memoir".
- Her other film credits include "Dead Man on the Run" (1975)(TV), "Mary White" (1977)(TV), "Jaws of Satan" (1981), "The Star Chamber" (1983), "Planes, Trains & Automobiles" (1987), "Cold Heaven" (1991) and "It Runs in the Family" (2003).
- Diana's other TV credits include "Medallion Theatre" (1953), "General Electric Theater" (1955), "Medic" (1956) 2 episodes, "West Point" (1956), "Naked City" (1959) 2 episodes, "Flipper" (1964), "Ben Casey" (1965), "Hawkins" (1973) 2 episodes, "The Streets of San Francisco" (1974), "Cannon" (1974-75) 2 episodes, "The Waltons" (1979) 3 episodes, "Knots Landing" (1980) 2 episodes, "Lou Grant" (1977-82) 2 episodes, "Capitol" (1982), "Dynasty" (1981-84) 3 episodes, "The West Wing" (2004) and "Cold Case" (2007).

- **Jim Davis** was born Marlin Jim Davis on August 26, 1909 in Edgerton, Missouri.
- He made his film debut in an uncredited role in "Cairo" in 1942.
- Jim then appeared in a number of "B" Westerns for Republic Pictures including "The

Fabulous Texan" (1947), "The Showdown" (1950), "Ride the Man Down" (1952) and "Woman They Almost Lynched" (1953).

- In 1954, he was cast as "Matt Clark" in the TV series "Stories of the Century". He appeared in 39 episodes from 1954 to 1955.
- Then in 1958, he was cast as "Wes Cameron" in the TV series "Rescue 8". He appeared in 73 episodes from 1958 to 1960.
- After "Rescue 8" finished Jim guest starred on a number of TV shows including "The Tall Man" (1960), "The Deputy" (1961), "Laramie" (1963), "Branded" (1966), "Bonanza" (1968), "The Virginian" (1971) and Gunsmoke" (1974).
- In 1978, he was cast as "Jock Ewing" in the popular TV series "Dallas". He appeared in 77 episodes from 1978 to 1981 (his death).
- Jim was married to Blanche Hammerer from 1945 until his death in 1981. They had one daughter, Tara Diane Davis, who was killed in a car accident in 1970 (17 years old).
- From the late 1970's Jim was a voice actor in commercials for the American Beef Council.
- Jim has a Star on the Hollywood Walk of Fame for his contribution to the television industry.
- His other film credits include "Hell's Outpost" (1954), "The Last Command" (1955), "The Quiet Gun" (1957), "The Toughest Gun in Tombstone" (1958), "Fort Utah" (1967), "Rio

Lobo" (1970), "The Parallax View" (1974) and "The Day Time Ended" (1980).

- Jim's other TV credits include "Dangerous Assignment" (1952) 5 episodes, "Cowboy G-Men" (1952-53) 4 episodes, "Fireside Theatre" (1951-54) 9 episodes, "Playhouse 90" (1957), "The Silent Service" (1957-58) 3 episodes, "Tales of Wells Fargo" (1957-62) 3 episodes, "Wagon Train" (1960-64) 4 episodes, "Death Valley Days" (1953-69) 12 episodes, "Daniel Boone" (1966-69) 4 episodes, "The Oregon Trail" (1977) and "Disneyland" (1972-78) 3 episodes.

- **A. Martinez** was born Adolfo Larrve Martinez III on September 27, 1948 in Glendale, California.
- He began his career at twelve years of age, winning a singing competition at the Hollywood Bowl.
- Adolfo graduated from Verdugo High School, Los Angeles and then furthered his acting at U.C.L.A.
- He made his acting debut in the film "The Young Animals" in 1968.
- Following this, he guest starred in a number of TV shows including "The Outcasts" (1969), "Mission: Impossible" (1969), "The New People" (1969), "Ironside" (1969) 2 episodes, "Adam-12" (1970), "Bonanza" (1970), "The Man and the City" (1971), "The Sixth Sense"

(1972), "Hawaii Five-O" (1973) and "Kodiak" (1974).

- In 1974, he was cast as "Cimarron" in the TV series "The Cowboys". He appeared in 12 episodes.
- In 1979, he appeared (3 episodes) as "Tranquilino Marquez" in the TV mini-series "James A. Michener's Centennial".
- Then in 1982, he was cast as "Benny Silva" in the TV series "Cassie & Co." The show only lasted 13 episodes.
- Following this in 1983, he was cast as "Lt. Neal Quinn" in the TV series "Whiz Kids". He appeared in 17 episodes from 1983 to 1984.
- In 1984, he started his daytime soap career in the TV series "Santa Barbara". He played the character "Cruz Castillo" in 1,048 episodes from 1984 to 1992.
- In 1990, he begun a recurring role as "Daniel Morales" in the TV series "L.A. Law". He appeared in 39 episodes from 1990 to 1994.
- Adolfo was cast in another recurring role in the 1996 TV series "The Profiler". He played the character "Agent Nick 'Coop' Cooper" in 9 episodes from 1996 to 1997.
- In 2002, he returned to daytime TV in "General Hospital". He played "Roy DiLucca" in 95 episodes.

- Another TV series he appeared in was "For the People". He played "Michael Olivas" in 17 episodes from 2002 to 2003.
- In 2008, he was cast as "Ray Montez" in the TV series "One Life to Live". He appeared in 52 episodes from 2008 to 2009.
- He joined the cast of "The Bold and the Beautiful" in 2011 and played the recurring character of "Dr. Ramon Montgomery" in 12 episodes.
- Then in 2012, he was cast in the recurring role of "Jacob Nighthorse" in the TV series "Longmire". He appeared in 23 episodes from 2012 to 2016.
- Adolfo has been married twice – Mare Winningham (1982-82) and Leslie Bryans (1982-present). He has three children with Ms. Bryans.
- In his younger years he played five seasons of semi-pro baseball.
- When he was in high school he played in a rock band and also ran track.
- In 1990, he won a daytime Emmy Award (Outstanding Lead Actor in a Drama Series) for his role in "Santa Barbara".
- Adolfo's other film credits include "Hunters Are for Killing" (1970)(TV), "The Cowboys" (1972), "Starbird and Sweet William" (1973), "Once Upon a Scoundrel" (1974), "Joe Panther" (1976), "Roughnecks" (1980), "Walking the

Edge" (1985), "One Night Stand" (1995), "The Cherokee Kid" (1996)(TV), "Ordinary Sinner" (2001), "Born in the U.S.A." (2007)(TV), "California Winter" (2012) and "In Embryo" (2015).

- His other TV credits include "McCloud" (1975), "Columbo" (1976), "The Streets of San Francisco" (1972-76) 3 episodes, "All in the Family" (1977) 2 episodes, "Barnaby Jones" (1976-79) 3 episodes, "Barney Miller" (1979-81) 2 episodes, "Romance Theatre" (1982) 5 episodes, "The Magnificent Seven" (1999), "Huff" (2006) 2 episodes, "C.S.I." (2005-07) 3 episodes, "Criminal Minds" (2009) and "The Night Shift" (2014).

- **Robert Reed Carradine** was born on March 24, 1954 in Hollywood, California.
- He is the son of actress and artist Sonia Sorel (nee Henius) and Actor John Carradine. His parents divorced when he was two years old.
- Robert has two full brothers (Christopher and Keith Carradine) and three half-brothers (Bruce and David Carradine and Michael Bowen).
- His maternal great-grandfather was biochemist Max Henius.
- Whilst still in high school he lived with his brother David and pursued his two major interests – race car driving and music.

- He and David belonged to a musical quartet and performed in small clubs in Los Angeles and San Francisco.
- In 1971, he made his acting debut in an episode ("A Home for Jamie") of "Bonanza".
- His film debut was in the movie "The Cowboys" in 1972.
- In 1974, he was cast as "Slim" in the TV series "The Cowboys". He appeared in 12 episodes before the series was canceled.
- Then in 2001, he was cast as "Sam McGuire" in the TV series "Lizzie McGuire". He appeared in 65 episodes from 2001 to 2004.
- Robert has been married to Edith Mani since 1990. They have two children, Marcia and Ian. He also has one daughter, Ever, with Susan Snyder.
- He is probably best remembered as the character "Lewis Skolnick" from the "Revenge of the Nerds" movies.
- Robert's other film credits include "Mean Streets" (1973), "Aloha, Bobby and Rose" (1975), "Cannonball!" (1976), "Orca" (1977), "Coming Home" (1978), "The Long Riders" (1980), "Number One with a Bullet" (1987), "Clarence" (1990)(TV), "The Killers Within" (1995), "Gunfighter" (1999), "The Lizzie McGuire Movie" (2003), "Deep Winter" (2008) and "Django Unchained" (2012).

- His other TV credits include "Kung Fu" (1972), "Monte Carlo" (1986) 2 episodes, "Disneyland" (1987), "Dark Skies" (1996), "NYPD Blue" (1997), "Nash Bridges" (1997-2000) 2 episodes, "Law & Order: Criminal Intent" (2005) and "Robot Chicken" (2008).

- **Clay O'Brien** was born Clay O'Brien Cooper on May 6, 1961 in Ray, Arizona.
- He grew up being a little cowboy on the family ranch in the San Fernando Valley. His stepfather, Gene O'Brien, worked as a wrangler on Western movies and television shows.
- He made his acting debut in the film "The Cowboys" in 1972. He played the character "Hardy Fimps".
- In 1974, he was cast as "Weedy" in the TV series "The Cowboys". He appeared in 12 episodes before the series was canceled.
- His last acting appearance, to date, was in an episode ("The Whiz Kid and the Carnival Caper") of "Disneyland" in 1976.
- Clay is married to Beth O'Brien and they have two daughters, Bailey and Quinn.
- After he quit acting Clay returned to a rodeo career, where he has managed to win seven world titles in roping.
- Clay's other film credits include "One Little Indian" (1973), "Cahill U.S. Marshal" (1973),

"Hog Wild" (1974)(TV), "The Apple Dumpling Gang" (1975) and "Mackintosh and T.J." (1975)

- His other TV credits include "Marcus Welby, M.D." (1972), "Gunsmoke" (1972-73) 3 episodes and "Little House on the Prairie" (1975).

- **Clinton 'Clint' Howard** was born on April 20, 1959 in Burbank, California.
- He is the son of actors Rance Howard and Jean Speegle Howard. Clint is also the brother of actor/producer/director Ron Howard.
- Clint attended school at R.L. Stevenson Elementary in Burbank, California.
- He made his uncredited acting debut in an episode ("The Jinx") of "The Andy Griffith Show" in 1962.
- Clint's film debut was in the movie "The Courtship of Eddie's Father" (1963), starring Glenn Ford and his brother Ron.
- He had a recurring role as "Leon" on "The Andy Griffith Show" from 1962 to 1964.
- In 1964, he was cast as "Stanley" in the TV series "The Baileys of Balboa". He appeared in 26 episodes from 1964 to 1965.
- In 1967, he was cast as "Mark Wedloe" in the TV series "Gentle Ben". He appeared in 56 episodes from 1967 to 1969.

- Then in 1974, he was cast as "Steve" in the TV series "The Cowboys". He appeared in 12 episodes before the series was canceled.
- In 1986, he was cast as "Googie" in the short-lived TV series "Gung Ho". He appeared in 9 episodes.
- Another short-lived TV series he appeared in was "Space Rangers" (1993-94). He played the character "Mimmer" in 6 episodes.
- Clint has been married to his present wife, Melanie, since 1995.
- He is only one of five actors that appeared in "Star Trek" (1966) and "Star Trek: Enterprise" (2001).
- Clint is an avid golfer.
- In 1998, he was presented with the MTV Lifetime Achievement Award at the MTV Movie Awards.
- Clint's other film credits include "An Eye for an Eye" (1966), "Gentle Giant" (1967), "The Wild Country" (1970), "The Red Pony" (1973)(TV), "Grand Theft Auto" (1977), "Night Shift" (1982), "Cocoon" (1985), "Parenthood" (1989), "Tango & Cash" (1989), "Backdraft" (1991), "Apollo 13" (1995), "The Grinch" (2000), "Cinderella Man" (2005), "Halloween" (2007), "Frost/Nixon" (2008) and "The Funhouse Massacre" (2015).
- His other TV credits include "The Fugitive" (1964-65) 2 episodes, "Bonanza" (1965), "The

Patty Duke Show" (1966), "Laredo" (1966),
"The Odd Couple" (1970), "The F.B.I." (1965-
70) 2 episodes, "The Virginian" (1966-71) 3
episodes, "The Rookies" (1973), "Disneyland"
(1975), "Happy Days" (1976-80) 2 episodes,
"Hunter" (1990), "Seinfeld" (1992), "The Outer
Limits" (1996), "Crossing Jordan" (2003), "My
Name is Earl (2006-08) 2 episodes, "Arrested
Development" (2003-13) 2 episodes and "Still
the King" (2016) 2 episodes.

"Custer"

Years : 1967

Episodes : 17 (1 season)

Cast :-

Wayne Maunder (b. 1935) - Played Lt. Col.
George Armstrong Custer

Robert F. Simon (b. 1908 d. 1992) - Played Gen.
Alfred Terry

Peter Palmer (b. 1931) - Played Sgt. James
Busterd

Slim Pickens (b. 1919 d. 1983) - Played California
Joe Milner

Michael Dante (b. 1931) - Played Crazy Horse

Synopsis :-
Story about the famous American George
Armstrong Custer.

Trivia & Tidbits :-

"The Show"

- **"Custer"** premiered on ABC on September 6, 1967 and last aired on December 27, 1967.
- The show ran for one season with a total of 17 episodes.
- The series was created by Samuel A. Peeples and David Weisbart and produced by 20th Century Fox.
- The theme music was composed by Leith Stevens and the music supervisor was Lionel Newman.
- Filming took place at the 20th Century Fox Ranch, California.
- The end credits included the following reference - "Series Suggested by Larry Cohen".
- The show aired opposite "The Virginian" on NBC and "Lost in Space" on CBS.
- Sean Penn's father, Leo, directed three episodes.

"In Memoriam"

- **Robert F. Simon** died of a heart attack on November 29, 1992 (83) in Tarzana, California.
- **Slim Pickens** died of a brain tumor on December 8, 1983 (64) in Modesto, California.

"The Stars"

- **Wayne E. Maunder** was born on December 19, 1935 in New Brunswick, Canada.

- His family moved to Bangor, Maine when he was four years old.
- Wayne attended Bangor High School, where he played football and baseball.
- After several unsuccessful tryouts with MLB teams he entered Compton Junior College where he studied psychiatry and then drama.
- Following this he studied acting with Stella Adler in New York.
- Wayne appeared in several plays in the New York area and then headed to Hollywood.
- He made his TV debut in an episode ("Race for the Rainbow") of "The Monroes" in 1967.
- Again in 1967, he was cast as "Lt. Col. George Armstrong Custer" in the TV series "Custer". He appeared in 17 episodes.
- Wayne made his movie debut in the film "The Legend of Custer" in 1968.
- In 1968, he was cast as "Scott Lancer" in the TV series "Lancer". He appeared in 51 episodes from 1968 to 1970.
- Then in 1973, he was cast as "Sgt. Sam MacCray" in the TV series "Chase". He appeared in 21 episodes from 1973 to 1974.
- His last acting appearance, to date, was in the film "Porky's" in 1981.
- Wayne married Lucia Maisto in 1967 and they have one son, Dylan T. Maunder.
- His other film credit is "The Seven Minutes" (1971).
- Wayne's other TV credits include "Kung Fu" (1972), "The Rookies" (1973), "Police Story" (1975) 2 episodes, "The Streets of San

Francisco" (1975) and "Barnaby Jones" (1977).

- **Robert F. Simon** was born on December 2, 1908 in Mansfield, Ohio.
- He was a traveling salesman before entering the acting profession.
- Robert was involved within the Cleveland Play House and then trained at the Actors Studio in New York.
- He had a ten year run on Broadway and appeared in such plays as "Uncle Harry" (1942), "Apology" (1943), "Mrs. January and Mr. X" (1944), "Brighten the Corner" (1945), "All My Sons" (1947), "Sundown Beach" (1948), "Death of a Salesman" (1949) and "Of Thee I Sing" (1952).
- Robert made his uncredited movie debut in the film "Where the Sidewalk Ends" in 1950.
- Then in 1951, he made his TV debut in an episode ("Valley Forge") of "Pulitzer Prize Playhouse".
- Following this, he appeared as a guest star in several TV shows including "The Philco Television Playhouse" (1951-54) 4 episodes, "Out There" (1952), "Man Against Crime" (1953), "Mayor of the Town" (1954), "Topper" (1955), "Alfred Hitchcock Presents" (1955), "Kraft Television Theatre" (1953-56) 4 episodes, "Broken Arrow" (1957), "Climax!" (1954-58) 5 episodes, "Playhouse 90" (1957-

58) 4 episodes, "Disneyland" (1958) 2 episodes, "Zane Grey Theatre" (1959), "Laramie" (1959), "Cheyenne" (1957-59) 2 episodes, "Johnny Ringo" (1959), "The Texan" (1959-60) 2 episodes, "Tombstone Territory" (1960) 2 episodes, "Bat Masterson" (1960), "Lawman" (1959-61) 2 episodes, "Have Gun – Will Travel" (1957-62) 4 episodes and "The Dick Powell Show" (1961-62) 4 episodes.

- In 1962, he was cast in the recurring role of "Dave Tabak" in the TV series "Saints and Sinners". He appeared in 13 episodes from 1962 to 1963.
- In 1967, he was cast as "Gen. Alfred Terry" in the TV series "Custer". He appeared in 17 episodes.
- Then in 1970, he was cast as "Uncle Everett McPherson" in the TV series "Nancy". He appeared in 17 episodes from 1970 to 1971.
- From 1964 to 1971, he had the recurring role of "Frank Stephens" in the TV series "Bewitched". He appeared in 5 episodes.
- In 1978, he was cast as "J. Jonah Jameson" in the TV series "The Amazing Spider-Man". He appeared in 13 episodes from 1978 to 1979.
- His last acting appearance was in an episode ("Airwolf II") of "Airwolf" in 1985.
- Robert was married and had two daughters (Barbara and Susan) and two sons (Robert and James).

- His other film credits include "The Black Dakotas" (1954), "Seven Angry Men" (1955), "The Benny Goodman Story" (1956), "Gunman's Walk" (1958), "Operation Petticoat" (1959), "The Man Who Shot Liberty Valance" (1962), "Wall of Noise" (1963), "Captain Newman, M.D." (1963), "Blindfold" (1965), "Private Duty Nurses" (1971) and "Tail Gunner Joe" (1977)(TV).
- Robert's other TV credits include "The Dakotas" (1963), "Daniel Boone" (1964), "Profiles in Courage" (1965) 2 episodes, "Dr. Kildare" (1965) 2 episodes, "Gunsmoke" (1957-66) 7 episodes, "Laredo" (1965-67) 2 episodes, "The Virginian" (1963-68) 4 episodes, "Bonanza" (1960-70) 2 episodes, "Nichols" (1971), "M.A.S.H." (1973) 3 episodes, "Hawaii Five-O" (1975), "The Streets of San Francisco" (1972-76) 7 episodes and "Quincy M.E." (1977-82) 4 episodes.

- **Peter Webster Palmer** was born on September 20, 1931 in Milwaukee, Wisconsin.
- He attended the University of Illinois where he played football and was a member of the team that won the Rose Bowl in 1952.
- Whilst at university Peter studied voice under Bruce Foote.
- In 1956, he was cast in the play "Li'l Abner" on Broadway. He stayed with the production for two years.

- In 1959, he made his movie debut in the film "Li'l Abner".
- Then in 1960, he made his TV debut in an episode ("Clem Kadiddlehopper in Dog Patch") of the "Red Skelton Show".
- A few more TV guest appearances followed including "The Texan" (1960), "The Bell Telephone Hour" (1960), "The Bill Dana Show" (1964) 2 episodes and "The John Forsythe Show" (1966).
- In 1967, He was cast as "Sgt. James Bustard" in the TV series "Custer". He appeared in 17 episodes.
- In 1977, he was cast as "Oscar Heinz" in the TV series "The Kallikaks". The show only lasted 5 episodes.
- His last acting appearance, to date, was in an episode ("Blast Off") of "Thunder in Paradise" in 1994.
- Peter has been married twice – Jackie Gleason (1954-65) and Mary Lou (Aniko) Farrell (? – 2011). He had five children with Ms. Gleason and one daughter with Ms. Farrell.
- He appeared in two more Broadway plays – "Brigadoon" (1963) and "Lorelei" (1974).
- Peter's other film credits include "The Legend of Custer" (1968), "The Hostage Heart" (1977)(TV), "A Time of Destiny" (1988) and "Edward Scissorhands" (1990).
- His other TV credits include "Lancer" (1969-70) 2 episodes, "The Rockford Files" (1976), "Three's Company" (1977), "Charlie's Angels" (1978), "M.A.S.H." (1978), "Simon & Simon" (1983), "Dallas" (1986), "Still the Beaver" (1989) and "Superboy" (1988-91) 2 episodes.

- **Slim Pickens** was born Louis Burton Lindley Jr. on June 29, 1919 in Kingsburg, California.
- He was the son of Sally Mosher (nee Turk) and Louis Bert Lindley Sr.
- Slim graduated from Hanford High School, California and joined the rodeo. He eventually became a well-known rodeo clown.
- After twenty years on the rodeo circuit he made his movie debut in the film "Rocky Mountain" (1950).
- Many more film roles followed including "Colorado Sundown" (1952), "The Story of Will Rogers" (1952), "Down Laredo Way" (1953), "The Boy from Oklahoma" (1954) and "The Outcast" (1954).
- Slim made his TV debut in an episode ("The Wild Bunch of Wyoming") of "Stories of the Century" in 1954.
- Following this, he guest starred in many TV shows including "Buffalo Bill Jr." (1956), "The Lone Ranger" (1956), "Circus Boy" (1956), "Annie Oakley" (1956) 4 episodes, "Cheyenne" (1957), "Frontier Doctor" (1959), "Overland Trail" (1960), "Sugarfoot" (1957-60) 3 episodes, "Riverboat" (1960), "Maverick" (1958-61) 3 episodes and "Bronco" (1961).
- In 1961, he was cast as "Slim" in the TV series "Outlaws". He appeared in 20 episodes from 1961 to 1962.
- In 1962, he was cast as "Slim Walker" in the TV series "Wide Country". He appeared in 6 episodes from 1962 to 1963.

- Then in 1967, he was cast as "California Joe Milner" in the TV series "Custer". He appeared in 17 episodes.
- In 1979, he played the recurring character "Sgt. Beauregard Wiley" in the TV series "B.J. and the Bear". He appeared in 5 episodes from 1979 to 1981.
- His last role before he passed away was in the TV movie "Sawyer and Finn" (1983).
- Slim was married to Margaret Pickens for many years and they had three children.
- One of his most memorable roles was as "Major 'King' Kong" in the film "Dr. Strangelove or: How I Learned to Stop Worrying and Love the Bomb" (1964).
- In 1982, he was inducted into the Hall of Great Western Performers at the National Cowboy and Western Heritage Museum.
- In 2005, he was inducted into the Pro Rodeo Hall of Fame.
- Slim held a civilian pilot's licence with a multi-engine rating.
- His other film credits include "Santa Fe Passage" (1955), "The Sheepman" (1958), "One-Eyed Jacks" (1961), "Savage Sam" (1963), "Major Dundee" (1965), "In Harm's Way" (1965), "Stagecoach" (1966), "Will Penny" (1968), "The Legend of Custer" (1968), "The Cowboys" (1972), "Pat Garrett & Billy the Kid" (1973), "Blazing Saddles" (1974), "The Apple Dumpling Gang" (1975), "1941" (1979) and "Pink Motel" (1982).
- Slim's other TV credits include "The Tall Man" (1962), "Wagon Train" (1958-62) 2 episodes, "The Travels of Jaimie McPheeters" (1963),

"The Fugitive" (1964), "Rawhide" (1964), "Daniel Boone" (1966) 2 episodes, "Cimarron Strip" (1968), "The Outcasts" (1968), "Ironside" (1969), "Bonanza" (1963-70) 4 episodes, "The Virginian" (1963-71) 3 episodes, "Gunsmoke" (1964-72) 5 episodes, "Hawaii Five-O" (1973), "Disneyland" (1957-74) 18 episodes, "The Misadventures of Sheriff Lobo" (1979) and "Filthy Rich" (1982).

- **Michael Dante** was born Ralph Vitti on September 2, 1931 in Stamford, Connecticut.
- He attended Stamford High School where he played on the school baseball team.
- After graduating from high school he signed a bonus contract with the Boston Braves.
- Following this, he took drama classes at the University of Miami and bandleader Tommy Dorsey arranged a screen test for him at M.G.M.
- Michael made his uncredited movie debut in the film "Somebody Up There Likes Me" in 1956.
- In 1957, he made his TV debut in an episode ("Reluctant Hero") of "Sugarfoot".
- He then guest starred on many TV shows including "Colt .45" (1957-58) 2 episodes, "Cheyenne" (1957-58) 4 episodes, "Tales of the Texas Rangers" (1958), "Rescue 8" (1958), "Lawman" (1959), "The Adventures of Rin Tin Tin" (1959), "Maverick" (1957-59) 3 episodes, "The Texan" (1959) 4 episodes, "Checkmate" (1961), "The Detectives" (1961), "87th Precinct" (1962), "Hawaiian Eye" (1963),

"Perry Mason" (1959-65) 2 episodes, "Bonanza" (1965) and "Get Smart" (1966).

- In 1967, he was cast as "Crazy Horse" in the TV series "Custer". He appeared in 16 episodes.
- His last acting appearance, to date, was in the film "Unbelievable!!!!!" in 2016.
- At present, Michael lives with his wife, Mary Jane, in Rancho Mirage, California.
- Michael's other film credits include "Fort Dobbs" (1958), "Westbound" (1959), "Seven Thieves" (1960), "Kid Galahad" (1962), "Operation Bikini" (1963), "Apache Rifles" (1964), "Arizona Raiders" (1965), "The Legend of Custer" (1968), "Willard" (1971), "The Farmer" (1977), "The Messenger" (1986) and "Cage" (1989).
- His other TV credits include "Star Trek" (1967), "The Big Valley" (1968), "Death Valley Days" (1959-69) 2 episodes, "Daniel Boone" (1969), "My Three Sons" (1972), "Disneyland" (1980), "Knots Landing" (1982), "The Fall Guy" (1983-84) 2 episodes and "Cagney & Lacey" (1987).

"The Dakotas"

Years : 1963

Episodes : 20 (1 season)

Cast :-

Larry Ward (b. 1924 d. 1985) - Played Marshal Frank Ragan

Jack Elam (b. 1920 d. 2003) - Played Deputy J.D. Smith

Chad Everett (b. 1936 d. 2012) - Played Deputy Del Stark

Mike Greene (b. 1933) - Played Deputy Vance Porter

Synopsis :-
A marshal and his three deputies keep the peace in the Dakota Territory.

Trivia & Tidbits :-

"The Show"

- **"The Dakotas"** premiered on ABC on January 7, 1963 and last aired on September 9, 1963.

- The show ran for one season with a total of 20 black and white episodes.
- It was a spin-off of the popular TV Western "Cheyenne". All four characters initially appeared in the "Cheyenne" episode "A Man Called Ragan".
- The theme music was composed by Harold Levey and Kenneth S. Webb.
- The show was produced by Warner Bros. Television and filmed on Laramie Street, Warner Bros. Burbank Studios.
- The series was cancelled after viewers complained about the episode "Sanctuary at Crystal Springs" (violence).

"In Memoriam"

- **Larry Ward** died on February 16, 1985 (60) in Los Angeles, California.
- **Jack Elam** died of congestive heart failure on October 20, 2003 (82) in Ashland, Oregon.
- **Chad Everett** died of lung cancer on July 24, 2012 (75) in Los Angeles, California.

"The Stars"

- **Larry Ward** was born on October 3, 1924 in Columbus, Ohio.
- His father was a former college football coach and a member of the Ohio State Senate.
- After graduating from high school he attended a number of universities before enlisting in the

United States Navy, where he served for three years.

- Following his discharge, he enrolled in the American Theatre Wing under the G.I. Bill of Rights.
- Larry made his acting debut in the TV series "The Brighter Day". He played the character "Dr. Randy Hamilton" from 1954 to 1957.
- Following this, he appeared as a guest star on a number of TV shows including "Lawman" (1962), "Cheyenne" ("A Man Called Ragan") (1962), "Checkmate" (1962), "77 Sunset Strip" (1962) and "Have Gun – Will Travel" (1962).
- In 1963, he was cast as "Marshal Frank Ragan" in the TV series "The Dakotas". He appeared in 20 episodes.
- His final acting appearance was in an episode ("The Moon Is Not Blue") of "M.A.S.H." in 1982.
- Larry was married to Roberta Haynes.
- His film credits include "A Distant Trumpet" (1964), "The Iron Men" (1966)(TV), "Hombre" (1967), "Shadow of Death" (1969) and "The Deathbed Virgin" (1974).
- Larry's other TV credits include "Temple Houston" (1964) 2 episodes, "Rawhide" (1965), "The Loner" (1965), "Lost in Space" (1966), "The Time Tunnel" (1966), "The Road West" (1966), "Gunsmoke" (1963-66) 4 episodes, "The Virginian" (1969-70) 2 episodes, "Bonanza" (1968-72) 5 episodes, "Banacek" (1974), "Cannon" (1974-75) 2 episodes and "Wonder Woman" (1978).

- **Jack Elam (see "Temple Houston")**

- **Chad Everett** was born Raymon Lee Cramton on June 11, 1937 in South Bend, Indiana.
- He was the son of Virdeen Ruth Hopper and Harry Clyde 'Ted' Cramton. Chad's father was a race car driver, racing mechanic and auto parts salesman.
- Chad was raised in Dearborn, Michigan and attended Fordson High School.
- Following this he attended Wayne State University in Detroit and graduated with a degree in drama.
- After he graduated he moved to Hollywood and signed a contract with Warner Brothers.
- Chad made his acting debut in an episode ("High Tide") of "Surfside 6" in 1960.
- He then made his movie debut in the film "Caudelle Inglish" in 1961.
- Many guest appearances on TV shows followed including "Lawman" (1961) 2 episodes, "Bronco" (1960-62) 2 episodes, "77 Sunset Strip" (1961-62), "Cheyenne" (1962) and "Hawaiian Eye" (1960-62) 5 episodes.
- In 1963, he was cast as "Deputy Del Stark" in the TV series "The Dakotas". He appeared in 20 episodes.
- In 1969, he was cast as "Dr. Joe Gannon" in the TV series "Medical Center". He appeared in 170 episodes from 1969 to 1976.

- Then in 1978, he was cast as "Major Maxwell Mercy" in the TV mini-series "James A. Michener's Centennial". He appeared in 12 episodes.
- Another TV series he appeared in was the short-lived "Hagen" (1980). He played "Paul Hagen" in 9 episodes.
- In 1983, he was cast as "Wyatt Earp III" in the TV series "The Rousters". He appeared in 13 episodes from 1983 to 1984.
- In 1994, he appeared as "Jack McKenna" in the short-lived TV series "McKenna". Although there were 13 episodes made, only 5 were aired.
- In 2000, he was cast as "Jake Manhattan" in the TV series "Manhattan AZ". The show only lasted 13 episodes.
- His last TV series was "Chemistry" (2011) in which he played the character "Vic". He appeared in 14 episodes.
- Chad's last acting appearance was in an episode ("The Blue Butterfly") of "Castle" in 2012.
- He was married to actress Shelby Grant from 1966 until her death in 2011. They had two children.
- In 1986, he was awarded a Star on the Hollywood Walk of Fame for his contribution to television.

- His name was changed to "Chad Everett" by his agent Henry Willson.
- Chad's other film credits include "Rome Adventure" (1962), "The Singing Nun" (1966), "Return of the Gunfighter" (1967), "The Firechasers" (1971), "Give Me My Money" (1977), "Malibu" (1983)(TV), "The Rousters" (1983)(TV), "Heroes Stand Alone" (1989), "Star Command" (1996)(TV), "Psycho" (1998), "Mulholland Dr." (2001), "Unspoken" (2006) and "Break" (2008).
- His other TV credits include "Redigo" (1963), "Branded" (1965), "The F.B.I." (1968), "Ironside" (1969), "Police Story" (1978), "The Love Boat" (1986) 2 episodes, "Murder, She Wrote" (1986-93) 4 episodes, "Diagnosis Murder" (1997), "Melrose Place" (1998) 4 episodes, "The Mountain" (2004), "Cold Case" (2006) and "Undercovers" (2010-12) 3 episodes.

- **Michael Harris Greene** was born on November 4, 1933 in San Francisco, California.
- He is the son of Gladys Pugh and Henry Greene.
- Michael made his uncredited acting debut in an episode ("East Is East") of "Johnny Ringo" in 1960.
- Several more TV guest spots followed including "Gunsmoke" (1960), "The Westerner" (1960), "Riverboat" (1960),

"Wanted: Dead or Alive" (1961), "Outlaws" (1961), "The Rifleman" (1962) and "Cheyenne" (1962) 2 episodes.

- In 1963, he was cast as "Deputy Vance Porter" in the TV series "The Dakotas". He appeared in 19 episodes.
- His last acting appearance, to date, was in the TV movie "The Day Reagan Was Shot" in 2001.
- Michael was married to Patricia Donovan but they have since divorced.
- His film credits include "This Is Not a Test" (1962), "Mickey and the Contessa" (1963)(TV), "The Last Movie" (1971), "The Clones" (1973), "California Split" (1974), "Harry and Walter Go to New York" (1976), "The Ordeal of Patty Hearst" (1979)(TV), "The Mountain Men" (1980), "Moscow on the Hudson" (1984), "Lost in America" (1985), "Down and Out in Beverly Hills" (1986), "Stranded" (1987), "Lord of the Flies" (1990), "For the Boys" (1991), "Gunsmoke: The Long Ride" (1993)(TV) and "The Politics of Desire" (1998).
- Michael's other TV credits include "The Big Valley" (1965), "Batman" (1966) 2 episodes, "The Virginian" (1966), "Laredo" (1967), "The Outcasts" (1968), "Gunsmoke" (1966-71) 3 episodes, "Bonanza" (1972), "Kung Fu" (1973-74) 2 episodes, "The A-Team" (1983), "The Fall Guy" (1986), "Chicken Soup" (1989), "Hunter" (1990), "F.B.I.: The Untold Stories" (1991), "Melrose Place" (1995) and "Baywatch" (1994-97) 2 episodes.

"Daniel Boone"

Years : 1964 - 1970

Episodes : 165 (6 seasons)

Cast :-

Fess Parker (b. 1924 d. 2010) - Played Daniel Boone

Patricia Blair (b. 1931 d. 2013) - Played Rebecca Boone

Ed Ames (b. 1927) - Played Mingo

Darby Hinton (b. 1957) - Played Israel Boone

Veronica Cartwright (b. 1949) - Played Jemima Boone

Dallas McKennon (b. 1919 d. 2009) - Played Cincinnatus

Synopsis :-
The exploits of the legendary frontier hero Daniel Boone.

Trivia & Tidbits :-

"The Show"

- **"Daniel Boone"** premiered on NBC on September 24, 1964 and last aired on September 10, 1970.
- The show ran for six seasons with a total of 165 episodes.
- "Daniel Boone" called his wife "Tick Licker".
- The theme song was written by Vera Matson (lyrics) and Lionel Newman (music).
- The pilot episode was titled "Ken-Tuck-E".
- Production companies involved in the show were Arcola Pictures, Fespar Enterprises, NBC and 20th Century Fox Television.
- Filming locations included Big Bear Lake, California; Iverson Ranch, California; Kanab Movie Ranch, Utah and Walt Disney's Golden Oak Ranch, California.
- Actor Albert Salmi portrayed "Daniel's" sidekick "Yandkin" in season one only.
- Some of the other semi-regular characters were "Josh Clements" (played by singer-actor Jimmy Dean) and "Gabe Cooper" (played by NFL footballer Roosevelt 'Rosey' Grier).
- Fess Parker ("Daniel Boone") wore a coonskin cap in the show, however, the real life Daniel did not.
- Although the "Boone's" had two children in the show, they actually had ten children.
- Daughter "Jemima" (played by Veronica Cartwright) "disappeared" from the show towards the end of the second season.

- There were three versions of the theme song written by Matson and Newman. The "groovy version" was sung by the group "The Imperials".
- Walt Disney made an earlier mini-series of "Daniel Boone" starring Dewey Martin in the title role.

"In Memoriam"

- **Fess Parker** died of natural causes on March 18, 2010 (85) in Santa Ynez, California.
- **Patricia Blair** died of breast cancer on September 9, 2013 (80) in North Wildwood, New Jersey.
- **Dallas McKennon** died on July 14, 2009 (89) in Raymond, Washington.

"The Stars"

- **Fess Elisha Parker** was born on August 16, 1924 in Fort Worth, Texas.
- He was raised on a farm near San Angelo, Texas.
- After graduating from high school in 1942 he joined the U.S. Navy. He tried to become a pilot but was found to be too tall (6 feet 6 inches). Fess eventually became a radio operator on a minesweeper in the South Pacific.
- Fess was discharged from the Navy in 1946 and enrolled at Hardin-Simmons University on

the G.I. Bill. He then transferred to the University of Texas in 1947 as a history major.

- After graduation he headed for California and studied drama at the University of Southern California.
- He made his show business debut as the voice of "Leslie the Chauffeur" in the 1950 film "Harvey".
- Fess was then an extra in the play "Mister Roberts".
- In 1952, he made his first credited appearance in the film "Untamed Frontier".
- In 1954, he made his TV debut in an episode ("The Big Winchester") of "Dragnet".
- Later on in 1954, he made his first appearance as "Davy Crockett" in an episode of "Disneyland". The title of the episode was "Davy Crockett: Indian Fighter".
- He would go on to appear in another four episodes as "Davy Crockett".
- In 1962, he was cast as "Sen. Eugene Smith" in the TV series "Mr. Smith Goes to Washington". He appeared in 25 episodes from 1962 to 1963.
- Then in 1964, he was cast as "Daniel Boone" in the TV series of the same name. He appeared in 165 episodes from 1964 to 1970.
- His last acting appearance was in the TV short "The Fess Parker Show" in 1974.
- Fess was married to Marcella Rinehart from 1960 until his death in 2010. They had two children, Fess and Ashley.
- In 1991, Fess was named a Disney Legend.

- After he retired from acting, he spent much of his time operating his Fess Parker Family Winery and Vineyards in Los Olivos, California.
- Fess' other film credits included "The Kid from Left Field" (1953), "Thunder Over the Plains" (1953), "Them!" (1954), "Battle Cry" (1955), "Old Yeller" (1957), "The Hangman" (1959), "Hell Is for Heroes" (1962), "Daniel Boone: Frontier Trail Rider" (1966) and "Climb an Angry Mountain" (1972)(TV).
- His other TV credits include "Stories of the Century" (1954), "Annie Oakley" (1954) 2 episodes, "City Detective" (1955), "Death Valley Days" (1954-62) 2 episodes, "Destry" (1964) and "The Red Skelton Show" (1970).

- **Patricia Blair** was born Patsy Lou Blake on January 15, 1933 in Fort Worth, Texas.
- She grew up in Dallas and became a teenage model from the Conover Agency.
- After a stint in summer stock she was signed by Warner Bros. and then moved to M.G.M. in 1959.
- Patricia made her movie debut in the film "Jump Into Hell" in 1955.
- In 1956, she made her TV debut on "The Bob Hope Show".
- In 1959, she played the part of "Goldy" in 5 episodes of the TV series "Yancy Derringer".
- Then in 1962, she was cast as "Lou Mallory" in the TV series "The Rifleman". She appeared in 22 episodes from 1962 to 1963.

- In 1964, she was cast as "Rebecca Boone" in the TV series "Daniel Boone". She appeared in 118 episodes from 1964 to 1970.
- Her last acting appearance was in the film "The Electric Horseman" in 1979.
- Patricia was married to Martin S. Colbert from 1965 to 1993.
- In later years, she produced trade shows in New York and New Jersey.
- Patricia's other film credits included "Crime Against Joe" (1956), "The Black Sheep" (1956), "City of Fear" (1959), "Cage of Evil" (1960), "Daniel Boone: Frontier Trail Rider" (1966) and "Left Hand of Gemini" (1972).
- Her other TV credits included "Telephone Time" (1956), "Mike Hammer" (1958), "Rescue 8" (1959), "Steve Canyon" (1959), "Follow the Sun" (1962), "Surfside 6" (1962), "The Virginian" (1963), "My Three Sons" (1963), "Perry Mason" (1963), "Bonanza" (1964), "Dusty's Trail" (1973) and "Petrocelli" (1975).

- **Ed Ames** was born Edmund Dantes Urick on July 9, 1927 in Malden, Massachusetts.
- He was the son of Sarah and David Urick, who had emigrated from the Ukraine. Ed was the youngest of nine children.
- Ed attended the Boston Latin School where he studied music and literature.
- After finishing high school, Ed and his brothers formed a singing group and eventually

performed under the name "The Ames Brothers".

- The group's first hit record was the doubled-sided "Rag Mop" and "Sentimental Me" released in 1950.
- The boys (Joe, Gene, Vic and Ed) then joined RCA Victor Records and had such hits as "It Only Hurts For a Little While", "You, You, You" and "The Naughty Lady of Shady Lane".
- The group disbanded in 1963 and Ed continued on with a solo career.
- Ed made his TV acting debut in an episode ("The Dancing Dowager") of "State Trooper" in 1957.
- Several more TV guest spots followed including "Mike Hammer" (1958), "The Rifleman" (1962), "Redigo" (1963) and "The Travels of Jaimie McPheeters" (1963).
- In 1964, he was cast as "Mingo" in the TV series "Daniel Boone". He appeared in 72 episodes from 1964 to 1968.
- Ed made his movie debut in the film "Daniel Boone: Frontier Trail Rider" in 1966.
- His last acting appearance, to date, was in an episode ("Little Odessa") of "The Marshal" in 1995.
- Ed has been married twice – Sara Cacheiro (1947-1970) and Jeanne Arnold (1998-present). He has three children with Ms. Cacheiro.

- He has appeared in several plays over the years including "The Crucible", "The Fantasticks", "Carnival!" and "One Flew Over the Cuckoo's Nest".
- In the 1960's, Ed had a number of hit records including "Try to Remember" (1965), "My Cup Runneth Over" (1967) and "Who Will Answer?" (1968).
- From 1968 to 1987, Ed had a part ownership in the Phoenix Suns professional basketball team.
- Ed sang the "Ballad of the War Wagon" in the John Wayne film "The War Wagon" in 1967.
- In 1975, Ed graduated from the University of California, Los Angeles with a degree in theater and cinema.
- Ed's other film credits include "Androcles and the Lion" (1967)(TV) and "Cricket on the Hearth" (1967)(TV).
- His other TV credits include "The Starlost" (1973), "Kodiak" (1974), "McCloud" (1974), "Murder, She Wrote" (1985), "In the Heat of the Night" (1988) and "Jake and the Fatman" (1990).

- **Darby Hinton** was born Edgar Raymond Darby Hinton on August 19, 1957 in Santa Monica, California.

- He is the son of Ed (an actor) and Marilynn Hinton. His father was killed in a plane crash when Darby was fourteen months old.
- Darby attended Emerson Junior High School in West Los Angeles and then transferred to the American School in Switzerland.
- Following this, he began college on a cruise ship, the World Campus Afloat Institute for Shipboard Education.
- He later continued his studies at the Pepperdine University near Malibu, California.
- Darby made his 'acting' debut at the age of six months old in the arms of Jayne Mansfield in the TV series "Playhouse 90".
- He made his movie debut in the film "Hero's Island" in 1962.
- In 1964, he was cast as "Israel Boone" in the TV series "Daniel Boone". He appeared in 110 episodes from 1964 to 1970.
- Several more TV guest appearances followed including "Wagon Train" (1964), "The Adventures of Ozzie & Harriet" (1966), "The Big Valley" (1967), "Disneyland" (1968) 2 episodes, "Owen Marshall, Counselor at Law" (1971) and "Hawaii Five-O" (1975).
- His last acting appearance, to date, was in the TV movie documentary "Dead of Winter: The Donner Party" in 2015.
- Darby has been married twice – Drana Preissman (divorced) and Shan Griffiths

(present). He has four children (Nick, Dakota, Ryder and India), two by each spouse.

- His son Nick is a member of the band "Badwater".
- Darby is involved in martial arts, and skilled in the JKD concept of fighting.
- His other film credits include "The Treasure of Jamaica Reef" (1975), "Hi-Riders" (1978), "Angel's Brigade" (1979), "Without Warning" (1980), "Wacko" (1982), "Malibu Express" (1985), "Dark Future" (1994), "They Crawl" (2001) and "Just for Kicks" (2003).
- Darby's other TV credits include "Magnum, P.I." (1981), "The Fall Guy" (1982-83) 2 episodes, "Jake and the Fatman" (1990), "Knots Landing" (1991), "Mike Hammer, Private Eye" (1997), "Rescue 77" (1999) and "Father Pete's Corner" (2015).

- **Veronica A. Cartwright** was born on April 20, 1949 in Bristol, England.
- She immigrated to the United States with her parents and sister (Angela Cartwright) in the early 1950's.
- Veronica began her career modelling and doing print ads for Kellogg's Corn Flakes.
- Her first acting appearance was an uncredited part in the film "In Love and War" (1958).
- This was followed by appearances in TV shows such as "Zane Grey Theatre" (1959), "One

Step Beyond" (1960), "The Betty Hutton Show" (1960), "Make Room for Daddy" (1959-61) 2 episodes, "Leave It To Beaver" (1959-63) 4 episodes, "The Bob Hope Show" (1962) and "The Dick Powell Show" (1963).

- In 1963, she appeared in the Alfred Hitchcock film "The Birds" followed by an uncredited part in the movie "Spencer's Mountain".
- In 1964, she was cast as "Jemima Boone" in the TV series "Daniel Boone". She appeared in 37 episodes from 1964 to 1966.
- Several more TV guest appearances followed including "Mannix" (1968), "Family Affair" (1969), "The Mod Squad" (1969), "Death Valley Days" (1970), "My Three Sons" (1970), "Serpico" (1976) and "Still the Beaver" (1985).
- In 1988, she played "Molly Hark" in the TV mini-series "Tanner 88". She appeared in 10 episodes.
- Then in 1989, she had a recurring role as "A.D.A. Margaret Flanagan" in the TV series "L.A. Law". She appeared in 9 episodes from 1989 to 1992.
- In 1998-9, she appeared in 4 episodes of the TV series "The X Files". She received two Emmy Award nominations for her role.
- Veronica has been married three times – Richard Gates (1968-72), Stanley Goldstein (1976-80) and Richard Compton (1982-2007). She has one son, Dakota, with Mr. Compton.

- Her character ("Violet Rutherford") on "Leave It To Beaver" gave "Beaver Cleaver" his first kiss.
- Veronica is best remembered for her roles in the science fiction films "Invasion of the Body Snatchers" (1978) and "Alien" (1979).
- Her other film credits include "The Children's Hour" (1961), "One Man's Way" (1964), "Inserts" (1975), "Goin' South" (1978), "The Right Stuff" (1983), "The Witches of Eastwick" (1987), "Valentino Returns" (1989), "Shoot the Moon" (1996), "My Engagement Party" (1998), "Scary Movie 2" (2001), "The Invasion" (2007), "Call of the Wild" (2009), "The Odd Way Home" (2013) and "The Dark Below" (2015).
- Veronica's other TV credits include "Miami Vice" (1987), "ER" (1997), "Chicago Hope" (1999), "Touched by an Angel" (2001), "Judging Amy" (2002), "Six Feet Under" (2004-05) 3 episodes, "Boston Legal" (2006), "Invasion" (2005-06) 5 episodes, "The Nine" (2006-07) 3 episodes, "Eastwick" (2009) 11 episodes, "Revenge" (2012) 2 episodes, "Resurrection" (2014) 5 episodes, "Bosch" (2015) 4 episodes and "Criminal Minds" (2016).

- **Dallas 'Dal' Raymond McKennon** was born on July 19, 1919 in La Grande, Oregon.

- His mother died when he was a teenager and because his father couldn't cope he and his two sisters were sent to live with family friends.
- Dal attended La Grande High School and during this time had a job at the local radio station.
- After graduation he joined the Army Corps of Engineers and was sent to Alaska and later Korea.
- Following his stint in the army he moved, with his wife, to Hollywood.
- In his early years in Hollywood he provided the voice on many animated features including "Buzz Buzzard" in Walter Lantz's "Woody Woodpecker" shorts.
- Dal provided the voices for many Disney characters and can be heard in films such as "Lady and the Tramp", "Sleeping Beauty", "One Hundred and One Dalmatians", "Mary Poppins" and "Bedknobs and Broomsticks".
- His first uncredited acting appearance was in the film "Bend of the River" in 1952.
- Dal's first TV appearance was in an episode ("The Big Lover") of "Dragnet" in 1953.
- He then appeared in "Lawman" (1959), "Colt .45" (1959) and "The Du Pont Show with June Allyson" (1959).

- In 1960, he supplied the voice of "Q.T. Hush" in the TV series of the same name. He provided the voice for 100 episodes.
- He then appeared in several more TV shows including "U.S. Marshal" (1960), "Sugarfoot" (1960), "Riverboat" (1960), "Holiday Lodge" (1961) and "The Tall Man" (1961).
- In 1960, he supplied the voices for "Courageous Cat/Minute Mouse/The Chief" in the TV series "Courageous Cat and Minute Mouse". He voiced 130 episodes from 1960 to 1962.
- From 1961 to 1962, he had a recurring role as "Dr. Blaney" in the TV series "87th Precinct". He appeared in 7 episodes.
- In 1964, he was cast as "Cincinnatus" in the TV series "Daniel Boone". He appeared in 81 episodes from 1964 to 1970.
- In 1965, he supplied the voices of "Sinbad Jr./Salty" in the TV series "Sinbad Jr." He voiced 20 episodes.
- Then in 1968, he voiced "Archie Andrews/Hot Dog/Mr. Weatherbee" in two series, "The Archie Show" (6 episodes) and "Archie's Funhouse" (23 episodes).
- Dal was married to Betty Warner from 1942 until his death in 2009. They had eight children.
- He supplied the voices in a number of Disney attractions such as "Big Thunder Mountain

Railroad", "It's a Small World" and "Epcot's The American Adventure".

- During the 1960's and 1970's he provided the original voices of "Tony the Tiger" for Kellogg's Frosties, "Corny the Rooster" for Kellogg's Cornflakes and "Snap, Crackle and Pop" for Kellogg's Rice Krispies.
- Dal's other film credits include "Good Day for a Hanging" (1959) uncredited, "The Silent Call" (1961), "Womanhunt" (1962), "House of the Damned" (1963), "The Birds" (1963) uncredited, "7 Faces of Dr. Lao" (1964), "Daniel Boone: Frontier Trail Rider" (1966), "The Andersonville Trial" (1970)(TV), "Hot Lead and Cold Feet" (1978) and "Mystery Mansion" (1983).
- His other TV credits include "The Untouchables" (1962), "Gunsmoke" (1961-62) 2 episodes, "Ben Casey" (1962), "The Virginian" (1962-63) 2 episodes, "The Rifleman" (1963) 2 episodes, "Wagon Train" (1960-64) 8 episodes, "My Three Sons" (1962-64) 2 episodes, "The Big Valley" (1965), "Bonanza" (1966), "Iron Horse" (1967) and "Cannon" (1971).

"Destry"

Years : 1964

Episodes : 13 (1 season)

Cast :-

John Gavin (b. 1931) - Played Harrison Destry

Synopsis :-

Destry, an innocent man sent to prison, searches for the men who framed him.

Trivia & Tidbits :-

"The Show"

- **"Destry"** premiered on ABC on February 14, 1964 and last aired on May 8, 1964.
- The show ran for one season with a total of 13 black and white episodes.
- "Destry" was based on the James Stewart (he played "Tom Destry") film "Destry Rides Again" (1939).
- In the TV series John Gavin plays "Harrison Destry", son of "Tom".
- The show was produced by Revue Studios at their studios in California.

- The "Destry" pilot ("The Solid Gold Girl") was directed by Don Siegel ("Dirty Harry").
- "Destry" was a mid-season replacement for the canceled series "77 Sunset Strip".

"The Star"

- **John Gavin** was born John Anthony Golenor on April 8, 1931 in Los Angeles, California.
- He is the son of Herald Ray Golenor (Spanish origin) and Delia Diana Pablos (Mexican origin).
- John attended St. John's Military Academy (Los Angeles) and Villanova Prep (Ojai, California).
- He earned a Bachelor of Arts degree from Stanford University.
- During the Korean War he was an air intelligence officer. He was discharged in 1955.
- After his discharge he signed a contract with Universal Studios and appeared in his first film, "Raw Edge", in 1956.
- Several more film roles followed including "Behind the High Wall" (1956), "Four Girls in Town" (1957), "Quantex" (1957), "A Time to Die" (1958), "Imitation of Life" (1959), "Psycho" (1960), "Spartacus" (1960), "Romanoff and Juliet" (1961) and "Tammy Tell Me True" (1961).
- John made his TV debut in an episode ("The Martyr") of "Insight" in 1960.
- In 1964, he was cast as "Harrison Destry" in the TV series "Destry". He appeared in 13 episodes.

- In 1965, he was cast as "Comdr. Dan Talbot" in the TV series "Convoy". He appeared in 13 episodes.
- His last acting appearance, to date, was in an episode ("Loving Strangers/Something Borrowed, Something Blue...") of "Fantasy Island" in 1981.
- John has been married twice – Cicely Evans (1957-65) and Constance Towers (1974-present). He and ex-wife Ms. Evans have two daughters. John also has two step-children with Ms. Towers.
- In 1959, he won a Golden Globe Award for Most Promising Newcomer – Male (shared with Bradford Dillman and Efrem Zimbalist Jr.).
- In 1961, he was appointed special adviser to the secretary general of the Organisation of American States.
- From 1971 to 1973 he was president of the Screen Actors Guild.
- Then in 1981, he was appointed U.S. Ambassador to Mexico by his friend President Ronald Reagan. He served until 1986.
- In 1971, he was signed to play "James Bond" in the film "Diamonds Are Forever", however, Sean Connery decided to return for the role.
- In 1973, John appeared on Broadway in the play "Seesaw".
- John's other film credits include "Back Street" (1961), "Thoroughly Modern Millie" (1967), "Niente rose per OSS 117" (1968), "Keep It in the Family" (1973), "Jennifer" (1978) and "Sophia Loren : Her Own Story" (1980)(TV).
- His other TV credits include "The Virginian" (1964), "The Alfred Hitchcock Hour" (1963-65)

2 episodes, "The Doris Day Show" (1971), "Medical Center" (1976), "The Love Boat" (1977) and "Flying High" (1978).

"Dirty Sally"

Years : 1974

Episodes : 13 (1 season)

Cast :-

Jeanette Nolan (b. 1911 d. 1998) - Played Sally Fergus

Dack Rambo (b. 1941 d. 1994) - Played Cyrus Pike

Synopsis :-
Sally and Cyrus head west to pan for gold.

Trivia & Tidbits :-

"The Show"

- **"Dirty Sally"** premiered on CBS on January 11, 1974 and last aired on April 5, 1974.
- The show ran for one season with a total of 13 episodes.
- "Dirty Sally" is a spin-off of a two-part 1971 episode of "Gunsmoke" titled "Pike".
- The series was produced by the Columbia Broadcasting System (CBS).
- In 1974, Jeanette Nolan was nominated for an Emmy Award for her role in the series.

- The original music was by Bruce Broughton and John Carl Parker.
- The show aired opposite "The Odd Couple" on ABC.

"In Memoriam"

- **Jeanette Nolan** died of a stroke-related illness on June 5, 1998 (86) in Los Angeles, California.
- **Dack Rambo** died of AIDS on March 21, 1994 (52) in Delano, California.

"The Stars"

- **Jeanette Nolan** was born on December 30, 1911 in Los Angeles, California.
- She graduated from Abraham Lincoln High School in Los Angeles.
- Jeanette made her acting debut at the Pasadena Playhouse and whilst a student at Los Angeles City College made her radio debut in 1932 in "Omar Khayyam".
- She went on to appear on several radio programs including "Young Dr. Malone" (1939-40), "Cavalcade of America" (1940-41), "One Man's Family" (1947-50) and "The Great Gildersleeve" (1949-52).
- Jeanette made her film debut in the movie "Macbeth" in 1948.
- Several more movie roles followed including "Words and Music" (1948), "Saddle Tramp"

(1950), "Kim" (1950), "The Secret of Convict Lake" (1951), "Hangman's Knot" (1952), "The Big Heat" (1953), "A Lawless Street" (1955), "Tribute to a Bad Man" (1956), "April Love" (1957) and "Wild Heritage" (1958).

- In 1959, she was cast as "Annette Deveraux" in the TV series "Hotel de Paree". She appeared in 29 episodes from 1959 to 1960.
- In 1967, she was cast as "Holly Grainger" in the TV series "The Virginian". She appeared in 27 episodes from 1967 to 1970.
- Her last acting role was in the film "The Horse Whisperer" in 1998.
- Jeanette was married to actor John McIntire ("Wagon Train" and "The Virginian") from 1935 until his death in 1991. They had two children, actor Tim and Holly.
- During her career she appeared in over 300 television episodes.
- Jeanette was nominated for four Emmy Awards - "The Richard Boone Show" (1964), "I Spy" (1966), "Dirty Sally" (1974) and "The Awakening Land" (1978).
- Her other film credits include "The Great Impostor" (1961), "Two Rode Together" (1961), "The Man Who Shot Liberty Valance" (1962), "Chamber of Horrors" (1966), "The Reluctant Astronaut" (1967), "Hijack!" (1973)(TV), "Babe" (1975)(TV), "Avalanche" (1978), "The Wild Women of Chastity Gulch" (1982)(TV) and "Going Home" (1996).
- Jeanette's other TV credits include "The Man Behind the Badge" (1955), "State Trooper" (1956), "Steve Canyon" (1959), "Lawman"

(1959), "Black Saddle" (1959), "Bat Masterson" (1961), "Hawaiian Eye" (1963), "Laramie" (1963), "Wagon Train" (1961-65) 3 episodes, "Perry Mason" (1958-65) 6 episodes, "My Three Sons" (1964-66) 4 episodes, "Laredo" (1965-67) 3 episodes, "Gunsmoke" (1957-72) 8 episodes, "Disneyland" (1966-75) 9 episodes, "The Waltons" (1978), "St. Elsewhere" (1986) and "Dear John" (1990).

- **Dack Rambo** was born Norman Jay Rambo on November 13, 1941 in Delano, California.
- He was the son of William Lester and Beatrice Rambo.
- Dack had a twin brother, Dirk (born Orman Ray), who was also an actor. Dirk was killed in a road accident on February 5, 1967.
- Early in his career Dack was a student of Lee Strasberg and Vincent Chase.
- In 1962, he was cast as "Peter Massey" in the TV series "The New Loretta Young Show. He appeared in 26 episodes from 1962 to 1963.
- His brother, Dirk, played "Paul Massey" in the same series.
- In 1966, he was cast as "Tim" in the TV series "Never Too Young". He appeared in 15 episodes.
- Then in 1967, he was cast as "Jeff Sonnett", opposite Walter Brennan, in the TV series "The Guns of Will Sonnett". He appeared in 50 episodes from 1967 to 1969.
- In 1974, he was cast as "Cyrus Pike" in the TV series "Dirty Sally" (a spin-off from

"Gunsmoke"). He appeared in 14 episodes before the show was canceled.

- Following this he appeared in another TV series. He was cast as the character "Jack Cole" in "Sword of Justice". The series only lasted 10 episodes.
- In 1983, he was cast as "Steve Jacobi" in the TV series "All My Children". He appeared in 7 episodes.
- Then in 1984, he played the character "Wesley Harper" in the TV series "Paper Dolls". He appeared in 13 episodes.
- In 1985, he was cast as "Jack Ewing" in the highly successful TV series "Dallas". He appeared in 51 episodes from 1985 to 1987.
- His last TV series was "Another World". He played the character "Grant Harrison" in 14 episodes from 1991 to 1992. He quit the show after being diagnosed HIV positive.
- Dack was bisexual and helped to establish an international data bank for AIDS research.
- His film credits include "Which Way to the Front?" (1970), "River of Gold" (1971)(TV), "Nightmare Honeymoon" (1974), "A Double Life" (1978)(TV), "The Spring" (1989) and "River of Diamonds" (1990).
- Dack's other TV credits include "Iron Horse" (1967), "Gunsmoke" (1970-71) 3 episodes, "Cannon" (1971), "The Rookies" (1975), "Fantasy Island" (1978-84) 6 episodes, "Hunter" (1988) and "Murder, She Wrote" (1984-90) 3 episodes.

"Dundee and the Culhane"

Years : 1967

Episodes : 13 (1 season)

Cast :-

John Mills (b. 1908 d. 2005) - Played Dundee

Sean Garrison (b. 1937) - Played The Culhane

Synopsis :-
A lawyer travels the West with his assistant.

Trivia & Tidbits :-

"The Show"

- **"Dundee and the Culhane"** premiered on CBS on September 7, 1967 and last aired on December 13, 1967.
- The show ran for one season with a total of 13 episodes.
- The series was produced by Filmways Television.

- In December, 1967 CBS replaced the show with "The Jonathan Winters Show".

"In Memoriam"

- **Sir John Mills** died of a chest infection on April 23, 2005 (97) in Denham, England.

"The Stars"

- **Sir John Mills** was born Lewis Ernest Watts Mills on February 22, 1908 in North Elmham, Norfolk, England.
- He grew up in Belton where his father was the headmaster of the village school.
- John was educated at Balham Grammar School in London, Sir John Leman High School in Beccles, Suffolk and Norwich High School for Boys.
- In 1939, he enlisted in the Royal Engineers (attaining the rank of Second Lieutenant) but was discharged in 1942 due to a stomach ulcer.
- After leaving school, John trained as a dancer and started his career by performing in music halls.
- Following this, he was discovered by Noel Coward and began appearing regularly on the London stage in revues.
- John made his movie debut in the film "The Midshipmaid" in 1932.

- Several more film roles followed including "The Ghost Camera" (1933), "The Lash" (1934), "Charing Cross Road" (1935), "Goodbye, Mr. Chips" (1939), "The Young Mr. Pitt" (1942), "Waterloo Road" (1945), "Great Expectations" (1946), "The History of Mr. Polly" (1949), "Mr. Denning Drives North" (1952), "The Colditz Story" (1955), "Around the World in Eighty Days" (1956), "Summer of the Seventeenth Doll" (1959), "Tunes of Glory" (1960), "The Parent Trap" (1961) and "The Valiant" (1962).
- In 1956, he made his TV debut in an episode ("The Letter") of "Producer's Showcase".
- In 1967, he was cast as "Dundee" in the TV series "Dundee and the Culhane". He appeared in 13 episodes.
- Then in 1974, he was cast as "Thomas 'The Elephant' Devon" in the TV series "The Zoo Gang". The series only lasted 6 episodes.
- In 1979, he played "Prof. Bernard Quatermass" in the TV mini-series "Quatermass".
- In 1980, he was cast as "Albert Collyer" in the TV series "Young at Heart". He appeared in 18 episodes from 1980 to 1982.
- Then in 1989, he played "Faversham" in the TV mini-series "Around the World in 80 Days".
- John was married twice - Aileen Raymond (1927-41) and Mary Hayley Bell (1941-2005). He had three children, Juliet, Hayley and Jonathan, with Ms. Bell.
- Both his daughters are actors with Hayley winning an Oscar in 1961 for her role in "Pollyanna" (1960).

- Juliet played the "Nanny" in the TV series "Nanny and the Professor" from 1970 to 1971.
- In 1997, John was ranked No.88 in Empire (UK) magazine's "The Top 100 Movie Stars of All Time".
- His grandson, Crispian Mills, is the lead singer in the band Kula Shaker.
- John was awarded a CBE (Commander of the Order of the British Empire) in 1960 and a Knight Bachelor of the Order of the British Empire in 1976.
- In 1971, he won a Best Supporting Actor Academy Award for his role in "Ryan's Daughter" (1970). He also won a Golden Globe Award in the same year.
- In 1962, he was nominated for a Tony Award for his role in the Broadway play "Ross".
- His favourite film he starred in was "Tunes of Glory" (1960).
- John was named a Disney Legend in 2002.
- His other film credits include "Operation Crossbow" (1965), "King Rat" (1965), "Chuka" (1967), "Ryan's Daughter" (1970), "Young Winston" (1972), "The Thirty Nine Steps" (1978), "Gandhi" (1982), "Sahara" (1983), "The Big Freeze" (1993), "Hamlet" (1996) and "Bright Young Things" (2003).
- John's other TV credits include "Nanny and the Professor" (1971), "The Love Boat" (1979), "Hotel" (1986), "Perfect Scoundrels" (1992) and "Great Performances" (1998).

- **Sean Garrison** was born on October 19, 1937 in New York City, New York.

- He made his TV debut in an episode ("A Time to Die") of "Colt .45" in 1957.
- Sean's first credited movie appearance was in the film "Violent Road" (1958).
- In 1967, he was cast as "The Culhane" in the TV series "Dundee and the Culhane".
- Sean's last acting appearance, to date, was in an episode ("The Hawk and the Hunter") of the TV series "CHiPs" in 1981.
- His other film credits include "Onionhead" (1958), "Up Periscope" (1959), "Splendor in the Grass" (1961), "Banning" (1967), "Breakout" (1970)(TV), "Midway" (1976) uncredited and "Power" (1980)(TV).
- Sean's other TV credits include "Cheyenne" (1958), "The Adventures of Ozzie & Harriet" (1958), "Sugarfoot" (1958), "The Big Valley" (1965), "Gunsmoke" (1966), "The Mod Squad" (1969), "Mannix" (1972), "The Rockford Files" (1977) and "Fantasy Island" (1980).

"Dusty's Trail"

Years : 1973-1974

Episodes : 26 (1 season)

Cast :-

Bob Denver (b. 1935 d. 2005) - Played Dusty

Forrest Tucker (b. 1919 d. 1986) – Played Mr. Callahan

Ivor Francis (b. 1918 d. 1986) – Played Mr. Carson Brookhaven

Jeannine Riley (b. 1940) – Played Lulu McQueen

Lori Saunders (b. 1941) – Played Betsy

Lyn Wood (b. 1930) – Played Mrs. Brookhaven

William Cort (b. 1936 d. 1993) – Played Andy

Synopsis :-
Five wagons heading west are separated from their friends.

Trivia & Tidbits :-

"The Show"

- **"Dusty's Trail"** premiered in syndication on September 11, 1973 and last aired on March 12, 1974.
- The show ran for one season with a total of 26 episodes.
- The series was created by Elroy and Sherwood Schwartz and produced by Metromedia Producers Corporation (MPC), Redwood Productions and Writer First Productions.
- "Dusty's" horse was named "Freckles" and "Callahan's" was "Blarney".
- The theme music was composed by Ross and Sherwood Schwartz.
- Due to poor ratings the show was canceled after 26 episodes.

"In Memoriam"

- **Bob Denver** died of complications from throat cancer on September 2, 2005 (70) in Winston-Salem, North Carolina.
- **Forrest Tucker** died of lung cancer and emphysema on October 25, 1986 (67) in Woodland Hills, Los Angeles, California.
- **Ivor Francis** died of multiple strokes on October 22, 1986 (67) in Los Angeles, California.
- **William Cort** died of cancer on September 23, 1993 (57) in Los Angeles, California.

"The Stars"

- **Bob Denver** was born Robert Osbourne Denver on January 9, 1935 in New Rochelle, New York.
- He was raised in Brownwood, Texas.
- After graduating from high school he moved to California and attended Loyola University in Los Angeles. One of his classmates was Dwayne Hickman ("The Many Loves of Dobie Gillis").
- In 1956, he broke his neck and was declared medically unfit to join the U.S. Army.
- After graduating from university, he worked as a mailman and then a teacher at Corpus Christi School in Pacific Palisades, California.
- Whilst teaching at Corpus Christi, he shot the pilot for the TV series "The Many Loves of Dobie Gillis".
- Bob actually made his TV debut in an episode ("The Tang's Last Shot") of "The Silent Service" in 1957.
- His film debut was in the movie "A Private's Affair" in 1959.
- In 1959, he was cast as "Maynard G. Krebs" in the TV series "The Many Loves of Dobie Gillis". He appeared in 144 episodes from 1959 to 1963.
- In 1964, he was cast as "Gilligan" in the TV series "Gilligan's Island". He appeared in 98

episodes from 1964 to 1967. One further episode ("Marooned") was made in 1992.

- Then in 1968, he was cast as "Rufus Butterworth" in the TV series "The Good Guys". He appeared in 42 episodes from 1968 to 1970.
- In 1973, he was cast as "Dusty" in the TV series "Dusty's Trail". He appeared in 26 episodes from 1973 to 1974.
- Bob supplied the voice of "Gilligan" in the animated TV series "The New Adventures of Gilligan". He voiced 24 episodes from 1974 to 1975.
- In 1975, he was cast as "Junior" in the TV series "Far Out Space Nuts". He appeared in 12 episodes.
- Following this, he appeared in three "Gilligan" TV movies – "Rescue from Gilligan's Island" (1978), "The Castaways on Gilligan's Island" (1979) and "The Harlem Globetrotters on Gilligan's Island" (1981).
- In 1982, he once again supplied the voice of "Gilligan" in the animated TV series "Gilligan's Planet". He voiced 13 episodes.
- Bob's last acting appearance was in an episode ("Mommy 'n' Meego") of "Meego" in 1997.
- He was married four times – Maggie Ryan (1960-66), Jean Webber (1967-70), Carole Abrahams (1972-75) and Dreama Peery Denver (1979-2005). He had two children with

Ms. Ryan, one child with Ms. Abrahams and one child with Ms. Peery.

- Bob appeared on Broadway in 1970 in the play "Play It Again Sam".
- Later on in life, he moved back to Princeton, West Virginia and became an FM radio personality.
- Bob's other film credits include "Take Her, She's Mine" (1963), "Who's Minding the Mint?" (1967), "The Sweet Ride" (1968), "Whatever Happened to Dobie Gillis?" (1977) (TV short), "Scamps" (1982)(TV), "High School U.S.A." (1983)(TV), "Back to the Beach" (1987) and "Bring Me the Head of Dobie Gillis" (1988)(TV).
- His other TV credits include "Dr. Kildare" (1963), "The Andy Griffith Show" (1964), "Make Room for Daddy" (1964), "I Dream of Jeannie" (1967), "Love, American Style" (1970-73) 4 episodes, "The Love Boat" (1979-82) 3 episodes, "Fantasy Island" (1980-83) 4 episodes, "The New Gidget" (1987), "Baywatch" (1992) and "Roseanne" (1995).

- **Forrest Tucker (see "F Troop")**

- **Ivor Francis** was born on October 26, 1918 in Toronto, Ontario, Canada.
- Ivor served in the Royal Air Force during the Second World War and then, after discharge, moved to the United States.

- He then appeared on Broadway in such plays as "JB" (1958-59), "The Devil's Advocate" (1961) and "Gideon" (1961-62)
- Ivor made his uncredited film debut in the movie "Splendor in the Grass" in 1961.
- His TV debut was in an episode ("The Locked Room") of "The Defenders" in 1962.
- He then appeared in several more Broadway productions including "The Fun Couple" (1962), "Lorenzo" (1963), "A Rainy Day in Newark" (1963) and "The Investigation" (1966).
- Ivor then moved back to Hollywood and guest starred on several TV shows including "Dark Shadows" (1967), "The Outcasts" (1968), "Get Smart" (1969), "Judd for the Defense" (1969), "I Dream of Jeannie" (1969), "Here Comes the Brides" (1969), "The Flying Nun" (1969-70) 2 episodes, "Ironside" (1970), "The Mary Tyler Moore Show" (1970), "Bonanza" (1969-71) 2 episodes, "Cannon" (1972), "Maude" (1972) and "Search" (1973).
- From 1969 to 1972, he had a recurring role as "Professor Mitchell" on the TV series "Bright Promise".
- From 1969 to 1974, he had a recurring role as "Kenneth Dragen" on the TV series "Room 222". He appeared in 18 episodes.
- In 1973, he was cast as "Mr. Carson Brookhaven" in the TV series "Dusty's Trail".

He appeared in 26 episodes from 1973 to 1974.

- His last acting appearance was in an episode ("Informed Consent") of "The Mississippi" in 1984.
- Ivor was married twice (Jacqueline Giroux and Rosemary Daley) and had four children.
- His daughter is actress Genie Francis.
- Ivor's other film credits include "In Name Only" (1969)(TV), "Hunters Are for Killing" (1970)(TV), "Pieces of Dreams" (1970), "The Steagle" (1971), "Killer by Night" (1972)(TV), "The World's Greatest Athlete" (1973), "Superdad" (1973), "Busting" (1974), "The Prisoner of Second Avenue" (1975), "Alien Zone" (1978) and "Will There Really Be a Morning" (1983)(TV).
- His other TV credits include "The Magician" (1974), "Hawaii Five-O" (1974), "Happy Days" (1974), "Kojak" (1974-75) 2 episodes, "Bronk" (1975-76) 2 episodes, "The Practice" (1976), "Barnaby Jones" (1977), "Fish" (1977) 2 episodes, "Meeting of Minds" (1979) 2 episodes, "Mrs. Columbo" (1979), "Hart to Hart" (1980), "Lou Grant" (1979-80) 2 episodes, "The Waltons" (1975-81) 4 episodes, "The Jeffersons" (1975-82) 2 episodes, "Barney Miller" (1976-82) 4 episodes and "Quincy M.E." (1977-83) 5 episodes.

- **Jeannine Brooke Riley** was born on October 1, 1940 in Madera, California.
- She made her uncredited acting debut in the film "Five Finger Exercise" in 1962.
- Several TV appearances followed including "Father of the Bride" (1962), "Route 66" (1962), "My Three Sons" (1962), "Wagon Train" (1963) and "The Virginian" (1963).
- In 1963, she was cast as "Billie Jo Bradley" in the TV series "Petticoat Junction". She appeared in 74 episodes from 1963 to 1965.
- Following this she guest starred on TV shows such as "Convoy" (1965), "The Adventures of Ozzie & Harriet" (1963-65) 2 episodes, "The Smothers Brothers Show" (1966) 3 episodes, "Mister Roberts" (1966), "Occasional Wife" (1966), "The Man from U.N.C.L.E." (1966-67) 2 episodes, "The Wild Wild West" (1967) and "Gomer Pyle" (1969).
- From 1969 to 1971, she appeared on the TV show "Hee Haw". She appeared in 50 episodes.
- In 1973, she was cast as "Lulu McQueen" in the TV series "Dusty's Trail". She appeared in 26 episodes from 1973 to 1974.
- Her last acting appearance, to date, was in the film "Timebomb" in 1991.
- Jeannine was married to Gary Groom but they have been divorced for some time.

- Her other film credits include "Strike Me Deadly" (1963), "The Big Mouth" (1967), "Sheriff Who" (1967), "Li'l Abner" (1967), "Fever Heat" (1968), "The Comic" (1968), "Electra Glide in Blue" (1973) and "Lone Star Bar & Grill" (1983).
- Jeannine's other TV credits include "Love, American Style" (1969-71) 3 episodes, "Nashville 99" (1977), "James at 15" (1978) and "High Mountain Rangers" (1988).

- **Lori Saunders** was born Linda Marie Hines on October 4, 1941 in Kansas City, Missouri.
- She studied for a time under acting coach Jeff Corey.
- Lori made her TV acting debut in an episode ("David Hires a Secretary") of "The Adventures of Ozzie & Harriet" in 1960.
- She went on to appear in another 4 episodes of "Ozzie & Harriet" between 1960 and 1962.
- Following this, she guest starred in "Burke's Law" (1964), "No Time for Sergeants" (1964) and "Bob Hope Presents the Chrysler Theatre" (1965).
- Lori made her film debut in the movie "The Girls on the Beach" in 1965.
- In 1965, she was cast as "Bobbie Jo Bradley" in the TV series "Petticoat Junction". She appeared in 148 episodes from 1965 to 1970.

- She appeared as the character "Bobbie Jo Bradley" in 3 episodes of "Green Acres" between 1965 and 1966.
- Between 1968 and 1971, Lori appeared in 7 episodes of "The Beverly Hillbillies". She played "Bobbie Jo Bradley" in 4 episodes and "Elizabeth Gordon" ("Mr. Drysdale's" secretary) in 3 episodes.
- In 1973, she was cast as "Betsy McGuire" in the TV series "Dusty's Trail". She appeared in 26 episodes from 1973 to 1974.
- Her last acting appearance, to date, was in the film "Captive" in 1980.
- Lori has been married to Bernard Sandler since 1961. They have two children, Stacy and Ronald.
- During her career, Lori has appeared in over 100 TV commercials.
- In the 1960's, Lori released a single record "Lonely Christmas" with "Out of Your Mind" on the B-side.
- She also formed a singing group with Linda Henning and Meredith MacRae. They performed as "The Girls from Petticoat Junction".
- Lori's other film credits include "Mara of the Wilderness" (1965), "Blood Bath" (1966), "Head On" (1971), "A Day at the White House" (1972), "Frasier, the Sensuous Lion" (1973) and "So Sad About Gloria" (1975).

- Her other TV credits include "Daniel Boone" (1970), "The Courtship of Eddie's Father" (1970), "Love, American Style" (1973), "Here We Go Again" (1973) and "The Young and the Restless" (1976).

- **Lynn Wood** was born on May 4, 1932 in the United States of America.
- She made her TV acting debut in an episode of "True Story" in 1961.
- Lynn made her film debut in the movie "Billy Rose's Jumbo" in 1962.
- This was followed by guest appearances in TV shows such as "My Three Sons" (1963), "Dr. Kildare" (1966), "Mission: Impossible" (1966), "Iron Horse" (1967), "It's About Time" (1967), "The Wild Wild West" (1967), "Hawaii Five-O" (1969), "The Doris Day Show" (1969), "The Mary Tyler Moore Show" (1971), "The F.B.I." (1972) and "Temperatures Rising" (1972).
- In 1973, she was cast as "Mrs. Brookhaven" in the TV series "Dusty's Trail". She appeared in 26 episodes from 1973 to 1974.
- Her last acting appearance, to date, was in an episode ("Professor Jonathan Higgins") of "Magnum, P.I." in 1985.
- Lynn was married to Iggie Wolfington from 1972 until his death in 2004.
- Her other film credits include "The Legend of Lizzie Borden" (1975)(TV), "The Ghost of

Flight 401" (1978)(TV), "It Lives Again" (1978) and "Stone" (1979)(TV).

- Lynn's other TV credits include "Apple's Way" (1974), "The Quest" (1976), "The Waltons" (1977), "Stone" (1979), "Hart to Hart" (1979), "Dallas" (1981-82) 2 episodes and "WKRP Cincinnati" (1982).

- **William 'Bill' Cort** was born William Phelps Greer III on July 8, 1936 in El Paso, Texas.
- He made his TV acting debut in an episode ("The Stone Guest") of "Route 66" in 1963.
- Bill made his film debut in the movie "Dear Heart" in 1964.
- Following this, he guest starred in a number of TV shows including "The Lieutenant" (1964) 2 episodes, "Hazel" (1964), "Combat!" (1965), "Branded" (1965), "Mister Roberts" (1965), "12 O'Clock High" (1964-66) 4 episodes, "Adam-12" (1968), "It Takes a Thief" (1969) and "The F.B.I." (1969-73) 3 episodes.
- In 1973, he was cast as "Andy" in the TV series "Dusty's Trail". He appeared in 26 episodes from 1973 to 1974.
- In 1975, he was cast as "Jim Cooney" in the TV series "The Montefuscos". He appeared in all 9 episodes.
- Then in 1978, he was cast as "Dr. Jerry Mackler" in the TV series "A.E.S. Hudson Street". He appeared in all 5 episodes.

- From 1990 to 1993, he had a recurring role as "Headmaster Wallace Thorvald" in the TV series "The Fresh Prince of Bel-Air". He appeared in 4 episodes.
- Bill's other film credits include "Banning" (1967), "Glass Houses" (1972), "Alex & the Gypsey" (1976), "Sammy" (1977), "Elvira: Mistress of the Dark" (1988), "Heathers" (1988), "Ghost" (1990), "Navy Seals" (1990) and "Maid for Each Other" (1992).

- His other TV credits include "Little House on the Prairie" (1974) 2 episodes, "Kojak" (1976), "Starsky and Hutch" (1977-78) 2 episodes, "The Ropers" (1979), "Lou Grant" (1979), "Dynasty" (1981), "Hart to Hart" (1983), "Three's Company" (1983-84) 2 episodes, "Matt Houston" (1985), "Family Ties" (1985), "Simon & Simon" (1986), "Our House" (1988), "Dallas" (1987-88) 3 episodes, "Empty Nest" (1990), "Homefront" (1991) and "Quantum Leap" (1993).

"F Troop"

Years : 1965 - 1967

Episodes : 65 (2 seasons)

Cast :-

Forrest Tucker (b. 1919 d. 1986) - Played Sgt. Morgan O'Rourke

Larry Storch (b. 1923) - Played Cpl. Randolph Agarn

Ken Berry (b. 1933) - Played Capt. Wilton Parmenter

Melody Patterson (b. 1949 d. 2015) - Played Wrangler Jane Angelica Thrift

Frank de Kova (b. 1910 d. 1981) - Played Chief Wild Eagle

James Hampton (b. 1936) - Played Hannibal Dobbs

Bob Steele (b. 1907 d. 1988) - Played Trooper Duffy

Joe Brooks (b. 1923 d. 2007) - Played Trooper Vanderbilt

Don Diamond (b. 1921 d. 2011) - Played Crazy Cat

Synopsis :-
The story of the cavalry at Fort Courage, Kansas.

Trivia & Tidbits :-

"The Show"

- **"F Troop"** premiered on ABC on September 14, 1965 and last aired on April 6, 1967.
- The show ran for two seasons with a total of 65 episodes.
- The first season (34 episodes) was filmed in black and white and the second season in color.
- The series was created by Seaman Jacobs, Ed James and Jim Barnett.
- The entire series was filmed on the Warner Bros. backlot in Burbank, California.
- The theme song was written by Irving Taylor and William Lava.

" In Memoriam"

- **Forrest Tucker** died of lung cancer on October 25, 1986 (67) in Woodland Hills, Los Angeles, California.

- **Melody Patterson** died from multiple organ failure on August 20, 2015 (66) in Hollister, Missouri.
- **Frank DeKova** died of natural causes on October 15, 1981 (71) in Sepulveda, California.
- **Bob Steele** died of emphysema on December 21, 1988 (81) in Burbank, California.
- **Joe Brooks** died on December 5, 2007 (83) in Los Angeles, California.
- **Don Diamond** died of heart failure on June 19, 2011 (90) in Los Angeles, California.

"The Stars"

- **Forrest Meredith Tucker** was born on February 12, 1919 in Plainfield, Indiana.
- He was the son of Forrest A. Tucker and Doris Heringlake.
- Forrest began performing at the age of 14 at the 1933 Chicago World's Fair. He pushed wicker chairs during the day and sang at night.
- The family then moved to Washington D.C. where he subsequently won an amateur contest at a burlesque theater. The manager gave him a job as master of ceremonies but it was soon discovered he was under age and therefore the job finished.
- Forrest graduated from Washington-Lee High School, Virginia in 1938.
- He moved to Hollywood in 1939 and made his acting debut in the film "The Westerner" in 1940.

- Several more film roles followed including "Emergency Landing" (1941), "New Wine" (1941), "Honolulu Lu" (1941), "Canal Zone" (1942), "Submarine Raider" (1942), "Counter-Espionage" (1942), "Boston Blackie Goes Hollywood" (1942) and "Keeper of the Flame" (1942).
- Forrest then joined the United States Army and eventually reached the rank of second lieutenant. He was discharged in 1945.
- He resumed his acting career in the film "Talk About a Lady" (1946).
- This was followed by a number of movie roles including "The Yearling" (1946), "Gunfighters" (1947), "Coroner Creek" (1948), "Two Guys from Texas" (1948), "The Last Bandit" (1949), "Sands of Iwo Jima" (1949) and "The Nevadan" (1950).
- Forrest made his TV debut in an episode ("The Hoosier School-Master") of "The Chevrolet Tele-Theatre" in 1950.
- In 1955, he was cast as "Crunch Adams" in the TV series "Crunch and Des". He appeared in 39 episodes from 1955 to 1956.
- In 1965, he was cast as "Sgt. Morgan O'Rourke" in the TV series "F Troop". He appeared in 65 episodes from 1965 to 1967.
- Then in 1973, he was cast as "Mr. Callahan" in the TV series "Dusty's Trail". He appeared in 26 episodes from 1973 to 1974.
- In 1975, he was cast as "Jake Kong" in the TV series "The Ghost Busters". He appeared in 15 episodes.

- In 1976, he played the character "Col. Avery" in the TV mini-series "Once an Eagle". He appeared in 4 episodes.
- His last acting appearance was in the TV movie "Timestalkers" in 1987. It was released after he had passed away.
- Forrest was married four times – Sandra Jolley (1940-50), Marilyn Johnson (1951-60), Marilyn Fisk (1961-85) and Sheila Forbes (1986). He had one child with Ms. Jolley and two children with Ms. Fisk.
- He appeared on Broadway in 1964 in the play "Fair Game for Lovers".
- In 1986, he was awarded a Star on the Hollywood Walk of Fame for his contribution to Motion Pictures.
- Forrest also appeared on stage in the production of "The Music Man". He played the character "Professor Harold Hill" 2,008 times over a five-year period.
- His other film credits include "California Passage" (1950), "Warpath" (1951), "Montana Belle" (1952), "Pony Express" (1953), "Jubilee Trail" (1954), "Rage at Dawn" (1955), "Stagecoach to Fury" (1956), "The Quiet Gun" (1957), "Fort Massacre" (1958), "Auntie Mame" (1958), "Doc" (1969)(TV), "Chisum" (1970), "Footsteps" (1972)(TV), "Jarrett" (1973)(TV), "Final Chapter: Walking Tall" (1977), "The Rebels" (1979)(TV), "Rare Breed" (1984) and "Thunder Run" (1986).
- Forrest's other TV credits include "Lux Video Theatre" (1956-57) 2 episodes, "Wagon Train" (1958), "Wide Country" (1963), "The Red

Skelton Show" (1957-63) 2 episodes, "Dr. Kildare" (1963), "Rawhide" (1963), "Death Valley Days" (1963), "The Virginian" (1965), "Hondo" (1967), "Daniel Boone" (1967-68) 2 episodes, "Bracken's World" (1970), "Love, American Style" (1970-71) 2 episodes, "Medical Center" (1970-71) 2 episodes, "Bonanza" (1971), "Gunsmoke" (1965-72) 6 episodes, "Columbo" (1972), "Little House on the Prairie" (1975), "Ellery Queen" (1976), "The Life and Times of Grizzly Adams" (1977), "Flo" (1980) 2 episodes, "Filthy Rich" (1982) 2 episodes, "The Love Boat" (1980-83) 3 episodes and "Murder, She Wrote" (1984).

- **Larry Storch** was born Lawrence Samuel Storch on January 8, 1923 in New York City, New York.
- He is the son of Alfred Storch, a realtor, and Sally Kupperman, a telephone operator.
- Larry attended DeWitt Clinton High School in The Bronx but never graduated due to hard times in the Great Depression. During this time he found work as a stand-up comic.
- Don Adams ("Get Smart") was a classmate and a lifelong friend.
- During the Second World War, Larry served in the United States Navy aboard the submarine tender USS Proteus.
- After the war, he started his career by appearing on "Toast of the Town" as a comedian.
- This was followed by a bit part in the movie "The Prince Who Was a Thief" in 1951.

- He then hosted two TV shows – "Cavalcade of Stars" (1950-52) and "The Larry Storch Show" (1953).
- Following this, he appeared on many TV shows including "The Colgate Comedy Hour" (1954), "The NBC Comedy Hour" (1956), "Stage Show" (1956), "The Steve Allen Show" (1957), "Playboy's Penthouse" (1959), "Toast of the Town" (1962) and "Tonight Starring Jack Paar" (1959-62).
- In 1962, he supplied the voices for "Koko the Clown" and "Mean Moe" in the TV series "Out of the Inkwell". He voiced 14 episodes.
- From 1962 to 1963, he supplied the voice of "Koko the Clown" in 99 TV shorts.
- From 1963 to 1966, he supplied the voices of "Phineas J. Whoopee/Rocky Maninoff/Red Beard in the TV series "Tennessee Tuxedo and His Tales". He voiced 70 episodes.
- In 1965, he was cast as "Cpl. Randolph Agarn" in the TV series "F Troop". He appeared in 65 episodes from 1965 to 1967.
- In 1969, he was cast as "Charles Duffy" in the TV series "The Queen and I". He appeared in 13 episodes.
- Then in 1970, he supplied voices in the TV series "Sabrina and the Groovie Goolies". He voiced 16 episodes.
- In 1971, he supplied voices in the TV series "Sabrina, the Teenage Witch". He voiced 9 episodes.
- Larry had the recurring role of "Duke Farentino" on the TV series "The Doris Day Show". He appeared in 4 episodes from 1970 to 1971.

- From 1972 to 1973, he supplied voices on the TV series "The Brady Kids". He voiced 22 episodes.
- In 1975, he was cast as "Eddie Spenser" in the TV series "The Ghost Busters". He appeared in 15 episodes.
- Then in 1987, he supplied voices in the TV series "Foofur". He voiced 13 episodes.
- His last acting appearance, to date, was in an episode of "Medium Rare" in 2010.
- Larry was married to Norma Grieve from 1961 until her death in 2003. They had one daughter, Candace.
- He has appeared on the Broadway stage in shows such as "The Littlest Revue" (1956), "Who Was That Lady I Saw You With?" (1958), "Porgy and Bess" (1983), "Arsenic and Old Lace" (1986-87), "Annie Get Your Gun" (1999-2001) and "Sly Fox" (2004).
- Larry released a comedy LP titled "Larry Storch at the Bon Soir" in the 1960's. This was followed by three more albums.
- His other film credits include "Gun Fever" (1958), "The Last Blitzkrieg" (1959), "40 Pounds of Trouble" (1962), "Captain Newman, M.D." (1963), "The Great Race" (1965), "The Funny Feeling" (1965), "The Great Bank Robbery" (1969), "The Woman Hunter" (1972)(TV), "Airport 1975" (1974), "Record City" (1978), "Without Warning" (1980), "Fake-Out" (1982), "A Fine Mess" (1986), "Medium Rare" (1987) and "Funny Valentine" (2005).
- Larry's other TV credits include "Phil Silver's Show" (1958-59) 2 episodes, "Hennesey"

(1959), "Car 54, Where Are You?" (1962-63) 4 episodes, "The Alfred Hitchcock Hour" (1963), "The Greatest Show on Earth" (1964), "Gilligan's Island" (1965), "I Dream of Jeannie" (1967), "Get Smart" (1968), "He & She" (1968) 2 episodes, "Gomer Pyle, U.S.M.C." (1967-68) 2 episodes, "The Flying Nun" (1969), "Alias Smith and Jones" (1972), "All in the Family" (1973), "Love, American Style" (1969-74) 5 episodes, "Mannix" (1968-74) 2 episodes, "Columbo" (1974), "McCloud" (1975), "Phyllis" (1976), "The Love Boat" (1978) 3 episodes, "Chips" (1979-80) 3 episodes, "Fantasy Island" (1979-82) 3 episodes, "The Fall Guy" (1984) and "Married With Children" (1995).

- **Ken Berry** was born Kenneth Ronald Berry on November 3, 1933 in Moline, Illinois.
- He is the son of Darrell Berry, an accountant, and Bernice Berry.
- Ken learned tap dancing at an early age and at age 15 won a talent competition and joined "The Horace Heidt Youth Opportunity Program". He toured the U.S. and Europe for fifteen months.
- After his high school graduation, he joined the United States Army. He spent one year in the Artillery division and then the final year in the Special Services Corps.
- Whilst in the army, Ken entered the All-Army talent contest and, after finishing third, appeared on the TV show "Toast of the Town".

- Following his army service, he moved to California to study acting.
- In 1959, he appeared on the Broadway stage in "Billy Barnes Revue".
- Ken made his TV acting debut in an episode ("Young Man's World") of Harrigan and Son" in 1960.
- From 1960 to 1961, he had the recurring role of "Woody" in the TV series "The Ann Sothern Show". He appeared in 11 episodes.
- In 1961, he was cast in the recurring role of "Dr. John Kapish" in the TV series "Dr. Kildare". He appeared in 25 episodes from 1961 to 1964.
- He made his uncredited film debut in the movie "Two for the Seesaw" in 1962.
- From 1962 to 1963, he had the recurring role of "Lt. Melton" in the TV series "Ensign O'Toole". He appeared in 5 episodes.
- Then in 1965, he was cast as "Capt. Wilton Parmenter" in the TV series "F Troop". He appeared in 65 episodes from 1965 to 1967.
- In 1968, he appeared as the character "Sam Jones" in the TV series "The Andy Griffith Show". He appeared in 4 episodes (one of the episodes was titled "Mayberry R.F.D.").
- It was then decided by the network to spin-off a series titled "Mayberry R.F.D." Ken again played "Sam Jones" in 78 episodes from 1968 to 1971.

- In 1983, he was cast as "Vinton Harper" in the TV series "Mama's Family". He appeared in 130 episodes from 1983 to 1990.
- His last acting appearance, to date, was in an episode ("Sometimes You Feel Like a Nut") of "Maggie Winters" in 1999.
- Ken was married to Jackie Joseph from 1960 to 1976. They have two adopted children, John and Jennifer.
- He appeared again on Broadway ("The Billy Barnes People") in 1961.
- In 1970, he released a record album entitled "Ken Berry RFD".
- From the mid 1970's to the early 1980's he appeared in TV commercials for "Kinney Shoes".
- Ken's other film credits include "Calhoun: County Agent" (1964)(TV), "Hello Down There" (1969), "Li'l Abner" (1971)(TV), "Every Man Needs One" (1972)(TV), "Herbie Rides Again" (1974), "Guardian of the Wilderness" (1976), "The Cat from Outer Space" (1978) and "Eunice" (1982)(TV).
- His other TV credits include "Hennesey" (1961), "Burke's Law" (1963), "Combat!" (1964), "The Dick Van Dyke Show" (1964) 2 episodes, "Hazel" (1964), "No Time for Sergeants" (1964-65) 3 episodes, "12 O'Clock High" (1964-65) 2 episodes, "The Danny Thomas Hour" (1967), "The Lucy Show"

(1968), "Love, American Style" (1971-73) 3 episodes, "The Brady Bunch" (1974), "Ellery Queen" (1976), "The Life and Times of Grizzly Adams" (1977), "The Love Boat" (1979), "Fantasy Island" (1978-82) 7 episodes, "The Golden Girls" (1992) and "The New Batman Adventures" (1997)(voice).

- **Melody Patricia Patterson** was born on April 16, 1949 in Inglewood, California.
- She was the daughter of Pat Patterson, a machinist, and Rosemary Wilson, an official in the Miss Universe contest.
- At a young age, Melody wrote and directed a play and also appeared as a photographer's model.
- In the ninth grade, she enrolled in the Hollywood Professional School.
- She continued her education at the Warner Bros. School whilst acting in "F Troop".
- Melody made her uncredited film debut in the movie "Bye Bye Birdie" in 1963.
- She made her TV debut in an episode ("You Can Fight City Hall") of "Wendy and Me" in 1965.
- In 1965, she was cast as "Wrangler Jane Angelica Thrift" in the TV series "F Troop". She appeared in 65 episodes from 1965 to 1967.
- Her last acting appearance was in the video "The Immortalizer" in 1990.

- She was married three times – James MacArthur (1970-75), Robert Seaton (1976-93) and Vern Miller (1998-2015).
- Melody entertained troops in Vietnam with the Johnny Grant Christmas tour.
- In 1999, she graduated from Sierra Nevada College with a Bachelor's Degree.
- Melody's other film credits include "The Angry Breed" (1968), "The Cycle Savages" (1969), "Blood and Lace" (1971) and "The Harrad Experiment" (1973) uncredited.
- Her other TV credits include "The Monkees" (1967), "Adam-12" (1968), "Green Acres" (1968) and "Hawaii Five-O" (1969-74) 3 episodes.

- **Frank de Kova** was born on March 17, 1910 in New York City, New York.
- He gave up teaching in New York to join a Shakespearean repertory group. Frank made his Broadway debut in "The Detective Story" and was discovered by director Elia Kazan.
- Frank made his TV debut in an episode ("The Ghost of Gravel Gertie") of "Dick Tracy" in the early 1950's.
- His uncredited film debut was in the movie "Up Front" in 1951.
- This was followed by many film roles including "Viva Zapata!" (1952) uncredited, "Holiday for Sinners" (1952), "Pony Soldier" (1952)

uncredited, "The Desert Song" (1953), "Arrowhead" (1953), "King of the Khyber Pass" (1953), "They Rode West" (1954), "The Man from Laramie" (1955), "The Lone Ranger" (1956), "The Ten Commandments" (1956), "Run of the Arrow" (1957), "Cowboy" (1958), "Apache Territory" (1958) and "Day of the Outlaw" (1959).

- During this period, Frank also guest starred on many TV shows including "Your Favorite Story" (1953) 2 episodes, "Big Town" (1956), "Tales of the 77th Bengal Lancers" (1956), "The Adventures of Rin Tin Tin" (1957) 2 episodes, "The Restless Gun" (1958), "Union Pacific" (1958), "Buckskin" (1959), "Black Saddle" (1959), "The Californians" (1958-59) 2 episodes, "Gunsmoke" (1956-59) 5 episodes, "The Deputy" (1959), "Tales of Wells Fargo" (1957-60) 3 episodes, "The Rifleman" (1959-60) 2 episodes, "Lawman" (1960), "Hong Kong" (1961), "Hawaiian Eye" (1960-61) 2 episodes, "Rawhide" (1959-61) 2 episodes, "Gunslinger" (1961), "Maverick" (1961), "The Gallant Men" (1962), "Cheyenne" (1957-62) 7 episodes, "The Untouchables" (1959-62) 8 episodes, "Laramie" (1959-63) 4 episodes, "77 Sunset Strip" (1958-63) 3 episodes, "Wagon Train" (1957-65) 8 episodes and "Daniel Boone" (1964-65) 2 episodes.

- In 1965, he was cast as "Chief Wild Eagle" in the TV series "F Troop". He appeared in 63 episodes from 1965 to 1967.
- His last acting job was providing the voice of "Old Vinnie" in the animated film "Hey Good Lookin'" in 1982 (released after his death).
- Frank's other film credits include "The Rise and Fall of Legs Diamond" (1960), "Portrait of a Mobster" (1961), "Follow That Dream" (1962), "Those Calloways" (1965), "The Greatest Story Ever Told" (1965), "The Wild Country" (1970), "The Mechanic" (1972), "The Don Is Dead" (1973), "Johnny Firecloud" (1975), "Mafia on the Bounty" (1980) and "American Pop" (1981).
- His other TV credits include "The High Chaparral" (1968), "Hawaii Five-O" (1969), "Death Valley Days" (1962-69) 3 episodes, "The F.B.I." (1973) 2 episodes, "Disneyland" (1968-75) 2 episodes, "Cannon" (1976), "The Rockford Files" (1977), "Little House on the Prairie" (1979) 2 episodes and "The Incredible Hulk" (1980).

- **James Wade Hampton** was born on July 9, 1936 in Oklahoma City, Oklahoma.
- He was raised in Dallas, Texas where his father, Ivan, operated a cleaning business. His mother's name was Edna.

- James majored in theatre arts at the University of North Texas, Denton.
- After a series of different jobs he joined the United States Army and was stationed in Germany where he performed with the USO.
- Following his service he performed in summer stock in Texas and then moved to New York City.
- He studied acting under Michael Howard in New York and then Leonard Nimoy in Los Angeles.
- James made his acting debut in the film short "The Cliff Dwellers" in 1962.
- He made his TV debut in an episode ("Jeb") of "Gunsmoke" in 1963.
- James guest starred in TV shows such as "Dr. Kildare" (1963), "Death Valley Days" (1964), "Gomer Pyle, U.S.M.C." (1965), "Gunsmoke" (1963-65) 2 episodes and "Rawhide" (1965).
- In 1965, he was cast as "Trooper Hannibal Dobbs" in the TV series "F Troop". He appeared in 65 episodes from 1965 to 1967.
- He made his film debut in the TV movie "Fade-In" in 1968.
- From 1968 to 1971, he had a recurring role as "LeRoy B. Simpson" in the TV series "The Doris Day Show". He appeared in 30 episodes.
- In 1977, he appeared in 5 episodes of the TV series "The Red Hand Gang".

- In 1981, he was cast as "Len Weston" in the TV series "Maggie". The series only lasted 8 episodes.
- From 1986 to 1987, he voiced the character "Harold Howard" in the animated TV series "Teen Wolf". He voiced 21 episodes.
- James' last acting appearance, to date, was in the video "The Association" in 2015.
- He has been married to Mary Deese since 2002.
- James was nominated for a Golden Globe Award (Most Promising Newcomer – Male) in 1975 for his performance in "The Longest Yard" (1974).
- His other film credits include "Soldier Blue" (1970), "Justin Morgan Had a Horse" (1972), "Force Five" (1975)(TV), "Macintosh and T.J." (1975), "Hustle" (1975), "The Amazing Howard Hughes" (1977)(TV), "The Cat from Outer Space" (1978), "The China Syndrome" (1979), "Condorman" (1981), "Teen Wolf" (1985), "Teen Wolf Too" (1987), "Pump Up the Volume" (1990), "Sling Blade" (1996), "Fire from Below" (2009) and "Divine Access" (2015).
- James' other TV credits include "Cimarron Strip" (1967), "Bracken's World" (1970), "Disneyland" (1972) 2 episodes, "Love, American Style" (1971-74) 4 episodes, "Mannix" (1975), "Kaz" (1979), "The Dukes of

Hazzard" (1980), "The Greatest American Hero" (1983), "Matt Houston" (1984) 2 episodes, "Who's the Boss?" (1984-85) 2 episodes, "Murder, She Wrote" (1984-86) 2 episodes, "Punky Brewster" (1986-87) 2 episodes, "Newhart" (1990), "Full House" (1989-90) 3 episodes, "Melrose Place" (1994) and "Fired Up" (1997).

- **Bob Steele** was born Robert Adrian Bradbury on January 23, 1907 in Portland, Oregon.
- His parents were Robert North Bradbury, an actor and director, and Nieta Catherine Quinn. Bob had a twin brother, Bill, who was also an actor.
- Bob started his acting career, with his brother Bill, in his father's film "The Adventures of Bob and Bill" in 1920.
- He and Bill then appeared in a series of short films, directed by their father, and included "Trapping the Wildcat" (1921), "Outwitting the Timber Wolf" (1921), "The Fox" (1921), "The Mountain Lion" (1921), "A Day in the Wilds" (1921) and "The Opossum" (1922).
- Bob was educated at Glendale High School, California where one of his classmates was John Wayne.
- He made his feature film debut in the movie "Just Plain Folks" in 1925.

- This was followed by a series of Western films including "Daniel Boone Thru the Wilderness" (1926), "Davy Crockett at the Fall of the Alamo" (1926), "The Mojave Kid" (1927), "Trail of Courage" (1928), "A Texas Cowboy" (1929), "The Oklahoma Sheriff" (1930), "The Nevada Buckaroo" (1931), "Law of the West" (1932), "Ranger's Code" (1933), "A Demon for Trouble" (1934), "Tombstone Terror" (1935), "The Law Rides" (1936), "The Trusted Outlaw" (1937), "Durango Valley Raiders" (1938) and "Riders of the Sage" (1939).
- From 1940 to 1941, he appeared in 6 films as the character "Billy the Kid". They were "Billy the Kid Outlawed" (1940), "Billy the Kid in Texas" (1940), "Billy the Kid's Gun Justice" (1940), "Billy the Kid's Range War" (1941), "Billy the Kid's Fighting Pals" (1941) and "Billy the Kid in Santa Fe" (1941).
- From 1940 to 1943, he appeared as the character "Tucson Smith" in 20 "Three Mesquiteers" films. Some of the films were "Under Texas Skies" (1940), "Lone Star Raiders" (1940), "Prairie Pioneers" (1941), "Pals of the Pecos" (1941), "Outlaws of the Cherokee Trail" (1941), "Code of the Outlaw" (1942), "Westward Ho" (1942), "Thundering Trails" (1943) and "Riders of the Rio Grande" (1943).

- Following this, he continued to appear in Westerns including "Death Valley Rangers" (1943), "Arizona Whirlwind" (1944), "The Utah Kid" (1944), "Navajo Kid" (1945), "Northwest Trail" (1945), "Six Gun Man" (1946), "Cheyenne" (1947), "Bandits of Dark Canyon" (1947), "Fort Worth" (1951), "Rose of Cimarron" (1952), "Column South" (1953) and "The Outcast" (1954).
- Bob made his TV debut in an episode ("Arroyo") of "Screen Directors Playhouse" in 1955.
- He then guest starred on a number of TV shows including "The Life and Legend of Wyatt Earp" (1955) 4 episodes, "Cheyenne" (1956), "Colt .45" (1957), "Sugarfoot" (1957), "Cimarron City" (1958), "Maverick" (1957-58) 3 episodes, "The Californians" (1958-59) 2 episodes, "Death Valley Days" (1958-59) 3 episodes, "The Rebel" (1959) 2 episodes, "Hotel de Paree" (1959-60) 2 episodes, "Rawhide" (1959-60) 3 episodes, "Disneyland" (1959-61) 6 episodes, "Whispering Smith" (1961), "Wide Country" (1962), "Gunsmoke" (1963-64) 2 episodes and "Daniel Boone" (1965).
- In 1965, he was cast as "Trooper Duffy" in the TV series "F Troop". He appeared in 63 episodes from 1965 to 1967.

- Bob's last acting appearance was in the film "Nightmare Honeymoon" in 1974.
- He was married three times – Louise Chessman (1931-33), Alice Petty Hackley (1935-38) and Virginia Nash Tatem (1939-88).
- Bob appeared in 6 films with classmate John Wayne – "Island in the Sky" (1953), "Rio Bravo" (1959), "The Comancheros" (1961), "The Longest Day" (1962), "McLintock!" (1963) and "Rio Lobo" (1970).
- His other film credits include "The Big Sleep" (1946), "Killer McCoy" (1947), "Gun for a Coward" (1957), "Pork Chop Hill" (1959), "Hell Bent for Leather" (1960), "4 for Texas" (1963), "Shenandoah" (1965) uncredited, "The Bounty Killer" (1965), "Hang 'Em High" (1968) and "Charley Varrick" (1973) uncredited.
- Bob's other TV credits include "Judd for the Defense" (1967), "Then Came Bronson" (1969) and "Family Affair" (1970).

- **Joe Brooks** was born John Joseph Brooks Jr. on December 14, 1923 in Los Angeles, California.
- After graduating from high school he became an actor.
- This was interrupted during the Second World War where he fought in the South Pacific.
- After the war, he resumed his acting career and made his uncredited acting debut in the film "Fighting Seabees" in 1944.

- A series of uncredited film roles followed including "The All American" (1953), "East of Eden" (1955), "The Sea Chase" (1955), "Tall Man Riding" (1955), "The McConnell Story" (1955) and "The Enemy Below" (1957).
- Joe made his TV debut in an episode ("Renegades") of "Cheyenne" in 1958.
- Following this, he appeared in several more uncredited film roles including "The Young Lions" (1958), "Rock-a-Bye Baby" (1958), "The Young Philadelphians" (1959), "Flaming Star" (1960), "Bachelor Flat" (1961) and "Rome Adventure" (1962).
- A number of guest appearances followed on TV shows such as "Rawhide" (1962) 4 episodes, "Temple Houston" (1963), "Grindl" (1964), "The Munsters" (1964), "Slattery's People" (1965) and "I Dream of Jeannie" (1965).
- In 1965, he was cast as "Trooper Vanderbilt" in the TV series "F Troop". He appeared in 48 episodes from 1965 to 1967.
- His last acting appearance was in the film "Eye of the Tiger" in 1986.
- Joe was married to Betty Jean Davis from 1948 until her death in 1991.
- His other film credits include "Critic's Choice" (1963) uncredited, "Robin and the 7 Hoods" (1964) uncredited, "Cheyenne Autumn" (1964) uncredited, "Harlow" (1965) uncredited, "Paint Your Wagon" (1969) uncredited, "Bite the

Bullet" (1975), "The Bad News Bears" (1976), "The Big Bus" (1976), "Gremlins" (1984) and "Vendetta" (1986).

- Joe's other TV credits include "Batman" (1966-67) 4 episodes, "Love, American Style" (1972), "The Six Million Dollar Man" (1975-77) 2 episodes and "The Fall Guy" (1983).

- **Don Diamond** was born on June 4, 1921 in Brooklyn, New York.
- His father was Russian-born and a veteran of the U.S. Army in the First World War (his mother was born in New Jersey).
- Don studied drama at the University of Michigan from 1938 to 1942.
- He made his TV debut on "The Lone Ranger" (1949) and film debut in "Borderline" (1950).
- In 1951, he was cast as "El Toro" in the TV series "The Adventures of Kit Carson". He appeared in 103 episodes from 1951 to 1955.
- In 1957, he was cast as "Cpl. Reyes" in the hit TV series "Zorro". He appeared in 50 episodes from 1957 to 1959.
- Then in 1965, he was cast as "Crazy Cat" in the TV series "F Troop". He appeared in 50 episodes from 1965 to 1967.
- His last acting appearance was in an episode ("The 100 Year Old Weekend") of "Our House" in 1987.

- Don was married to Louisa Tassler, a Spanish teacher, from 1965 until his death in 2011. They had one daughter, Roxanne.
- His other film credits include "The Old Man and the Sea" (1958), "How Sweet It Is!" (1968), "Herbie Goes Bananas" (1980) and "The Kid With the Broken Halo" (1982)(TV).
- Don's other TV credits include "Circus Boy" (1957), "Adventures of Superman" (1957), "26 Men" (1958), "Frontier Justice" (1961), "Redigo" (1963), "The Big Valley" (1969), "The Odd Couple" (1975) and "Lou Grant" (1979).

"Frontier Circus"

Years : 1961 - 1962

Episodes : 26 (1 season)

Cast :-

Chill Wills (b. 1902 d. 1978) - Played Colonel Casey Thompson

John Derek (b. 1926 d. 1998) - Played Ben Travis

Richard Jaeckel (b. 1926 d. 1997) - Played Tony Gentry

Synopsis :-
Stories of a traveling circus out West in the 1880's.

Trivia & Tidbits :-

"The Show"

- **"Frontier Circus"** premiered on CBS on October 5, 1961 and last aired on September 6, 1962. The first episode was titled "The Depths of Fear".
- The show ran for one season with a total of 26 black and white episodes.

- "Frontier Circus" was created by Samuel A. Peeples.
- The series was produced by Calliope Productions and distributed by the Columbia Broadcasting System (CBS).
- It was filmed at Revue Studios, California, Corriganville, Ray Corrigan Ranch, California and Red Rock Canyon State Park, California.
- The show ran opposite "The Adventures of Ozzie & Harriet" and "The Donna Reed Show" on ABC and "The Outlaws" on NBC.

"In Memoriam"

- **Chill Wills** died of cancer on December 15, 1978 (76) in Encino, California.
- **John Derek** died of heart problems on May 22, 1998 (71) in Santa Maria, California.
- **Richard Jaeckel** died of malignant melanoma on June 14, 1997 (70) in Woodland Hills, California.

"The Stars"

- **Chill Wills** was born Theodore Childress 'Chill' Wills on July 18, 1902 in Seagoville, Texas.
- From early childhood, Chill was a performer and in the 1930's formed the singing group "Chill Wills and His Avalon Boys".
- They made their film debut in the movie "It's a Gift" in 1934.
- Several films followed including "Bar 20 Rides Again" (1935), "Anything Goes" (1936),

- "Hideaway Girl" (1936), "Way Out West" (1937) and "Nobody's Baby" (1937).
- Chill disbanded the group in 1938 and set out on a solo career.
- He then appeared in several films including "Lawless Valley" (1938), "Arizona Legion" (1939), "Trouble in Sundown" (1939), "Racketeers of the Range" (1939), "Allegheny Uprising" (1939), "Boom Town" (1940), "The Westerner" (1940), "Western Union" (1941), "Billy the Kid" (1941), "Tarzan's New Adventure" (1942), "Apache Trail" (1942), "A Stranger in Town" (1943), "Meet Me in St. Louis" (1944), "I'll Be Seeing You" (1944), "The Harvey Girls" (1946), "The Yearling" (1946), "Northwest Stampede" (1948), "Tulsa" (1949) and "Red Canyon" (1949).
- In 1950, he supplied the voice of "Francis the Talking Mule" in the film "Francis".
- He voiced another five "Francis" movies – "Francis Goes to the Races" (1951), "Francis Goes to West Point" (1952), "Francis Covers the Big Town" (1953), "Francis Joins the WACS" (1954) and "Francis in the Navy" (1955).
- Chill made his TV debut in an episode ("The Gray Dude") of "The Gene Autry Show" in 1950.
- After appearing in several more films he guest starred on a number of TV shows including "Alfred Hitchcock Presents" (1958), "Wagon Train" (1958), "Trackdown" (1959), "The Texan" (1959) and "Assignment: Underwater" (1960).

- In 1961, he was cast as "Colonel Casey Thompson" in the TV series "Frontier Circus". He appeared in 26 episodes from 1961 to 1962.
- In 1966, he was cast as "Jim Ed Love" in the TV series "The Rounders". He appeared in 17 episodes from 1966 to 1967.
- His last acting appearance was in the TV movie "Stubby Pringle's Christmas" in 1978.
- Chill was married twice – Hattie Elizabeth 'Betty' Chappelle (1928-71) and Novadeen Googe (1973-78). He had two children, Jill and Will, with Ms. Chappelle.
- He composed the song "The Blue-Eyed Sailor Man" that he performed in the 1942 MGM film "Stand By for Action".
- In 1960, he was awarded a Star on the Hollywood Walk of Fame for his contribution to Motion Pictures.
- In 1961, he was nominated for an Academy Award (Best Actor in a Supporting Role) for "The Alamo" (1960).
- In 1968, he supported George Wallace in the presidential election.
- Chill's other film credits include "Rio Grande" (1950), "Oh! Susanna" (1951), "Ride the Man Down" (1952), "The Man from the Alamo" (1953), "Kentucky Rifle" (1955), "Giant" (1956), "Gun Glory" (1957), "From Hell to Texas" (1958), "Where the Boys Are" (1960), "Young Guns of Texas" (1962), "McLintock!" (1963), "The Rounders" (1965), "Fireball 500" (1966), "The Over-the-Hill Gang" (1969)(TV), "The Over-the-Hill Gang Rides Again"

(1970)(TV), "Pat Garrett & Billy the Kid" (1973) and "Mr. Billion" (1977).

- His other TV credits include "Route 66" (1964) 2 episodes, "Rawhide" (1964) 2 episodes, "Burke's Law" (1963-65) 3 episodes, "Tarzan" (1968), "Gunsmoke" (1962-68) 3 episodes, "The Virginian" (1971), "Alias Smith and Jones" (1972) and "Hec Ramsey" (1974).

- **John Derek** was born Derek Delevan Harris on August 12, 1926 in Hollywood, California.
- He was the son of Lawson Harris, actor/director, and Dolores Johnson, actress.
- He was groomed for a movie career by David O. Selznick and his agent Henry Willson.
- At the beginning of his career his agent gave him the stage name "Dare Harris". He subsequently appeared in three films under this name – "The Nest" (1943) (short), "Since You Went Away" (1944) uncredited and "I'll Be Seeing You" (1944).
- In 1944, he was drafted into the United States Army and served his time in the Philippines during the last days of the Second World War.
- After the war, his stage name was changed to "John Derek" and he appeared in an uncredited role in the film "A Double Life" (1947).
- He then appeared in a number of films including "Knock on Any Door" (1949), "All The King's Men" (1949), "Rogues of Sherwood

Forest" (1950), "Mask of the Avenger" (1951), "Scandal Sheet" (1952), "Prince of Pirates" (1953), "Ambush at Tomahawk Gap" (1953), "The Last Posse" (1953) and "Mission Over Korea" (1953).

- John made his TV debut in an episode ("Tomorrow's Men") of "The Ford Television Theatre" in 1953.
- He then continued appearing in movies such as "The Outcast" (1954), "Prince of Players" (1955), "An Annapolis Story" (1955), "The Ten Commandments" (1956), "Massacre at Sand Creek" (1956), "Omar Khayyam" (1957), "Private of the Half Moon" (1959) and "Exodus" (1960).
- In 1961, he was cast as "Ben Travis" in the TV series "Frontier Circus". He appeared in 26 episodes from 1961 to 1962.
- Following this, he directed and starred in three films – "The 26th Cavalry" (1965), "Nightmare in the Sun" (1965) and "Once Before I Die" (1966).
- He then concentrated on directing films such as "Childish Things" (1969), "Love You!" (1979), "Fantasies" (1981), "Tarzan the Ape Man" (1981), "Bolero" (1984) and "Ghosts Can't Do It" (1989).
- His last acting appearance was in an episode ("A Mischevious Offence") of "Janus" in 1994.

- John was married four times – Pati Behrs (1948-56), Ursula Andress (1957-66), Linda Evans (1968-75) and Bo Derek (1976-98). He had two children, Russell and Sean Catherine, with Ms. Behrs.
- In 1960, he was awarded a Star on the Hollywood Walk of Fame for his contribution to the television industry.
- He directed the music videos for Shania Twain's "Whose Bed Have Your Boots Been Under?" and "Any Man of Mine".
- John's other TV credits include "Lux Video Theatre" (1954), "The Ford Television Theatre" (1956), "Playhouse 90" (1956), "Zane Grey Theatre" (1957-61) 2 episodes and "Flair" (1990) (mini-series).

- **Richard Hanley Jaeckel** was born on October 10, 1926 in Long Island, New York.
- He graduated from Hollywood High School.
- Richard's career basically started at age 17. He was working in the mail room at 20th Century Fox when a casting director auditioned him for a part in the film "Guadalcanal Diary" (1943). He won the part.
- He then appeared in the film "Wing and a Prayer" (1944).
- From 1944 to 1948, he served in the U.S. Navy.

- After his discharge, he appeared in several films including "Jungle Patrol" (1948), "Battleground" (1949), "Sands of Iwo Jima" (1949), "The Gunfighter" (1950), "Wyoming Mail" (1950) and "Fighting Coast Guard" (1951).
- He made his TV debut in an episode ("T.K.O.") of "Bigelow Theatre" in 1951.
- In 1961, he was cast as "Tony Gentry" in the TV series "Frontier Circus". He appeared in 26 episodes from 1961 to 1962.
- In 1972, he was cast as "Lt. Pete McNeil" in the TV series "Banyon". He appeared in 8 episodes.
- Then in 1974, he was cast as "Hank Myers" in the TV series "Firehouse". He appeared in 13 episodes.
- In 1979, he was cast as "Jack Klinger" in the TV series "Savage 1". He appeared in 13 episodes.
- In 1983, he was cast as "Maj. Hawkins" in the TV series "At Ease". He appeared in 14 episodes.
- In 1985, he was cast as "Lt. Martin Quirk" in the TV series "Spenser: For Hire". He appeared in 47 episodes from 1985 to 1987.
- From 1991 to 1994, he had the recurring role of "Ben Edwards" in the TV series "Baywatch". He appeared in 28 episodes.

- Richard was married to Antoinette Marches from 1947 until his death in 1997. They had two children, Barry and Richard Jr.
- His son, Barry, was a professional golfer.
- In 1972, he was nominated for an Academy Award (Best Actor in a Supporting Role) for his performance in the film "Sometimes a Great Notion" (1970).
- Richard's other film credits include "Come Back, Little Sheba" (1952), "The Violent Men" (1955), "Attack" (1956), "3:10 to Yuma" (1957), "The Naked and the Dead" (1958), "The Gallant Hours" (1960), "Flaming Star" (1960), "The Young and the Brave" (1963), "4 for Texas" (1963), "Once Before I Die" (1966), "The Dirty Dozen" (1967), "The Devil's Brigade" (1968), "Chisum" (1970), "Pat Garrett & Billy the Kid" (1973), "The Drowning Pool" (1975), "Grizzly" (1976), "Twilight's Last Gleaming" (1977), "The Dark" (1979), "Herbie Goes Bananas" (1980), "Blood Song" (1982), "Starman" (1984), "Black Moon Rising" (1986) and "Ghetto Blaster" (1989).
- His other TV credits include "Stories of the Century" (1954), "West Point" (1956-57) 2 episodes, "The Gray Ghost" (1958), "Cimarron City" (1958), "The Texan" (1959), "Trackdown" (1959), "The Rebel" (1960) 2 episodes, "The Tall Man" (1961), "Lawman" (1961), "Wagon Train" (1961-63) 2 episodes,

"The Dakotas" (1963), "The Virginian" (1964), "Perry Mason" (1963-66) 2 episodes, "The Wild Wild West" (1966-67) 2 episodes, "Bonanza" (1964-67) 2 episodes, "Ironside" (1972), "The F.B.I." (1971-74) 2 episodes, "Gunsmoke" (1963-75) 4 episodes, "Big Hawaii" (1977), "Lou Grant" (1979), "Little House on the Prairie" (1976-81) 3 episodes, "Matt Houston" (1983), "Dallas" (1983) 2 episodes, "Murder, She Wrote" (1987) and "China Beach" (1991).

"The Great Adventure"

Years : 1963 - 1964

Episodes : 26 (1 season)

Cast :-

Van Heflin (b. 1910 d. 1971) - Narrator

Russell Johnson (b. 1924 d. 2014) - Narrator

Synopsis :-
Anthology series about famous historical events.

Trivia & Tidbits :-

"The Show"

- **"The Great Adventure"** premiered on CBS on September 27, 1963 and last aired on May 1, 1964.
- The show ran for one season with a total of 26 black and white episodes.
- The series was produced by the Columbia Broadcasting System.
- The theme music was composed by Richard Rodgers.

"In Memoriam"

- **Van Heflin** died of a heart attack on July 23, 1971 (60) in Hollywood, California.
- **Russell Johnson** died of kidney failure on January 16, 2014 (89) in Bainbridge Island, Washington State.

"The Stars"

- **Van Heflin** was born Emmett Evan Heflin Jr. on December 13, 1910 in Walters, Oklahoma.
- He was the son of Fanny Bleecker (nee Shippey) and Dr. Emmett Evan Heflin, a dentist.
- Van attended Classen High School in Oklahoma City and then the University of Oklahoma.
- After leaving school Van spent a few years at sea aboard merchant ships.
- He made his acting debut in the Broadway play "The Bride of Torozko" in 1934.
- Van's first movie role was in the film "A Woman Rebels" in 1936.
- Following this he appeared in many movies including "Flight from Glory" (1937), "Santa Fe Trail" (1940), "Johnny Eager" (1941), "Tennessee Johnson" (1942), "The Strange Love of Martha Ivers" (1946), "The Three Musketeers" (1948) and "East Side, West Side" (1949).

- In 1950, he made his TV debut in an episode ("A Double-Dyed Deceiver") of "Nash Airflyte Theatre".
- In 1963, he was the host of the TV series "The Great Adventure". He hosted the show for 13 episodes from 1963 to 1964.
- His last acting appearance was in the TV movie "The Last Child" in 1971.
- During the Second World War, Van served as a combat cameraman in the Ninth Air Force in Europe.
- In 1943, he won an Oscar for Best Actor in a Supporting Role for the film "Johnny Eager".
- Another bit of trivia - his film "Cry of Battle" (1963) was playing at the Dallas theatre where Lee Harvey Oswald took refuge after assassinating President John F. Kennedy on November 22, 1963.
- Van has two Stars on the Hollywood Walk of Fame. One for his contribution to Motion Pictures and one for television.
- He was married twice, the first to Eleanor Scherr and the second to Frances Neal. Van had three children with Ms. Neal.
- Van's other film roles include "Shane" (1953), "Battle Cry" (1955), "3:10 to Yuma" (1957), "They Came to Cordura" (1959), "The Greatest Story Ever Told" (1965), "Stagecoach" (1966) and "Airport" (1970).
- His other TV credits include "Robert Montgomery Presents" (1950), "Playhouse 90" (1957-60) 3 episodes, "The Dick Powell Show" (1961) and "The Danny Thomas Hour" (1968).

- **Russell David Johnson** was born on November 10, 1924 in Ashley, Pennsylvania.
- After his father died he was sent, along with his brothers, to Girard College, a private boarding school in Philadelphia.
- Following this he joined the United States Army Air Forces during the Second World War. His plane was subsequently shot down in 1945 and he broke both his ankles. He was awarded several medals including the Purple Heart and Bronze Star.
- Russell studied acting after the war and became friends with Audie Murphy.
- He made his film debut in "For Men Only" (1952).
- In 1959, he was cast as "Marshal Gib Scott" in the TV series "Black Saddle". He appeared in 44 episodes from 1959 to 1960.
- After "Black Saddle" finished he appeared in numerous films and guest starred in several TV shows.
- In 1964, he was cast as "Professor Roy Hinkley" in the TV series "Gilligan's Island". He appeared in 98 episodes from 1964 to 1967.
- Russell was married three times and had two children from his second marriage to Kay Cousins and one stepson from his third marriage to Constance Dane.
- His son David (39) died of AIDS in 1994.
- Russell was discovered by director/actor Paul Henreid.
- He auditioned for the title role in the TV series "Ben Casey", but lost out to Vince Edwards.

- Russell was also known for narrating the long running animation series "Robotech" (1985).
- His other film credits include "Column South" (1953), "Ma and Pa Kettle at Waikiki" (1955), "The Greatest Story Ever Told" (1965), "MacArthur" (1977) and "Blue Movies" (1988).
- Russell's other TV credits include "Superman" (1953), "The Silent Service" (1957), "Lawman" (1959), "Route 66" (1962), "Death Valley Days" (1968), "Mannix" (1974) and "Lou Grant" (1978).

"The Guns of Will Sonnett"

Years : 1967 - 1969

Episodes : 50 (2 seasons)

Cast :-

Walter Brennan (b. 1894 d. 1974) - Played Will Sonnett

Dack Rambo (b. 1941 d. 1994) - Played Jeff Sonnett

Jason Evers (b. 1922 d. 2005) - Played James 'Jim' Sonnett

Synopsis :-
Will Sonnett and his grandson, Jeff, search for Will's son, Jim
.

Trivia & Tidbits :-

"The Show"

- **"The Guns of Will Sonnett"** premiered on ABC on September 8, 1967 and last aired on September 15, 1969.

- The show ran for two seasons with a total of 50 episodes.
- The series was produced by Brenco Productions and Thomas/Spelling Productions and created by Aaron Spelling.
- "Will Sonnett's" horse was named "Marauder".
- The series was filmed around Griffith Park, California and Desilu-Paramount Studios.

"In Memoriam"

- **Walter Brennan** died of emphysema on September 21, 1974 (80) in Oxnard, California.
- **Dack Rambo** died of AIDS on March 21, 1994 (52) in Delano, California.
- **Jason Evers** died of heart failure on March 13, 2005 (83) in Los Angeles, California.

"The Stars"

- **Walter Brennan** was born on July 25, 1894 in Swampscott, Massachusetts.
- He is regarded as one of the most successful character actors of American sound films.
- Walter won three Academy Awards for Best Supporting Actor - "Come and Get It" (1936), "Kentucky" (1938) and "The Westerner" (1940).
- He was married to Ruth Wells for fifty four years and they had three children.
- After World War 1 Walter moved to Los Angeles and made a fortune from real estate.

However, when the market took a downturn he lost almost everything.

- During World War 1, although never wounded, he was exposed to poison gas which ruined his vocal chords, leaving him with a high pitched voice texture.
- John Ford (director) and Walter didn't get along and Ford was one of only a few directors Brennan didn't collaborate with more than once during his film career.
- Walter had four Top 100 singles during his career including Top 5 hit "Old Rivers" which first hit the charts in April, 1962. This song spent eleven weeks on the Billboard charts and peaked at No.5.
- In 1970, Walter was inducted into the Hall of Great Western Performers at the National Cowboy and Western Heritage Museum in Oklahoma.
- Walter has a Star on the Hollywood Walk of Fame for his contribution to Motion Pictures.
- He appeared in over 230 film and TV roles over a period of nearly five decades.
- Walter appeared in three other TV series after "The Real McCoys" finished - "The Tycoon" (1964), "The Guns of Will Sonnett" (1967) and "To Rome with Love" (1970).
- He was regarded as a Hollywood Republican. He campaigned for Senator Barry Goldwater in the 1964 presidential election after the senator voted against the Civil Rights Act.
- Walter campaigned for Ronald Reagan to become Governor of California in 1966.

- He supported George Wallace (Independent Party) in his campaigns for the Presidency in 1968 and 1972.
- Walter's other TV credits include "The Ford Television Theatre" (1956), "Zane Grey Theatre" (1957), "The Red Skelton Show" (1970) and "Alias Smith and Jones" (1972).
- His other film credits include "Three Godfathers" (1936), "The Pride of the Yankees" (1942), "Tammy and the Bachelor" (1957), "Rio Bravo" (1959) and "How the West Was Won" (1962).

- **Dack Rambo (see "Dirty Sally")**

- **Jason Evers (see "Wrangler")**

"Gunslinger"

Years : 1961

Episode : 12 (1 season)

Cast :-

Tony Young (b. 1937 d. 2002) - Played Cord

Preston Foster (b. 1900 d. 1970) - Played Capt. Wingate

Midge Ware (b. 1927) - Played Amby Hollister

John Pickard (b. 1913 d. 1993) - Played Sgt. Major Murdock

Charles H. Gray (b. 1921 d. 2008) - Played Pico McGuire

Synopsis :-
A young gunfighter works undercover for the local army garrison commander.

Trivia & Tidbits :-

"The Show"

- **"Gunslinger"** premiered on CBS on February 9, 1961 and last aired on May 18, 1961.
- The show ran for one season with a total of 12 black and white episodes.
- The series was produced by the CBS Television Network and Emirau Productions.
- The theme song was written by Ned Washington (lyrics) and Dimitri Tiomkin (music) and sung by Frankie Laine.
- The series was filmed at the MGM Studios, Culver City.

"In Memoriam"

- **Tony Young** died of lung cancer on February 26, 2002 (64) in Hollywood, California.
- **Preston Foster** died on July 14, 1970 (69) in La Jolla, California.
- **John Pickard** died due to an animal attack on August 4, 1993 (80) in Rutherford County, Tennessee.
- **Charles H. Gray** died on August 2, 2008 (86) in San Bernardino, California.

"The Stars"

- **Tony Young** was born Carleton L. Young on June 28, 1937 in New York City, New York.
- His father was film and television character actor Carleton G. Young.
- Tony graduated from Los Angeles City College and also served in the United States Air Force.

- His acting career began in 1959 with appearances in four TV Western shows – "Bronco", "Fury", "Lawman" and "Maverick".
- In 1961, he was cast as "Cord" in the TV series "Gunslinger". He appeared in 12 episodes before the series was cancelled.
- Tony's last acting appearance was in an episode ("Goodbye Norma Jean – April 4, 1960") of "Quantum Leap" in 1993.
- He was married three times – Connie Mason (1958-62), Madlyn Rhue (1962-70) and Sondra Currie (1976-86). Tony had one daughter named Julie.
- Tony's film credits include "Walk Like a Dragon" (1960), "He Rides Tall" (1964), "Taggart" (1964), "Charro!" (1969), "A Man Called Sledge" (1970), "Black Gunn" (1972), "Policewomen" (1974), "Tuff Tuff" (1985) and "Up Your Alley" (1989).
- His other TV credits include "Tombstone Territory" (1960), "Laramie" (1960), "The Deputy" (1960), "Cheyenne" (1960-62) 2 episodes, "Death Valley Days" (1963), "Wagon Train" (1964), "Star Trek" (1968), "The Virginian" (1967-71) 2 episodes, "Mannix" (1972-73) 3 episodes, "Police Woman" (1974), "Fantasy Island" (1978), "Knight Rider" (1984) and "Mike Hammer" (1986).

- **Preston Foster** was born on August 24, 1900 in Pitman, New Jersey.
- He started his career by appearing on the Broadway stage. Preston starred in shows such as "Congratulations" (1929), "Seven"

(1929), "Ladies All" (1930), "Two Seconds" (1931) and "Adam Had Two Sons" (1932).

- During the Second World War he served with the United States Coast Guard and rose to the rank of captain. He eventually held the honorary rank of commodore.
- Preston made his acting debut in the film short "Pusher-in-the-Face" in 1929.
- Several more film roles followed including "Heads Up" (1930), "Two Seconds" (1932), "I Am a Fugitive from a Chain Gang" (1932), "The Band Plays On" (1934), "Annie Oakley" (1935), "Submarine Patrol" (1938), "Geronimo" (1939), "My Friend Flicka" (1943), "Bud Abbott and Lou Costello in Hollywood" (1945), "I Shot Jesse James" (1949) and "Montana Territory" (1952).
- In 1954, he was cast as "Cap'n John Herrick" in the TV series "Waterfront". He appeared in 78 episodes from 1954 to 1955.
- In 1961, he was cast as "Capt. Zachary Wingate" in the TV series "Gunslinger". He appeared in 12 episodes before the show was canceled.
- His last acting appearance was in the film "Chubasco" in 1967.
- Preston was married twice – Gertrude Warren (1926-45) and Sheila Darcy (1946-70). He had one daughter, Stephanie, with Ms. Warren.
- He has a Star on the Hollywood Walk of Fame for his services to television.
- Preston had a secondary career as a vocalist. He used to perform in a trio with his wife Sheila and guitarist Gene Leis.

- His other film credits include "Destination 60,000" (1957), "The Man from Galveston" (1963) and "You're Got to Be Smart" (1967).
- Preston's other TV credits include "Outlaws" (1961), "Going My Way" (1963), Eleventh Hour" (1963) and "77 Sunset Strip" (1964).

- **Midge Ware** was born Midge Ware Bendelson on October 20, 1927 in The Bronx, New York.
- She made her acting debut in an episode ("Honey for Your Tea") of "Front Page Detective" in 1951.
- From 1955 to 1957 she had a recurring role on "The Phil Silvers Show" as the character "WAC Corporal Mallory".
- In 1961, she was cast as "Amby Hollister" in the TV series "Gunslinger". She appeared in 12 episodes before the show was canceled.
- Her last acting appearance, to date, was in an episode ("The Hope of Elkwood") of "Quincy M.E." in 1980.
- Midge has been married twice – Arthur Batanides and David Moessinger. She has one daughter, Amy, with Mr. Moessinger.
- Her other film credits include "The Prince Who Was a Thief" (1951), "Untamed Women" (1952), "Five Minutes to Live" (1961), "The Cincinnati Kid" (1965), "All Woman" (1967) and "Faces" (1968).
- Midge's other TV credits include "Mike Hammer" (1958), "The Rifleman" (1960), "The

Donna Reed Show" (1961), "The Virginian" (1962), "Ben Casey" (1963) 2 episodes, "Iron Horse" (1967), "The F.B.I." (1969) and "Serpico" (1976).

- **John Pickard** was born on June 25, 1913 in Lascassas, Tennessee.
- He graduated from the Nashville Conservatory in Nashville, Tennessee.
- John made his acting debut (uncredited) in the film "Mary of Scotland" in 1936.
- From 1942 to 1946, he served in the U.S. Navy. He was the model for naval recruitment posters during the Second World War.
- After the war, he resumed his acting career and appeared in films such as "Wake of the Red Witch" (1948) uncredited, "White Heat" (1949) uncredited, "Stage to Tucson" (1950) uncredited, "Oh! Susanna" (1951), "Little Big Horn" (1951), "Trail Guide" (1952), "Hellgate" (1952), "Above and Beyond" (1952), "Arrowhead" (1953), "Bitter Creek" (1954), "Black Horse Canyon" (1954), "Shotgun" (1955), "The McConnell Story" (1955), "Fort Yuma" (1955) and "The Lone Ranger" (1956).
- In 1957, he was cast as "Capt. Shank Adams" in the TV series "Boots and Saddles". He appeared in 38 episodes from 1957 to 1958.

- In 1961, he was cast as "Sgt. Major Murdoch" in the TV series "Gunslinger". He appeared in 12 episodes before the show was canceled.
- His last acting appearance was in an episode ("Ancient Echoes") of "Simon & Simon" in 1987.
- John was married to wife Ann and they had one child.
- He was almost cast as "Marshal Dillon" in "Gunsmoke", but lost out to James Arness.
- John was killed by a bull on the family farm in 1993.
- His other film credits include "War Drums" (1957), "Outlaw's Son" (1957), "Cimarron" (1960) uncredited, "Gun Street" (1961), "A Gathering of Eagles" (1963), "Country Boy" (1966), "Ride to Hangman's Tree" (1967), "Charro!" (1969), "True Grit" (1969), "Chisum" (1970) and "Rape Squad" (1974).
- John's other TV credits include "The Adventures of Rin Tin Tin" (1954-57) 3 episodes, "The Lone Ranger" (1952-57) 7 episodes, "Sergeant Preston of the Yukon" (1955-57) 4 episodes, "Flight" (1959) 4 episodes, "Tales of Wells Fargo" (1957-59) 3 episodes, "The Life and Legend of Wyatt Earp" (1957-59) 4 episodes, "Zane Grey Theatre" (1957-61) 4 episodes, "Laramie" (1959-63) 8 episodes, "Perry Mason" (1958-63) 4 episodes, "Rawhide" (1959-65) 10 episodes, "Branded"

(1965-66) 6 episodes, "The Wild Wild West" (1966-69) 4 episodes, "Death Valley Days" (1958-69) 10 episodes, "The Virginian" (1965-69) 6 episodes and "Gunsmoke" (1960-75) 12 episodes.

- **Charles H. Gray** was born on November 27, 1921 in St. Louis, Missouri.
- He made his uncredited acting debut in the film "One Desire" in 1955.
- In 1956, he was cast as "Officer Edwards" in the TV series "Highway Patrol". He appeared in 5 episodes.
- In 1959, he was cast as "Clay Forrester" in the TV series "Rawhide". He appeared in 47 episodes from 1959 to 1964.
- Then in 1961, he was cast as "Pico McGuire" in the TV series "Gunslinger". He appeared in 11 episodes before the show was canceled.
- His last acting appearance was in the film "Prophecy" in 1979.
- Charles' other film credits include "The Black Whip" (1956), "Trooper Hook" (1957), "Ride a Violent Mile" (1957), "Desert Hell" (1958), "Charro!" (1969), "Wild Rovers" (1971), "Junior Bonner" (1972) and "And I Alone Survived" (1978)(TV).
- His other TV credits include "The Life and Legend of Wyatt Earp" (1956), "Superman" (1957), "Navy Log" (1957), "The Texan" (1959), "Zane Grey Theatre" (1957-59) 2

episodes, "Riverboat" (1959-60) 2 episodes, "Death Valley Days" (1960-61) 2 episodes, "Gunsmoke" (1956-64) 5 episodes, "Perry Mason" (1964), "The Road West" (1966) 2 episodes, "The Virginian" (1970), "Bonanza" (1972), "Banacek" (1974) and "Ike" (1979) 2 episodes.

"Hec Ramsey"

Years : 1972 - 1974

Episodes : 10 (2 seasons)

Cast :-

Richard Boone (b. 1917 d. 1981) - Played Dep. Sheriff Hec Ramsey

Rick Lenz (b.1939) - Played Police Chief Oliver B. Stamp

Harry Morgan (b. 1915 d. 2011) - Played Doc. Amos B. Coogan

Dennis Rucker - Played Constable Arne Tornquist

Synopsis :-
Ex-gunfighter Hec Ramsey settles down in Oklahoma.

Trivia & Tidbits :-

"The Show"

- **"Hec Ramsey"** premiered on NBC on October 8, 1972 and last aired on April 7, 1974.

- The show ran over two seasons (5 episodes each) with a total of 10 episodes.
- The series was created by Harold Jack Bloom and produced by Mark V11 Ltd and Universal TV.
- Filming took place on the Universal Studios Backlot.
- The theme music for "Mystery Movie" was composed by Henry Mancini.
- Jack Webb ("Dragnet") was the executive producer on the show.
- Despite good ratings the show was canceled after two seasons because of differences between Richard Boone and Universal Studios.

"In Memoriam"

- **Richard Boone** died of throat cancer on January 10, 1981 (63) in St. Augustine, Florida.
- **Harry Morgan** died of pneumonia on December 7, 2011 (96) in Brentwood, California.

"The Stars"

- **Richard Allen Boone** was born on June 18, 1917 in Los Angeles, California,
- He was the son of Kirk E. Boone, a corporate lawyer, and Cecile Beckerman. He is the uncle of Randy Boone ("The Virginian") and cousin of actor-singer Pat Boone.

- Richard graduated from Hoover High School and attended Stanford University but left before graduation.
- He tried oil-rigging, bartending, painting and writing before joining the U.S. Navy in 1941. Richard served on three ships during the Second World War.
- After the war, he studied acting at the Actor's Studio, New York and debuted on Broadway in the play "Medea" (1947).
- He then appeared in two other plays – "Macbeth" (1948) and "The Man" (1950).
- Richard made his TV debut in an episode ("You're Breaking My Heart") of "Actor's Studio" in 1949.
- He made his film debut in the movie "Halls of Montezuma" in 1950.
- Several more movie roles followed including "The Desert Fox : The Story of Rommel" (1951), "Red Skies of Montana" (1952), "The Robe" (1953), "Beneath the 12-Mile Reef" (1953), "Dragnet" (1954), "Man Without a Star" (1955) and "Away All Boats" (1956).
- In 1954, he was cast as "Dr. Konrad Styner" in the TV series "Medic". He appeared in 59 episodes from 1954 to 1956.
- Then in 1957, he was cast as "Paladin" in the TV series "Have Gun – Will Travel". He appeared in 225 episodes from 1957 to 1963.
- In 1963, he appeared in his own show "The Richard Boone Show". He appeared in 25 episodes from 1963 to 1964.

- In 1972, he appeared as "Hec Ramsey" in the TV series of the same name. He appeared in 10 episodes from 1972 to 1974.
- His last acting appearance was in the film "The Bushido Blade" in 1981.
- Richard was married three times – Jane Hopper (1937-1940), Mimi Kelly (1949-1950) and Clair McAloon (1951-1981). He had one son with Ms. McAloon.
- In 1955, Richard received an Emmy Award nomination (Best Actor) for "Medic".
- He received two more Emmy Award nominations in 1959 and 1960 for "Have Gun – Will Travel" and one for "The Richard Boone Show" in 1964.
- Richard was offered the role of "Steve McGarrett" in "Hawaii Five-O" but turned it down. The role went to Jack Lord.
- His other film credits include "The Garment Jungle" (1957), "Ocean's Eleven" (1960), "The Alamo" (1960), "The War Lord" (1965), "Hombre" (1967), "The Kremlin" (1970), "Big Jake" (1971), "The Shootist" (1976) and "The Big Sleep" (1978).
- Richard's other TV credits include "Suspense" (1950), "Frontier" (1956), "Studio One" (1957) and "Cimarron Strip" (1967).

- **Rick Lenz** was born on November 21, 1939 in Springfield, Illinois.
- He attended the University of Michigan and New York University.
- After graduation he spent two years as a director at the Michigan Civic Theater.

- Following this, he travelled to New York to seek work as an actor.
- In 1965, he made his Broadway debut in "Mating Game" and followed this up with a part in the hit play "Cactus Flower".
- Rick made his TV debut in an episode ("The Agricultural Student") of "Green Acres" in 1968.
- In 1969, he made his film debut as "Igor Sullivan" in "Cactus Flower" (the same role he played on Broadway).
- In 1972, he was cast as "Police Chief Oliver B. Stamp" in the TV series "Hec Ramsey". He appeared in 10 episodes from 1972 to 1974.
- Then in 1987, he had a recurring role as "Benjamin Baxter Sr." in the TV series "The New Adventures of Beans Baxter".
- His last acting appearance, to date, was in an episode ("Mannequins") of "Treelore Theatre" in 2012.
- Rick has been married twice – Jessica Rains (1966-77) and Linda Kurth (1982-present). He has three children with Ms. Rains.
- After his acting roles started to dry up, Rick concentrated on writing and painting.
- In 1973, his first play, "The Epic of Buster Friend", was produced at the Theatre De Lys in New York City.
- Then in 1981, he co-wrote the pilot for the ABC television series "Aloha Paradise".
- Rick published his memoir "North of Hollywood" in 2012.
- His other film credits include "Doc" (1969)(TV), "Scandalous John" (1971), "Ladies of the Corridor" (1975)(TV), "The Shootist"

(1976), "The Little Dragons" (1979), "Reunion" (1980)(TV), "Malice in Wonderland" (1985)(TV), "Perry Mason : The Case of the Telltale Talk Show Host" (1993)(TV) and "Home Room" (2002).

- Rick's other TV credits include "Green Acres" (1969) 3 episodes, "Ironside" (1972), "Lucas Tanner" (1974), "The Six Million Dollar Man" (1975-76) 3 episodes, "The Bionic Woman" (1976), "Dynasty" (1981) 3 episodes, "Lou Grant" (1982), "The Greatest American Hero" (1983), "Happy Days" (1984), "Simon & Simon" (1983-85) 3 episodes, "Falcon Crest" (1986) 2 episodes, "Baywatch" (1997) and "The Practice" (2003).

- **Harry Morgan** was born Harry Bratsburg on April 10, 1915 in Detroit, Michigan.
- He was married to Eileen Detchon for 45 years, until her death in 1985. They had four sons. In 1986, he married Barbara Bushman, granddaughter of silent screen star Francis X. Bushman.
- Harry is of Norwegian descent, his grandparents were immigrants from Scandinavia.
- He was raised in Muskegon, Michigan, and graduated from Muskegon High School in 1933, where he achieved distinction as a statewide debating champion.
- He originally wanted to be a lawyer, but began acting while a junior at the University of Chicago in 1935 and found that he liked it.
- He began acting on stage under his birth name, joining the Group Theatre in New York

City in 1937. He appeared in the original production of the Clifford Odets play "Golden Boy", followed by a host of successful Broadway roles.

- Morgan made his screen debut in the 1942 movie "To the Shores of Tripoli".
- In 1942, Harry had a small part in the film "Orchestra Wives" (1942) featuring Glenn Miller. In 1953, he co-starred with James Stewart in "The Glenn Miller Story" (1954).
- Harry continued to play a number of significant roles on the big screen in such films as "The Ox-Bow Incident" (1943), Dragonwyck" (1946), "High Noon" (1952), "Inherit the Wind" (1960), "How the West Was Won" (1962) and "Frankie and Johnny" (1966).
- In 1954, he was cast as "Pete Porter" in the TV series "December Bride". He appeared in 111 episodes from 1954 to 1959.
- He then continued this role in a new series called "Pete and Gladys". This show was on air from 1960 to 1962, a total of 72 episodes.
- In the 1964-65 season, Harry co-starred as "Seldom Jackson" in the 26 week NBC comedy/drama "Kentucky Jones" starring Dennis Weaver.
- His next series began in 1967. He was cast as "Bill Gannon" in "Dragnet 1967". He co-starred with Jack Webb and appeared in 98 episodes from 1967 to 1970.
- In 1975, he was cast as "Col. Sherman T. Potter" in the TV series "M.A.S.H." He appeared in 180 episodes from 1975 to the show's finish in 1983.

- After "M.A.S.H." finished in 1983 a spin-off series called "AfterMASH" was created. Harry appeared in this show during the first season (a total of 20 episodes).
- In several episodes of "M.A.S.H.", "Col. Potter" is seen painting portraits of different characters. These portraits were actually painted by him.
- Harry appeared with Lee J. Cobb, the father of his future daughter-in-law Julie Cobb, in "How the West Was Won" (1962).
- In 2006, Harry was inducted into the Hall of Great Western Performers at the National Cowboy & Western Heritage Museum.
- His son Christopher is a TV producer and his grandson, Spencer Morgan, is a columnist at the New York Observer.
- Harry's other TV credits include "The Amazing Mr. Malone" (1951), "The 20th Century-Fox Hour" (1957), "The Untouchables" (1962), "The Virginian" (1963), "Dr. Kildare" (1965), "The Partridge Family" (1972), "Gunsmoke" (1975), "The Love Boat" (1985), "The Twilight Zone" (1988) and "3rd Rock from the Sun" (1997).
- His other film credits include "State Fair" (1945), "Boots Malone" (1952), "Strategic Air Command" (1955), "Cimarron" (1960), "The Barefoot Executive" (1971), "The Shootist" (1976), "Dragnet" (1987) and "Crosswalk" (1999).

- **Dennis Wayne Rucker** was born on October 23, 1946 in Dallas, Texas.

- He made his acting debut in an episode ("The People vs. Saydo") of "The D.A." in 1971.
- In 1972, he was cast as "Constable Arne Tornquist" in the TV series "Hec Ramsey". He appeared in 8 episodes from 1972 to 1974.
- His last acting appearance, to date, was in the film "Wrong Bet" in 1990.
- Dennis' other film credits include "A Very Missing Person" (1972)(TV), "Death Race" (1973)(TV), "The Sex Symbol" (1974)(TV), "Midway" (1976), "Coming Home" (1978), "An Officer and a Gentleman" (1982), "Sunset" (1988) and "The China Lake Murders" (1990)(TV).
- His other TV credits include "Columbo" (1971), "Adam-12" (1971-72) 2 episodes, "Alias Smith and Jones" (1971-72) 3 episodes, "Cannon" (1972), "Ironside" (1971-73) 2 episodes, "Toma" (1974), "Police Woman" (1977), "The Dukes of Hazzard" (1980), "Hart to Hart" (1981) and "Dallas" (1986).

"Here Come the Brides"

Years : 1968 - 1970

Episodes : 52 (2 seasons)

Cast :-

Robert Brown (b. 1926) - Played Jason Bolt

Bobby Sherman (b. 1943) - Played Jeremy Bolt

David Soul (b. 1943) - Played Joshua Bolt

Mark Lenard (b. 1924 d. 1996) - Played Aaron Stempel

Bridget Hanley (b. 1941) - Played Candy Pruitt

Joan Blondell (b. 1906 d. 1979) - Played Lottie Hatfield

Synopsis :-
100 prospective brides travel from Massachusetts to Seattle.

Trivia & Tidbits :-

"The Show"

- **"Here Come the Brides"** premiered on ABC on September 25, 1968 and last aired on April 3, 1970.
- The show ran for two seasons with a total of 52 episodes.
- The series was loosely based on the "Mercer Girls" from Seattle, and inspired by the movie "Seven Brides for Seven Brothers" (1954).
- The theme song "Seattle" was written by Hugo Montenegro, Jack Keller and Ernie Sheldon, and sung by "The New Establishment".
- The series was produced by Screen Gems Television.
- Joan Blondell was nominated for two (1969 and 1970) Emmy Awards for "Outstanding Continued Performance by an Actress in a Leading Role in a Dramatic Series".
- The series was filmed at the Columbia/Sunset Gower studios and the Columbia/Warner Bros. Ranch, California.
- Martial arts expert Bruce Lee guest starred in a 1969 episode titled "Marriage Chinese Style".

"In Memoriam"

- **Mark Lenard** died of multiple myeloma on November 22, 1996 (72) in New York City, New York.
- **Joan Blondell** died of leukemia on December 25, 1979 (73) in Santa Monica, California.

"The Stars"

- **Robert Brown** was born Robin Adair MacKenzie Brown on November 17, 1926 in Trenton, New Jersey.
- He is the son of William and Margaret Brown. Robert has an older brother, Harold.
- Robert served in the U.S. Navy at the end of the Second World War.
- He studied acting in New York City at the New School for Social Research's Dramatic Workshop and American Theater Wing.
- Robert made his uncredited acting debut in the film "The Challenge" in 1948.
- He made his TV acting debut in an episode ("The Quest of Quesnay") of "Matinee Theatre" in 1958.
- Robert then guest starred on several TV shows including "The Silent Service" (1958), "Wagon Train" (1960), "The Case of the Dangerous Robin" (1960), "The Lawless Years" (1961) 2 episodes, "Bonanza" (1962), "The Dick Powell Show" (1963), "Perry Mason" (1960-64) 3 episodes, "12 O'Clock High" (1965), "Shane" (1966), "Star Trek" (1967), "Run for Your Life" (1967) and "The Danny Thomas Show" (1968).
- In 1968, he was cast as "Jason Bolt" in the TV series "Here Come the Brides". He appeared in 52 episodes from 1968 to 1970.
- In 1971, he was cast as "Carter Primus" in the TV series "Primus". He appeared in 26 episodes from 1971 to 1972.
- His last acting appearance, to date, was in an episode ("Poor Relations") of "In the Heat of the Night" in 1994.

- Robert has been marries four times – Leila Brown (1949-54), Mary Elizabeth Sellers (1961-67), Anna Gonyaw (1969-80) and Elisse Pogofsky-Harris (1986-present). He has three children.
- In recent years he has done voiceover work for radio and television.
- Robert's other film credits include "Appointment in Honduras" (1953) uncredited, "The Flame Barrier" (1958), "Tower of London" (1962), "J.T." (1969)(TV), "The Last Hurrah" (1977)(TV) and "Brass" (1985)(TV).
- His other TV credits include "Bewitched" (1970), "Mannix" (1973), "Columbo" (1975), "Police Story" (1975) 2 episodes, "Archie Bunker's Place" (1979) and "Fantasy Island" (1984).

- **Bobby Sherman** was born Robert Cabot Sherman Jr. on July 22, 1943 in Santa Monica, California.
- He is the son of Robert Cabot Sherman Sr. and Juanita 'Nita' Sherman (nee Freeman).
- Bobby grew up in Van Nuys, California (after moving there in 1951) along with his sister Darlene.
- At age 11, he learned to play the trumpet and then went onto master another 15 musical instruments.
- He graduated from Birmingham High School, Van Nuys in 1961 and then attended Pierce College in Woodland Hills, California.

- In 1962, he became a protégé of actor Sal Mineo and also released his first single record titled "Judy, You'll Never Know".
- In 1964, he began singing on the TV show "Shindig!" In all, he would stay for two years and a total of 43 episodes.
- In 1965, he made his acting debut in an episode ("The Princess and the Paupers") of "Honey West".
- He made his uncredited film debut in the movie "Wild in the Streets" in 1968.
- In 1968, he was cast as "Jeremy Bolt" in the TV series "Here Come the Brides". He appeared in 52 episodes from 1968 to 1970.
- In 1971, he was cast as "Bobby Conway" in the TV series "Getting Together". He appeared in 14 episodes from 1971 to 1972.
- Then in 1986, he was cast as "Frankie Rondell" in the TV series "Sanchez of Bel Air". He appeared in all 13 episodes.
- His last acting appearance, to date, was in an episode ("The Unnatural") of "Frasier" in 1997.
- Bobby has been married twice – Patti Carnel (1971-79) and Brigitte Poublon (2011-present). He has two children with Ms. Carnel.
- In 1969, he achieved his first hit record with "Little Woman" (gold record). Other hit records include "Julie, Do Ya Love Me?" (platinum record) and "Easy Come, Easy Go" (gold record).
- After his entertainment career, he became an Emergency Medical Technician (EMT) and worked with the Los Angeles Police Department, giving CPR and first aid classes.

- In 1996, he co-wrote, with Dena Hill, his best-selling autobiography "Still Remembering You".
- In 1998, he performed in concert as part of "The Teen Idol Tour" with Peter Noone ("Herman's Hermits") and Davy Jones ("The Monkees").
- In 2001, he performed his last concert as a solo performer in Lincoln, Rhode Island.
- In 2005, he was ranked No.8 in TV Guide's list of "TV's 25 Greatest Teen Idols".
- Bobby's other film credits included "Skyway to Death" (1974)(TV), "He Is My Brother" (1975), "The Gossip Columnist" (1980)(TV) and "Get Crazy" (1983).
- His other TV credits include "The Monkees" (1967), "The F.B.I." (1968), "The Partridge Family" (1971), "Cade's County" (1972), "The Mod Squad" (1972) 2 episodes, "Ellery Queen" (1976), "Flying High" (1979), "Fantasy Island" (1981), "The Love Boat" (1978-82) 2 episodes, "Murder, She Wrote" (1985) and "Blacke's Magic" (1986).

- **David Soul** was born David Richard Solberg on August 28, 1943 in Chicago, Illinois.
- He is the son of June Johnanne (nee Nelson), a teacher, and Dr. Richard w. Solberg, a Lutheran minister.
- David attended Augustana College, the University of the Americas in Mexico City and the University of Minnesota.

- He turned down a professional baseball contract with the Chicago White Sox to study political science.
- Whilst in Mexico, he learned to play the guitar and decided to follow his passion for music.
- In 1967, he appeared on "The Merv Griffin Show" as a singer.
- He made his acting debut in an episode ("The Firing Line: Part 1") of "Flipper" in 1967.
- In 1968, he was cast as "Joshua Bolt" in the TV series "Here Come the Brides". He appeared in 52 episodes from 1968 to 1970.
- In 1975, he was cast as "Det. Ken 'Hutch' Hutchinson" in the TV series "Starsky and Hutch". He appeared in 92 episodes from 1975 to 1979.
- Then in 1983, he was cast as "Rick Blaine" in the TV series "Casablanca". The series only lasted 5 episodes.
- Also in 1983, he was cast as "Roy Champion" in the TV series "The Yellow Rose". He appeared in 22 episodes from 1983 to 1984.
- In 1989, he was cast as "John Westley 'Westy' Grayson" in the TV series "Unsub". He appeared in 8 episodes.
- His last acting appearance, to date, was in the film "Filth" in 2013.
- David has been married five times – Mim Russeth (1963-65), Karen Carlson (1968-77), Patti Carnel Sherman (1980-86), Julia Nickson

(1987-93) and Helen Snell (2010-present). He has four children as well as two step-children.

- Between 1976 and 1982, he recorded four albums. He had No.1 hits with "Don't Give Up On Me Baby" (1976), "Silver Lady" (1977) and "Going In With My Eyes Open" (1977).
- In 2004, he became a United Kingdom citizen.
- David's other film credits include "The Secret Sharer" (1967), "Johnny Got His Gun" (1971), "Magnum Force" (1973), "The Disappearance of Flight 412" (1974)(TV), "Dogpound Shuffle" (1975), "The Stick Up" (1977), "Swan Song" (1980)(TV), "Through Naked Eyes" (1983)(TV), "The Hanoi Hilton" (1987), "Appointment with Death" (1988), "Prime Target" (1989)(TV), "Tides of War" (1990), "Perry Mason: The Case of the Fatal Framing" (1992)(TV), "Pentathlon" (1994), "Tabloid" (2001), "Jerry Springer: The Opera" (2005)(TV) and "Farewell" (2009).
- His other TV credits include "Star Trek" (1967), "Dan August" (1971), "All in the Family" (1971), "The F.B.I." (1972), "Owen Marshall, Counselor at Law" (1971-74) 5 episodes, "Cannon" (1973-74) 2 episodes, "Medical Center" (1974), "Partners in Crime" (1984), "Crime Story" (1987), "The Young Riders" (1990) 2 episodes, "Jake and the Fatman" (1988-92) 2 episodes, "Murder, She Wrote" (1991-93) 2 episodes, "High Tide"

(1994), "Holby City" (2001-02) 2 episodes and "Lewis" (2012).

- **Mark Lenard** was born Leonard Rosenson on October 15, 1924 in Chicago, Illinois.
- He was the son of a Russian/Jewish immigrant, Abraham and his wife, Bessie.
- Mark was raised in South Haven, Michigan, where his family owned a tourist resort.
- He joined the United States Army in 1943 and trained to be a paratrooper during the Second World War. He did not see actual combat and was discharged in 1946.
- After his discharge, he earned a master's degree in theater and speech from the University of Michigan.
- Mark worked in theater in New York City for a number of years before moving his family to Los Angeles.
- He made his TV debut in an episode ("I, Don Quixote") of "The DuPont Show of the Month" in 1959.
- Mark made his film debut in the TV movie "Family Classics: The Three Musketeers" in 1960.
- Several TV guest appearances followed including "Armstrong Circle Theatre" (1960-62) 2 episodes, "Lamp Unto My Feet" (1963), "The Defenders" (1964), "The Nurses" (1964), "Another World" (1964) 2 episodes, "Days of

Our Lives" (1965), "Jericho" (1966), "Iron Horse" (1967), "Star Trek" (1966-67) 2 episodes, "The Wild Wild West" (1967), "Run for Your Life" (1968), "Gunsmoke" (1968) and "Cimarron Strip" (1968).

- In 1967, he was cast as the character "Sarek" in an episode ("Journey to Babel") of "Star Trek". He went onto play the character in three movies – "Star Trek III: The Search for Spock" (1984), "Star Trek IV: The Voyage Home" (1986) and "Star Trek VI: The Undiscovered Country" (1991). Mark also played the character in 2 episodes of the TV series "Star Trek: The Next Generation" (1990-91).
- In 1968, he was cast as "Aaron Stempel" in the TV series "Here Come the Brides". He appeared in 52 episodes from 1968 to 1970.
- In 1974, he was cast as "Urko" in the TV series "Planet of the Apes". He appeared in 11 episodes.
- Mark's last acting appearance was in an episode ("Legacy") of "In the Heat of the Night" in 1993.
- He was married to Ann Amouri from 1960 until his death in 1996. They had two daughters, Roberta and Catherine.
- Mark's other film credits include "The Greatest Story Ever Told" (1965), "Hang 'Em High" (1968), "Noon Sunday" (1970), "Outrage"

(1973)(TV), "Annie Hall" (1977), "Star Trek: The Motion Picture" (1979) and "The Radicals" (1990).

- His other TV credits include "Mission: Impossible" (1966-70) 4 episodes, "Alias Smith and Jones" (1971), "Mannix" (1973), "Chopper One" (1974), "Little House on the Prairie" (1976), "Hawaii Five-O" (1969-77) 4 episodes, "Greatest Heroes of the Bible" (1978) 2 episodes, "How the West Was Won" (1979) and "Buck Rogers in the 25th Century" (1981).

- **Bridget Ann Elizabeth Hanley** was born on February 3, 1941 in Minneapolis, Minnesota.
- She is the daughter of Leland Hanley, an All-American football player at Northwestern University and United States Marine Corps veteran, and Doris Nihlroos.
- When she was four years old the family moved to Edmonds, Washington (state).
- After graduating from Edmonds High School she went to San Francisco College for Women and then the University of Washington.
- She graduated from university with honors and a B.A. in drama.
- Bridget started her acting career in Repertory Theater and landed the role of "Robin" in a touring company production of "Under the Yum Yum Tree".

- She made her TV debut in an episode ("My Fair Co-Ed") of "Hank" in 1965.
- Several TV guest appearances followed including "Gidget" (1966), "The Farmer's Daughter" (1966), "Love on a Rooftop" (1966), "Occasional Wife" (1967), "Iron Horse" (1967), "The Second Hundred Years" (1967) 3 episodes and "The Flying Nun" (1968).
- In 1968, she was cast as "Candy Pruitt" in the TV series "Here Comes the Brides". She appeared in 52 episodes from 1968 to 1970.
- Bridget's film debut was in the TV movie "Mad Mad Scientist" in 1968.
- In 1981, she was cast as "Wanda Reilly Taylor" in the TV series "Harper Valley P.T.A." She appeared in 30 episodes from 1981 to 1982.
- Her last acting appearance, to date, was in an episode ("Storm Warning") of "Kung Fu: The Legend Continues" in 1996.
- Bridget was married to E.W. Swackhamer from 1969 until his death in 1994. They have two daughters, Bronwyn and Megan.
- Her other film credits include "Bell, Book and Candle" (1976)(TV), "Breaking Up Is Hard to Do" (1979)(TV), "Malibu" (1983)(TV) and "Chattanooga Choo Choo" (1984).
- Bridget's other TV credits include "The Odd Couple" (1970), "The Interns" (1970), "Cade's County" (1972), "Love, American Style" (1970-73) 5 episodes, "The Rookies" (1974),

"Insight" (1976), "Chips" (1978), "Riptide" (1985), "Simon & Simon" (1982-88) 2 episodes, "Columbo" (1990) and "The New Adam-12" (1991).

- **Joan Blondell** was born Rose Joan Blondell on August 30, 1906 in Manhattan, New York.
- She was the daughter of vaudeville comedian Ed Blondell and Kathryn Cain. She had one sister, Gloria (also an actress) and a brother, Ed Blondell Jr.
- In her early years, she worked as a fashion model and entered several beauty pageants. In 1926, she won the Miss Dallas pageant.
- About 1927, she returned to New York City, joined a stock company to become an actress and performed on the Broadway stage in the play "The Trial of Mary Dugan" (1927-28).
- She then appeared in two more Broadway plays – "Maggie the Magnificent" (1929) and "Penny Arcade" (1930).
- In 1930, she made her feature film debut in the movie "The Office Wife".
- This was followed by several movie roles including "Other Men's Women" (1931), "The Public Enemy" (1931), "Blonde Crazy" (1931), "Make Me a Star" (1932), "Big City Blues" (1932), "Central Park" (1932), "Gold Diggers of 1933" (1933), "Kansas City Princess" (1934), "Stage Struck" (1936), "Stand-In"

(1937), "Two Girls on Broadway" (1940), "Topper Returns" (1941), "A Tree Grows in Brooklyn" (1945), "Christmas Eve" (1947) and "The Blue Veil" (1951).

- She made her TV debut in an episode ("Pot o' Gold") of "Nash Airflyte Theatre" in 1951.
- Several more TV guest appearances followed including "Suspense" (1953), "Fireside Theatre" (1955), "The United States Steel Hour" (1955), "Studio One" (1958), "Playhouse 90" (1957-59) 2 episodes, "Adventures in Paradise" (1960), "The Untouchables" (1961), "The Dick Powell Show" (1962), "Death Valley Days" (1963), "The Real McCoys" (1963) 3 episodes, "The Virginian" (1963), "Burke's Law" (1963-64) 2 episodes, "Bonanza" (1964), "Disneyland" (1965), "The Lucy Show" (1965) 2 episodes, "My Three Sons" (1965), "The Man from U.N.C.L.E." (1966), "Family Affair" (1967) and "That Girl" (1968).
- In 1968, she was cast as "Lottie Hatfield" in the TV series "Here Come the Brides". She appeared in 52 episodes from 1968 to 1970.
- In 1972, she was cast as "Peggy Revere" in the TV series "Banyon". She appeared in 8 episodes.
- Her last acting appearance was in the film "The Woman Inside" in 1981 (released after she had passed away).

- Joan was married three times – George Barnes (1933-36), Dick Powell (1936-44), and Michael Todd (1947-50). She had one son, Norman, with Mr. Barnes and one daughter, Ellen, with Mr. Powell.
- She appeared twice more in Broadway plays – "The Naked Genius" (1943) and "The Rope Dancers" (1957-58).
- In 1960, she was awarded a Star on the Hollywood Walk of Fame for her contribution to Motion Pictures.
- In 1972, she wrote a novel titled "Center Door Fancy" (some think it is a thinly disguised autobiography).
- Joan was nominated twice (1969 and 1970) for an Emmy Award for her role in "Here Comes the Brides".
- She made six movies with James Cagney at Warner Brothers.
- Joan's other film credits include "The Opposite Sex" (1956), "Lizzie" (1957), "Desk Set" (1957), "Angel Baby" (1961), "The Cincinnati Kid" (1965), "Ride Beyond Vengeance" (1966), "Winchester 73" (1967)(TV), "Support Your Local Gunfighter" (1971) "Winner Take All" (1975)(TV), "The Baron" (1977), "Grease" (1978) and "The Champ" (1979).
- Her other TV credits include "The Name of the Game" (1970), "McCloud" (1971), "Love, American Style" (1971-73) 2 episodes, "The

New Dick Van Dyke Show" (1973), "Police Story" (1975), "Starsky and Hutch" (1976) 2 episodes, "The Love Boat" (1978) and "Fantasy Island" (1979).

"The High Chaparral"

Years : 1967 - 1971

Episodes : 98 (4 seasons)

Cast :-

Leif Erickson (b. 1911 d. 1986) - Played Big John Cannon

Cameron Mitchell (b. 1918 d. 1994) - Played Buck Cannon

Mark Slade (b. 1939) - Played Billy Blue Cannon

Linda Cristal (b. 1934) - Played Victoria Cannon

Henry Darrow (b. 1933) - Played Manolito Montoya

Don Collier (b. 1928) - Played Sam Butler

Robert F. Hoy (b. 1927 d. 2010) - Played Joe Butler

Roberto Contreras (b. 1928 d. 2000) - Played Pedro

Synopsis :-

The story of a ranching family in the Arizona Territory during the 1870's.

Trivia & Tidbits :-

"The Show"

- **"The High Chaparral"** premiered on NBC on September 10, 1967 and last aired on March 12, 1971.
- The show ran for four seasons with a total of 98 episodes.
- The series was made by Xanadu Productions in association with NBC Productions and created by David Dortort (of "Bonanza" fame).
- The theme song was written by David Rose (music) with lyrics by Joe Lubin and David Dortort.
- The outdoor scenes for the series were filmed at the Old Tucson Studios, Arizona, whilst, indoor scenes were completed in Hollywood.
- For the four years the show was on air it never rated in the top thirty programs.
- The series won one Golden Globe Award (Linda Crystal - Best Actress), one Western Heritage Award (Fictional TV Drama) and nominated for two Emmy Awards.
- During the four years of production "The High Chaparral" had a total of 53 writers and 29 directors.

"In Memoriam"

- **Leif Erickson** died of cancer on January 29, 1986 (74) in Pensacola, Florida.
- **Cameron Mitchell** died of lung cancer on July 6, 1994 (75) in Pacific Palisades, California.
- **Robert F. Hoy** died of cancer on February 8, 2010 (82) in Northridge, California.
- **Roberto Contreras** died on July 18, 2000 (71) in Los Angeles, California.

"The Stars"

- **Leif Erickson** was born William Wycliffe Anderson on October 27, 1911 in Alameda, California.
- He studied at the University of Southern California and began his career as a singer and trombonist with Ted Fio Rito and his orchestra.
- Leif made his film debut in the movie "The Sweetheart of Sigma Chi" in 1933.
- Several film roles followed including "Air Tonic" (1933) (short), "Wanderer of the Wasteland" (1935), "Nevada" (1935), "Desert Gold" (1936), "College Holiday" (1936), "Waikiki Wedding" (1937), "Ride a Crooked Mile" (1938), "Nothing But the Truth" (1941), "The Fleet's In" (1942), "Eagle Squadron" (1942) and "Arabian Nights" (1942).
- During the Second World War, Leif joined the United States Navy as a combat photographer. He served as an instructor and was shot down and wounded twice.

- After the war, he resumed his career and appeared in films such as "Blonde Savage" (1947), "The Gangster" (1947), "Sorry, Wrong Number" (1948), "The Gay Intruders" (1948), "Joan of Arc" (1948) and "The Lady Gambles" (1949).
- He made his TV debut in an episode ("The Lady or the Tiger") of "Your Show Time" in 1949.
- This was followed by several more film roles including "Stella" (1950), "The Showdown" (1950), "Dallas" (1950), "Show Boat" (1951), "The Cimarron Kid" (1952), "Carbine Williams" (1952), "Abbott and Costello Meet Captain Kidd" (1952), "Born to the Saddle" (1953), "Captain Scarface" (1953), "On the Waterfront" (1954), "The Fastest Gun Alive" (1956) and "Istanbul" (1957).
- He then started to appear on more TV shows such as "Climax!" (1955-57) 4 episodes, "Matinee Theatre" (1958) 2 episodes, "The Millionaire" (1956-58) 2 episodes, "The Rifleman" (1958), "Hotel de Paree" (1959), "Zane Grey Theatre" (1958-60) 2 episodes, "Playhouse 90" (1957-60) 4 episodes, "Rawhide" (1959-61) 2 episodes, "The New Breed" (1962), "Wagon Train" (1963), "Hazel" (1963), "The Travels of Jaimie McPheeters" (1964), "The Great Adventure" (1963-64) 2 episodes, "Burke's Law" (1964), "The Alfred Hitchcock Hour" (1964-65) 2 episodes, "A Man Called Shenandoah" (1965), "Bonanza" (1961-65) 2 episodes, "The Virginian" (1964-65) 3 episodes, "Branded" (1966), "Daniel Boone"

(1965-66) 2 episodes and "Gunsmoke" (1967).

- In 1967, he was cast as "Big John Cannon" in the TV series "The High Chaparral". He appeared in 97 episodes from 1967 to 1971.
- His last acting appearance was in an episode ("Goin' on Home/Ambitious Lady") of "Fantasy Island" in 1984.
- Leif was married three times – Frances Farmer (1936-42), Margaret Hayes (1942) and Ann Diamond (1945-86). He had two children with MS. Diamond.
- During the 1960's, when acting roles were scarce, he became a yacht broker.
- In 1967, he visited soldiers fighting in Vietnam.
- Over the years, Leif appeared on the Broadway stage in plays such as "All the Living" (1938), "Margin for Error" (1939-40), "Higher and Higher" (1940), "Tea and Sympathy" (1953-55) and "The World of Carl Sandburg" (1960).
- Leif's other film credits include "Shootout at Big Sag" (1962), "A Gathering of Eagles" (1963), "The Carpetbaggers" (1964), "Roustabout" (1964), "Terror in the Sky" (1971)(TV), "The Family Rico" (1972)(TV), "Abduction" (1975), "Winterhawk" (1975), "Twilight's Last Gleaming" (1977) and "Savage in the Orient" (1983)(TV).
- His other TV credits include "The Sixth Sense" (1972), "The Mod Squad" (1972), "Night Gallery" (1971-73) 2 episodes, "The Streets of San Francisco" (1973), "Ironside" (1974),

"Medical Center" (1974), "Mannix" (1974), "Cannon" (1974), "Hunter" (1977) and "The Rockford Files" (1979).

- **Cameron Mitchell** was born Cameron McDowell Mitzell on November 4, 1918 in Dallastown, Pennsylvania.
- His parents were Reverend Charles and Kathryn Mitzell. The family moved to Chicora, Pennsylvania in 1921 so that his father could take up the position of pastor.
- Cameron graduated from Greenwood High School, Millerstown, Pennsylvania in 1936.
- He attended the Theater School of Dramatic Arts in New York City.
- Between the two world wars, he worked as a young actor in Alfred Lunt and Lynn Fontanne's National Theater Company.
- He made his Broadway debut in the play "Jeremiah" in 1939.
- During the Second World War, he served as a bombardier with the United States Army Air Forces.
- Cameron made his movie debut in the film short "The Last Installment" in 1945.
- This was followed by a number of film roles including "What Next, Corporal Hargrove?" (1945), "They Were Expendable" (1945), "Cass Timberlane" (1947), "Homecoming" (1948), "Adventures of Gallant Bess" (1948) and "Command Decision" (1948).
- Cameron made his TV debut in an episode ("The Old Lady Shows Her Medals") of "The Philco Television Playhouse" in 1948.

- Several more TV roles followed including "Stars Over Hollywood" (1951) 2 episodes, "Gruen Guild Playhouse" (1951), "Campbell Playhouse" (1952), "The Fisher Family" (1952), "The 20th Century-Fox Hour" (1955) 2 episodes, "Climax!" (1956-57) 2 episodes, "Studio One" (1956-58) 2 episodes, "Colt .45" (1958), "Wagon Train" (1959), "The Untouchables" (1959), "Zane Grey Theatre" (1958-59) 3 episodes, "Bonanza" (1960) and "Death Valley Days" (1960).
- In 1962, he was cast as "John Lackland/Narrator" in the TV series "The Beachcomber". He appeared in 39 episodes.
- In 1967, he was cast as "Buck Cannon" in the TV series "The High Chaparral". He appeared in 97 episodes from 1967 to 1971.
- Then in 1975, he was cast as "Jeremiah Worth" in the TV series "Swiss Family Robinson". He appeared in 20 episodes from 1975 to 1976.
- In 1976, he had a recurring role as "Coulee John Brinkerhoff" in the TV series "How the West Was Won". He appeared in 4 episodes from 1976 to 1978.
- His last acting appearance was in the film "Jack-O" in 1995 (the film was released after he had passed away).
- Cameron was married three times – Johanna Mendel (1940-60), Lissa Jacobs Gertz and Margaret Mozingo (1973-76). He had a total of six children.
- He appeared in a number of other Broadway plays including "The Trojan Women" (1941), "Death of a Salesman" (1949-50), "Southern

Exposure" (1950), "Les Blancs" (1970) and "The November People" (1978).

- Cameron's other film credits include "Death of a Salesman" (1951), "Japanese War Bride" (1952), "Les Miserables" (1952), "Pony Soldier" (1952), "Garden of Evil" (1954), "The Tall Men" (1955), "Carousel" (1956), "Escapade in Japan" (1957), "Inside the Mafia" (1959), "The Last Gun" (1964), "Hombre" (1967), "The Andersonville Trial" (1970)(TV). "Buck and the Preacher" (1972), "Medusa" (1973), "The Klansman" (1974), "The Swiss Family Robinson" (1975), "The Quest" (1976)(TV), "Texas Detour" (1978), "The Silent Scream" (1979), "Captive" (1980), "Blood Link" (1982), "Kenny Rogers as The Gambler: The Adventure Continues" (1983)(TV), "Night Train to Terror" (1985), "Hollywood Cop" (1987), "Return to Justice" (1990) and "Crossing the Line" (1990).
- His other TV credits include "Daniel Boone" (1966) 2 episodes, "The Mod Squad" (1971), "Cade's County" (1971), "The F.B.I." (1971), "Alias Smith and Jones" (1972), "Night Gallery" (1972) 2 episodes, "Search" (1973), "Kodiak" (1974), "Ironside" (1972-74) 3 episodes, "Medical Center" (1974) 2 episodes, "Gunsmoke" (1974), "Cannon" (1975), "The Quest" (1976), "Hunter" (1977), "Police Story" (1973-77) 2 episodes, "Flying High" (1978), "Hawaii Five-O" (1974-79) 2 episodes, "Mrs. Columbo" (1980), "The Littlest Hobo" (1980), "Charlie's Angels" (1979-80) 2 episodes, "Magnum, P.I." (1981), "Fantasy Island" (1978-81) 4 episodes, "Knight Rider" (1984),

"Murder, She Wrote" (1985), "Matlock" (1987) and "Mama's Boy" (1988).

- **Mark Slade** was born Mark Van Blarcom Slade on May 1, 1939 in Salem, Massachusetts.
- He is the son of Elinor Van Blarcom and William A. Slade, a Boston businessman and watercolor artist.
- In 1956, he enrolled in Worcester Academy, Massachusetts to study art, however, after one of his classmates fell ill, he substituted in a play ("The Male Animal") and then decided to study acting.
- Mark then moved to New York City to attend the American Academy of Dramatic Arts.
- He made his Broadway debut in the play "There Was a Little Girl" in 1960.
- Mark made his TV debut in an episode ("Deadline") of "My Three Sons" in 1961.
- Following this, he appeared in the film "Voyage to the Bottom of the Sea" (1961).
- He then appeared as a guest star on a number of TV shows such as "The Dick Powell Show" (1962), "Alcoa Premiere" (1962), "Stoney Burke" (1963), "The Fugitive" (1964), "Channing" (1964), "Perry Mason" (1964) and "Rawhide" (1961-64) 2 episodes.
- In 1964, he had the recurring role of "Malone" in the TV series "Voyage to the Bottom of the Sea". He appeared in 5 episodes.

- Also in 1964, he had the recurring role of "Eddie" in the TV series "Gomer Pyle U.S.M.C." He appeared in 8 episodes.
- Then in 1965, he was cast as "Radioman Patrick Hollis" in the TV series "The Wackiest Ship in the Army". He appeared in 29 episodes from 1965 to 1966.
- In 1967, he was cast as "Billy Blue Cannon" in the TV series "The High Chaparral". He appeared in 80 episodes from 1967 to 1970.
- In 1974, he was cast as "Taylor Reed" in the TV series "Salty". He appeared in 19 episodes from 1974 to 1975.
- His last acting appearance, to date, was in an episode ("Stress") of "Cagney & Lacey" in 1985.
- Mark has been married to Melinda Marie Riccilli since 1968. They have two children.
- In the early 1960's, he served in the United States Army Reserve.
- Mark has published four novels – "Going Down Maine" (2012), "Of Pain and Coffee" (2014), "Someone's Story" (2014) and "Hangin' With the Truth" (2016).
- Since his acting career he has concentrated on creating and selling his own artworks.
- Mark's other film credits include "13 West Street" (1962), "Drag Racer" (1971), "Salty" (1973), "Message to My Daughter" (1973)(TV), "Benji" (1974), "The Return of

Mod Squad" (1979)(TV), "Waikiki" (1980)(TV) and "Flashpoint" (1984).

- His other TV credits include "The Alfred Hitchcock Hour" (1964), "Mr. Novak" (1964-65) 3 episodes, "The Donna Reed Show" (1965), "Bonanza" (1966), "The Wild Wild West" (1967), "The Mod Squad" (1972), "The Rookies" (1972-75) 3 episodes, "S.W.A.T." (1976), "The Life and Times of Grizzly Adams" (1978), "Charlie's Angels" (1981), "Today's F.B.I." (1981) and "Chips" (1979-82) 2 episodes.

- **Linda Cristal** was born Marta Victoria Moya Burges on February 23, 1934 in Buenos Aires, Argentina.
- She was born to a French father and an Italian mother. Both her parents died in what was considered a suicide pact.
- After appearing in several Mexican films she made her U.S. film debut in the movie "Comanche" in 1956.
- This was followed by roles in films such as "The Last of the Fast Guns" (1958), "The Fiend Who Walked the West" (1958) and "The Perfect Furlough" (1958).
- Linda made her TV debut in an episode ("Incident of a Burst of Evil") of "Rawhide" in 1959.
- She then guest starred on many TV shows including "The Tab Hunter Show" (1961),

"Alcoa Premiere" (1963), "General Hospital" (1963), "Voyage to the Bottom of the Sea" (1964), "T.H.E. Cat" (1966) and "Iron Horse" (1967).

- In 1967, she was cast as "Victoria Cannon" in the TV series "The High Chaparral". She appeared in 96 episodes from 1967 to 1971.
- Her last acting appearance, to date, was in the Argentinian TV soap "Rosse" in 1985.
- Linda has been married three times. She has two sons, Gregory and Jordan.
- She won two Golden Globe Awards – 1959 (Most Promising Newcomer – Female) for "The Perfect Furlough" and 1970 (Best TV Actress – Drama) for "The High Chaparral".
- Linda's other film credits include "Seven Sins" (1959), "Cry Tough" (1959), "The Alamo" (1960), "Two Rode Together" (1961), "Panic in the City" (1968), "Call Home" (1972)(TV), "Mr. Majestyk" (1974), "The Dead Don't Die" (1975)(TV) and "Love and the Midnight Auto Supply" (1977).
- Her other TV credits include "Cade's County" (1971), "Bonanza" (1971), "Search" (1972), "Police Story" (1974), "Barnaby Jones" (1979), "The Love Boat" (1981) and "Fantasy Island" (1981).

- **Henry Darrow** was born Enrique Tomas Delgado on September 15, 1933 in New York City, New York.
- He is the son of Gloria and Enrique Pio Delgado. His father worked in the restaurant and clothing businesses.
- When he was eight years old, he performed in a school play and the experience made up his mind to become an actor.
- Henry graduated from Academia del Perpetuo Socorro High School in Miramar, Puerto Rico and then enrolled in the University of Puerto Rico to study political science and acting.
- He then moved to Los Angeles and enrolled in the Pasadena Playhouse. He graduated with a Bachelor of Arts in theater arts.
- Henry made his uncredited film debut in the movie "Curse of the Undead" in 1959.
- This was followed by roles in the films "Holiday for Lovers" (1959) uncredited and "Revenge of the Virgins" (1959).
- He made his TV debut in an episode ("The Stagecoach Story") of "Wagon Train" in 1959.
- Henry then guest starred on many TV shows including "The Dick Powell Show" (1961), "Stoney Burke" (1963), "The Outer Limits" (1963), "Channing" (1964), "Voyage to the Bottom of the Sea" (1964), "Iron Horse" (1966), "The Wild Wild West" (1967), "T.H.E. Cat" (1966-67) 2 episodes, "Bonanza" (1967),

"Gunsmoke" (1966-67) 2 episodes and "Daniel Boone" (1967).

- In 1967, he was cast as "Manolito Montoya" in the TV series "The High Chaparral". He appeared in 97 episodes from 1967 to 1971.
- In 1973-74, he had the recurring role of "Alex Montenez" in the TV series "The New Dick Van Dyke Show". He appeared in 5 episodes.
- In 1974-75, he had the recurring role of "Lt. Manuel 'Manny' Quinlan" in the TV series "Harry O". He appeared in 14 episodes.
- Then in 1981, he supplied the voice of "Don Diego" in the animated TV series "The New Adventures of Zorro". He voiced 13 episodes.
- In 1983, he played "Don Diego de Vega" in the TV series "Zorro and Son". The series only lasted 5 episodes.
- In 1985, he played "Lt. Rojas" in the TV series "Me and Mom". The series only lasted 6 episodes.
- In 1989, he was cast as "Rafael Castillo" in the daytime soap "Santa Barbara". He appeared in 61 episodes from 1989 to 1990.
- In 1990, he was cast as "Don Alejandro de la Vega" in the TV series "Zorro". He appeared in 63 episodes from 1990 to 1993.
- He was cast as the character "Dr. Carlos Nunez" in the TV soap "The Bold and the Beautiful". He appeared in 14 episodes from 1998 to 2001.

- Henry's last acting appearance, to date, was in the film "Soda Springs" in 2012.
- He has been married twice – Louise DePuy (1956-79) and Lauren Levinson (1982-present). He has two children with Ms. DePuy.
- In 1990, he won a Daytime Emmy (Outstanding Supporting Actor in a Drama Series) for "Santa Barbara".
- Henry was a member of the board of directors of the Screen Actors Guild.
- In 2015, he co-authored, with Jan Pippins, his autobiography titled "Henry Darrow: Lightning in the Bottle".
- Henry's other film credits include "Sniper's Ridge" (1961), "The Glass Cage" (1964), "The Dream of Hamish Mose" (1969), "Cancel My Reservation" (1972), "Badge 373" (1973), "Night Games" (1974)(TV), "Exit Dying" (1976)(TV), "Where's Willie?" (1978), "A Life of Sin" (1979), "Birds of Paradise" (1981), "Rooster" (1982)(TV), "The Hitcher" (1986), "In Dangerous Company" (1988), "The Last of the Finest" (1990), "Maverick" (1994), "Empire" (1995)(TV), "Enemy Action" (1999), "Runaway Jury" (2003) and "Primo" (2008).
- His other TV credits include "Bearcats!" (1971) 2 episodes, "The Mod Squad" (1972), "Kung Fu" (1973), "Kojak" (1974), "The Streets of San Francisco" (1976), "Sara" (1976), "Hawaii Five-O" (1971-77) 3 episodes, "Wonder

Woman" (1977) 2 episodes, "The Waltons" (1979), "The Incredible Hulk" (1981), "Quincy M.E." (1976-82) 3 episodes, "Hart to Hart" (1979-83) 2 episodes, "Dallas" (1983) 2 episodes, "Scarecrow and Mrs. King" (1983-84) 2 episodes, "The Fisher Family" (1984-85) 2 episodes, "T.J. Hooker" (1982-86) 3 episodes, "Simon & Simon" (1981-88) 2 episodes, "Time Trax" (1993) 2 episodes, "Sisters" (1995) 2 episodes, "Night Man" (1997), "Family Law" (2000), "Just Shoot Me" (2002) and "One Tree Hill" (2005).

- **Don Collier (see "Outlaws")**

- **Robert Francis Hoy** was born on April 3, 1927 in New York City, New York.
- He served in the U.S. Marines during the Second World War.
- Robert's career spanned 55 years as first a stuntman, then an actor and director.
- He made his uncredited acting debut in the film "Ambush" in 1950.
- This was followed by many film roles including "The Lawless Breed" (1953) uncredited, "Taza, Son of Cochise" (1954), "A Star Is Born" (1954) uncredited, "Francis in the Navy" (1955) uncredited, "To Hell and Back" (1955) uncredited, "Gun for a Coward" (1957) and "Twilight for the Gods" (1958).

- Robert made his TV debut in an episode ("Song Plugging") of "December Bride" in 1957.
- He followed this with guest appearances on many TV shows including "Sea Hunt" (1958) 2 episodes, "Have Gun – Will Travel" (1958), "The Life and Legend of Wyatt Earp" (1959), "Steve Canyon" (1959) 3 episodes, "Walt Disney's Wonderful World of Color" (1958-59) 6 episodes, "U.S. Marshal" (1959), "Johnny Ringo" (1960), "Tombstone Territory" (1960), "Zane Grey Theatre" (1958-60) 6 episodes, "Peter Gunn" (1961), "The Tall Man" (1961), "Bat Masterson" (1960-61) 2 episodes, "The Jack Benny Program" (1961-62) 3 episodes, "Laramie" (1963), "The Rifleman" (1960-63) 3 episodes, "Branded" (1965) 2 episodes, "The Virginian" (1966), "Shane" (1966), "The Wild Wild West" (1966) 3 episodes, "The Man from U.N.C.L.E." (1965-66) 3 episodes, "Laredo" (1965-67) 2 episodes and "Star Trek" (1967).
- In 1967, he was cast as "Joe Butler" in the TV series "The High Chaparral". He appeared in 63 episodes from 1967 to 1971.
- In 1982, he had the recurring role of "Detective Howard" in the TV series "Dallas". He appeared in 4 episodes.
- Then in 1986, he had another recurring role as "Cliff" in the TV series "Our House". He appeared in 12 episodes from 1986 to 1988.

- His last acting appearance was in an episode ("Lost & Found") of "N.C.I.S." in 2007.
- Robert was married twice – Eleanor Barrett (1963-?) and Kiva Lawrence (1987-2010). He had one son, Christopher, with Ms. Barrett.
- In 1961, he became a co-founding member of The Stuntman's Association of Motion Pictures.
- Robert's other film credits include "Operation Petticoat" (1959), "Spartacus" (1960) uncredited, "Tickle Me" (1965) uncredited, "Tobruk" (1967), "The Love Bug" (1968), "A Man for Hanging" (1972)(TV), "Toke" (1973), "Bite the Bullet" (1975), "The Outlaw Josey Wales" (1976), "The Enforcer" (1976), "Steel Cowboy" (1978)(TV), "Bronco Billy" (1980), "The Legend of the Lone Ranger" (1981), "Assassin" (1986)(TV), "Houston: The Legend of Texas" (1986)(TV), "Bonanza: The Next Generation" (1988)(TV) and "Detective" (2005)(TV).
- His other TV credits include "Bonanza" (1960-71) 12 episodes, "Cade's County" (1972), "Hec Ramsey" (1972), "Kung Fu" (1972-73) 2 episodes, "The New Perry Mason" (1973), "The Cowboys" (1974), "Mannix" (1968-74) 3 episodes, "Police Story" (1974-75) 2 episodes, "Barbary Coast" (1975), "Cannon" (1972-75) 2 episodes, "The Streets of San Francisco" (1973-75) 2 episodes, "The Quest" (1976), "McMillan & Wife" (1977), "The Six Million

Dollar Man" (1974-78) 2 episodes, "Switch" (1977-78) 2 episodes, "Wonder Woman" (1978-79) 2 episodes, "Hawaii Five-O" (1980), "Little House on the Prairie" (1975-82) 3 episodes, "Simon & Simon" (1982-84) 2 episodes, "The Fall Guy" (1982-85) 3 episodes, "Magnum, P.I." (1981-86) 4 episodes, "The Young Riders" (1989-91) 2 episodes and "Walker, Texas Ranger" (1995).

- **Roberto Contreras** was born on December 12, 1928 in St. Louis, Missouri.
- He was the son of director Jaime Contreras.
- Roberto made his uncredited U.S. film debut in the movie "The Beast of Hollow Mountain" in 1956.
- He made his TV debut in an episode ("Strange Vendetta") of "Have Gun – Will Travel" in 1957.
- Several TV guest appearances followed including "Telephone Time" (1958), "Broken Arrow" (1958), "Maverick" (1958) 2 episodes, "The Adventures of Jim Bowie" (1958) 2 episodes, "Zorro" (1958) 2 episodes, "Border Patrol" (1959), "Sugarfoot" (1959), "26 Men" (1959), "Riverboat" (1960), "Law of the Plainsman" (1959-60) 3 episodes, "The Texan" (1959-60) 2 episodes, "The Westerner" (1960), "Gunslinger" (1961), "Mister Ed" (1961), "Have Gun – Will Travel" (1959-61) 2

episodes, "Zane Grey Theatre" (1959-61) 2 episodes, "Ripcord" (1961), "Outlaws" (1961-62) 2 episodes, "Tales of Wells Fargo" (1962), "Cheyenne" (1962) 2 episodes, "77 Sunset Strip" (1960-62) 3 episodes, "Dr. Kildare" (1964), "Wendy and Me" (1965), "Rawhide" (1959-65) 3 episodes, "Get Smart" (1965), "Laredo" (1965-67) 2 episodes, "The Big Valley" (1966-67) 2 episodes and "The Fugitive" (1963-67) 2 episodes.

- In 1967, he was cast as "Pedro" in the TV series "The High Chaparral". He appeared in 61 episodes from 1967 to 1971.
- His last acting appearance was in the film "Blood In, Blood Out" in 1993.
- Roberto is the father of actor Luis Contreras who passed away in 2004 (53 years old).
- His other film credits include "The Flame Barrier" (1958), "The Magnificent Seven" (1960) uncredited, "Gold of the Seven Saints" (1961), "California" (1963), "Mara of the Wilderness" (1965), "The Professionals" (1966) uncredited, "Topaz" (1969), "Pets" (1973), "Black Samurai" (1977), "Barbarosa" (1982), "Scarface" (1983), "Blue City" (1986) and "The Under Achievers" (1987).
- Roberto's other TV credits include "Death Valley Days" (1966-69) 3 episodes, "Ironside" (1971), "Mission: Impossible" (1969-72) 3 episodes, "The Cowboys" (1974), "Cannon"

(1971-74) 2 episodes, "Kung Fu" (1975), "Chico and the Man" (1978), "Simon & Simon" (1984-85) 2 episodes and "Amazing Stories" (1986).

"Hondo"

Years : 1967

Episodes : 17 (1 season)

Cast :-

Ralph Taeger (b. 1936 d. 2015) - Played Hondo Lane

Noah Beery Jr. (b. 1913 d. 1994) – Played Buffalo Baker

Michael Pate (b. 1920 d. 2008) – Played Chief Vittoro

William Bryant (b. 1924 d. 2001) – Played Colonel Crook

Gary Clarke (b. 1933) – Played Captain Richards

Kathie Browne (b. 1930 d. 2003) – Played Angie Dow

Buddy Foster (b. 1957) – Played Johnny Dow

Synopsis :-
The story of a cavalry scout during the Indian Wars.

Trivia & Tidbits :-

"The Show"

- **"Hondo"** premiered on ABC on September 8, 1967 and last aired on December 29, 1967.
- The show ran for one season with a total of 17 episodes.
- The series was based on a film of the same name starring John Wayne.
- "Hondo" was not very successful because it was up against two top rating shows on the other networks – "Gomer Pyle, U.S.M.C." (CBS) and "Star Trek" (NBC).
- The show was produced by Andrew J Fenady Productions, Batjac Productions and MGM Television.
- "Hondo's" dog was named Sam.

"In Memoriam"

- **Ralph Taeger** died after a long illness on March 11, 2015 (78) in Placerville, California.
- **Noah Beery Jr.** died of a cerebral thrombosis on November 1, 1994 (81) in Tehachapi, California.
- **Michael Pate** died of pneumonia on September 1, 2008 (88) in Sydney, Australia.
- **William Bryant** died on June 26, 2001 (77) in Woodland Hills, California.
- **Kathie Browne** died of natural causes on April 8, 2003 (72) in Beverly Hills, California.

"The Stars"

- **Ralph Taeger (see "Klondike")**

- **Noah Lindsey Beery Jr.** was born on August 10, 1913 in New York City, New York.
- He was the son of actor Noah Beery Sr. and Margarite Lindsey. His uncle was the famous actor Wallace Beery.
- After living in New York for two years the family moved to California so his father could begin acting in motion pictures.
- Following a short stint in Los Angeles the family moved to a ranch in the San Fernando Valley.
- Noah made his screen debut in the film "The Mutiny of the Elsinore" (1920) followed up with an uncredited role in "The Mark of Zorro" (1920), starring Douglas Fairbanks and his father.
- For the next thirty five years he appeared in numerous films including "Gold Diggers of Broadway" (1929) uncredited, "Heroes of the West" (1932), "The Three Musketeers" (1933) serial, "The Trail Beyond" (1934), "Devil's Canyon" (1935), "Ace Drummond" (1936), "Bad Lands" (1939), "20 Mule Team" (1940), "Sergeant York" (1941), "Overland Mail" (1942), "Under Western Skies" (1945), "Red River" (1948), "Davy Crockett, Indian Scout" (1950), "The Cimarron Kid" (1952), "The Story

of Will Rogers" (1952), "The Yellow Tomahawk" (1954) and "White Feather" (1955).

- In 1956, he was cast as "Uncle Joey" in the TV series "Circus Boy". He appeared in 49 episodes from 1956 to 1957.
- In 1960, he was cast as "Bill Blake" in the TV series "Riverboat". He appeared in 13 episodes from 1960 to 1961 (he was brought in to the series to replace Burt Reynolds).
- Then in 1967, he was cast as "Buffalo Baker" in the TV series "Hondo". He appeared in 17 episodes.
- In 1974, he was cast as "Joseph 'Rocky' Rockford" in the TV series "The Rockford Files". He appeared in 121 episodes from 1974 to 1980.
- In 1983, he was cast as "Luther Dillard" in the TV series "The Yellow Rose". He appeared in 22 episodes from 1983 to 1984.
- His last acting appearance was in an episode ("Hello Emily/The Tour Guide/The Winner Number") of "The Love Boat" in 1986.
- Noah was married twice – Maxine Jones (1940-65) and Lisa Thorman (1968-94). He had three children, Bucklind (actor), Muffett and Melissa, with Ms. Jones.
- His first wife, Maxine, was the daughter of cowboy star Buck Jones.
- In 2004, his character in "The Rockford Files", "Rocky Rockford", was ranked No.45 in TV

Guide's list of the "50 Greatest TV Dads of all Time".

- Noah's favorite movie was "Red River" (1948).
- He has a Star on the Hollywood Walk of Fame for his contribution to the television industry.
- Noah's other film credits include "The Fastest Gun Alive" (1956), "Escort West" (1958), "7 Faces of Dr. Lao" (1964), Journey to Shiloh" (1968), "Little Fauss and Big Halsy" (1970), "Walking Tall" (1973), "The Bastard" (1978)(TV), "The Asphalt Cowboy" (1980)(TV) and "The Best Little Whorehouse in Texas" (1982).
- His other TV credits include "Climax!" (1957), "Rawhide" (1959), "The Real McCoys" (1961), "The Wide Country" (1962), "Death Valley Days" (1963), "Wagon Train" (1960-64) 3 episodes, "Gunsmoke" (1964-66) 2 episodes, "Bonanza" (1965-68) 2 episodes, "The Virginian" (1966-70) 3 episodes, "Doc Elliott" (1973), "The Waltons" (1974), "Fantasy Island" (1981) and "Murder, She Wrote" (1985).

- **Michael Pate** was born Edward John Pate on February 26, 1920 in Drummoyne, New South Wales, Australia.
- In 1938, he began his career in radio, writing and broadcasting a program called "Youth Speaks" for ABC Radio.
- For the next few years he continued to work in radio drama.

- In 1940, he made his uncredited film debut in the movie "40,000 Horsemen".
- His career was interrupted by the Second World War. He joined the Australian Army and served in the South West Pacific Area.
- After the war, he returned to radio and appeared in many plays and serials.
- In 1950, he appeared in two more Australian films, "Sons of Matthew" and "Bitter Springs".
- In 1951, he traveled to the U.S. to appear in the film "Thunder on the Hill".
- Several more film roles followed including "Ten Tall Men" (1951), "Face to Face" (1952), "Target Hong Kong" (1953), "The Desert Rats" (1953) uncredited, "Julius Caesar" (1953), "All the Brothers Were Valiant" (1953), "Hondo" (1953) and "Secret of the Incas" (1954).
- Michael made his TV debut in an episode ("The Assassination of Julius Caesar (March 15, 44 B.C.)") of "You Are There" in 1953.
- Many more TV guest star roles followed including "The Lone Wolf" (1954) 2 episodes, "Schlitz Playhouse of Stars" (1954-55) 2 episodes, "Passport to Danger" (1956), "Broken Arrow" (1956) 3 episodes, "Wire Service" (1957), "The Adventures of Jim Bowie" (1957), "Zorro" (1958) 4 episodes, "The Frank Sinatra Show" (1958), "Climax!" (1954-58) 2 episodes, "Alcoa Theatre" (1957-58) 3 episodes, "Sugarfoot" (1958), "The Adventures of Rin Tin Tin" (1959), "Black Saddle" (1959), "The Texan" (1958-60) 2

episodes, "Zane Grey Theatre" (1956-60) 4 episodes, "Hawaiian Eye" (1960), "Maverick" (1961), "The Tall Man" (1961), "Lawman" (1961), "Ripcord" (1962), "Laramie" (1960-62) 3 episodes, "Have Gun – Will Travel" (1957-62) 3 episodes, "The Rifleman" (1958-62) 5 episodes, "Cheyenne" (1957-62) 3 episodes, "Rawhide" (1959-64) 5 episodes, "Perry Mason" (1963-64) 2 episodes, "Gunsmoke" (1957-64) 4 episodes, "Lassie" (1965), "Wagon Train" (1958-65) 2 episodes, "Branded" (1966) 3 episodes, "Daktari" (1966) 2 episodes, "Daniel Boone" (1964-66) 2 episodes, "Death Valley Days" (1962-66) 6 episodes, "Rango" (1967) and "Tarzan" (1967) 2 episodes.

- In 1967, he was cast as "Chief Vittoro" in the TV series "Hondo". He appeared or was credited in 17 episodes.
- In 1971, he was cast as "Det. Sgt. Vic Maddern" in the Australian TV series "Matlock Police". He appeared in 192 episodes from 1971 to 1975.
- His last acting job was in the comedy short "Down Rusty Down" (1997). He supplied the voice of "Rusty".
- Michael was married twice – Margaret Pate and Felippa Rock (1951-2008). He had one son, Christopher, with Ms. Rock.
- In 1970, he published his textbook on acting titled "The Film Actor".

- In 1979, he won an Australian Writer's Guild award for the film "Tim" (1979), starring Mel Gibson.
- In 1997, he was awarded the O.A.M. (Order of Australian Medal) for his services to the performing arts.
- Michael's other film credits include "The Silver Chalice" (1954), "The Court Jester" (1955), "7th Cavalry" (1956), "The Oklahoman" (1957), "Westbound" (1959), "Walk Like a Dragon" (1960), "Sergeants 3" (1962), "PT 109" (1963), "Major Dundee" (1965), "The Great Sioux Massacre" (1965), "The Singing Nun" (1966), "Return of the Gunfighter" (1967), "Mad Dog Morgan" (1976), "Death of a Soldier" (1986), "Howling III" (1987) and "Official Denial" (1993)(TV).
- His other TV credits include "Voyage to the Bottom of the Sea" (1964-68) 3 episodes, "Riptide" (1969) 2 episodes, "The Virginian" (1963-70) 2 episodes, "Homicide" (1970), "Division 4" (1970), "Power Without Glory" (1976) and "Mission: Impossible" (1989).

- **William Bryant** was born William Robert Klein on January 31, 1924 in Detroit, Michigan.
- He made his uncredited film debut in the movie "Twelve O'Clock High" in 1949.
- This was followed by other uncredited parts including "When Willie Comes Marching Home" (1950), "My Blue Heaven" (1950), "People Will Talk" (1951) and "Purple Heart Diary" (1951).

- In 1952, he made his TV debut in an episode ("Appointment with the Past") of "Schlitz Playhouse of Stars".
- Following this, he appeared in a number of films including "The 49th Man" (1953), "Sky Commando" (1953), "Battle of Rogue River" (1954), "A Bullet for Joey" (1955), "King Dinosaur" (1955), "Massacre at Sand Creek" (1956)(TV), "Escape from san Quentin" (1957), "The Missouri Traveler" (1958), "Las Vegas Beat" (1961), "Experiment in Terror" (1962) and "The Great Race" (1965).
- During this time, he also guest starred on a number of TV shows including "Waterfront" (1955), "Navy Log" (1955), "Damon Runyon Theater" (1955-56) 2 episodes, "The Adventures of Rin Tin Tin" (1956), "Frontier" (1956), "Whirlybirds" (1957), "Casey Jones" (1957), "The Gray Ghost" (1958), "The Life and Legend of Wyatt Earp" (1955-58) 2 episodes, "Adventures of Wild Bill Hickok" (1955-58) 3 episodes, "The Silent Service" (1957-58) 3 episodes, "Maverick" (1958), "Steve Canyon" (1958-59) 2 episodes, "Sugarfoot" (1959), "Hotel de Paree" (1959), "Zane Grey Theatre" (1960), "Outlaws" (1960), "Lock-Up" (1959-60) 3 episodes, "Two Faces West" (1961), "The Rebel" (1959-61) 9 episodes, "Bronco" (1961), "The Rifleman" (1958-62) 4 episodes, "Laramie" (1959-63) 7 episodes, "Wagon Train" (1963), "The

Virginian" (1963), "Temple Houston" (1964) and "Rawhide" (1964-65) 2 episodes.

- Between 1965 and 1966, he had a recurring role as "President Ulysses S. Grant" in the TV series "Branded". He appeared in 8 episodes.
- Between 1966 and 1967, he had a recurring role as "McCall" in the TV series "Combat!" He appeared in 6 episodes.
- In 1967, he was cast as "Col. Crook" in the TV series "Hondo". He appeared or was credited in 16 episodes.
- Between 1972 and 1978, he appeared in 19 episodes of the TV series "Emergency!"
- In 1977, he was cast as "Lt. Stafford Shilton" in the TV series "Switch". He appeared in 12 episodes from 1977 to 1978.
- In 1982, he was cast in a recurring role as "The Director" in the TV series "The Fall Guy". He appeared in 14 episodes from 1982 to 1983.
- His last acting appearance was in the film "Metal" in 2001.
- William was married to his wife Patricia from 1958 until his death in 2001. They had three children.
- His other film credits include "Ride Beyond Vengeance" (1966), "Heaven with a Gun" (1969), "The Animals" (1970), "Chisum" (1970), "Wild Rovers" (1971), "The New Healers" (1972)(TV), "McQ" (1974), "The Other Side of the Mountain" (1975), "The Other Side of the Mountain: Part II" (1978),

"Steel Cowboy" (1978)(TV), "The Legend of the Golden Gun" (1979)(TV), "Gridlock" (1980)(TV) and "Hell Squad" (1986).

- William's other TV credits include "The Monroes" (1966), "The Guns of Will Sonnett" (1968), "The Wild Wild West" (1969), "Death Valley Days" (1962-69) 2 episodes, "Lancer" (1968-69) 4 episodes, "The Name of the Game" (1969-71) 2 episodes, "Alias Smith and Jones" (1971) 2 episodes, "Cade's County" (1972), "Bonanza" (1967-72) 5 episodes, "McCloud" (1970-73) 4 episodes, "The F.B.I." (1971-73) 3 episodes, "Ironside" (1972-74) 2 episodes, "Columbo" (1973-74) 2 episodes, "Gunsmoke" (1957-74) 8 episodes, "Cannon" (1975) 2 episodes, "The Rockford Files" (1974-75) 2 episodes, "Barnaby Jones" (1973-76) 3 episodes, "Once an Eagle" (1976) (mini-series) 4 episodes, "Hawaii Five-O" (1978), "How the West Was Won" (1976-79) 2 episodes, "CBS Afternoon Playhouse" (1980) 5 episodes, "Lou Grant" (1978-81) 3 episodes, "Dallas" (1983) 2 episodes, "Simon & Simon" (1981-89) 5 episodes and "Murder, She Wrote" (1989).

- **Gary Clarke (see "The Virginian")**

- **Kathie Browne** was born Jacqueline Katherine Browne on September 19, 1930 in San Luis Obispo, California.
- In her teens, she moved to Hollywood to study at Los Angeles City College.

- She was discovered whilst appearing in the Los Angeles production of Tennessee Williams' play "Cat on a Hot Tin Roof".
- Kathie made her TV acting debut in an episode ("Gambling Syndicate") of "Big Town" in 1955.
- This was followed by guest appearances in TV shows such as "The Gray Ghost" (1957), "The Sheriff of Cochise" (1957), "Gunsmoke" (1957), "The D.A.'s Man" (1959), "Lock Up" (1960) 2 episodes, "The Man from Blackhawk" (1960), "Tombstone Territory" (1960), "Two Faces West" (1960), "Cheyenne" (1961), "Sea Hunt" (1960-61) 3 episodes, "Rawhide" (1961) 3 episodes, "Bronco" (1961), "Lawman" (1962), "Ben Casey" (1962), "Shannon" (1961-62) 2 episodes, "Surfside 6" (1962) 2 episodes, "Ripcord" (1962-63) 2 episodes, "The Real McCoys" (1963), "Laramie" (1962-63) 2 episodes, "Hawaiian Eye" (1963), "Wagon Train" (1960-63) 2 episodes, "The Virginian" (1963), "77 Sunset Strip" (1961-64) 4 episodes, "Bonanza" (1961-64) 6 episodes, "Hazel" (1962-65) 2 episodes, "Perry Mason" (1960-65) 4 episodes, "Slattery's People" (1965) 2 episodes, "Branded" (1966) 3 episodes, "Laredo" (1966) and "The Wild Wild West" (1965-67) 2 episodes.
- Kathie made her film debut in the movie "Murder by Contract" in 1958.
- In 1967, she was cast as "Angie Dow" In the TV series "Hondo". She appeared or was credited in 17 episodes.

- Her last acting appearance was in a two-part episode ("The Family Plan/The Promoter/May the Best Man Win/Forever Engaged/The Judges") of "The Love Boat" in 1980.
- Kathie was married to actor Darren McGavin ("Riverboat") from 1969 until her death in 2003. She had four step-children.
- Her other film credits include "City of Fear" (1959), "The Slowest Gun in the West" (1960)(TV), "The Underwater City" (1962), "Man's Favorite Sport?" (1964), "The Brass Bottle" (1964), "Brainstorm" (1965), "Berlin Affair" (1970)(TV), "Happy Mother's Day, Love George" (1973) and "The Suicide's Wife" (1979)(TV).
- Kathie's other TV credits include "The Big Valley" (1968), "The Name of the Game" (1968) 2 episodes, "Star Trek" (1968), "The Outsider" (1968-69) 2 episodes, "Mannix" (1971), "Longstreet" (1972), "Cade's County" (1972), "Ironside" (1968-74) 3 episodes, "The Rockford Files" (1975), "The Oregon Trail" (1977) and "Fantasy Island" (1979).

- **Buddy Foster** was born Lucius Fisher Foster IV on July 12, 1957 in Los Angeles, California.
- His parents are Lucius Fisher Foster III and Evelyn Ella Almond. Buddy has three sisters, the most famous being Jodie Foster (two-time Academy Award winner).

- Buddy made his TV debut in an episode ("Temperature! Temperature!") of "Petticoat Junction" in 1967.
- In 1967, he was cast as "Johnny Dow" in the TV series "Hondo". He appeared or was credited in 17 episodes.
- In 1968, he appeared in two episodes of "The Andy Griffith Show", playing the character "Mike Jones".
- Then he was cast as "Mike Jones" in the TV series "Mayberry R.F.D." (spin-off from "The Andy Griffith Show"). He appeared in 42 episodes from 1968 to 1971.
- His last acting appearance, to date, was in the film "Foxes" in 1980.
- Buddy is married to Leah Foster. They have two children.
- He authored a book in 1997 titled "Foster Child".
- Buddy's other film credits include "Angel in My Pocket" (1969), "The Point" (1971)(TV), "Black Noon" (1971)(TV) and "Sixteen" (1973).
- His other TV credits include "Green Acres" (1966-67) 2 episodes, "Land of the Giants" (1969), "Dragnet 1967" (1969), "Adam-12" (1970-71) 2 episodes, "Emergency!" (1972), "Alias Smith and Jones" (1972), "The Six Million Dollar Man" (1975), "Isis" (1975) and "The Rockford Files" (1976).

"How the West Was Won"

Years : 1977 - 1979

Episodes : 28 + pilot (aired 1976) (3 seasons)

Cast :-

James Arness (b. 1923 d. 2011) - Played Zeb Macahan

Fionnula Flanagan (b. 1941) - Played Molly Culhane

Bruce Boxleitner (b. 1950) - Played Luke Macahan

Kathryn Holcomb (b. ????) - Played Laura Macahan

William Kirby Cullen (b. 1952) - Played Josh Macahan

Vicki Schreck (b. 1961) - Played Jessica Macahan

Synopsis :-
The story of the Macahan family and their move out west.

Trivia & Tidbits :-

"The Show"

- **"How the West Was Won"** premiered on ABC on February 6, 1977 and last aired on April 23, 1979.
- The show ran for three seasons with a total of 28 episodes.
- The original pilot episode aired on January 19, 1976.

"In Memoriam"

- **James Arness** died of heart failure on June 3, 2011 (88) in Los Angeles, California.

"The Stars"

- **James Arness** was born James King Aurness on May 26, 1923 in Minneapolis, Minnesota.
- He was the son of Rolf Cirkler Aurness, a businessman, and Ruth Duesler, a journalist. His brother, actor Peter Graves, died in 2010.
- James attended John Burrows Grade School, Washburn High School and West High School in Minneapolis.
- He graduated from high school in 1942 and worked as a courier for a jewelry wholesaler, loading and unloading railway boxcars at the Minneapolis freight-yards and logging in Pierce, Idaho.
- In 1942, he enlisted in the U.S. Army and was deployed to Italy in 1944. He was severely

- wounded in the leg and eventually honourably discharged in 1945.
- He was subsequently awarded the Bronze Star and Purple Heart.
- After he was discharged he undertook a radio course at the University of Minnesota and was recommended, by his teacher, for an announcer's job at a Minneapolis radio station.
- His next move was to hitch-hike to Hollywood with a friend in the hope of getting work as a film extra.
- James studied at the Bliss-Hayden Theatre School and was noticed by agent Leon Lance.
- Lance got him a role in the film "The Farmer's Daughter" in 1947.
- For the next eight years he appeared in a number of films including "Roses Are Red" (1947), "Battleground" (1949), "Wagon Master" (1950), "Sierra" (1950), "Wyoming Mail" (1950), "Two Lost Worlds" (1951), "The Thing from Another World" (1951), "Carbine Williams" (1952), "Big Jim McLain" (1952), "The Lone Hand" (1953), "Hondo" (1953), "Them!" (1954), "Her Twelve Men" (1954), "The Sea Chase" (1955) and "Many Rivers to Cross" (1955).
- In 1955, he was cast as "Marshal Matt Dillon" in the TV series "Gunsmoke". He appeared in 635 episodes from 1955 to 1975.
- In 1977, he was cast as "Zeb Macahan" in the TV series "How the West Was Won". The series ran for 28 episodes from 1977 to 1979.

- Then in 1981, he was cast as "Det. Jim McClain" in the TV series "McClain's Law". He appeared in 16 episodes from 1981 to 1982.
- His last acting appearance was in the TV movie "Gunsmoke: One Man's Justice" in 1994.
- James was married twice – Virginia Chapman (1948-1963) and Janet Surtrees (1978-2011). He had three children, Jenny Lee, Rolf and Craig with Ms. Chapman.
- His daughter, Jenny Lee, committed suicide in 1975 and son Craig died in 2004.
- In 1981, he was inducted (with other "Gunsmoke" cast members) into the Hall of Great Western Performers at the National Cowboy and Western Heritage Museum.
- He has a Star on the Hollywood Walk of Fame for his contribution to the television industry.
- In 2006, he was inducted into the Santa Clarita Walk of Western Stars.
- In 1989 (50th anniversary of television, People Magazine chose James as No.6 in their list of "The Top 25 Television Stars of All Time".
- He was nominated for three Emmy Awards (1957, 1958 and 1959).
- James Arness' natural hair color was blond.
- In 2001, James with James E. Wise Jr. published his autobiography titled "James Arness: An Autobiography".
- James' other film roles included "Flame of the Islands" (1956), "Gun the Man Down" (1956), "The Macahans" (1976)(TV), "The Alamo : Thirteen Days to Glory" (1987)(TV) and "Red River" (1988)(TV).

- His other TV credits included "The Lone Ranger" (1950), "Lux Video Theatre" (1954), "Hallmark Hall of Fame" (1955) and "Front Row Center" (1956).

- **Fionnula Flanagan** was born Fionnghuala Manon Flanagan on December 10, 1941 in Dublin, Ireland.
- She is the daughter of Rosanna McGuirk and Terence Niall Flanagan, an Irish Army officer and Communist.
- Fionnula was educated in Switzerland and England. She trained at the Abbey Theatre in Dublin and travelled throughout Europe before settling in Los Angeles in 1968.
- She made her Irish film debut in the TV movie "Deirdre" in 1965.
- This was followed by several Irish/U.K. TV roles including "Knock on Any Door" (1965), "Insurrection" (1966) (mini-series), "Broome Stages" (1966) (mini-series), "The Wednesday Play" (1966-67) 2 episodes, "Callan" (1967) and "Cold Comfort Farm" (1968) (mini-series).
- She also appeared in two U.K. films – "Ulysses" (1967) and "Sinful Davey" (1969).
- Fionnula made her U.S. TV debut in an episode ("Heritage of Anger") of "Bonanza" in 1972.
- Following this, she guest starred on a number of TV shows including "Mannix" (1972), "Gunsmoke" (1972), "The New Perry Mason" (1973), "The Rookies" (1974), "Hec Ramsey"

(1974), "Police Story" (1975), "The Streets of San Francisco" (1976), "Marcus Welby, M.D." (1972-76) 3 episodes, "Kojak" (1976) and "Serpico" (1976).

- In 1978, she was cast as "Molly Culhane" in the TV series "How the West Was Won". She appeared in 21 episodes from 1978 to 1979.
- In 1987, she was cast as "Lt. Guyla Cook" in the TV series "Hard Copy". She appeared in 4 episodes.
- Then in 1990, she was cast as "Kathleen Meacham" in the TV series "H.E.L.P." She appeared in 6 episodes.
- In 1998, she was cast as "Fiona McGrail" in the TV series "To Have & To Hold". She appeared in 13 episodes.
- In 2007, she was cast as "Peig Sayers" in the TV series "Paddywhackery". She appeared in 6 episodes.
- From 2006 to 2008, she had the recurring role of "Rose Caffee" in the TV series "Brotherhood". She appeared in 25 episodes.
- She had another recurring role in the TV series "Lost". She played "Eloise Hawking" in 7 episodes from 2007 to 2010.
- In 2013, she played the character "Nicky" in the TV series "Defiance". She appeared in 8 episodes.
- Her last acting appearance, to date, was in the film "Little Secret" in 2016.

- Fionnula was married to Dr. Garrett O'Connor from 1972 until his death in 2015. Garrett was the cousin of actor Carroll O'Connor ("All in the Family").
- She has appeared on Broadway in three plays – "Lovers" (1968), "The Incomparable Max" (1971) and "Ulysses in Nighttown" (1974). Fionnula received a Tony Award nomination for "Ulysses".
- In 1976, she won a Primetime Emmy Award (Outstanding Single Performance by a Supporting Actress in Comedy or Drama Series) for her performance in "Rich Man, Poor Man".
- Fionnula's other film credits include "The Picture of Dorian Gray" (1973)(TV), "The Legend of Lizzie Borden" (1975)(TV), "Mary White" (1977)(TV), "Mr. Patman" (1980), "Through Naked Eyes" (1983)(TV), "Reflections" (1984), "James Joyce's Women" (1985), "Youngblood" (1986), "Final Verdict" (1991)(TV), "Money for Nothing" (1993), "Some Mother's Son" (1996), "Waking Ned Devine" (1998), "The Others" (2001), "Tears of the Sun" (2003), "Transamerica" (2005), "Yes Man" (2008), "The Payback" (2009), "Kill the Irishman" (2011) and "Trash Fire" (2016).
- Her other TV credits include "Trapper John, M.D." (1981), "Benson" (1982), "Fame" (1984), "Simon & Simon" (1984-88) 2

episodes, "Columbo" (1989), "Beauty and the Beast" (1990) 2 episodes, "Murder, She Wrote" (1987-95) 4 episodes, "Chicago Hope" (1999), "Poltergeist: The Legacy" (1998-99) 3 episodes, "Law & Order: S.V.U." (2003), "Revelations" (2005) (mini-series) 4 episodes and "Gortimer Gibbon's Life on Normal Street" (2014-16) 4 episodes.

- **Bruce William Boxleitner** was born on May 12, 1950 in Elgin, Illinois.
- He is the son of a public accountant and attended Prospect High School in Illinois. Later on, he went to the Goodman Theater School of Drama in Chicago.
- Bruce trained on the stage and appeared on Broadway in the play "Status Quo Vadis" in 1973.
- He then relocated to Los Angeles and made his TV debut in an episode ("I Gave at the Office") of "The Mary Tyler Moore Show" in 1973.
- Bruce made his film debut in the TV movie "The Chadwick Family" in 1974.
- Following this, he appeared in several other movies including "A Cry for Help" (1975)(TV), "Sixpack Annie" (1975), "The Macahans" (1976)(TV) and "Kiss Me, Kill Me" (1976)(TV).
- During this time, he also guest starred on a number of TV shows such as "Gunsmoke" (1975), "Police Woman" (1975), "Baretta" (1976) and "Hawaii Five-O" (1974-76) 3 episodes.

- In 1976, he was cast as "Luke Macahan" in the TV series "How the West Was Won". He appeared in 25 episodes from 1976 to 1979.
- In 1982, he was cast as "Frank Buck" in the TV series "Bring 'Em Back Alive". He appeared in 17 episodes from 1982 to 1983.
- Then in 1983, he was cast as "Lee Stetson" in the TV series "Scarecrow and Mrs. King". He appeared in 89 episodes from 1983 to 1987.
- In 1994, he was cast as "President John Sheridan" in the TV series "Babylon 5". He appeared in 88 episodes from 1994 to 1998.
- In 2005, he appeared in the TV mini-series "Young Blades". He played the character "Captain Martin Duval" in 13 episodes.
- Bruce provided the voice for "Tron" in the TV series "TRON: Uprising". He voiced 17 episodes from 2012 to 2013.
- In 2013, he had the recurring role of "Bob Beldon" in the TV series "Cedar Cove". He appeared in 29 episodes from 2013 to 2015.
- His last acting appearance, to date, was in the TV movie "Wedding Bells" in 2016.
- Bruce has been married three times – Kathryn Holcomb (1977-87), Melissa Gilbert (1995-2012) and Verena King (2016-present). He has two children, Sam and Lee, with Ms. Holcomb and one child, Michael, with Ms. Gilbert.
- From 1986 to 1989, Bruce appeared in advertisements for Estee Lauder's "Lauder for Men".

- Bruce has written two science fiction novels with a Western theme – "Frontier Earth" (1999) and "Frontier Earth: Searcher" (2001).
- Bruce has also been a member of the Board of Governors of the National Space Society.
- In 2012, he was inducted into the Hall of Great Western Performers at the National Cowboy and Western Heritage Museum in Oklahoma.
- Bruce's other film credits include "Murder at the World Series" (1977)(TV), "Happily Ever After" (1978)(TV), "Kenny Rogers as The Gambler" (1980)(TV), "TRON" (1982), "I Married Wyatt Earp" (1983)(TV), "Kenny Rogers as The Gambler: The Adventure Continues" (1983)(TV), "Kenny Rogers as The Gambler, Part III: The Legend Continues" (1987)(TV), "Red River" (1988)(TV), "Breakaway" (1990), "Kuffs" (1992), "The Babe" (1992), "The Secret" (1992)(TV), "Gunsmoke: One Man's Justice" (1994)(TV), "Babylon 5: In the Beginning" (1998)(TV), "Babylon 5: Thirdspace" (1998)(TV), "Babylon: A Call to Arms" (1999)(TV), "Contagion" (2002), "Gods and Generals" (2003), "Brilliant" (2004), "Detective" (2005)(TV), "Pandemic" (2007)(TV), "Shadows in Paradise" (2010), "TRON: Legacy" (2010), "Smokewood" (2012)(TV) and "The Thanksgiving House" (2013)(TV).

- His other TV credits include "East of Eden" (1981) (mini-series), "Till We Meet Again" (1989) (mini-series), "Tales from the Crypt" (1991), "Touched by an Angel" (1998), "Dead Man's Gun" (1999), "She Spies" (2003) 4 episodes, "Crossing Jordan" (2005), "Commander in Chief" (2005), "Cold Case" (2007), "Chuck" (2008-09) 2 episodes, "Heroes" (2008-09) 3 episodes, "N.C.I.S." (2010) and "Good Christian Bitches" (2012) 4 episodes.

- **Kathryn Holcomb** made her acting debut in the film "Supersonic Supergirls" in 1973.
- She then appeared in the film "Our Time" (1974) and the TV movie "The Macahans" (1976).
- In 1976, she was cast as "Laura Macahan" in the TV series "How the West Was Won". She appeared in 25 episodes from 1976 to 1979.
- In 1980, she was cast as "Patricia Skagska" in the TV series "Skag". The series only lasted 6 episodes.
- Her last acting appearance, to date, was in the film "Rock-A-Doodle" in 1991.
- Kathryn has been married twice – Bruce Boxleitner (1977-87) and Ian Ogilvy (1992-present). She has two children, Sam and Lee, with Mr. Boxleitner.

- Her other film credit is "Detour to Terror" (1980)(TV).
- Kathryn's other TV credits include "Chips" (1978), "Fantasy Island" (1978), "Supertrain" (1979), "Mike Hammer" (1986), "Houston Knights" (1987) and "Simon & Simon" (1988).

- **William Kirby Cullen** was born on March 9, 1952 in Santa Ana, California.
- He made his acting debut in the film "Multiple Maniacs" in 1970.
- Also in 1970, he made his TV debut in an episode ("Captain of the Team") of "Room 222".
- Several TV guest appearances followed including "The Rookies" (1973), "Shazam!" (1974), "Lucas Tanner" (1975), "S.W.A.T." (1976) and "Insight" (1976).
- He then played "Jed Macahan" in the TV movie "The Macahans" (1976).
- In 1976, he was cast as "Josh Macahan" in the TV series "How the West Was Won". He appeared in 25 episodes from 1976 to 1979.
- His last acting appearance, to date, was in an episode ("The Good Doctor") of "Highway to Heaven" in 1985.
- William's other film credits include "The Force of Evil" (1977)(TV), "When Hell Was in Session" (1979)(TV), "Power" (1980)(TV),

"Fugitive Family" (1980)(TV) and "Blood Song" (1982).

- His other TV credits include "One Day at a Time" (1976) 5 episodes, "Code R" (1977), "Eight Is Enough" (1977), "David Cassidy – Man Undercover" (1978), "Barnaby Jones" (1979) and "Airwolf" (1984).

- **Vicki Schreck** was born on November 14, 1961 in Los Angeles, California.
- She made her acting debut in the film "Dream No Evil" in 1970.
- Vicki made her TV debut in an episode ("You Can't Win 'Em All") of "The Brady Bunch" in 1973.
- In 1976, she was cast as "Jessie Macahan" in the TV series "How the West Was Won". She appeared in 25 episodes from 1976 to 1979.
- Her last acting appearance, to date, was in the TV movie "Big Bend Country" in 1981.
- It has been reported that she lives in Glendale, California and has two boys.
- Vicki's other film credits include "What's the Matter with Helen?" (1971), "The Easter Promise" (1975)(TV), "The Macahans" (1976)(TV) and "Freaky Friday" (1976).
- Her other TV credits include "Love, American Style" (1973), "The Waltons" (1976) and "Sara" (1976).

"The Iron Horse"

Years : 1966 - 1968

Episodes : 47 (2 seasons)

Cast :-

Dale Robertson (b. 1923 d. 2013) - Played Ben Calhoun

Robert Ramdon (b. 1943) - Played Barnabas Rogers

Gary Collins (b. 1938 d. 2012) - Played Dave Tarrant

Synopsis :-
The building of a railroad during the 1870's.

Trivia & Tidbits :-

"The Show"

- **"The Iron Horse"** premiered on ABC on September 12, 1966 and last aired on January 6, 1968.
- The show ran for two seasons with a total of 47 episodes.

- The external sequences, involving trains, were filmed on the historic Sierra Railroad in and around Jamestown and Sonora, California.
- The show was produced by Dagonet Productions and Screen Gems Television.
- Ben's horse was "Hannibal" and his raccoon was "Ulysses".

"In Memoriam"

- **Dale Robertson** died of pneumonia on February 27, 2013 (89) in San Diego, California.
- **Gary Collins** died of natural causes on October 13, 2012 (74) in Biloxi, Mississippi.

"The Stars"

- **Dale Robertson** was born Dayle Lymoine Robertson on July 14, 1923 in Harrah, Oklahoma.
- He went to Claremore Military Academy and served in a tank crew and the combat engineers during the Second World War (he was wounded twice).
- Dale's first movie role was the character "Jesse James" in "Fighting Man of the Plains" (1949).
- In 1957, he was cast as "Jim Hardie" in the TV series "Tales of Wells Fargo". He appeared in 201 episodes from 1957 to 1962.

- In 1966, he was cast as "Ben Calhoun" in the TV series "The Iron Horse". He appeared in 48 episodes from 1966 to 1968.
- Also in the 1960's, Dale was one of the hosts on "Death Valley Days".
- In 1981, he was cast as "Walter Lankershim" in the TV series "Dynasty". He only appeared in the first season before being written out.
- Then in 1987, he appeared as "Jerome Jeremiah 'J.J.' Starbuck" in the "J.J. Starbuck" TV series. The show only lasted 16 episodes and finished in 1988.
- Dale has been married a number of times and is presently married to Susan Robertson.
- In 1983, he was inducted into the Hall of Great Western Performers at the National Cowboy and Western Heritage Museum.
- Then in 1985, he was the recipient of the Golden Boot Award.
- Dale also has a Star on the Hollywood Walk of Fame for his contribution to the television industry.
- His other film credits include "Two Flags West" (1950), "Sitting Bull" (1954), "Hell Canyon Outlaws" (1957), "Law of the Lawless" (1964) and "The Last Ride of the Dalton Gang" (1979)(TV).
- Dale's other TV credits include "The Ford Television Theatre" (1956), "The Red Skelton Show" (1968), "Dallas" (1982), "Murder, She Wrote" (1989) and "Harts of the West" (1994).

- **Robert Ramdon** was born Robert Chambers on January 29, 1943 in Chilliwack, British Columbia, Canada.
- He made his TV debut in an episode ("What's Different About Today?") of "Dr. Kildare in 1964.
- Several more TV guest appearances followed including "The Man from U.N.C.L.E." (1964), "Branded" (1965), "Mr. Novak" (1964-65) 2 episodes, "The Dick Van Dyke Show" (1965), "The Legend of Jesse James" (1965), "Ben Casey" (1965) 2 episodes, "Lassie" (1964-65) 2 episodes, "Daniel Boone" (1965) 2 episodes and "Gidget" (1965) 2 episodes.
- In 1966, he was cast as "Barnabas Rogers" in the TV series "The Iron Horse". He appeared in 44 episodes from 1966 to 1968.
- Bob made his first credited movie appearance in the film "Village of the Giants" in 1965.
- His last acting role, to date, was in the film "Danger Zone 111: Steel Horse War" in 1990.
- Bob was married to Ida Cunningham, but they have since divorced.
- His former wife was nominated for an Oscar in 1988 (Art Direction for the film "Rain Man").
- Bob's other film credits include "The Restless Ones" (1965), "This Property Is Condemned" (1966), "A Time for Dying" (1969), "The Other Side of the Wind" (1972), "Time Walker" (1982) and "Vampire at Midnight" (1988).
- His other TV credits include "Cimarron Strip" (1968), "The Virginian" (1965-68) 2 episodes, "Hawaii Five-O" (1968), "Gunsmoke" (1965-71) 7 episodes, "Cannon" (1974) and "Get Christie Love!" (1975).

- **Gary Ennis Collins** was born on April 30, 1938 in Venice, California.
- He was raised by his single mother who worked as a waitress and factory worker.
- In 1955, Gary graduated from Venice High School and then attended Santa Monica City College.
- Following this, he enlisted in the U.S. Army and served in Europe, where he was a radio and television performer for the Armed Forces Network.
- After his discharge from the army he performed at the Barter Theatre in Virginia.
- Gary made his movie debut in the film "The Pigeon That Took Rome" in 1962.
- In 1965, he was cast as "Lt. Richard P. 'Rip' Ripley" in the TV series "The Wackiest Ship in the Army". He appeared in 29 episodes from 1965 to 1966.
- In 1966, he was cast as "Dave Tarrant" in the TV series "Iron Horse". He appeared in 43 episodes from 1966 to 1968.
- Then in 1972, he was cast as "Dr. Michael Rhodes" in the TV series "The Sixth Sense". He appeared in 24 episodes.
- In 1974, he was cast as "George Adamson" in the TV series "Born Free". The series only lasted 13 episodes.
- His last acting appearance was in an episode ("The Bad Guy") of "Dirty Sexy Money" in 2009.
- Gary hosted the talk show "Hour Magazine" from 1980 to 1988 and co-hosted the ABC

television series "The Home Show" from 1989 to 1994.

- From 1982 to 1990 he hosted the Miss America Pageant.
- Gary was married twice – Susan Peterson (1964 to 1967) and Mary Ann Mobley (1967 to 2012). He had two children with Ms. Peterson and one child with Ms. Mobley.
- In 1985, Gary published "The Hour Magazine Cookbook".
- Gary won a "Daytime Emmy" in 1984 as the host of "Hour Magazine".
- Again in 1985, he received a Star on the Hollywood Walk of Fame for his contribution to television.
- Gary's other film credits include "Stranded" (1965), "Angel in My Pocket" (1969), "Airport" (1970), "Houston, We've Got a Problem" (1974)(TV), "Killer Fish" (1979), "Secrets" (1992)(TV) and "Beautiful" (2000).
- His other TV credits include "Perry Mason" (1965-66) 2 episodes, "The Virginian" (1969), "Ironside" (1968-69) 2 episodes, "Dan August" (1971), "Lassie" (1972), "Love, American Style" (1970-73) 4 episodes, "Insight" (1972-76) 3 episodes, "Thriller" (1974-76) 3 episodes, "The Quest" (1976), "The Love Boat" (1978) 2 episodes, "Disneyland" (1978-80) 3 episodes, "Fantasy Island" (1978-82) 3 episodes, "Burke's Law" (1994) and "Yes, Dear" (2000).

"Klondike"

Years : 1960 - 1961

Episodes : 17 (1 season)

Cast :-

Ralph Taeger (b. 1936 d. 2015) - Played Mike Halliday

James Coburn (b. 1928 d. 2002) - Played Jeff Durain

Mari Blanchard (b. 1923 d. 1970) - Played Kathy O'Hara

Synopsis :-
The story is set in 1897 around the gold rush town of Skagway in the Alaskan Klondike region.

Trivia & Tidbits :-

"The Show"

- **"Klondike"** premiered on NBC on October 10, 1960 and last aired on February 13, 1961.
- The show ran for one season with a total of 17 black and white episodes.

- The series was produced by ZIV Television Programs and United Artists Television.
- "Klondike" was filmed at the Paramount Ranch, California.
- Two notable directors on the series were Sam Peckinpah and William Conrad ("Cannon").
- The theme music was composed by Mann Curtis.

"In Memoriam"

- **Ralph Taeger** died after a long illness on March 11, 2015 (78) in Placerville, California.
- **James Coburn** died of a heart attack on November 18, 2002 (74) in Beverly Hills, California.
- **Mari Blanchard** died of cancer on May 10, 1970 (47) in Woodland Hills, Los Angeles, California.

"The Stars"

- **Ralph Taeger** was born on July 30, 1936 in Richmond Hill, Queens, New York.
- His first choice career was as a professional baseballer but due to knee injuries this did not eventuate.
- Ralph decided to try acting and enrolled at the American Academy of Dramatic Arts in New York City.
- Following this, he landed a role in a production at the Beverly Hills Playhouse. He was seen by an official at MGM and signed to a contract.

- Ralph made his uncredited acting debut in the film "It Started With a Kiss" in 1959.
- Several more TV guest spots followed including "Lock Up" (1960), "Men Into Space" (1960), "Bat Masterson" (1960), "Tombstone Territory" (1959-60) 2 episodes and "Sea Hunt" (1960).
- In 1960, he was cast as "Mike Halliday" in the TV series "Klondike". He appeared in 16 episodes from 1960 to 1961.
- In 1961, he was cast as "Patrick Malone" in the TV series "Acapulco". He appeared in 8 episodes.
- Then in 1967, he was cast as "Hondo Lane" in the TV series "Hondo". He appeared in 17 episodes.
- His last acting appearance was in an episode ("The Rockets' Red Glare") of "Father Murphy" in 1983.
- Ralph was married to Linda Jarrett from 1967 until his death and they have one son, Rich.
- His other film credits include "X-15" (1961), "The Carpetbaggers" (1964), "Stage to Thunder Rock" (1964), "A House Is Not a Home" (1964) and "The Hostage Heart" (1977)(TV).
- Ralph's other TV credits include "The New Breed" (1961), "King of Diamonds" (1961), "The Many Loves of Dobie Gillis" (1963), "The Man from U.N.C.L.E." (1965), "The Six Million Dollar Man" (1975) and "Quincy M.E." (1977-82) 2 episodes.

- **James Harrison Coburn 111** was born on August 31, 1928 in Laurel, Nebraska.
- He was the son of James Coburn Jr. and Mylet Johnson.
- James was raised in Compton, California and attended Compton Junior College.
- At age 22, he enlisted in the U.S. Army where he served as a truck driver and part-time as a disc jockey on the Army radio station.
- He was then deployed to Mainz, Germany and narrated Army training films.
- After his discharge he attended Los Angeles City College where he studied acting.
- Following this, he made his stage debut at the La Jolla Playhouse in the play "Billy Budd".
- James made his TV debut in an episode ("The Night America Trembled") of "Studio One" in 1957.
- Then in 1959, he made his movie debut in the film "Ride Lonesome" starring Randolph Scott.
- Several more TV guest spots followed including "Trackdown" (1959), "Black Saddle" (1959), "The Restless Gun" (1958-59) 2 episodes, "M Squad" (1959), "The Rough Riders" (1959), "The Californians" (1959) 2 episodes, "Johnny Ringo" (1959), "Tombstone Territory" (1959), "Disneyland" (1958-59) 3 episodes, "The Life and Legend of Wyatt Earp" (1959), "The Texan" (1960), "Bronco" (1959-60) 2 episodes, "Wichita Town" (1959-60) 2 episodes, "Bat Masterson" (1959-60) 2 episodes, "Sugarfoot" (1960), "Wanted : Dead or Alive" (1959-60) 3 episodes, "Death Valley Days" (1960) and "Lawman" (1960) 2 episodes.

- In 1960, he was cast as "Jeff Durain" in the TV series "Klondike". He appeared in 10 episodes from 1960 to 1961.
- In 1961, he was cast as "Gregg Miles" in the TV series "Acapulco". He appeared in 8 episodes.
- Then in 1990, he provided the voice for the character "Looten Plunder" in the TV series "Captain Planet and the Planeteers". He made 15 episodes from 1990 to 1992.
- His last acting appearance was in an episode ("The Immortal") of "Arli$$" in 2002.
- James was married twice – Beverly Kelly (1959-79) and Paula O'Hara (1993-2002). He had one son, James H. Coburn IV, with Ms. Kelly.
- In 1979, he developed severe rheumatoid arthritis that left him debilitated. In 1998, a holistic healer started him on a dietary supplement that improved his condition drastically.
- James appears on the cover of Paul McCartney's 1973 album "Band on the Run".
- He co-wrote two songs, "Melancholy Melon" and "Losin' the Blues for You" with Lynsey De Paul.
- In 1994, he was awarded a Star on the Hollywood Walk of Fame for his contribution to Motion Pictures.
- In 1999, he won an Oscar (Best Actor in a Supporting Role) for the film "Affliction" (1997).
- James' other film credits include "Face of a Fugitive" (1959), "The Magnificent Seven" (1960), "Hell Is for Heroes" (1962), "The Great

Escape" (1963), "Charade" (1963), "The Man from Galveston" (1963), "The Americanization of Emily" (1964), "Major Dundee" (1965), "Our Man Flint" (1966), "In Like Flint" (1967), "Hard Contract" (1969), "Pat Garrett & Billy the Kid" (1973), "Bite the Bullet" (1975), "Midway" (1976), "The Iron Cross" (1977), "Young Guns 11" (1990), "Deadfall" (1993), "Maverick" (1994), "The Nutty Professor" (1996), "Intrepid" (2000) and "American Gun" (2002).

- His other TV credits include "Cheyenne" (1961), "The Rifleman" (1958-61) 2 episodes, "Rawhide" (1962), "Perry Mason" (1961-62) 2 episodes, "Bonanza" (1959-62) 3 episodes, "Tales of Wells Fargo" (1958-62) 2 episodes, "Stoney Burke" (1963), "The Defenders" (1964), "Murder, She Wrote" (1992), "Picket Fences" (1995), "Profiler" (1997) 2 episodes and "Scene by Scene" (2000).

- **Mari Blanchard** was born Mary E. Blanchard on April 13, 1923 (some sources say 1927) in Long Beach, California.
- She was the daughter of an oil tycoon (father) and a psychotherapist (mother).
- At age nine she contracted poliomyelitis and it took her three years to make a full recovery.
- Later on, she attended the University of Southern California and graduated with a degree in international law. She decided not to pursue this as a career.
- Mari then worked as an advertising model and was spotted on the back page of the Hollywood Reporter and signed to a contract by Paramount.

- Her first movie role for Paramount was an uncredited part in the film "Mr. Music" (1950) starring Bing Crosby.
- Several more film roles followed including "No Questions Asked" (1951), "Ten Tall Men" (1951), "Overland Telegraph" (1951), "Back at the Front" (1952), "Abbott and Costello Go to Mars" (1953), "Rails Into Laramie" (1954), "Black Horse Canyon" (1954) and "Destry" (1954).
- Mari's TV debut was in an episode ("Worm in the Apple") of "Your Jeweler's Showcase" in 1952.
- A number of TV appearances followed including "Terry and the Pirates" (1952), "Climax!" (1955), "Casablanca" (1956), "The Millionaire" (1957), "Shotgun Slade" (1959), "The Texan" (1959), "Sugarfoot" (1959), "Bachelor Father" (1959), "Tales of Wells Fargo" (1960), "Laramie" (1960), "Bronco" (1960), "Sea Hunt" (1960) and "Rawhide" (1959-61) 2 episodes.
- In 1960, she was cast as "Kathy O'Hara" in the TV series "Klondike". She appeared in 12 episodes from 1960 to 1961.
- Her last acting appearance was in an episode ("Totally by Design") of "It Takes a Thief" in 1968.
- Mari was married three times – Reese Hale Taylor Jr. (1960-61), George Shepard (1965-66) and Vincent J. Conti (1967-70).
- Her beautiful looks inspired cartoonist Al Capp to create the character "Stupefyin' Jones" for the popular "L'il Abner" comic strip.
- Mari always answered all her own fan mail.

- Her last movie role was in the John Wayne film "McLintock!" in 1963.
- Mari's other film credits include "Son of Sinbad" (1955), "The Crooked Webb" (1955), "Stagecoach to Fury" (1956), "Machete" (1958), "Karasu" (1958) and "Don't Knock the Twist" (1962).
- Her other TV credits include "The Roaring 20's" (1961), "Gunslinger" (1961), "Hawaiian Eye" (1961), "The Detectives" (1962), "Perry Mason" (1962), "Burke's Law" (1965) and "The Virginian" (1967).

"Kung Fu"

Years : 1972 - 1975

Episodes : 63 (3 seasons)

Cast :-

David Carradine (b. 1936 d. 2009) - Played Kwai Chang Caine

Radames Pera (b.1960) - Played Young Caine ("Grasshopper")

Keye Luke (b. 1904 d. 1991) - Played Master Po

Philip Ahn (b. 1905 d. 1978) - Played Master Kan

Synopsis :-
Adventures of a Shaolin Monk roaming the American West.

Trivia & Tidbits :-

"The Show"

- **"Kung Fu"** premiered on ABC on October 14, 1972 and last aired on April 26, 1975.
- The show ran for three seasons with a total of 63 episodes.

- The series was created by Ed Spielman and produced by Warner Bros. Television.
- Filming took place on the Warner Bros. backlot.
- The original series music was by Jim Helms.
- The adolescent "Kwai Chang Caine" was played by David Carradine's brother Keith.
- The series won three Emmy Awards - 1972 (Makeup) and 1973 (Directing and Cinematography).
- The show was preceded by a 90-minute TV movie that aired on February 22, 1972.
- The Shaolin Monastery which appeared in flashbacks was originally a set used for the film "Camelot" (1967).

"In Memoriam"

- **David Carradine** died of accidental asphyxiation on June 3, 2009 (72) in Bangkok, Thailand.
- **Keye Luke** died of a stroke on January 12, 1991 (86) in Whittier, California.
- **Philip Ahn** died from complications after surgery on February 28, 1978 (72) in Los Angeles, California.

"The Stars"

- **David Carradine (see "Shane")**

- **Radames Pera** was born on September 14, 1960 in New York City, New York.
- He is the son of actress Lisa Pera.
- Radames moved to Hollywood with his mother in 1963 so she could pursue her acting career.
- He made his movie debut in the film "A Dream of Kings" in 1969.
- Radames' TV acting debut was in an episode ("The Last Ten Yards") of "Medical Center" in 1969.
- He then appeared in several more TV shows including "The Red Skelton Show" (1969), "The Bill Cosby Show" (1970), "Family Affair" (1971), "Dan August" (1971), "The Interns" (1970-71) 2 episodes, "Cannon" (1971), "The Waltons" (1972) and "Lassie" (1972) 3 episodes.
- In 1972, he was cast as "Young Caine" in the TV series "Kung Fu". He appeared in 47 episodes from 1972 to 1975.
- From 1975 to 1977, he had a recurring role as "John Sanderson Edwards" in the TV series "Little House on the Prairie". He appeared in 8 episodes.
- His last acting appearance, to date, was in the film "Mojo Tango" in 2010.
- Radames has been married twice – Marsha Mann and Anne-Sophie Henault Pera.
- After the initial pilot for "Kung Fu" he had to have his head shaved and appeared bald in all other episodes.
- Radames quit acting in the late 1980's and formed his own company, All Systems Go! in Los Angeles. The company designed and

installed home theaters and residential sound systems.

- His other film credits include "Incident in San Francisco" (1971)(TV), "Gidget Gets Married" (1972)(TV), "The Six Million Dollar Man" (1973)(TV) uncredited, "Very Like a Whale" (1980)(TV) and "Red Dawn" (1984).
- Radames' other TV credits include "The Rookies" (1973), "Hawaii Five-O" (1973), "Marcus Welby, M.D." (1972-73) 2 episodes, "The Six Million Dollar Man" (1975), "Masquerade" (1984) and "Starman" (1987).

- **Keye Luke** was born on June 18, 1904 in Guangzhou, China.
- His father owned an art shop.
- Keye grew up in Seattle, Washington and attended Franklin High School, where he contributed cartoons and illustrations to school publications.
- Before becoming an actor Keye was a local artist in Seattle and Hollywood. He worked on several of the murals inside Grauman's Chinese Theatre.
- Keye made his uncredited movie debut in the film "The Painted Veil" in 1934.
- In 1935, he was cast as "Lee Chan" in the film "Charlie Chan in Paris". The character he played was "Charlie Chan's" son. He would go on to play this character in another ten "Charlie Chan" movies.

- During the 1930's and 1940's, he appeared in numerous films including "The Good Earth" (1937), "The Green Hornet" (1940), "Phantom of Chinatown" (1940), "The Green Hornet Strikes Again!" (1940), "Burma Convoy" (1941), "Mr. and Mrs. North" (1942), "The Falcon's Brother" (1942), "Dr. Gillespie's New Assistant" (1942), "Dr. Gillespie's Criminal Case" (1943), "Andy Hardy's Blonde Trouble" (1944), "Between Two Women" (1945) and "Tokyo Rose" (1946).
- Keye made his TV debut in an episode ("Shadow of the Avenger") of "Mysteries of Chinatown" in 1950.
- In 1972, he supplied the voice of "Charlie Chan" in the TV series "The Amazing Chan and the Chan Clan". He voiced 14 episodes.
- Again in 1972, he was cast as "Kralahome" in the TV series "Anna and the King". He appeared in 13 episodes.
- Still in 1972, he was cast as "Master Po" in the TV series "Kung Fu". He appeared in 46 episodes from 1972 to 1975.
- From 1978 to 1980, he supplied the voices for "Zoltar/The Great Spirit/Colonel Cronus" in the TV series "Battle of the Planets". He voiced 85 episodes.
- In 1983, he supplied voices in the TV series "Alvin & the Chipmunks". He voiced 13 episodes.

- In 1986, he was cast as "Sabasan" in the TV series "Sidekicks". He appeared in 23 episodes from 1986 to 1987.
- His last acting appearance was in the Woody Allen film "Alice" in 1990.
- Keye was married to Ethel Davis from 1942 until her death in 1979.
- In 1958, he appeared on Broadway in the musical "Flower Drum Song". He performed the part of "Wang Chi Yang" for two years.
- In 1990, he was awarded a Star on the Hollywood Walk of Fame for his contribution to Motion Pictures.
- In 2012, writer and filmmaker Timothy Tau wrote, directed and produced a short film about Keye Luke's earlier life and work entitled "Keye Luke".
- Keye's other film credits include "The Congregation" (1952), "Fair Wind to Java" (1953), "Nobody's Perfect" (1968), "The Chairman" (1969), "The Hawaiians" (1970), "The Amsterdam Kill" (1977), "Fly Away Home" (1981)(TV), "Gremlins" (1984), "Kung Fu: The Movie" (1986)(TV), "Dead Heat" (1988) and "Gremlins 2: The New Batch" (1990).
- His other TV credits include "Terry and the Pirates" (1952-53) 3 episodes, "The New Adventures of China Smith" (1954) 4 episodes, "Annie Oakley" (1955), "Gunsmoke" (1955),

"Jungle Jim" (1956), "Wire Service" (1957), "The Californians" (1958), "Trackdown" (1958), "Follow the Sun" (1961), "Fair Exchange" (1962), "Perry Mason" (1962-65) 2 episodes, "The Green Hornet" (1966), "Dragnet 1967" (1967-69) 2 episodes, "Hawaii Five-O" (1969), "Marcus Welby, M.D." (1971) 2 episodes, "The F.B.I." (1966-73) 4 episodes, "Cannon" (1974-75) 2 episodes, "Charlie's Angels" (1980), "Goldie Gold and Action Jack" (1981)(voice) 13 episodes, "Bret Maverick" (1981), "Falcon Crest" (1983) 2 episodes, "Mike Hammer" (1984), "Night Court" (1986-87) 2 episodes and "Superboy" (1989).

- **Philip Ahn** was born Pi Lip Ahn on March 29, 1905 in Highland Park, Los Angeles, California.
- His father, Dosan Ahn Chang-ho, was an educator and an activist for Korean independence.
- Philip's parents immigrated to the United States in 1902, however, the father, Dosan, returned to live in Korea in 1926.
- After graduating from high school in 1923, Philip went to work in rice fields around Colusa, California.
- The rice fields eventually failed, due to floods, so he started a job as an elevator operator in Los Angeles.

- In 1934, he attended the University of Southern California and remained there for two years. He then quit his studies and decided to try acting full-time.
- During the Second World War, Philip enlisted in the United States Army but was discharged early due to an ankle injury.
- Philip had two uncredited film roles, "Desirable" (1934) and "Shanghai" (1935), before he made his acting debut in the film "A Scream in the Night" in 1935.
- Several more film roles followed including "The General Died at Dawn" (1936), "The Good Earth" (1937) uncredited, "China Passage" (1937), "Daughter of Shanghai" (1937), "Thank You, Mr. Moto" (1937), "Charlie Chan in Honolulu" (1938), "Barricade" (1939), "The Shadow" (1940) uncredited, "Submarine Raider" (1942), "China Girl" (1942), "The Story of Dr. Wassell" (1944), "Back to Bataan" (1945), "The Chinese Ring" (1947), "The Creeper" (1948), "Boston Blackie's Chinese Venture" (1949), "Halls of Montezuma" (1951), "Japanese War Bride" (1952) and "Fair Wind to Java" (1953).
- In 1952, he made his TV debut in an episode ("Souvenir from Singapore") of Schlitz Playhouse.
- Following this, he appeared in several more films including "China Venture" (1953), "His

Majesty O'Keefe" (1954), "Hell's Half Acre" (1954), "The Shanghai Story" (1954), "Love Is a Many-Splendored Thing" (1955) and "The Left Hand of God" (1955).

- In 1955, he switched to television and guest starred on a number of shows including "TV Reader's Digest" (1955) 2 episodes, "Crossroads" (1955-56) 3 episodes, "Jungle Jim" (1956), "Four Star Playhouse" (1955-56) 2 episodes, "The New Adventures of Charlie Chan" (1957), "Navy Log" (1956-57) 2 episodes, "Dragnet" (1958), "The Eve Arden Show" (1958), "The Californians" (1957-58) 2 episodes, "Lawman" (1958), "The Adventures of Rin Tin Tin" (1959), "Have Gun – Will Travel" (1958-60) 2 episodes, "The Rebel" (1960), "Wanted: Dead or Alive" (1960), "Mr. Garlund" (1960) 3 episodes, "Hong Kong" (1960-61) 2 episodes, "Follow the Sun" (1961-62) 2 episodes, "Adventures in Paradise" (1959-62) 4 episodes, "Hawaiian Eye" (1960-62) 4 episodes, "Perry Mason" (1962), "Stoney Burke" (1963), "Bonanza" (1960-64) 3 episodes, "Laredo" (1967), "The Big Valley" (1968), "My Three Sons" (1968), "The F.B.I." (1966-72) 2 episodes, "Hawaii Five-O" (1968-72) 4 episodes and "The Streets of San Francisco" (1972).

- In 1972, he was cast as "Master Kan" in the TV series "Kung Fu". He appeared in 39 episodes from 1972 to 1975.
- His last acting role was in the film "Portrait of a Hitman" (1979). This film was released after he had passed away.
- Philip never married.
- In 1984, he was awarded (posthumously) a Star on the Hollywood Walk of Fame for his contribution to Motion Pictures.
- In the 1950's, he opened a restaurant with his sister, Soorah, called "Phil Ahn's Moongate Restaurant". They operated this in the San Fernando Valley for over thirty years.
- In 1968, he made a USO tour of Vietnam.
- Philip's other film credits include "Battle Hymn" (1957), "Hong Kong Confidential" (1958), "Never So Few" (1959), "The Great Impostor" (1961), "One-Eyed Jacks" (1961), "Diamond Head" (1962), "Paradise, Hawaiian Style" (1966), "Thoroughly Modern Millie" (1967), "The World's Greatest Athlete" (1973) and "The Killer Who Wouldn't Die" (1976)(TV).
- His other TV credits include "Love, American Style" (1974), "The Magician" (1974), "Sanford and Son" (1977), "M.A.S.H." (1976-77) 3 episodes, "Wonder Woman" (1977), "Switch" (1978) and "Police Woman" (1977-78) 2 episodes.

"Lancer"

Years : 1968 - 1970

Episodes : 51 (2 seasons)

Cast :-

James Stacy (b. 1936 d. 2016) - Played Johnny
Madrid Lancer

Andrew Duggan (b. 1923 d. 1988) - Played
Murdoch Lancer

Wayne Maunder (b. 1935) - Played Scott Lancer

Paul Brinegar (b. 1917 d. 1995) - Played Jelly
Hoskins

Elizabeth Baur (b. 1947) - Played Teresa O'Brien

Synopsis :-
The story of the Lancer family in California's San
Joaquin Valley.

Trivia & Tidbits :-

"The Show"

- **"Lancer"** premiered on CBS on September 24, 1968 and last aired on May 19, 1970.
- The show ran for two seasons with a total of 51 episodes.
- The series was produced by 20th Century Fox Television.
- "Lancer" was created by Samuel A. Peeples.
- The theme music was composed by Jerome Moross.
- Scriptwriter Andy Lewis won the Western Writers of America 'Spur Award' for the episode titled "Zee" starring Stefanie Powers.

"In Memoriam"
- **James Stacy** died from an allergic reaction on September 9, 2016 (79) in Ventura, California.
- **Andrew Duggan** died of throat cancer on May 15, 1988 (64) in Westwood, California.
- **Paul Brinegar** died of emphysema on March 27, 1995 (77) in Los Angeles, California.

"The Stars"

- **James Stacy** was born Maurice William Elias on December 23, 1936 in Los Angeles, California.
- His father (Louie) was a Lebanese immigrant and his mother (Lois), although born in America, was of Irish-Scottish descent.
- James made his acting debut in an episode ("The Banjo Player") of "The Adventures of Ozzie & Harriet" in 1956. He played the character "Marshall".

- His film debut was in an uncredited part in "Sayonara" (1957).
- In 1958, he was cast as the character "Fred" in the TV series "The Adventures of Ozzie & Harriet". He appeared in 27 episodes from 1958 to 1964.
- In 1968, he was cast as "Johnny Madrid Lancer" in the TV series "Lancer". He appeared in 51 episodes from 1968 to 1970.
- Then in 1990, he was cast as "Ed/Mark Rogosheske" in the TV series "Wiseguy". He appeared in 5 episodes.
- His last acting appearance was in an episode ("Can't We Get Along") of "The New WKRP in Cincinnati" in 1992.
- James was married twice – Connie Stevens (1963-66) and Kim Darby (1968-69). He had one daughter, Heather, with Ms. Darby.
- In 1973, James had a serious motorcycle accident and lost his left arm and left leg.
- He made his acting comeback in the film "Posse" in 1975. The role was created for him by the film's director, Kirk Douglas.
- In 1995, James was sent to prison for 6 years for molesting an 11 year-old girl.
- James' other film credits include "South Pacific" (1958), "Like Father, Like Son" (1961), "Summer Magic" (1963), "The Sheriff" (1966)(TV), "Flareup" (1969), "Heat of Anger" (1972)(TV) and "Matters of the Heart" (1990)(TV).
- His other TV credits include "Have Gun – Will Travel" (1962), "Cheyenne"(1962), "The Donna Reed Show" (1962) 3 episodes, "Perry

Mason" (1964-66) 2 episodes, "Cimarron Strip" (1968), "Gunsmoke" (1964-73) 5 episodes, "Hotel" (1985) and "Highway to Heaven" (1987).

- **Andrew Duggan** was born on December 28, 1923 in Franklin, Indiana.
- He was raised in Texas and went to college at Indiana University.
- During the Second World War he served in the United States Army. His company was led by actor Melvyn Douglas.
- After the war he decided to go into acting and made his debut in an episode ("Heat Lightning") of "The Chevrolet Tele-Theatre" in 1949.
- Several more TV appearances followed including "NBC Presents" (1949) 3 episodes, "Armstrong Circle Theatre" (1950), "The Gabby Hayes Show" (1951), "Suspense" (1953), "I Spy" (1955), "Medic" (1956), "Lux Video Theatre" (1950-56) 5 episodes, "Playhouse 90" (1956), "Wire Service" (1957), "Wagon Train" (1957), "Colt .45" (1957), "Tombstone Territory" (1958), "Have Gun – Will Travel" (1958) and "Omnibus" (1959).
- In 1959, he was cast as "Cal Calhoun" in the TV series "Bourbon Street Beat". He appeared in 38 episodes from 1959 to 1960.
- In 1962, he was cast as "George Rose" in the TV series "Room for One More". He appeared in 26 episodes.
- Then in 1965, he had a recurring role as "Maj. Gen. Ed Britt" in the TV series "12 O'Clock

High". He appeared in 17 episodes from 1965 to 1967.

- In 1968, he was cast as "Murdoch Lancer" in the TV series "Lancer". He appeared in 51 episodes from 1968 to 1970.
- Another recurring role was in the TV series "Medical Center". He played the character "Dr. Oliver Garson" in 4 episodes from 1970 to 1973.
- His last acting appearance was in the film "A Return to Salem's Lot" in 1987.
- Andrew was married to Elizabeth 'Betty' Logue from 1953 until his death in 1988. They had three children – Richard, Nancy and Melissa. His wife passed away less than a month after his death.
- In the 1950's, Andrew appeared in several Broadway plays – "The Rose Tattoo" (1951), "Gently Does It" (1953), "Anniversary Waltz" (1954-55), "Fragile Fox" (1954) and "Third Best Sport" (1958-59).
- Andrew's other film credits include "Patterns" (1956), "Decision at Sundown" (1957), "Westbound" (1959), "Merrill's Marauders" (1962), "The Incredible Mr. Limpet" (1964), "Seven Days in May" (1964), "In Like Flint" (1967), "The Secret War of Harry Frigg" (1968), The Homecoming : A Christmas Story" (1971)(TV), "It Lives Again" (1978), "Frankenstein Island" (1981) and "J. Edgar Hoover" (1987)(TV).
- His other TV credits include "Bronco" (1962), "Maverick" (1961-62) 2 episodes, "Lawman" (1961-62) 2 episodes, "Cheyenne" (1956-62) 6 episodes, "The Dakotas" (1963), "Hawaiian

Eye" (1962-63) 2 episodes, "77 Sunset Strip" (1959-63) 6 episodes, "Bonanza" (1964), "The Great Adventure" (1964) 2 episodes, "Gunsmoke" (1956-65) 3 episodes, "The Virginian" (1966), "The Big Valley" (1965-67) 2 episodes, "Cimarron Strip" (1967-68) 3 episodes, "Banacek" (1973), "Disneyland" (1957-75) 8 episodes, "Cannon" (1971-76) 3 episodes, "Insight" (1970-79) 3 episodes, "Hawaii Five-O" (1968-79) 7 episodes, "Chips" (1979-81) 3 episodes and "Falcon Crest" (1984-85) 4 episodes.

- **Wayne Maunder (see "Custer")**

- **Paul Brinegar** was born on December 19, 1917 in Tucumcari, New Mexico.
- He made his acting debut (uncredited) in the film "Abilene Town" in 1946.
- For the next ten years he appeared in numerous films including "Larceny" (1948), "Sword in the Desert" (1949) uncredited, "A Ticket to Tomahawk" (1950) uncredited, "Journey Into Light" (1951), "Here Comes the Nelsons" (1952) uncredited, "The Captive City" (1952), "Captain Scarface" (1953) and "Dawn at Socorro" (1954).
- In 1955, he played the recurring character "Jim 'Dog' Kelly" in the TV series "The Life and Legend of Wyatt Earp". He appeared in 19 episodes from 1956 to 1958.
- In 1959, he was cast as "Wishbone" in the TV series "Rawhide". He appeared in 215 episodes from 1959 to 1965.

- Then in 1968, he played the recurring character "Jelly Hoskins" in the TV series "Lancer". He appeared in 36 episodes from 1968 to 1970.
- In 1982, he played the recurring character "Lamar Pettybone" in the TV series "Matt Houston". He appeared in 10 episodes from 1982 to 1983.
- His last acting appearance was in the film "Wyatt Earp: Return to Tombstone" in 1994. He reprised his role of "Jim 'Dog' Kelly" from the original TV series.
- Paul's other film credits include "Flight to Hong Kong" (1956) uncredited, "The Vampire" (1957), "Cattle Empire" (1958), "How to Make a Monster" (1958), "Country Boy" (1966), "Charro!" (1969), "High Plains Drifter" (1973), "I Wonder Who's Killing Her Now" (1975), "The Wild Women of Chastity Gulch" (1982)(TV), "Life Stinks" (1991) and "Maverick" (1994).
- His other TV credits include "The Lone Ranger" (1954), "The Man Behind the Badge" (1955) 3 episodes, "Tales of the Texas Rangers" (1956), "Cheyenne" (1956), "Tales of Wells Fargo" (1957), "State Trooper" (1958), "Lawman" (1959), "Perry Mason" (1958-66) 2 episodes, "Death Valley Days" (1966) 2 episodes, "Bonanza" (1967), "Cannon" (1974), "Emergency!" (1974-76) 3 episodes, "Little House on the Prairie" (1976), "Disneyland" (1977), "Chips" (1977-82) 2 episodes, "Knight Rider" (1985) and "The Adventures of Brisco County Jr." (1993) 2 episodes.

- **Elizabeth Baur** was born on December 1, 1947 in Los Angeles, California.
- Her father, Jack Baur, was a veteran casting director at 20th Century Fox.
- Elizabeth attended Immaculate Heart High School in Los Angeles and spent over a year at Los Angeles Valley College.
- After college she joined the 20th Century Fox program for trainee actors.
- She made her TV acting debut in an episode ("Nora Clavicle and the Ladies' Crime Club") of "Batman" in 1968.
- Her film debut was in the movie "The Boston Strangler" in 1968.
- In 1968, she was cast as "Teresa O'Brien" in the TV series "Lancer". She appeared in 51 episodes from 1968 to 1970.
- In 1971, she was cast as "Officer Fran Belding" in the TV series "Ironside". She appeared in 89 episodes from 1971 to 1975.
- Her last acting appearance, to date, was in the TV movie "The Return of Ironside" in 1993.
- Elizabeth's other TV credits include "Daniel Boone" (1970), "The Young Rebels" (1970), "Room 222" (1971), "Emergency!" (1972), "Police Woman" (1978), "Fantasy Island" (1981) and "Remington Steele" (1984).

"Laredo"

Years : 1965 - 1967

Episodes : 56 (2 seasons)

Cast :-

Neville Brand (b. 1920 d. 1992) - Played Reese Bennett

William Smith (b. 1933) - Played Joe Riley

Peter Brown (b. 1935 d. 2016) - Played Chad Cooper

Philip Carey (b. 1925 d. 2009) - Played Capt. Ed Parmalee

Synopsis :-
The story of four Texas Rangers.

Trivia & Tidbits :-

"The Show"

- **"Laredo"** premiered on NBC on September 16, 1965 and last aired on April 7, 1967.
- The show ran for two seasons with a total of 56 episodes.

- The series was produced by Universal Television.
- Claude Akins played "Ranger Cotton Buckmeister" in five episodes but was never a regular cast member.
- Three of the episodes from Season 1 of the series were edited into the feature film "Three Guns for Texas" (1968).
- Peter Brown used his own horse, "Amigo", on the series.

"In Memoriam"

- **Neville Brand** died of emphysema on April 16, 1992 (71) in Sacramento, California.
- **Peter Brown** died from Parkinson's disease on March 21, 2016 (80) in Phoenix, Arizona.
- **Philip Carey** died of lung cancer on February 6, 2009 (83) in New York City, New York.

"The Stars"

- **Neville Brand** was born Lawrence Neville Brand on August 13, 1920 in Griswold, Iowa.
- He was the son of Leo Thomas Brand, an electrician, and Helen Louise Davis.
- Neville was raised in Kewanee, Illinois, where he attended high school. After he left school he worked as a soda jerk, waiter and shoe salesman.
- In 1941, he enlisted in the United States Army and trained at Fort Carson.

- During the Second World War he participated in many campaigns over Europe. He was wounded in 1945 and received the Silver Star and Purple Heart.
- In 1946, after his discharge, he worked on a U.S. Army Signal Corps film with Charleton Heston.
- Following this, he enrolled at the American Theater Wing and worked off-Broadway.
- Neville then moved to California and attended the Geller Drama School in Los Angeles on the G.I. Bill.
- He made his movie debut (uncredited) in the film "Port of New York" in 1949. Several more film roles followed including "D.O.A." (1950), "Halls of Montezuma" (1950), "Only the Valiant" (1951), "The Mob" (1951) and "Red Mountain" (1951).
- Neville made his TV debut in an episode ("The Man Who Had Nothing to Lose") of "The Bigelow Theatre" in 1950.
- More film roles followed including "Kansas City Confidential" (1952), "Stalag 17" (1953), "The Man from the Alamo" (1953), "Gun Fury" (1953), "The Lone Gun" (1954), "Fury at Gunsight Pass" (1956), "Love Me Tender" (1956), "The Tin Star" (1957) and "Badman's Country" (1958).
- Neville played the notorious gangster Al Capone on five separate occasions – "The Scarface Mob" (1959)(TV), "The Untouchables" (pilot episode – 1959), "Westinghouse Desilu Playhouse" (two part episode "The Untouchables" – 1959), "The Untouchables"

(two part episode "The Big Train" – 1961) and "The George Raft Story" (1961).

- In an episode ("We've Lost a Train") of the TV series "The Virginian" in 1965, he was cast as "Reese Bennett", a Texas Ranger. This was effectively the pilot episode for the TV series "Laredo".

- Later on in the year he was cast as "Reese Bennett" in the TV series "Laredo". He appeared in 56 episodes from 1965 to 1967.

- He played the character "Reese Bennett" once more in the film "Three Guns for Texas" in 1968.

- Neville's last acting appearance was in the film "Evils of the Night" in 1985.

- He was married to Mae Brand for many years and they had three daughters.

- Neville was an avid reader and amassed a collection of 30,000 books over the years, however, many were destroyed when a fire engulfed his Malibu home in 1978.

- In 1955, he was nominated for a BAFTA film award for his role in "Riot in Cell Block II" (1954).

- Neville's other film credits include "All the King's Men" (1958)(TV), "Birdman of Alcatraz" (1962), "That Darn Cat!" (1965), "The Desperados" (1969), "Cahill U.S. Marshal" (1973), "The Quest" (1976)(TV) and "The Return" (1980).

- His other TV credits include "Zane Grey Theatre" (1959), "Death Valley Days" (1962), "Rawhide" (1960-63) 2 episodes, "Destry" (1964), "Wagon Train" (1964) 2 episodes,

"Gunsmoke" (1965), "Daniel Boone" (1967), "Bonanza" (1960-71) 3 episodes, "Barbary Coast" (1975), "McCloud" (1972-75) 3 episodes, "Baretta" (1977) and "Fantasy Island" (1980).

- **William Smith** was born on March 24, 1933 in Columbia, Missouri.
- He spent his early life on a cattle ranch but due to severe dust storms (known as "The Dust Bowl") the family ended up losing everything and moved to California.
- William began his acting career at the age of eight and appeared in several popular films (uncredited roles) including "The Ghost of Frankenstein" (1942), "The Song of Bernadette" (1943), "Going My Way" (1944), "A Tree Grows in Brooklyn" (1945) and "Gilda" (1946).
- After graduating from high school he enlisted in the United States Air Force in 1951.
- Because he could speak several languages (Russian, German, French and Serbo-Croatian) he was recruited by the N.S.A. and flew secret missions over Russia during the Korean War.
- After his discharge he studied at Syracuse University, the University of Munich, the Sorbonne in Paris and finally U.C.L.A. where he received a Master's degree in Russian Studies.
- Following this, he taught Russian at U.C.L.A. but gave this up after being offered a contract with M.G.M.

- William made his TV debut in an episode ("Edie and the Princess") of "Kraft Television Theatre" in 1954.
- His first M.G.M. movie was an uncredited role in the film "High School Confidential!" in 1958.
- In 1961, he was cast as "Sgt. Danny Keller" in the TV series "The Asphalt Jungle". He appeared in 13 episodes.
- In 1962, he was cast as "Jimmy Delaney" in the TV series "Zero One". He appeared in 31 episodes from 1962 to 1965.
- Then in 1965, he was cast as "Joe Riley" in the TV series "Laredo". He appeared in 56 episodes from 1965 to 1967.
- In 1976, he played the character "Falconetti" in the TV mini-series "Rich Man, Poor Man".
- He continued the role in the TV series "Rich Man, Poor Man – Book II". He appeared in 18 episodes from 1976 to 1977.
- In 1979, he appeared in the final season of "Hawaii Five-O" as the character "Det. James 'Kimo' Carew". He appeared in 19 episodes from 1979 to 1980.
- Then in 1983, he had a recurring role as "Col. Willie Shell" in the TV series "Emerald Point N.A.S." He appeared in 6 episodes.
- Another recurring role was as "Brodie Hollister" in the TV series "Wildside". He appeared in 6 episodes in 1985.
- His last acting role, to date, was in the film "Island of Witches" in 2014.
- William has been married twice – Michele Smith and Joan Cervelli.
- He played the "Marlboro Man" in the final Marlboro cigarette commercial.

- William is an honorary member of the Stuntman's Association of Motion Pictures.
- He studied Kung Fu for eight years with Jimmy Woo and Kenpo Karate master Ed Parker.
- Whilst living in France he stunt doubled for former Tarzan, Lex Barker.
- William's other film credits include "Mail Order Bride" (1964), "Three Guns for Texas" (1968), "Grave of the Vampire" (1972), "Invasion of the Bee Girls" (1973), "Hollywood Man" (1976), "Seven" (1979), "Any Which Way You Can" (1980), "Conan the Barbarian" (1982), "Red Dawn" (1984), "Commando Squad" (1987), "Terror in Beverly Hills" (1989), "Highway Warrior" (1990), "Maverick" (1994), "The Shooter" (1997), "Hell to Pay" (2005) and "Tiger Cage" (2012).
- His other TV credits include "Stoney Burke" (1963), "Combat!" (1963-64) 2 episodes, "Wagon Train" (1964) 2 episodes, "The Virginian" (1963-68) 5 episodes, "Daniel Boone" (1967-70) 5 episodes, "Death Valley Days" (1969-70) 4 episodes, "The Mod Squad" (1969-71) 3 episodes, "Gunsmoke" (1972-75) 2 episodes, "Matt Houston" (1982), "The Fall Guy" (1982-83) 3 episodes, "Airwolf" (1987), "Hunter" (1985-89) 3 episodes, "Due South" (1994) and "Justice League" (2002) 2 episodes.

- **Peter Brown** was born Pierre Lind de Lappe on October 5, 1935 in New York City, New York.

- His mother, Mina Reaume, was a stage and radio actress and his father died when he was four years old. Peter has three other brothers.
- Peter took the name "Brown" from his stepfather, Albert 'Bud' Brown.
- He graduated from North Central High School, Spokane, Washington.
- During his U.S. Army service in Alaska, he became involved in writing, directing and acting in plays to entertain the troops.
- After his discharge, he studied drama at U.C.L.A.
- Whilst pumping gas on Sunset Strip he met Jack L. Warner and wangled a screen test at Warner Bros.
- He was put under contract and made his TV debut in an episode ("The Peacemaker") of "Colt .45" in 1957.
- Peter made his film debut in the Warner's movie "Darby's Rangers" in 1958.
- In 1958, he was cast as "Deputy Johnny McKay" in the TV series "Lawman". He appeared in 155 episodes from 1958 to 1962.
- During this time he also appeared in episodes of "Sugarfoot" ("The Trial of the Canary Kid" – 1959) and "Maverick" ("Hadley's Hunters" – 1960) as "Deputy Johnny McKay".
- In 1965, he was cast as "Chad Cooper" in the TV series "Laredo". He appeared in 56 episodes from 1965 to 1967.
- He also appeared in an episode ("We've Lost a Train") of "The Virginian" (1965) as "Chad Cooper".
- In 1971, he started his 'soap' career, appearing in "Days of Our Lives" (1971-79),

"The Young and the Restless" (1981-82; 1989-91), "Loving" (1983-84), "One Life to Live" (1986-87) and "Bold and the Beautiful" (1991-92).

- His last acting appearance was in the film "Hell to Pay" in 2005.
- Peter was married five times and had one long-term relationship – Diane Jergens (1958-59); Sandy Edmundson 1964-?); Yvette Safargy (1971-74); Amber Karlson (1974-79) not married; Mary Kathleen Gauba (1986-99) and Kerstin Kern (2008-16). He had two sons, Matthew and Joshua.
- He dyed his hair peroxide blond for his role in "Ride the Wild Surf" (1964) with Tab Hunter and Fabian.
- Had his own production company called "Handshake Films".
- Peter's other film credits include "Merrill's Marauders" (1962), "A Tiger Walks" (1964), "Three Guns for Texas" (1968), "Attack at Dawn" (1970), "Piranha" (1972), "Sunburst" (1975), "The Concrete Jungle" (1982), "The Wedding Planner" (2001) and "Three Bad Men" (2005).
- His other TV credits include "Hawaiian Eye" (1962), "Cheyenne" (1962), "The Gallant Men" (1963), "Wagon Train" (1964), "My Three Sons" (1971), "Police Story" (1974), "Charlie's Angels" (1978), "Dallas" (1982), "The Fall Guy" (1984) and "Babylon 5" (1997).

- **Philip Carey** Was born Eugene Joseph Carey on July 15, 1925 in Hackensack, New Jersey.

- He grew up on Long Island, New York and later served with the Marine Corps during the Second World War and then the Korean War.
- Following his discharge he briefly attended New York's Mohawk University and then studied drama at the University of Miami.
- Whilst he was playing summer stock in New England a talent scout offered him a contract with Warner Bros.
- Philip made his movie debut in the film "Operation Pacific" (1951), starring John Wayne.
- Several more film roles followed including "I Was a Communist for the F.B.I." (1951), "The Tanks Are Coming" (1951), "Cattle Town" (1952), "Springfield Rifle" (1952), "The Man Behind the Gun" (1953), "Gun Fury" (1953), "Calamity Jane" (1953) and "The Nebraskan" (1953).
- Philip made his TV debut in an episode ("Two Lives Have I") of "Schlitz Playhouse of Stars" in 1953.
- In 1956, he was cast as "Lieutenant Michael Rhodes" in the TV series "Tales of the 77th Bengal Lancers". He appeared in 26 episodes from 1956 to 1957.
- In 1959, he was cast as "Philip Marlowe" in the TV series of the same name. He appeared in 26 episodes from 1959 to 1960.
- Then in 1965, he was cast as "Capt. Edward Parmalee" in the TV series "Laredo". He appeared in 56 episodes from 1965 to 1967.
- In 1979, he was cast in the recurring role of "Asa Buchanan" in the TV soap "One Life to

Live". He appeared in the show from 1979 to 2008.

- Philip was married twice – Maureen Peppler (1949 - ?) and Colleen Welch (1976-2009). He had three children with Ms. Peppler and two with Ms. Welch.
- Carey's character ("Michael Rhodes") in "Bengal Lancers" was portrayed as a Canadian because he, reportedly, could not master a British accent.
- Philip appeared in television commercials for "Granny Goose" potato chips.
- His other film credits include "They Rode West" (1954), "Mister Roberts" (1955), "Tonka" (1958), "The Trunk" (1961), "The Great Sioux Massacre" (1965), "Three Guns for Texas" (1968), "The Rebel Rousers" (1970) and "Monster" (1980).
- Philip's other TV credits include "The Ford Television Theatre" (1953-57) 10 episodes, "Zane Grey Theatre" (1961), "Stagecoach West" (1961), "The Rifleman" (1961), "Lawman" (1962), "Bronco" (1962), "Cheyenne" (1962) 2 episodes, "77 Sunset Strip" (1962-63) 4 episodes, "The Virginian" (1963-65) 2 episodes, "Cimarron Strip" (1968), "All in the Family" (1971), "Gunsmoke" (1971), "McCloud" (1975) and "The Betty White Show" (1977).

"The Legend of Jesse James"

Years : 1965 - 1966

Episodes : 34 (1 season)

Cast :-

Christopher Jones (b. 1941 d. 2014) - Played Jesse James

Allen Case (b. 1934 d. 1986) - Played Frank James

Synopsis :-
The story of notorious outlaws Jesse and Frank James.

Trivia & Tidbits :-

"The Show"

- **"The Legend of Jesse James"** premiered on ABC on September 13, 1965 and last aired on May 9, 1966.
- The show ran for one season with a total of 34 black and white episodes.
- The series was created by Samuel A. Peeples (he also created the TV series "Lancer") and produced by 20th Century Fox Television.

- It was filmed at the Iverson Ranch in Chatsworth, California.
- The show was up against two top-rating programs on the other networks - "The Lucy Show" (CBS) and "Dr. Kildare" (NBC).

"In Memoriam"

- **Christopher Jones** died of cancer on January 31, 2014 (72) in Los Alamitos, California.
- **Allen Case** died of a heart attack on August 25, 1986 (51) in Truckee, California.

"The Stars"

- **Christopher Jones** was born William Franklin Jones on August 18, 1941 in Jackson, Tennessee.
- He was the son of J.G. Jones, a grocery clerk, and his mother Robbie, an artist.
- His mother was committed to a mental institution in 1945 and remained there until her death in 1960.
- Christopher had one older brother, Robert, and they were sent to Boys Town in 1947 because their father was unable to look after them.
- After he left Boys Town, Chris enlisted in the Army. He soon resented the decision and went AWOL. After stealing a car he headed for New York.
- In New York he turned himself in to the Army and was subsequently court-martialed. He

served six months on Grovernors Island in the East River.

- After his release he studied painting and then turned to acting, studying at the Actor's Studio under Lee Strasberg.
- Chris made his Broadway debut in 1961 in Tennessee William's "The Night of the Iguana", starring Shelley Winters.
- In 1963, he headed to Hollywood and was later cast as "Jesse James" in the TV series "The Legend of Jesse James". He appeared in 34 episodes from 1965 to 1966.
- His last acting role was in the film "Mad Dog Time" in 1996.
- Chris was married to Susan Strasberg from 1965 until their divorce in 1968. They had one daughter, Jenny.
- He had a relationship with Cathy Abernathy from 1974 to 1980 which produced a son, Christopher Jones Jr.
- Another relationship with Paula McKenna from 1984 to 1994 produced a further four children.
- During his time in Hollywood Chris became friends with Sharon Tate and her husband Roman Polanski. When Sharon was murdered by the Manson family in 1969 he was so devastated he abandoned his acting career.
- Chris was offered the role of "Zed" in "Pulp Fiction" (1994) by Quentin Tarantino but turned it down.
- His other film credits include "Chubasco" (1967), "Wild in the Streets" (1967), "Three in the Attic" (1968), "The Looking Glass War"

(1969), "A Brief Season" (1969) and "Ryan's Daughter" (1970).

- Chris' other TV credits include "Judd for the Defense" (1967) and "The Man from U.N.C.L.E." (1967).

- **Allen Case** was born on October 8, 1934 in Dallas, Texas.
- He was raised in Dallas and briefly attended the Southern Methodist University.
- Allen moved to New York and secured a singing spot on Arthur Godfrey's morning show.
- He then performed at several nightclubs and had parts in two musicals - "Reuben Reuben" and "Pleasure Dome".
- Allen then moved to Hollywood and made his film debut in "Damn Yankees!" (1958) (uncredited). He played a baseball player.
- His TV debut was in an episode ("The Besieged") of "Bronco" in 1958.
- Several other TV guest appearances followed including "Sugarfoot" (1958), "The Rifleman" (1958), "Wagon Train" (1959), "Have Gun - Will Travel" (1959), "Lawman" (1959) and "Colt .45" (1959).
- In 1959, he was cast as "Deputy Clay McCord" in the TV series "The Deputy". He appeared in 76 episodes from 1959 to 1961.
- Then in 1965, he was cast as "Frank James" in the TV series "The Legend of Jesse James". He appeared in 34 episodes from 1965 to 1966.
- In 1967, he went back to Broadway and appeared in the musical "Hallelujah Baby!"

- In 1980, he appeared as "Dean Knitzer" in the TV series "The Life and Times of Eddie Roberts".
- His last acting role was in an episode ("This Year's Riot") of "Chips" in 1982.
- Allen's other film credits include "The Ordeal of Patty Hearst" (1979) (TV), "Nero Wolfe" (1979) (TV) and "Murder Can Hurt You" (1980) (TV).
- His other TV credits include "The Virginian" (1962), "Perry Mason" (1964), "Gunsmoke" (1966), "Barnaby Jones" (1975), "Police Woman" (1976), "The Bob Newhart Show" (1978) and "Hill Street Blues" (1981).

"The Life and Times of Grizzly Adams"

Years : 1977 - 1978

Episodes : 37 (2 seasons)

Cast :-

Dan Haggerty (b. 1941 d. 2016) - Played James 'Grizzly' Adams

Denver Pyle (b. 1920 d. 1997) - Played Mad Jack

Don Shanks (b. 1950) - Played Nakoma

Synopsis :-
Stories of a man living in the mountains.

Trivia & Tidbits :-

"The Show"

- **"The Life and Times of Grizzly Adams"** premiered on NBC on February 9, 1977 and last aired on December 19, 1978.
- The show ran for two seasons with a total of 37 episodes plus one TV movie titled "The Capture of Grizzly Adams" (1982).

- The series was based on a book, "The Life and Times of Grizzly Adams", written by Charles E. Sellier Jr. in 1972.
- In 1974, a film of the same name was completed on a budget of $140,000 (the film subsequently earned $65 million at the box office).
- The series was produced by Sunn Classic Pictures, a company founded by Charles Sellier.
- The theme song, "Maybe", was written and sung by Thom Pace. The song was released as a single in Europe and went to No.1 on the charts.
- The show was filmed in the mountains near Ruidoso, New Mexico.
- The bear in the show was named "Ben" and the mule "Number 7".

"In Memoriam"

- **Dan Haggerty** died of cancer on January 15, 2016 (73) in Burbank, California.
- **Denver Pyle** died of lung cancer on December 25, 1997 (77) in Burbank, California.

"The Stars"

- **Dan Haggerty** was born Gene Jajonski on November 19, 1941 in Pound, Wisconsin.
- He made his movie debut in the film "Muscle Beach Party" (1964), starring Frankie Avalon and Annette Funicello.

- Several more film roles followed including "Girl Happy" (1965) uncredited, "Easy Rider" (1969) uncredited, "Angels Die Hard" (1970), "The Tender Warrior" (1971), "Pink Angels" (1972), "Hex" (1973), "When the North Wind Blows" (1974), "The Life and Times of Grizzly Adams" (1974) and "The Adventures of Frontier Fremont" (1976).
- In 1977, he was cast as "James 'Grizzly' Adams" in the TV series "The Life and Times of Grizzly Adams". He appeared in 37 episodes from 1977 to 1978.
- His last acting appearance was in the film "40 Nights" due for release in 2016.
- Dan had been married twice – Diane Rooker (1959-84) and Samantha Haggerty (1984-2008). He has two children with Diane and three children with Samantha.
- In his early days, Dan worked as an animal trainer and stuntman.
- A new book titled "The Life and Times of Dan Haggerty – the man who made Grizzly Adams famous!: The Preacher, the Pirate and the Pagan" was published in 2013 and written by Terry W. Bomar.
- In 1994, Dan was awarded a Star on the Hollywood Walk of Fame for his contribution to the television industry.
- Dan's other film credits include "Once Upon a Starry Night" (1978)(TV), "Condominium" (1980)(TV), "Legend of the Wild" (1981), "The Capture of Grizzly Adams" (1982)(TV), "Elves" (1989), "Macon County War" (1990), "Soldier's Fortune" (1991), "Cheyenne Warrior"

(1994)(TV), "Grizzly Mountain" (1997), "Escape to Grizzly Mountain" (2004) and "Big Stan" (1983).

- **Denver Dell Pyle** was born on December 25, 1920 in Bethune, Colorado.
- He was the son of Ben H. Pyle, a farmer, and his wife Maude.
- Denver graduated from high school and then attended Colorado State University, but dropped out to become a drummer.
- During the Second World War he enlisted in the U.S. Navy but after being wounded at Guadalcanal was medically discharged in 1943.
- After his discharge he worked at several jobs before landing a role in an amateur theater production. He was discovered by a talent scout and began training as an actor.
- He made his uncredited movie debut in the film "The Guilt of Janet Ames" in 1947.
- Several more film roles followed including "Train to Alcatraz" (1948), "Red Canyon" (1949), "Dynamite Pass" (1950), "Rough Riders of Durango" (1951), "Texas Bad Man" (1953), "Ride Clear of Diablo" (1954), "To Hell and Back" (1955) and "7th Cavalry" (1956).
- Denver made his TV debut in an episode ("Hypnotist Murder") of "The Cisco Kid" in 1951.
- Many more TV guest starring roles followed including "The Range Rider" (1951-53) 14 episodes, "The Roy Rogers Show" (1952-53) 4 episodes, "Hopalong Cassidy" (1952-54) 2 episodes, "Annie Oakley" (1954) 2 episodes,

"The Adventures of Kit Carson" (1952-54) 7 episodes, "The Gene Autry Show" (1951-54) 10 episodes, "Buffalo Bill Jr." (1955) 2 episodes, "You Are There" (1953-56) 8 episodes, "The Lone Ranger" (1951-56) 7 episodes, "The Adventures of Jim Bowie" (1956-57) 3 episodes, "Fury" (1955-58) 2 episodes, "The Texan" (1959-60) 4 episodes, "The Life and Times of Wyatt Earp" (1955-60) 10 episodes, "Have Gun – Will Travel" (1957-60) 7 episodes and "Zane Grey Theatre" (1956-61) 7 episodes.

- In 1963, he started a recurring role as "Briscoe Darling" in the TV series "The Andy Griffith Show". He appeared in 6 episodes from 1963 to 1966.
- In 1965, he was cast as "Grandpa Tarleton" in the TV series "Tammy". He appeared in 26 episodes from 1965 to 1966.
- Then in 1968, he was cast as "Buck Webb" in the TV series "The Doris Day Show". He appeared in 53 episodes from 1968 to 1970.
- In 1977, he was cast as "Mad Jack" in the TV series "The Life and Times of Grizzly Adams". He appeared in 37 episodes from 1977 to 1978.
- In 1979, he was cast as "Uncle Jesse" in the TV series "The Dukes of Hazzard". He appeared in 146 episodes from 1979 to 1985.
- In 1983, he supplied the voice of "Uncle Jesse Duke" in the animated TV series "The Dukes". The series lasted 20 episodes.
- His last acting appearance was in the TV movie "The Dukes of Hazzard: Reunion!" in 1997.

- Denver was married twice – Marilee Carpenter (1955-67) and Tippie Johnston (1983-97). He had two sons, David and Tony, with Ms. Carpenter.
- He was the brother of animator Willis Pyle and cousin of writer Ernie Pyle.
- Denver was a friend of John Wayne and appeared in several of his movies including "The Horse Soldiers" (1959), "The Alamo" (1960), "The Man Who Shot Liberty Valance" (1962) and "Cahill U.S. Marshal" (1973).
- In 1997, he received a Star on the Hollywood Walk of Fame for his contribution to Motion Pictures.
- Denver's other film roles included "Gun Duel in Durango" (1957), "The Left Handed Gun" (1958), "Geronimo" (1962), "Mail Order Bride" (1964), "Shenandoah" (1965), "The Great Race" (1965), "Tammy and the Millionaire" (1967), "Bonnie and Clyde" (1967), "Bandolero!" (1968), "Guardian of the Wilderness" (1976), "Maverick" (1994) and "Father and Scout" (1994)(TV).
- His other TV credits included "The Rifleman" (1959-61) 5 episodes, "Bronco" (1961) 4 episodes, "Cheyenne" (1961-62) 3 episodes, "Laramie" (1959-63) 5 episodes, "Wagon Train" (1957-65) 2 episodes, "Perry Mason" (1958-66) 6 episodes, "Death Valley Days" (1953-66) 7 episodes, "Bonanza" (1961-72) 8 episodes, "Gunsmoke" (1956-73) 14 episodes, "Disneyland" (1959-78) 7 episodes and "Dallas" (1990) 2 episodes.

- **Donald L. Shanks** was born on February 26, 1950 in Piasa, Illinois.
- He of Cherokee and Choctaw descent.
- As well as acting he has also worked as a stunt coordinator.
- Don made his acting debut in the film "The Life and Times of Grizzly Adams" in 1974. He played the character "Nakoma".
- In 1977, he was cast as the same character ("Nakoma") in the TV series "The Life and Times of Grizzly Adams". He appeared in 36 episodes from 1977 to 1978.
- Don's other film credits include "The Adventures of Frontier Fremont" (1976), "Last of the Mohicans" (1977)(TV), "The Ghost Dance" (1980), "Legend of the Wild" (1981), "Revenge of the Ninja" (1983), "Halloween 5" (1989), "The Indian Runner" (1991), "Wind Dancer" (1993), "Primary Suspect" (2000), "No Dogs Allowed" (2002), "Little Bear and the Master" (2008), "Smothered" (2014) and "Like Son" (2015).
- His other TV credits include "How the West Was Won" (1979), "The Chisholms" (1979), "Werewolf" (1988), "Hollywood Detective" (1991) and "Touched by an Angel" (2001).

"Little House on the Prairie"

Years : 1974 - 1983

Episodes : 203 (plus 4 TV films)

Cast :-

Michael Landon (b. 1936 d. 1991) - Played Charles Ingalls

Karen Grassle (b. 1942) - Played Caroline Ingalls

Melissa Gilbert (b. 1964) - Played Laura Ingalls

Melissa Sue Anderson (b. 1962) - Played Mary Ingalls

Sidney/Lindsay Greenbush (b. 1970) - Played Carrie Ingalls

Matthew Laborteaux (b. 1966) - Played Albert Quinn Ingalls

Katherine "Scottie" MacGregor (b. 1925) - Played Harriet Oleson

Richard Bull (b. 1924 d. 2014) - Played Nels Oleson

Alison Arngrim (b. 1962) - Played Nellie Oleson

Jonathan Gilbert (b. 1968) - Played Willie Oleson

Kevin Hagen (b. 1928 d. 2005) - Played Dr. Hiram Baker

Dabbs Greer (b.1917 d. 2007) - Played Rev. Robert Alden

Trivia & Tidbits :-

"The Show"

- **"Little House on the Prairie"** premiered on NBC on September 11, 1974 and last aired on March 21, 1983.
- The show ran for nine seasons with a total of 203 episodes and 4 TV films.
- During the 1982-83 season, with the departure of Michael Landon, the series was broadcast with a new title - "Little House: A New Beginning".
- A three-hour compilation special called "The Little House Years" was aired in 1979.
- The series was preceded by a two-hour pilot movie that first aired on March 30, 1974.
- The show was loosely based on Laura Ingalls Wilder's best-selling series of "Little House on the Prairie" books.
- Many girls auditioned for the part of "Laura Ingalls", however, Michael Landon was so

convinced Melissa Gilbert was the perfect candidate, he only sent her screen test to the producers at NBC.

- Before Alison Arngrim auditioned for the part of "Nellie Oleson", she had unsuccessfully auditioned for the parts of "Laura and Mary Ingalls".
- In the "Last Farewell" episode, the town of Walnut Grove was really blown up. One of the few buildings left standing was the church/schoolhouse.
- One of the other buildings left standing was the house the Ingalls' lived in. However, it was subsequently destroyed by the fires in California in 2003.
- In the episode "Here Comes the Brides", Scottie MacGregor was actually injured in the scene where "Mrs. Oleson" falls off the horse. Because Scottie was unable to do the next sequence, Ruth Foster (who plays "Mrs. Foster" in the show) dressed in "Mrs. Oleson's" costume and filmed the sequence for her.
- In 2004, the character "Charles Ingalls" was ranked No.4 in TV Guide's list of the "50 Greatest TV Dads of All Time".
- In 2005, the character "Nellie Oleson" was ranked No.3 in TV Guide's list of "TV's 10 Biggest Brats".
- "Mary's" husband, "Adam Kendall", was studying law when he went blind. Just before he regained his sight, he passed the bar. He went on to practice law in Walnut Grove.

- The theme song was written by David Rose. He is best known for the 1962 Burlesque classic, "The Stripper".
- Because Walnut Grove had no jail, "Nels Oleson's" ice house served as such for anyone awaiting trial.
- The first dog the "Ingalls's" owned was "Jack". After he died, they adopted a stray black and white dog named "Bandit".
- "Laura's" favorite perfume was lemon verbena. "Mr. Edwards" gave it to her in two episodes.
- Actor E.J. Andre appeared on the series 7 times, in 5 different roles.
- In the episode "Christmas at Plum Creek", "Laura's" horse "Bunny" is referred to as being male. However, in the episodes "Bunny", "The Race" and "Journey in the Spring", the same horse is referred to as being female.
- In the episode "The Lord is My Shepherd", "Laura" ran away from home and stays on top of a mountain, even though there are no mountains in Walnut Grove, Minnesota.
- After the series finished there were three made-for-television movies shot - "Little House: Look Back to Yesterday" (1983), "Little House: Bless All the Dear Children" (1983) and "Little House: The Last Farewell" (1984).
- Over the nine seasons, the show was only out of the Top 30 programs once. The ratings for each season were - 1974/75 (No.13), 1975/76 (-), 1976/77 (No.16), 1977/78 (No.7), 1978/79 (No.14), 1979/80 (No.16), 1980/81 (No.10), 1981/82 (No.25) and 1982/83 (No.29).

- The show won 3 Emmy Awards (1978, 1979 and 1982).

"In Memoriam"

- **Michael Landon** died of pancreatic cancer on July 1, 1991 (54) in Malibu, California.
- **Richard Bull** died of pneumonia on February 3, 2014 (89) in Calabasas, California.
- **Kevin Hagen** died of esophageal cancer on July 9, 2005 (77) in Grants Pass, Oregon.
- **Dabbs Greer** died of a kidney and heart ailment on April 28, 2007 (90) in Pasadena, California.

"The Stars"

- **Michael Landon** was born Eugene Maurice Orowitz on October 31, 1936 in Forest Hills, Queens, New York.
- His father, Eli Maurice Orowitz (died of a heart attack in 1959), was a Jewish American actor and movie theatre manager, and his mother, Peggy O'Neill (died in 1981), was an Irish American Roman Catholic dancer and comedienne. He was the younger of two children.
- In 1941, when Michael was 4 years old, he and the family moved to Collingswood, New Jersey, where he later attended Collingswood High School. He graduated in 1954.

- His running made him very good at track in high school and won him a scholarship to the University of Southern California. Unfortunately, he tore his shoulder ligaments and was unable to throw the javelin and was no longer able to participate with the USC track team.
- He claimed he picked his stage name, Michael Landon, out of the Los Angeles telephone directory.
- Before he became a successful actor, he worked in a warehouse and a gas station.
- After changing his name to Landon he soon became one of the more popular and enduring young actors of the late 1950's, making his first uncredited appearance in the film "These Wilder Years" (1956).
- In 1959, at the age of 22, Michael had his first starring TV role as "Little Joe Cartwright" on "Bonanza". He appeared in all 14 seasons of the western, which totalled 430 episodes.
- In 1962, he released a "Bonanza" related single, "Gimme A Little Kiss/Be Patient With Me", on Columbia Records.
- The year after "Bonanza" was canceled, Michael went on to star in the pilot of what would become another successful television series, "Little House on the Prairie", again for NBC.
- Michael's third successful TV series was "Highway to Heaven", which ran from 1984 to 1989 and a total of 111 episodes.

- "Highway to Heaven" was the only show throughout his long career in television that he owned outright.
- Actress Melissa Gilbert's son, Michael, was named after him.
- Former U.S. President Ronald Reagan and his wife, Nancy Davis Reagan, attended Michael's memorial service the day after his death. The service was attended by many celebrities including Brian Keith and Ernest Borgnine.
- Like his "Bonanza" co-star Lorne Greene he was a staunch supporter of the Republican Party.
- Michael was inducted, with the rest of the "Little House" cast, into the Hall of Great Western Performers at the National Cowboy and Western Heritage Museum in 1998.
- He never legally adopted his stepdaughter, Cheryl, because of her birth father's objections.
- Michael started having grey hair at the age of 20.
- Comedian and ex-talk show host, Johnny Carson was a lifetime friend.
- Before his death, he appeared on "The Tonight Show Starring Johnny Carson" to talk about his brave battle against cancer and his life, it was the highest-rated show of all time.
- He studied karate under Chuck Norris, as did the children of his "Bonanza" co-star Dan Blocker.
- Michael wrote and directed two movies that were semi-autobiographical: "The Loneliest Runner" (1976) (TV) and "Sam's Son" (1984).

- 12 years after his death, his sister, Evelyn, died on New Years' Day, 2003.
- He smoked 4 packs of unfiltered menthol cigarettes a day during his lifetime.
- Michael wore lifts in "Bonanza" so he would not be dwarfed by considerably taller co-stars Dan Blocker and Lorne Greene.
- He had an IQ of 159.
- Michael was married three times and had a total of eight children. His first marriage was to Dodie Levy Fraser and lasted six years before they were divorced in 1962.
- His second wife, Marjorie Lynn Noe, was one of the few people who refused to attend his funeral, because she told her children that the divorce had already been like a death to her. When Michael filed for divorce from Lynn, it cost him $26 million.
- His last wife was former make-up artist, Cindy Clerico, whom he met near the end of the "Little House" run in 1981, and married two years later.
- A community building at Malibu's Bluffs Park was named The Michael Landon Center following his death.
- Michael's other TV acting credits include "Sheriff of Cochise" (1956), "Wire Service" (1956), "Crossroads" (1957), "Tales of Wells Fargo" (1957), "Cheyenne" (1958), "The Texan" (1958), "Wanted Dead or Alive" (1959), "The Rifleman" (1959) and "The Red Skelton Show" (1970).
- His film credits include "Fight for the Title" (1957), "I Was a Teenage Werewolf" (1957),

"High School Confidential!" (1958), "The Legend of Tom Dooley" (1959), "Luke and the Tenderfoot" (1965) (TV), "Love is Forever" (1983) (TV), "Where Pigeons Go to Die" (1990) (TV) and "Us" (1991) (TV).

- **Karen Grassle** was born on February 25, 1942 in Berkeley, California.
- Her father, Gene Grassle, ran a gas station and her mother managed a restaurant.
- Karen was known as the miracle baby in her family because, previous to her birth, her mother had 4 miscarriages.
- She has been married three times. Her first husband was actor Leon Russom. In 1982, she married J. Allen Radford, a real estate developer, with whom she adopted a daughter, Lily. In 1991, she married Dr. Scott T. Sutherland, a psychiatrist.
- Karen graduated from Ventura High School in 1959 and afterwards enrolled in the University of California, Berkeley. She graduated with two BA degrees in 1965, one in English and the other in Dramatic Art.
- She then received a scholarship to the Royal Academy of Dramatic Art in London and eventually became head of its Voice Department.
- Karen's first acting job in New York City was in the play "Gingham Tree". It was at this point she started calling herself "Gabriel Tree".
- In 1974, she auditioned for the role of "Caroline Ingalls" in "Little House on the Prairie". She won the role from 47 other

actresses and Michael Landon convinced her to revert back to her birth name. In all, she appeared in 166 episodes from 1974 to 1982.

- After the series ended, she moved to Louisville, Kentucky, where she remained active in theater. She later became co-founder and artistic director of Santa Fe's Resource Theatre Company and starred in "Wit" at the Arizona Theatre Company.
- A long-involved advocate for women's rights, she wrote and co-starred in the mini-movie "Battered" (1978) (TV), which dealt with the issues of domestic violence.
- She was inducted into the Hall of Great Western Performers at the National Cowboy and Western Heritage Museum in 1998.
- In 2006, she performed in "Driving Miss Daisy" in the starring role of "Miss Daisy" at the Manitoba Theatre Centre in Winnipeg, Manitoba, Canada.
- In 2008, Karen appeared in commercials for Premier bathtubs.
- Karen's other TV credits include "Gunsmoke" (1974), "The Love Boat" (1981), "Hotel" (1983) and "Murder, She Wrote" (1988).
- Her film credits include "Emily, Emily" (1977) (TV), "The President's Mistress" (1978) (TV), "Harry's War" (1981), "Cocaine: One Man's Seduction" (1983) (TV), "Little House: The Last Farewell" (1984) (TV) and "Wyatt Earp" (1994).
- Karen now lives in Pacific Palisades, California with her daughter.

- **Melissa Ellen Gilbert** was born on May 8, 1964 in Los Angeles, California.
- She was born to a Jewish family but was adopted by actor Paul Gilbert (born Paul MacMahon) and his wife, Barbara Cowan, when she was one day old. She had two siblings, Sara Gilbert, who played "Darlene Conner" on the popular television series "Roseanne", and Jonathan Gilbert, with whom she co-starred in "Little House on the Prairie".
- Melissa has been married twice and is presently wed to actor Bruce Boxleitner. She has two children and two step-children.
- In 1974, Melissa won the role of "Laura Ingalls" over 500 other young actresses. She went on to appear in 189 episodes from 1974 to 1983, and also starred in the three subsequent TV movies.
- She is the youngest person ever to receive a Star on the Hollywood Walk of Fame.
- Melissa had a highly publicised relationship with Rob Lowe during the eighties.
- She was inducted into the Hall of Great Western Performers at the National Cowboy and Western Heritage Museum in 1998.
- In 2001, Melissa was elected President of the Screen Actors Guild and re-elected in 2003. She announced, in 2005, that she would not seek a third term.
- Both her ex-spouses, Bo Brinkman and Bruce Boxleitner, played Confederate officers in "Gods and Generals" (2003).
- Melissa was ranked No.31 in VH 1's list of the "100 Greatest Kid Stars".

- In 2006, she was co-host, with Leeza Gibbons, of an infomercial for "Sheer Cover" cosmetics.
- In 2007, was co-host with Chaz Dean, of an infomercial for Chaz's "Wen" healthy hair care system.
- In 2008, she played "Caroline 'Ma' Ingalls" in "Little House on the Prairie", a musical adaptation for the stage at the Guthrie Theatre, Minneapolis, Minnesota.
- Melissa regularly keeps in contact with her friend Alison Arngrim, who played her nemesis "Nellie Oleson" on "Little House".
- Her other TV credits include "Gunsmoke" (1972), "Emergency!" (1972), "The Love Boat" (1978), "The Hidden Room" (1991), "Stand by Your Man" (1992), "Batman" (1994), "Babylon 5" (1996), "Touched by an Angel" (1998), "Adoption" (2003) and "Nip/Tuck" (2006).
- Melissa's film credits include "The Miracle Worker" (1979) (TV), "Splendor in the Grass" (1981) (TV), "Sylvester" (1985), "Donor" (1990) (TV), "Dying to Remember" (1993) (TV), "Christmas in My Hometown" (1996) (TV), "Sanctuary" (2001) (TV), "Spring Thaw" (2007) (TV) and "Betrayal of Trust" (2008).

- **Melissa Sue Anderson** was born on September 26, 1962 in Berkeley, California.
- She was born to Jim, a salesman, and Marion, a housewife, Anderson.
- Melissa and her older sister and their parents moved around California quite frequently until they decided to settle in Los Angeles. Her

- parents subsequently divorced when she was 12.
- Her show business career got underway when a dance teacher urged her parents to find an agent for her. She began by doing TV commercials.
- Melissa's first TV guest appearance was in "Bewitched" (1972) and her second was in "The Brady Bunch" (1973), where she played "Millicent", the girl who kissed "Bobby".
- She attended California Parochial High School in Burbank when she wasn't filming "Little House".
- In 1974, she was cast as "Mary Ingalls" in "Little House on the Prairie". She went on to appear in 131 episodes from 1974 to 1981.
- In the later years of "Little House" she cut her hair short and wore a brown wig for the episodes after that.
- She won a Daytime Emmy Award for her performance in "Which Mother Is Mine?" an "ABC Afternoon Special" (1979).
- Melissa was offered the Brooke Shields role in "Blue Lagoon" (1980) but turned it down due to "overexposure".
- Her first movie role was in the Montreal-made horror film, "Happy Birthday To Me" (1981), opposite Glenn Ford.
- Melissa's first publicly known romance was with actor Lorenzo Lamas, with whom she made an appearance in the TV series "The Love Boat".
- At 18, Melissa dated Frank Sinatra Jr., who was then 35.

- At the age of 19, she made her stage debut at Burt Reynolds' Dinner Theatre in Jupiter, Florida, in Neil Simon's "The Gingerbread Lady".
- She was the "1984 NATO Female Star of the Year" for her starring role in the feature film "Chattanooga Choo Choo" (1984).
- When she was on "Little House", her nickname was "Missy".
- Melissa has been married to producer/writer Michael Sloan since 1990, and they have two children, Piper and Griffin.
- She was the associate producer for the next to last TV project Michael Landon made before dying: "Where Pigeons Go to Die" (1990).
- Melissa has a Star on the Hollywood Walk of Fame and in 1998, was inducted into the Hall of Great Western Performers at the National Cowboy and Western Heritage Museum.
- Her other TV acting credits include "Shaft" (1973), "A New Kind of Family" (1979), "Fantasy Island" (1980), "Murder, She Wrote" (1984), "The Love Boat" (1986), "The Equalizer" (1988), "Alfred Hitchcock Presents" (1989), "X-Men" (1994) and "Partners" (1999).
- Melissa's film credits include "Little House on the Prairie" (1974) (TV), "James at 15" (1977) (TV), "An Innocent Love" (1982) (TV), "The Suicide Club" (1988), "The Return of Sam McCloud" (1989) (TV), "Forbidden Nights" (1990) (TV), "Killer Lady" (1995), "10.5 : Apocalypse" (2006) (TV) and "Marco Polo" (2007) (TV) (voice).

- In 2002, Melissa, Michael and the kids moved to Montreal, Canada to live.
- On July 1, 2007 (Canada Day) they became Canadian citizens.

- **Sidney Greenbush** was born Sidney Robin Danae Bush on May 25, 1970 in Hollywood, California.
- Her parents were Billy Green and Carol Kay Bush. Her brother is actor Clay Bush.
- Shared the role of "Carrie Ingalls" in "Little House" with her identical twin, Lindsay.
- Appeared in the movie "Sunshine" (1973) (TV) with Lindsay (shared role) and this brought them to the attention of the "Little House" producers.
- In 1974, they were cast in "Little House on the Prairie", appearing in 181 episodes from 1974 to 1982.
- Sidney started taking formal riding lessons when she was 13, and has been in equestrian competitions. She later barrel-raced with her college rodeo team, before moving on to pro-rodeo and becoming a member of the Women's Professional Rodeo Association.
- In 2001, she was considered the West Coast's top-ranked barrel racer.
- Sidney Graduated from Santa Monica High School in 1988.
- She also earned an associate's degree in animal science from Pierce College in Woodland Hills, California.

- In 1998, she was inducted into the Hall of Great Western Performers at the National Cowboy and Western Heritage Museum.
- In 1996, she married machinist Charles Caraccilo but they divorced in 2000. She then married Rocky Foster, who trains horses for TV and movies.
- Sidney and Rocky live on their ranch in Visalia, California.
- She has also put together a line of original designer jewellery that she sells to her fans.
- Sidney's other movie roles include "Little House on the Prairie" (1974) (TV), "Little House Years" (1979) (TV) and "Hambone and Hillie" (1983).

- **Lindsay Greenbush** was born Rachel Lindsay Rene Bush on May 25, 1970 in Hollywood, California.
- After graduating from Santa Monica High School in 1988, she went to Santa Monica College.
- She has been married to Frank Dornan since 2001, but they are now separated.
- Worked at a ski resort in Taos, New Mexico in 1993-95. It was here she met the father of her daughter, Katlynn Danae, but she no longer has any contact with him.
- In 1974, she was cast, with her sister, as "Carrie Ingalls" in the TV series "Little House on the Prairie". She played in 181 episodes from 1974 to 1982.
- The episode "The Godsister" was the only episode that featured Lindsay and Sidney at

the same time. They played "Carrie" and god sister "Alyssa".

- In 1998, she was inducted into the Hall of Great Western Performers at the National Cowboy and Western Heritage Museum.
- In addition to acting, she has many other interests and pursuits, including as an amateur boxer, having competed in her first bout on August 4, 2007.
- Lindsay is also actively involved with Kids Gloves Boxing Studios in Simi Valley, California, working with kids and adults.
- She has only appeared in one other TV series and that was "Matt Houston" (1983).
- Her film credits include "Little House on the Prairie" (1974) (TV) and "Little House Years" (1979) (TV).

- **Matthew Charles Laborteaux** was born on December 8, 1966 in Los Angeles, California.
- He was born with autism and a hole in the heart.
- Matthew is the adopted son of Frances Marshall Laborteaux and brother of actor Patrick Labyorteaux and actress Jane Laborteaux.
- In 1978, he was cast as "Albert Quinn Ingalls" in "Little House on the Prairie". He played in 87 episodes from 1978 to 1983.
- On "Little House" a few seasons before he played the "Ingalls" adopted son "Albert" he played a young "Charles Ingalls" (Michael Landon) in an episode where "Charles" remembers his past.

- In 1992, he and his brother, Patrick, with whom he founded the Youth Rescue Fund, a charity dedicated to helping runaways, appeared before a House sub-committee to plead the case of runaways and raised $11 million for youth shelters across America.
- Matthew's other TV credits include "The Rookies" (1975), "Mulligan's Stew" (1977), "Lou Grant" (1979), "The Love Boat" (1982), "Whiz Kids" (1983-84) 18 episodes, "Highway to Heaven" (1985), "Night Court" (1989) and "Spider-Man" (1995-97) (voice).
- His film credits include "A Woman Under the Influence" (1974), "A Circle of Children" (1977) (TV), "Killing Stone" (1978) (TV), "Little House : Look Back to Yesterday" (1983) (TV), "Deadly Friend" (1986), "The Last to Go" (1991) (TV), "Everyone's Hero" (2006) (voice) and "Bride Wars" (2009) (voice).
- Matthew has also worked as a voice actor for video games.

- **Katherine "Scottie" MacGregor** was born Dorlee Deane MacGregor on January 12, 1925 in Glendale, California.
- She lived in Denver, Colorado for a time as a child.
- Scottie was briefly married to Bert Remsen.
- Her first movie role was an uncredited part in "On the Waterfront" (1954) starring Marlon Brando.
- Before moving to Los Angeles in 1970 she worked as a stage actress on Broadway, off

Broadway and in regional theater in and around New York City.

- In 1974, she was cast as "Harriet Oleson" in "Little House on the Prairie". She appeared in 151 episodes from 1974 to 1983.
- She could not appear in the final feature TV movie "Little House: The Last Farewell" (1984), because she was on a pilgrimage in India.
- Her other TV credits include "Love of Life" (1951), "Play of the Week" (1959), "Mannix" (1971), "Emergency!" (1972), "All in the Family" (1973) and "Ironside" (1974).
- Scottie's film credits include "The Student Nurses" (1970), "The Traveling Executioner" (1970) uncredited, "The Death of Me Yet" (1971) (TV), "The Girls of Huntington House" (1973) (TV) and "Tell Me Where It Hurts" (1974) (TV).
- She is happy, retired, in excellent health and living in Hollywood.

- **Richard Bull** was born on June 26, 1924 in Zion, Illinois.
- He was married to Barbara "Bobbi" Collentine from 1948 until his death in 2014.
- Richard began his stage career at the famous Goodman Theatre in Chicago.
- He had a recurring role as a ship's doctor on the mid-60's fantasy series "Voyage to the Bottom of the Sea".
- In 1974, he was cast as "Nels Oleson" in "Little House on the Prairie". He appeared in 145

episodes from 1974 to 1983. Richard also appeared in the three subsequent TV movies.

- Over the years Richard made over 100 film and TV appearances.
- Richard's other TV credits include "Perry Mason" (1958), "Highway Patrol" (1959), "Harrigan and Son" (1961), "Ben Casey" (1964), "My Three Sons" (1966), "The Andy Griffith Show" (1967), "Family Affair" (1969), "The Partridge Family" (1972), "Barnaby Jones" (1976), "Amazing Stories" (1985) and "ER" (1999).
- His film credits include "Full of Life" (1956) uncredited, "Della" (1964), "Hour of the Gun" (1967), "The Thomas Crown Affair" (1968), "Lawman" (1971), "High Plains Drifter" (1973), "The Parallax View" (1974), "A Death in California" (1985) (TV), "Where Pigeons Go to Die" (1990) (TV), "Osso Bucco" (2007) and "Witless Protection" (2008).
- Richard lived in his hometown of Chicago, Illinois. He moved back there in 1994 with his wife, after years of living in Los Angeles.

- **Alison Margaret Arngrim** was born on January 18, 1962 in New York City, New York.
- She is the daughter of Thor Arngrim (a well-known Hollywood manager) and Norma MacMillan (a voice actress).
- Alison has been married twice and is presently wed to Robert Paul Schoonover (a musician). She has a 22 year old step-daughter.
- After unsuccessful auditions for the roles of "Mary and Laura Ingalls", she was cast as

"Nellie Oleson" in "Little House on the Prairie". She went on to appear in 105 episodes from 1974 to 1982.

- Her signature "Nellie Oleson" curls were a wig, which were held so tightly to her head that her scalp bled.
- Since "Little House" finished, Alison has appeared on TV shows such as "The Tonight Show with Jay Leno", "Extra", "Entertainment Tonight", "Larry King Live" and "Today".
- Alison worked as a poster model for three years after leaving "Little House".
- Following the AIDS-related death of her "Little House" husband, actor Steve Tracy, she began working as an AIDS activist.
- She is on the national advisory committee of the National Association to Protect Children.
- In 2000, she routinely appeared as a stand-up comic in Los Angeles clubs.
- In 2005, she was No.96 on VH 1's "100 Greatest Kid Stars".
- In 2006, she won a TV Land Award for the "Character Most Desperately in Need of a Timeout" ("Nellie Oleson").
- Alison is a vegetarian.
- She made a comedy record album in which she portrayed Amy Carter, the only daughter of ex-President Jimmy Carter. The record was called "Heeere's Amy - Alison Arngrim as Amy Carter".
- Alison's stage credits include "Butterflies Are Free", "In One Bed and Out the Other", "The Wool Gatherers" and "Hidden in the Laughter".

Recently she has been seen in Celebration Theatre's "Suena Queen of the Tango".

- Her TV show credits include "Room 222", "Fantasy Island" and "The Love Boat".
- Whilst her film credits include "Throw Out the Anchor!" (1974), "I Married Wyatt Earp" (1983) (TV), "For the Love of May" (2000), "The Last Place on Earth" (2000), "Deal Le" (2007) and "Make the Yuletide Gay" (2009).
- Since both Alison's parents were always working, her Aunt Marion King was her guardian during her shooting days on the "Little House" set.
- Alison now lives in Marion's house up in the Hollywood hills with her husband and their cat "Hannibal".

- **Jonathan Gilbert** was born on July 10, 1968 in the United States of America.
- He is the adopted son of actress Barbara Crane and Paul Gilbert, and brother of Sara and Melissa Gilbert.
- In 1974, he was cast as "Willie Oleson" in "Little House on the Prairie". He appeared in 140 episodes from 1974 to 1983 and the two movie sequels.
- He is one of only six actors to appear throughout the entire series (from season one to the TV movie sequels).
- Jonathan's film credits include "The Miracle Worker" (1979) (TV) and "Brubaker" (1980) uncredited.
- Since "Little House" ended production, Jonathan attended and graduated from

Hamilton College with a B.A. degree followed by an M.B.A. in Finance from Bernard M. Baruch College's Zicklin School of Business.

- He is now working as a stockbroker in New York City.

- **Kevin Hagen** was born on April 3, 1928 in Chicago, Illinois.
- He was the son of professional ballroom dancers, Haakon Olaf Hagen and Marvel Lucile Wadsworth.
- His father left the family when he was five. Kevin was raised by his mother, two aunts and a grandmother, with some help from his uncle, a physician.
- The family moved to Portland, Oregon when Kevin was a teenager and he played baseball and football at Jefferson High School. He attended Oregon State University before enlisting in the U.S. Navy after the Second World War, and served in San Diego.
- Kevin did not start acting until he was 27, by which time he had worked for the U.S. State Department in Germany, earning a degree in international relations from the University of Southern California.
- He was spotted in a production of Eugene O'Neill's "Desire Under the Elms" and given a guest role on the classic 1950's TV series "Dragnet".
- Kevin considered his big break was the role of a Confederate soldier who kills James Stewart's son and daughter-in-law in the 1965 film "Shenandoah".

- In 1974, he was cast as "Dr. Hiram Baker" in "Little House on the Prairie". He appeared in 113 episodes from 1974 to 1983.
- He performed and toured in a one-man show he wrote based on the "Doc Baker" character called "A Playful Dose of Prairie Wisdom". While performing that show he met his fourth wife, Jan. They were married in 1993.
- In 1992, he moved to Grants Pass, Oregon and continued his acting career.
- In 2004, he was diagnosed with esophageal cancer.
- Kevin was married four times and had one son.
- His son Kristopher Hagen (b. 1971) is a Special Education teacher and a high school basketball coach in Bakersfield, California.
- Kevin appeared in over 100 TV shows including "The Gray Ghost" (1957), "Tales of Wells Fargo" (1957), "Yancy Derringer" (1958-59) as "John Colton" in 18 episodes, "Sugarfoot" (1960), "Bat Masterson" (1961), "77 Sunset Strip" (1962), "Perry Mason" (1965), "Bonanza" (1967), "The Virginian" (1969), "Bracken's World" (1969), "Ironside" (1972), "M.A.S.H." (1978) and "Matlock" (1987).
- His film credits include "Gunsmoke in Tucson" (1958), "Pork Chop Hill" (1959), "The Man from Galveston" (1963), "The Learning Tree" (1969), "The Delphi Bureau" (1972) (TV), "The Hunter" (1980), "Bonanza : The Next Generation" (1988) (TV) and "The Ambulance" (1990).

- **Dabbs Greer** was born Robert William Greer on April 2, 1917 in Fairview, Missouri.
- He was the son of Bernice Irene Dabbs, a speech teacher, and Randall Alexander Greer, a druggist.
- Dabbs first acting experience was on stage in a children's theatre production when he was eight years old.
- He attended Drury College in Springfield, Missouri, where he earned a B.A. degree.
- Dabbs joined the Pasadena Playhouse in California as an actor, instructor and administrator from 1943 to 1950.
- He made his film debut in "Reign of Terror" (1949) in an uncredited bit part.
- Dabbs appeared in three separate episodes of "Adventures of Superman", including the very first episode titled "Superman on Earth" (1952).
- His other two appearances were in the episodes "Five Minutes to Doom" (1953) and "The Superman Silver Mine" (1958).
- He was often cast as a minister, he performed the marriages of "Rob and Laura Petrie" in "The Dick Van Dyke Show" and of "Mike and Carol Brady" in "The Brady Bunch".
- In 1974, Dabbs was cast as "Reverend Alden" in "Little House on the Prairie". He appeared in 76 episodes from 1974 to 1983, and the two subsequent TV movies.
- Dabbs was one of the great TV and film character actors, with over 250 appearances.

- His other TV credits include "Dick Tracy" (1950), "The Lone Ranger" (1952), "Father Knows Best" (1955), "Cheyenne" (1956), "Fury" (1957), "The Restless Gun" (1958), "Troubleshooters" (1959), "Bus Stop" (1961), "Peyton Place" (1965), "Hank" (1965), "Bonanza" (1971), "The Greatest American Hero" (1982), "Roseanne" (1989), "Picket Fences" (1992-96) as "Reverend Henry Novotny" in 20 episodes and "Lizzie McGuire" (2003).
- Dabbs film credits include "Bitter Creek" (1954), "The McConnell Story" (1955), "Last Train from Gun Hill" (1959) uncredited, "Roustabout" (1964), "Shenandoah" (1965), "Rage" (1972), "Two Moon Junction" (1988), "Con Air" (1997) and "The Green Mile" (1999).

"The Loner"

Years : 1965 - 1966

Episodes : 26 (1 season)

Cast :-

Lloyd Bridges (b. 1913 d. 1998) - Played William Colton

Synopsis :-
An ex-soldier encounters various problems after the Civil War.

Trivia & Tidbits :-

"The Show"

- **"The Loner"** premiered on CBS on September 18, 1965 and last aired on March 12, 1966.
- The show ran for one season with a total of 26 black and white episodes.
- The series was created by Rod Serling ("The Twilight Zone") and produced by Greenway Productions, Interlaken Productions, CBS Television Network and 20th Century Fox Television.
- Filming took place at the Iverson Movie Ranch, California.

- The theme music was composed by Jerry Goldsmith.
- Both Philip Morris and Proctor & Gamble sponsored the series.

"In Memoriam"

- **Lloyd Bridges** died of natural causes on March 10, 1998 (85) in Los Angeles, California.

"The Star"

- **Lloyd Bridges** was born Lloyd Vernet Bridges Jr. on January 15, 1913 in San Leandro, California.
- He was the son of Harriet Evelyn (nee Brown) and Lloyd Vernet Bridges Snr., a man involved in the hotel business. He also once owned a movie theatre.
- Lloyd graduated from Petaluma High School and studied political science at the University of California, Los Angeles.
- He made his acting debut in an uncredited part in the film "Freshman Love" (1936).
- Lloyd then made his Broadway debut in a production of Shakespeare's Othello in 1937.
- Several more movie roles followed including "Harmon of Michigan" (1941), "Blondie Goes to College" (1942), "Saddle Leather Law" (1944), "A Walk in the Sun" (1945), "Abilene Town" (1946), "Colt .45" (1950) and "High Noon" (1952).

- He made his TV debut in an episode ("Man's First Debt") of "The Bigelow Theatre" in 1951.
- In 1958, he was cast as "Mike Nelson" in the TV series "Sea Hunt". He appeared in 155 episodes from 1958 to 1961.
- In 1962, he hosted and appeared in his own TV series "The Lloyd Bridges Show". He appeared in 28 episodes from 1962 to 1963.
- Then in 1965, he was cast as "William Colton" in the TV series "The Loner". He appeared in 26 episodes from 1965 to 1966.
- In 1975, he was cast as "Joe Forrester" in the TV series of the same name. He appeared in 23 episodes from 1975 to 1976.
- Lloyd appeared as "Evan Brent" in Alex Haley's TV mini-series "Roots" in 1977.
- Another TV mini-series he appeared in was "How the West Was Won" (1978). He played the character "Orville Gant" in 4 episodes.
- In 1982, he was cast as "Ben Geyser" in the TV mini-series "The Blue and the Gray". He appeared in 3 episodes.
- Then in 1984, he appeared as "Caleb Quinn" in 3 episodes of the TV mini-series "George Washington".
- Following this, Lloyd played the character "Grant Harper" in the TV series "Paper Dolls". He appeared in 13 episodes in 1984.
- After this series, he appeared as "Jefferson Davis" in the TV mini-series "North and South, Book II" (1986). He appeared in 6 episodes.
- In 1990, he was cast as "Jonathan Turner" in the TV series "Capital News". He appeared in 13 episodes.

- His last TV series, "Harts of the West" (1993-94), was as character "Jake Tyrell". He appeared in 7 episodes.
- Lloyd's last acting appearance was in the film "Meeting Daddy".
- He was married to Dorothy Dean Bridges for nearly sixty years (1938-1998). They had four children - Beau, Garrett, Jeff and Cindy. Garrett died (1948) of SIDS when he was only a few months old.
- Lloyd's two other sons, Beau and Jeff, are actors. Jeff won the Oscar for best actor in 2010. The film was "Crazy Heart" (2009).
- During the Second World War, Lloyd enlisted in the U.S. Coast Guard.
- In the 1950's, he was briefly blacklisted by the House Un-American Activities Committee for his links to the Actors' Lab (a group linked to the Communist Party). He was subsequently cleared by the F.B.I.
- Lloyd has a Star on the Hollywood Walk of Fame for his contribution to television.
- He was nominated for two primetime Emmy awards, once for "The Alcoa Hour" in 1957 and once for "Seinfeld" in 1998.
- Lloyd's other film credits include "The Tall Texan" (1953), "Wichita" (1955), "Around the World Under the Sea" (1966), "Running Wild" (1973), "Flying High" (1980), "Flying High II : The Sequel" (1982), "Hot Shots!" (1991), "Hot Shots! 2" (1993) and "Jane Austen's Mafia!" (1998).
- His other TV credits include "Crossroads" (1955), "The Frank Sinatra Show" (1958),

"Zane Grey Theatre" (1957-61) 4 episodes, "Mission: Impossible" (1966), "Here's Lucy" (1972, "Battlestar Galactica" (1978), "Matt Houston" (1983), "Disneyland" (1986) and "Seinfeld" (1997).

"A Man Called Shenandoah"

Years : 1965 - 1966

Episodes : 34 (1 season)

Cast :-

Robert Horton (b. 1924 d. 2016) - Played Shenandoah

Synopsis :-
A man has amnesia after being shot and roams the West in search of his identity.

Trivia & Tidbits :-

"The Show"

- **"A Man Called Shenandoah"** premiered on ABC on September 13, 1965 and last aired on May 16, 1966.
- The show ran for one season with a total of 34 black and white episodes.
- The series was created by E. Jack Neuman and produced by Bronze Enterprises and MGM Television.
- Location scenes were filmed in California's High Sierras and Mojave Desert.

- Robert Horton composed new lyrics for the traditional song "Oh Shenandoah" and sang the theme song.
- In 1965, Robert Horton recorded the song for Columbia Records.
- The ring "Shenandoah" wears belonged to his brother "Walter", killed during the Civil War.

"In Memoriam"

- **Robert Horton** died of natural causes on March 9, 2016 (89) in Los Angeles, California.

"The Star"

- **Robert Horton** was born Meade Howard Horton Jr. on July 29, 1924 in Los Angeles, California.
- He has been married to Marilynn Bradley for forty eight years and they have no children.
- Robert appeared in a number of TV shows before he took the role of "Flint McCullough" in "Wagon Train". The most notable was the TV version of "Kings Row" (1955). The show featured Jack Kelly ("Maverick") and ran for seven episodes as part of the "Warner Bros. Presents" series.
- In 1957, he was cast as "Flint McCullough" in "Wagon Train". He appeared in 189 episodes from 1957 to 1962.

- He also starred in seven "Alfred Hitchcock Presents" episodes from 1956 to 1960.
- To prepare for the role as "Flint McCullough", Robert got in his car and drove the route the wagon trains actually travelled to get a feel for the terrain.
- Robert owned the Appaloosa horse he used to ride in the show. He named the horse "Stormy Night" after he bought it on a stormy night at a rodeo in Idaho.
- In 1962, after five seasons, Robert left "Wagon Train" to pursue his career in musical theatre.
- He was replaced by Robert Fuller ("Laramie" 1959-1963) who played "Cooper Smith".
- After "Wagon Train" he played in two more TV series - "A Man Called Shenandoah" (1965-1966) and "As the World Turns" (1983-1984).
- For many years, after "Wagon Train", Robert performed in theatres and nightclubs all over America and Australia.
- In 2006, Robert received the Cowboy Spirit Award at the 16th Annual Bison Homes Festival held in Phoenix, Arizona.
- Robert's favourite movie is "Uncertain Glory" (1944) and favourite actors are Errol Flynn and Myrna Loy.
- His hobbies include flying and collecting fancy cars. He owned a Piper Comanche 250 airplane from 1957 to 1998 and he logged over 1,000 hours whilst flying all across the country.
- Robert and his wife live in Encino, California.
- His other TV credits include "The Lone Ranger" (1954), "Meet Mr. McNulty" (1955), "Sheriff of

Cochise" (1956), "The Red Skelton Show" (1963) and "Murder, She Wrote" (1989).

- Robert's other film credits include "Return of the Texan" (1952), "Pony Soldier" (1952), "The Man Is Armed" (1956), "The Green Slime" (1968) and "Red River" (1988) (TV).

"The Monroes"

Years : 1966 - 1967

Episodes : 26 (1 season)

Cast :-

Michael Anderson Jr. (b. 1943) - Played Clayt Monroe

Barbara Hershey (b. 1948) - Played Kathy Monroe

Keith Schultz (b. 1953) - Played Jefferson Monroe

Kevin Schultz (b. 1953) - Played Fennimore Monroe

Tammy Locke (b. 1959) - Played Amy Monroe

Synopsis :-
The story of five orphans trying to survive as a family in Wyoming.

Trivia & Tidbits :-

"The Show"

- **"The Monroes"** premiered on ABC on September 7, 1966 and last aired on March 15, 1967.
- The show ran for one season with a total of 26 episodes.
- The series was set around the Grand Teton National Park near Jackson, Wyoming.
- Milt Rosen created the series and it was produced by Qualis Productions and 20th Century Fox Studios.
- The show faced stiff competition on the other networks - "The Virginian" (NBC) and "Lost in Space" and "The Beverly Hillbillies" (CBS).

"The Stars"

- **Michael Anderson Jr.** was born on August 6, 1943 in Hillingdon, Middlesex, England.
- He is the son of film director Michael Anderson Sr. and stepson of actress Adrienne Ellis.
- Michael attended the Arts Education School where he studied drama and ballet.
- He made his TV acting debut in an episode ("A Matter of Justice") of "The Count of Monte Cristo" in 1956.
- Michael made his film debut in the movie "The Moonraker" in 1958.
- Several more film appearances followed including "The Sundowners" (1960), "Reach for Glory" (1962), "The Greatest Story Ever Told" (1965), "Major Dundee" (1965), "The Sons of Katie Elder" (1965) and "The Glory Guys" (1965).

- In 1966, he was cast as "Clayt Monroe" in the TV series "The Monroes". He appeared in 26 episodes from 1966 to 1967.
- In 1982, he was cast as "Martin" in the TV series "Romance Theatre". He appeared in 5 episodes.
- His last acting appearance, to date, was in the TV movie "Rescuers: Stories of Courage: Two Families" in 1998.
- Michael has been married three times – Maria O'Brien, Victoria Harrington and Marina Anderson. He has one child with Ms. O'Brien and three children with Ms. Harrington.
- His other film credits include "WUSA" (1970), "The Last Movie" (1971), "Evel Knievel" (1974)(TV), "Logan's Run" (1976), "Nightkill" (1980), "Sunset Grill" (1993), "Terminal Rush" (1996) and "Elvis Meets Nixon" (1997)(TV).
- Michael's other TV credits include "Ivanhoe" (1958), "Stoney Burke" (1963), "The Name of the Game" (1969), "Medical Center" (1970-72) 2 episodes, "The Mod Squad" (1972) 2 episodes, "Ironside" (1974) 2 episodes, "Cannon" (1976), "Hawaii Five-O" (1971-76) 4 episodes, "Fantasy Island" (1978-79) 2 episodes, "Chips" (1982), "Magnum, P.I." (1984), "Sweating Bullets" (1991) and "Highlander" (1995).

- **Barbara Hershey** was born Barbara Lynn Herzstein on February 5, 1948 in Hollywood, California.

- She is the daughter of Melrose (nee Moore) and Arnold Nathan Herzstein. Her father was a horse racing columnist.
- Barbara attended Hollywood High School until, at age 17, she decided to pursue an acting career.
- She made her acting debut in an episode ("Chivalry Isn't Dead") of "Gidget" in 1965.
- This was followed by two more appearances on "Gidget" and two appearances on "The Farmer's Daughter".
- In 1966, she was cast as "Kathy Monroe" in the TV series "The Monroes". She appeared in 26 episodes from 1966 to 1967.
- Barbara's first film appearance was as "Stacey Iverson" in the film "With Six You Get Eggroll" (1968).
- In 1973, she changed her stage name to "Barbara Seagull". By 1976 she had changed her name back to "Hershey".
- In 1993, she appeared as "Clara Allen" in 4 episodes of the TV mini-series "Return to Lonesome Dove".
- Then in 1995, she was cast as "Dr. Francesca Alberghetti" in the TV series "Chicago Hope". She appeared in 25 episodes from 1999 to 2000.
- In 2004, she was cast as "Gennie Carver" in the TV series "The Mountain". She appeared in 13 episodes from 2004 to 2005.
- In 2012, she was cast in a recurring role as "Cora Mills" in the TV series "Once Upon a Time". She has appeared in 15 episodes from 2012 to 2016.

- In 2016, she was cast as "Ann Rutledge" in the TV series "Damien". To date she has appeared in 10 episodes.
- Barbara has been married once to Stephen Douglas (1992-93), however, she had two other long-term relationships – David Carradine (1969-75) and Naveen Andrews (1999-2009). She has one son, Tom, with Mr. Carradine.
- In 1991, she won a Golden Globe Award for her performance in the TV movie "A Killing in a Small Town.
- In 1997, she was nominated for an Academy Award for her performance in "A Portrait of a Lady" (Best Actress in a Supporting Role).
- Barbara is the first performer to win back to back awards at the Cannes Film Festival.
- Her other film credits include "Last Summer" (1969), "The Pursuit of Happiness" (1971), "Boxcar Bertha" (1972), "You and Me" (1974), "The Stunt Man" (1980), "The Right Stuff" (1983), "The Natural" (1984), "Hannah and Her Sisters" (1986), "Hoosiers" (1986), "Beaches" (1988), "Falling Down" (1993), "Passion" (1999), "Lantana" (2001), "Riding the Bullet" (2004), "Albert Schweitzer" (2009), "Black Swan" (2010) and "The 9th Life of Louis Drax" (2016).
- Barbara's other TV credits include "Daniel Boone" (1967), "Run for Your Life" (1968), "Love Story" (1973), "Kung Fu" (1974) 2 episodes, "American Playhouse" (1982) 2 episodes, "Agatha Christie's Poirot" (2010) and "Once Upon a Time in Wonderland" (2014).

- **Keith Sean Schultz** was born on September 16, 1953 in Santa Monica, California.
- His parents are Earl and Evelyn Schultz.
- Keith made his acting debut, at age 2, in the movie "The Long Grey Line" (1955).
- In 1966, he was cast as "Jefferson Monroe" in the TV series "The Monroes". He appeared in 26 episodes from 1966 to 1967.
- His last acting appearance, to date, was in an episode ("Two-Timin' Man") of "Brothers" in 1986.
- In 1967, he formed a musical group, "The Monroe Doctrine", with his brother Kevin.
- After he finished his acting career, Keith became a professional photographer with his brother Kevin. They are still at it in 2016.
- Keith's other TV credits include "Gunsmoke" (1967), "The Flying Nun" (1968) and "Cannon" (1973).

- **Kevin Edward Schultz** was born on September 16, 1953 in Santa Monica, California.
- His parents are Earl and Evelyn Schultz.
- Like his brother, Keith, he made his acting debut in the film "The Long Grey Line" (1955).
- In 1966, he was cast as "Fennimore Monroe" in the TV series "The Monroes". He appeared in 26 episodes from 1966 to 1967.
- In 1968, he was cast as "Tom Sawyer" in the TV series "The New Adventures of Huckleberry

Finn". He appeared in 20 episodes from 1968 to 1969.

- His last acting appearance, to date, was in an episode ("Two-Timin' Man") of "Brothers" in 1986.
- In 1967, he formed a musical group, "The Monroe Doctrine", with his brother Keith.
- Following his acting career he became a professional photographer with his brother Keith. They are still in the business as at 2016.
- In 1978, he played a surfer in the hit film "Big Wednesday".
- Kevin's other TV credits include "Iron Horse" (1967), "Lucas Tanner" (1975) and "Eight Is Enough" (1980) 2 episodes.

- **Tammy Locke** was born on September 19, 1959 in California.
- Her parents, Lola and Earl, both worked for the Northrop Corporation.
- Tammy made her acting debut as "Sally Laurents" in an episode ("The Voice of Charlie Pont") of "Alcoa Premiere" in 1962.
- In 1966, she was cast as "Amy Monroe" in the TV series "The Monroes". She appeared in 26 episodes from 1966 to 1967.
- Her last acting appearance before she took a break was in an episode ("Baker's Dozen") of "Gunsmoke" in 1967.

- Tammy has been married to Tom Arriola since 1996. They have one son, Robert.
- From 1962 to 1968, Tammy appeared in several TV commercials.
- In 1974, Tammy began her musical career which lasted for many years. She toured with the band "California Express" for 5-6 years.
- In 1979, at age 19, she became a professional Roller Derby skater with the Detroit Devils.
- Following this she had her own radio show called "The Tammy Jean Show".
- In 2010, she resumed her acting career with a guest appearance in an episode ("War") of "Private Practice".
- Tammy's other film credits include "The Naked Kiss" (1964) uncredited, "Once a Thief" (1965), "Meet Me in St. Louis" (1966)(TV), "Matted" (2010)(TV) and "The Murder of Hi Good" (2012).
- Her other TV credits include "The Middle" (2011), "Medium" (2011), "Franklin & Bash" (2012), "Kickin' It" (2012) and "Your Honor?" (2014).

"Nichols"

Years : 1971 - 1972

Episodes : 24 (1 season)

Cast :-

James Garner (b. 1928 d. 2014) - Played Frank Nichols

Margot Kidder (b. 1948) - Played Ruth

Neva Patterson (b. 1920 d. 2010) - Played Ma Ketcham

John Beck (b. 1943) - Played Ketcham

Stuart Margolin (b. 1940) - Played Mitch

Synopsis :-
A soldier returns to his home town in Arizona.

Trivia & Tidbits :-

"The Show"

- **"Nichols"** premiered on NBC on September 16, 1971 and last aired on March 14, 1972.

- The show ran for one season with a total of 24 episodes.
- The series was created by Frank Pierson and produced by Cherokee Productions and Warner Bros. Television.
- Filming took place at Warner Bros. Studios, California.
- The original series music was by Bernardo Segall.

"In Memoriam"

- **James Garner** died of acute myocardial infarction on July 19, 2014 (86) in Brentwood, California.
- **Neva Patterson** died of complications from a broken hip on December 14, 2010 (90) in Brentwood, California.

"The Stars"

- **James Garner** was born James Scott Bumgarner on April 7, 1928 in Norman, Oklahoma.
- He was the son of Weldon Warren Bumgarner, a carpet layer, and Mildred Meek (part Cherokee Indian). He was the youngest of three brothers.
- James' mother died when he was five years old. His father remarried but the children disliked their "wicked stepmother".

- The marriage eventually broke down and his father moved away to Los Angeles. The children were left with relatives.
- After a stint in the Unites States Merchant Marine, James joined his father in Los Angeles and enrolled in Hollywood High School.
- Later, he joined the National Guard and served seven months.
- Following this, he enlisted in the U.S. Army and served fourteen months in Korea. He was wounded twice and awarded two Purple Hearts.
- After the war a friend got him a non-speaking part in the Broadway stage play "The Caine Mutiny Court-Martial" (1954).
- The play led to small television roles, television commercials and eventually a contract with Warner Bros.
- He made his TV acting debut in an episode ("Mountain Fortress") of "Cheyenne" in 1955.
- In 1957, he was cast as "Bret Maverick" in the TV series "Maverick". He appeared in 57 episodes from 1957 to 1960.
- In 1971, he was cast as "Nichols" in the TV series of the same name. He appeared in 24 episodes from 1971 to 1972.
- Then in 1974, he was cast as "Jim Rockford in the TV series "The Rockford Files". He appeared in 122 episodes from 1974 to 1980.
- In 1981, he was cast as "Bret Maverick" in the TV series of the same name. This was an attempt to revive the old series but it only lasted one season.

- In 1991, he was cast as "Councilman Jim Doyle" in the short-lived TV series "Man of the People". The series only lasted 10 episodes.
- In 2000, he provided the voice of "God" in the TV series "God, the Devil and Bob". He appeared in 13 episodes.
- In 2002, he was cast as "Chief Justice Thomas Brankin" in the TV series "First Monday". The series only lasted 13 episodes.
- In 2003, he was cast as "Jim Egan" in the TV series "8 Simple Rules...for Dating My Teenage Daughter" (he replaced John Ritter who had passed away). He appeared in 45 episodes from 2003 to 2005.
- His last acting appearance was in the video "DC Showcase Original Shorts Collection" in 2010. He provided the voice for "Shazam".
- James was married to Lois Clarke from 1956 until his death in 2014. They had two children, Kimberly and Gigi. He adopted his wife's nine year old daughter Kimberly after they were married.
- In 1978, he was inducted into the Off-Road Motorsports Hall of Fame.
- In 1986, James was inducted into the Oklahoma Hall of Fame.
- In 1990, he was inducted into the Hall of Great Western Performers at the National Cowboy and Western Heritage Museum.
- He has a Star on the Hollywood Walk of Fame for his contribution to the television industry.
- James had quintuple heart bypass surgery in 1988.

- His favorite film was "The Americanisation of Emily" (1964).
- James was a big fan of the Oakland Raiders football team.
- He has won four Golden Globe Awards (1958 – "Most Promising Newcomer – Male"); (1987 – "Best Performance by an Actor in a Mini-Series or Motion Picture Made for TV" for the "Hallmark Hall of Fame" episode "Promise"); (1991 – "Best Performance by an Actor in a Mini-Series or Motion Picture Made for TV" for "Decoration Day" (1990)(TV)); (1994 – "Best Performance by an Actor in a Mini-Series or "Motion Picture Made for TV" for "Barbarians at the Gate" (1993)(TV)).
- He was nominated for an Academy Award in 1986 as "Best Actor in a Leading Role" for "Murphy's Romance" (1985).
- In the 1990's, he appeared in eight "Rockford Files" TV movies.
- James' other film credits include "Toward the Unknown" (1956), "Shoot-Out at Medicine Bend" (1957), "Sayonara" (1957), "Up Periscope" (1959), "Cash McCall" (1960), "The Great Escape" (1963), "The Thrill of It All" (1963), "Move Over, Darling" (1963), "36 Hours" (1965), "Duel at Diablo" (1966), "Grand Prix" (1966), "How Sweet It Is!" (1968), "Support Your Local Sheriff!" (1969), "Marlowe" (1969), "Support Your Local Gunfighter" (1971), "The New Maverick" (1978)(TV), "Victor Victoria" (1982), "Sunset" (1988), "Maverick" (1994), "Twilight" (1998), "Space Cowboys" (2000), "Mark Twain's

Roughing It" (2002)(TV) and "The Notebook" (2004).

- His other TV credits include "Zane Grey Theatre" (1956), "Cheyenne" (1955-57) 4 episodes, "Hallmark Hall of Fame" (1986-89) 2 episodes and "Chicago Hope" (2000) 4 episodes.

- **Margot Kidder** was born Margaret Ruth Kidder on October 17, 1948 in Yellowknife, Northwest Territories, Canada.
- Her parents were Jocelyn Mary 'Jill' (nee Wilson), a history teacher, and Kendall Kidder, a mining engineer.
- Margot attended eleven schools over a twelve year period, eventually graduating from Havergal College in 1966.
- She made her acting debut in an episode ("After All, Who's Art Morrison Anyway?") of "Wojeck" in 1968.
- Her film debut was in the movie "The Best Damn Fiddler from Calabogie to Kaladar" in 1969.
- Several more TV appearances followed including "Festival" (1969), "Corwin" (1969), "McQueen" (1969) 3 episodes, "The Mod Squad" (1970) and "Adventures in Rainbow Country" (1969-70) 2 episodes.
- In 1971, she was cast as "Ruth" in the TV series "Nichols". She appeared in 24 episodes from 1971 to 1972.
- She then appeared in a number of films including "The Bounty Man" (1972)(TV), "Sisters" (1972), "The Gravy Train" (1974),

"Black Christmas" (1974), "The Great Waldo Pepper" (1975), "92 in the Shade" (1975) and "Shoot the Sun Down" (1978).

- In 1978, she was cast as "Lois Lane" in the film "Superman", starring Christopher Reeve. Three more movies followed – "Superman II" (1980), "Superman III" (1983) and "Superman 1V: The Quest for Peace" (1987).
- In 1987, she was cast as "Dinah/Jennie Jerome" in the TV series "Shell Game". She appeared in 6 episodes.
- Then in 1993, she supplied the voice for the character "Gaia" in the TV series "Captain Planet and the Planeteers". She voiced 16 episodes from 1993 to 1995.
- In 1994, she supplied the voice for the character "Rebecca Madison" in the TV series "Phantom 2040". She voiced 34 episodes from 1994 to 1996.
- In 1996, she had a recurring role as "Cookie de Varen" in the TV series "Boston Common". She appeared in 6 episodes from 1996 to 1997.
- Her last acting appearance, to date, was in the film "The Red Maple Leaf" in 2016.
- Margot has been married three times – Thomas McGuane (1976-77), John Heard (1979-80) and Philippe de Broca (1983-84). She has one daughter with Mr. McGuane.
- In 1990, she had a serious car accident that kept her from working for two years.
- Then in 1996, it was reported that she had a nervous breakdown.

- Margot has been a longtime supporter of democratic and liberal causes throughout her career.
- She became an American citizen in 2005.
- Margot won a Daytime Emmy Award in 2015 for her performance in an episode ("Mrs. Worthington") of "R.L. Stine's The Haunting Hour".
- Her other film credits include "The Amityville Horror" (1979), "Bus Stop" (1982)(TV), "Little Treasure" (1985), "Mob Story" (1989), "Aaron Sent Me" (1992), "Maverick" (1994) uncredited, "Windrunner" (1994), "The Planet of Junior Brown" (1997), "Tribulation" (2000), "Angel Blade" (2002), "A Single Woman" (2008) and "No Deposit" (2015).
- Margot's other TV credits include "Banacek" (1972), "Barnaby Jones" (1973), "Switch" (1976), "Tales from the Crypt" (1992), "Burke's Law" (1995), "The Hunger" (1997), "Touched by an Angel" (1998), "The Outer Limits" (2000), "Smallville" (2004) 2 episodes, "Robson Arms" (2005) 3 episodes and "Brothers & Sisters" (2007) 2 episodes.

- **Neva Louise Patterson** was born on February 10, 1920 on a farm near Nevada, Iowa.
- She graduated from Nevada High School in 1937 and worked at secretarial jobs in Des Moines before moving to New York.
- Neva appeared in two Broadway plays ("The Druid Circle" (1948) and "Strange Bedfellows" (1948)) before moving to the west coast.

- She made her TV acting debut in an episode ("St. Helena") of "The Philco Television Playhouse" in 1949.
- This was followed by several more TV guest appearances including "Colgate Theatre" (1949), "NBC Presents" (1949), "The Web" (1951), "Lux Video Theatre" (1951) 2 episodes, "Suspense" (1952) 2 episodes, "Short Short Dramas" (1952) and "The Doctor" (1952).
- Neva made her film debut in the movie "Taxi" in 1953.
- In 1969, she was cast as "Maggie McLeod" in the TV series "The Governor & J.J.". She appeared in 22 episodes from 1969 to 1970.
- In 1971, she was cast as "Sara 'Ma' Ketcham" in the TV series "Nichols". She appeared in 24 episodes from 1971 to 1972.
- Then in 1984, she appeared as "Eleanor Dupres" in the three part mini-series "V: The Final Battle".
- In 1987, she had a recurring role as "Marguerite Spooner" in the TV series "St. Elsewhere". She appeared in 4 episodes.
- Her last acting appearance was in an episode ("Fool for Love") of "In the Heat of the Night" in 1992.
- Neva was married three times – Thomas Gallagher, Michael Ellis (1953-56) and James

Lee (1957-2002). She had two adopted children with Mr. Lee.

- During her career Neva appeared in several more Broadway plays including "The Ivy Green" (1949), "Ring Round the Moon" (1950-51), "The Seven Year Itch" (1952-55), "Speaking of Murder" (1956-57) and "Romantic Comedy" (1979-80).
- Neva's other film credits include "The Solid Gold Cadillac" (1956), "Desk Set" (1957), "An Affair to Remember" (1957), "The Spiral Road" (1962), "Counterpoint" (1967), "The Runaways" (1975)(TV), "All the President's Men" (1976), "The Buddy Holly Story" (1978), "All of Me" (1984) and "Deadline: Madrid" (1988)(TV).
- Her other TV credits include "The Best of Broadway" (1954), "The Alcoa Hour" (1956), "Kraft Television Theatre" (1949-57) 4 episodes, "Goodyear Television Playhouse" (1952-57) 4 episodes, "Ben Casey" (1961), "Naked City" (1963), "The Defenders" (1962-64) 2 episodes, "The Patty Duke Show" (1964-65) 2 episodes, "Ironside" (1973), "The Rockford Files" (1975), "Barnaby Jones" (1973-77) 3 episodes, "The Waltons" (1979), "Brett Maverick" (1982), "Dynasty" (1983), "Webster" (1984-85) 3 episodes and "Hotel" (1986).

- **John Beck** was born on January 28, 1943 in Chicago, Illinois.
- He grew up in Joliet, Illinois and performed in plays at school.
- When he was 19, he moved to California and made his living by appearing in television commercials.
- John made his acting debut in an episode ("Russian Roulette") of "I Dream of Jeannie" in 1965.
- Several more TV guest appearances followed including "Days of Our Lives" (1965), "Hank" (1966), "Death Valley Days" (1969), "Mannix" (1969), "The F.B.I." (1969), "Lancer" (1970) 2 episodes, "Bonanza" (1969-70) 2 episodes and "Dan August" (1971).
- He made his film debut in the movie "Cyborg 2087" in 1966.
- In 1971, he was cast as "Ketcham" in the TV series "Nichols". He appeared in 24 episodes from 1971 to 1972.
- In 1980, he was cast as "Sam Curtis" in the TV series "Flamingo Road". He appeared in 38 episodes from 1980 to 1982.
- Then in 1983, he was cast as "Mark Graison" in the TV series "Dallas". He appeared in 67 episodes from 1983 to 1986.
- In 1995-97, he voiced 3 episodes of "Spider-Man".

- From 2001-03, he had a recurring role as "Bruce" in the TV series "Passions". He appeared in 23 episodes.
- His last acting appearance, to date, was in the movie short "Mesmerize Me" in 2009.
- John has been married to his wife, Tina Carter, since 1971. They have one son and three daughters.
- He was a very good boxer and won the heavyweight "Golden Gloves" of Chicago title in 1973.
- John was also a champion roller-skater. He performed many of his own stunts in the film "Rollerball" (1975).
- His other film credits include "Three in the Attic" (1968), "The Silent Gun" (1969)(TV), "Lawman" (1971), "Pat Garrett & Billy the Kid" (1973), "Sleeper" (1973), "The Law" (1974)(TV), "The Other Side of Midnight" (1977), "Crazy Dan" (1986)(TV), "In the Cold of the Night" (1990), "Black Day Blue Night" (1995), "The Alternate" (2000) and "Project Viper" (2002)(TV).
- John's other TV credits include "Hawaii Five-O" (1974), "Gunsmoke" (1970-75) 3 episodes, "Time Express" (1979), "Fantasy Island" (1983), "The Love Boat" (1985), "Hotel" (1985-86) 2 episodes, "Paradise" (1989-90) 3 episodes, "Santa Barbara" (1992) 3 episodes, "Trade Winds" (1993) 3 episodes, "Baywatch"

(1994) 2 episodes, "Matlock" (1986-94) 2 episodes, "Air America" (1999), "Walker" (1996-2000) 3 episodes and "Hunter" (2003).

- **Stuart Margolin** was born on January 31, 1940 in Davenport, Iowa.
- He graduated from South Oak Cliff High School, Dallas, Texas in 1958.
- Stuart made his acting debut in an episode ("Lonely Sunday") of "The Gertrude Berg Show" in 1961.
- This was followed by a recurring role as "Lt. Miller" in the TV series "Ensign O'Toole". He appeared in 4 episodes during 1962.
- Several more TV appearances followed including "The Lieutenant" (1963), "The Fugitive" (1964), "Ben Casey" (1964), "Branded" (1965), "Hey, Landlord" (1966), "Ironside" (1967), "The Virginian" (1968), "The Monkees" (1968), "That Girl" (1968-69) 3 episodes, "It Takes a Thief" (1968-69) 3 episodes and "Getting Together" (1971).
- He made his film debut in the movie "Women of the Prehistoric Planet" in 1966.
- In 1971, he was cast as "Deputy Mitch Mitchell" in the TV series "Nichols". He appeared in 24 episodes from 1971 to 1972.
- From 1969 to 1973 he appeared in 29 episodes of the TV series "Love, American Style".

- In 1974, he was cast as "Angel Martin" in the TV series "The Rockford Files". He appeared in 40 episodes from 1974 to 1979.
- In 1981, he was cast in a recurring role as "Philo Sandeen" in the TV series "Bret Maverick". He appeared in 8 episodes from 1981 to 1982.
- Then in 1983, he was cast as "Dr. Klein" in the TV series "Mr. Smith". He appeared in 13 episodes.
- From 1994 to 1997, he appeared as "Angel Martin" in seven "Rockford Files" TV movies.
- In 2002, he was cast as "Jack Welsh" in the TV series "Tom Stone". He appeared in 26 episodes from 2002 to 2004.
- His last acting appearance, to date, was in the film "The Second Time Around" in 2016.
- Stuart has been married three times – Patricia Ann Dunne, Terri Lynn McCortney and Joyce Eliason. He has three step-children.
- In 1979 and 1980 he won two Primetime Emmy Awards for his role in the "Rockford Files" (Outstanding Supporting Actor – Drama Series).
- Stuart is an accomplished director having directed over 50 TV episodes.
- He is also a respected songwriter. Stuart has written several songs with his longtime friend Jerry Riopelle.

- Stuart's other film credits include "Don't Just Stand There" (1968), "The Gamblers" (1970), "Kelly's Heroes" (1970), "Limbo" (1972), "The Stone Killer" (1973), "Death Wish" (1974), "Running Hot" (1984), "Deep Sleep" (1990), "The Hoax" (2006) and "Arbitrage" (2012).
- His other TV credits include "Mary Tyler Moore" (1973), "Gunsmoke" (1965-74) 3 episodes, "M.A.S.H." (1972-74) 2 episodes, "The Fall Guy" (1983), "Hill Street Blues" (1985), "Matlock" (1992) 2 episodes, "Touched by an Angel" (1997-2000) 2 episodes, "These Arms of Mine" (2000-01) 3 episodes, "Intelligence" (2006) 3 episodes, "The Bridge" (2010) and "N.C.I.S." (2014).

"The Oregon Trail"

Years : 1976 - 1977

Episodes : 14 (1 season)

Cast :-

Rod Taylor (b. 1930 d. 2015) - Played Evan Thorpe

Andrew Stevens (b. 1955) - Played Andrew Thorpe

Tony Becker (b. 1963) - Played William Thorpe

Gina Smika Hunter - Played Rachel Thorpe

Darlene Carr (b. 1950) - Played Margaret Devlin

Charles Napier (b. 1936 d. 2011) - Played Luther Sprague

Synopsis:-
A pioneer family heads west.

Trivia & Tidbits :-

"The Show"

- **"The Oregon Trail"** premiered on NBC on January 10, 1976 and last aired on November 30, 1977.
- The show ran for one season with a total of 14 episodes including the feature-length pilot.

"In Memoriam"

- **Rod Taylor** died of a heart attack on January 7, 2015 (84) in Beverly Hills, California.
- **Charles Napier** died of blood clots on October 5, 2011 (75) in Bakersfield, California.

"The Stars"

- **Rodney Sturt 'Rod' Taylor** was born on January 11, 1930 in Lidcombe, New South Wales, Australia.
- He was the only child of William Sturt Taylor, a contractor and commercial artist, and Mona Taylor (nee Thompson), a writer.
- Rod attended Parramatta High School before studying at East Sydney Technical and Fine Arts College.
- He began working as a commercial artist but then decided to try acting after seeing Sir Laurence Olivier in a touring production of "Richard III".
- In the early 1950's he decided to try his luck in Hollywood.
- Before leaving for America he made two films in Australia – "King of the Coral Sea" (1954) and "Long John Silver" (1954).

- Rod made his American acting debut in an episode ("The Black Sheep's Daughter") of "Studio 57" in 1955.
- Several more TV appearances followed including "Lux Video Theatre" (1955) 2 episodes, "Cheyenne" (1955), "Suspicion" (1957), "Studio One" (1958), "Playhouse 90" (1958-59) 5 episodes, "The Twilight Zone: The Original Series" (1959), "Zane Grey Theatre" (1960) and "Goodyear Theatre" (1960).
- In 1960, he was cast as "Glenn Evans" in the TV series "Hong Kong". He appeared in 26 episodes from 1960 to 1961.
- In 1971, he was cast as "Hank Brackett" in the TV series "Bearcats!" He appeared in 14 episodes.
- Then in 1976, he was cast as "Evan Thorpe" in the TV series "The Oregon Trail". He appeared in 14 episodes from 1976 to 1977.
- In 1983, he was cast as "Mr. Lavender" in the TV series "Masquerade". He appeared in 13 episodes from 1983 to 1984.
- Another short-lived TV series he appeared in was "Outlaws". He played "Sheriff Jonathan Grail" in 12 episodes from 1986 to 1987.
- Following this, he had a recurring role in the TV series "Falcon Crest". He appeared as "Frank Agretti" in 30 episodes from 1988 to 1990.
- Rod's final TV series was a recurring part in "Walker". He played "Gordon Cahill" in 4 episodes from 1996 to 2000.
- His final acting appearance was in the Quentin Tarantino film "Inglourious Basterds" (2009). He played "Winston Churchill".

- Rod was married three times – Peggy Williams (1951-54), Mary Beth Hilem (1963-69) and Carol Kikumura (1980-2015). He had one daughter, Felicia, with Ms. Hilem.
- He played "Tarzan" in an Australian children's radio serial in the early 1950's.
- In 2012, Stephen Vagg published a biography of Rod titled "Rod Taylor: An Aussie in Hollywood".
- In 2010, he received, with the rest of the cast, a Screen Actors Guild Award for "Inglourious Basterds".
- Rod's other film credits include "Top Gun" (1955), "Giant" (1956), "Raintree County" (1957), "Separate Tables" (1958), "The Time Machine" (1960), "101 Dalmatians" (1961), "The Birds" (1963), "The V.I.P.'s" (1963), "A Gathering of Eagles" (1963), "Sunday in New York" (1963), "36 Hours" (1964), "Young Cassidy" (1965), "The Liquidator" (1965), "Hotel" (1967), "Chuka" (1967), "Zabriskie Point" (1970), "The Train Robbers" (1973), "The Picture Show Man" (1977), "Mask of Murder" (1988), "Welcome to Woop Woop" (1997) and "Kaw" (2007).
- His other TV credits include "Bus Stop" (1961), "Tales of the Unexpected" (1980), "Murder, She Wrote" (1995) 3 episodes and "Pacific Blue" (1996).

- **Andrew Stevens** was born Herman Andrew Stephens on June 10, 1955 in Memphis, Tennessee.

- He is the only child of actress Stella Stevens and her former husband Noble Herman Stephens.
- After he graduated from high school, Andrew received a Bachelor's degree in psychology from Antioch University, Los Angeles.
- Andrew made his uncredited acting debut in the film "The Courtship of Eddie's Father" in 1963.
- His first credited part was in an episode ("Northeast Division") of "Adam-12" in 1973.
- Several more TV guest appearances followed including "Apple's Way" (1974), "The Wide World of Mystery" (1975), "Police Story" (1975), "Shazam!" (1976), "The Quest" (1976) and "Once an Eagle" (1976) mini-series 4 episodes.
- In 1976, he was cast as "Andrew Thorpe" in the TV series "The Oregon Trail". He appeared in 14 episodes from 1976 to 1977.
- In 1981, he was cast as "Ted Rorchek" in the TV series "Code Red". He appeared in 14 episodes from 1981 to 1982.
- Then in 1983, he was cast as "Lt. Glenn Matthews" in the TV series "Emerald Point N.A.S.". He appeared in 22 episodes from 1983 to 1984.
- In 1987, he was cast in a recurring role as "Casey Denault" in the TV series "Dallas". He appeared in 33 episodes from 1987 to 1989.

- His final acting appearance, to date, was in the TV movie "Mongolian Death Worm" in 2010.
- Andrew has been married twice – Kate Jackson (1978-80) and Robyn Stevens (1995-2010). He has three children from his second marriage.
- He is an accomplished producer, director, actor and writer.
- In the early 1990's he was owner and president of Royal Oak Entertainment.
- From 1997 to 2004, he was President/CEO of Franchise Pictures. The company filed for bankruptcy in 2004.
- At present, he operates Andrew Stevens Entertainment and Stevens Entertainment Group.
- Andrew's other film credits include "Shampoo" (1975), "Las Vegas Lady" (1975), "Vigilante Force" (1976), "The Fury" (1978), "Death Hunt" (1981), "The Seduction" (1982), "10 to Midnight" (1983), "The Terror Within" (1989), "Down the Drain" (1990), "Munchie" (1992), "Night Eyes Three" (1993), "Scorned" (1994), "Pursued" (2004) and "Fire from Below" (2009).
- His other TV credits include "Westside Medical" (1977), "Hollywood Wives" (1985) 3 episodes, "The Love Boat" (1985) 2 episodes, "Hotel" (1985-87) 2 episodes, "Murder, She Wrote"

(1984-89) 2 episodes, "Columbo" (1990) and "Swamp Thing" (1992).

- **Tony Becker** was born on September 14, 1963 in Los Angeles, California.
- He is the son of actor Kenneth Becker and actress Patti Kane.
- Tony attended Hollywood High School.
- He made his acting debut as a two year old in an episode ("Question: How Do You Catch a Cool Bird of Paradise?") of "Slattery's People" in 1965.
- In 1974, he was cast as "T.J. Wheeler" in the TV series "The Texas Wheelers". He appeared in 8 episodes from 1974 to 1975.
- In 1976, he was cast as "William Thorpe" in the TV series "The Oregon Trail". He appeared in 14 episodes from 1976 to 1977.
- Then in 1980, He had a recurring role as "Drew Cutter" in the TV series "The Waltons". He appeared in 8 episodes from 1980 to 1981.
- In 1983, he was cast as "Pvt. Utah Wilson" in the TV series "For Love and Honor". He appeared in 12 episodes from 1983 to 1984.
- In 1987, he was cast as "Cpl. Daniel 'Danny' Percell" in the TV series "Tour of Duty". He appeared in 57 episodes from 1987 to 1990.
- His last acting appearance, to date, was in the film "2016" (2016).

- Tony's dad, Ken, had the first on-screen fight with Elvis Presley in the film "Loving You" (1957).
- His mum, Patti, was Sandra Dee's best friend in the original "Gidget" (1959) film.
- Tony's other film credits include "The Other Side of the Mountain" (1975), "Bound for Glory" (1976), "Cody" (1977), "The Onion Field" (1979), "A Wedding on Walton's Mountain" (1982)(TV), "Mother's Day on Waltons Mountain" (1982)(TV), "The Alamo: Thirteen Days to Glory" (1987)(TV), "A Walton Thanksgiving Reunion" (1993)(TV), " Walton Wedding" (1995)(TV), "A Walton Easter" (1997)(TV) and "The Hunters" (2011).
- His other TV credits include "Marcus Welby, M.D." (1976), "Lou Grant" (1978), "Little House on the Prairie" (1979) 2 episodes, "Trapper John, M.D." (1982), "Matlock" (1987) 2 episodes, "Disneyland" (1980-87) 3 episodes, "Murder, She Wrote" (1992), "Walker" (1996) and "Justified" (2011).

- **Gina Smika Hunter** made her uncredited acting debut in the film "Last of the Red Hot Lovers" in 1972.
- In 1976, she was cast as "Rachel Thorpe" in the TV series "The Oregon Trail". She appeared in 14 episodes from 1976 to 1977.

- Her last acting appearance, to date, was in the TV movie "Between the Darkness and the Dawn" in 1985.
- Gina's other film credits include "The Sword and the Sorcerer" (1982) and "The Slumber Party Massacre" (1982).
- Her other TV credits include "Kojak" (1974), "Little House on the Prairie" (1978), "Friends" (1979), "The Bad News Bears" (1980), "The Two of Us" (1981) and "Trapper John, M.D." (1984).

- **Darlene Carr** was born Darlene Farnon on December 12, 1950 in Chicago, Illinois.
- She is the daughter of actress Rita Oehmen and composer Brian Farnon.
- Darlene is the sister of Charmian Carr (died September 17, 2016) who played "Liesl" in the film "The Sound of Music" (1965).
- Her acting debut was in an episode ("Little White Liar") of "The Littlest Hobo" in 1964.
- Several more TV guest appearances followed including "The John Forsythe Show" (1965) 2 episodes, "Mayberry R.F.D." (1968), "Family Affair" (1969), "The Virginian" (1969) and "To Rome with Love" (1969).
- In 1971, she was cast as "Cindy Smith" in the TV series "The Smith Family". She appeared in 39 episodes from 1971 to 1972.

- In 1976, she was cast as "Margaret Devlin" in the TV series "The Oregon Trail". She appeared in 13 episodes from 1976 to 1977.
- In 1976-77, she appeared as "Tommy Caldwell" in the seven-part mini-series "Once an Eagle".
- Darlene had a recurring role as "Jeannie Stone" in the TV series "The Streets of San Francisco". She appeared in 12 episodes from 1973 to 1977.
- In 1979, she was cast as "Susan Winslow" in the short-lived TV series "Miss Winslow and Son". She appeared in 6 episodes.
- In 1981, she was cast as "Mary Lou 'M.L.' Springer" in the TV series "Bret Maverick". She appeared in 18 episodes from 1981 to 1982.
- In 1991, she supplied voices in the TV series "The Pirates of Dark Water". She voiced 17 episodes from 1991 to 1993.
- Her last acting appearance, to date, was in the film "Eight Days a Week" in 1997.
- Darlene has been married twice – Jason Laskay (1974-77) and Jameson Parker (1992-present).
- She dubbed the children's singing voices in "The Sound of Music" (1965).
- Darlene was nominated for a Golden Globe Award for her performance in the mini-series "Once an Eagle" (1976).

- She is an accomplished singer and released an album "The Carr-DeBelles Band" in 1988.
- Charlene's other film credits include "Monkeys, Go Home!" (1967), "The Jungle Book" (1967)(voice), "Death of a Gunfighter" (1969), "All My Darling Daughters" (1972)(TV), "Law of the Land" (1976)(TV), "Young Joe, the Forgotten Kennedy" (1977)(TV), "Back to the Streets of San Francisco" (1992)(TV) and "Piranha" (1995).
- Her other TV credits include "The F.B.I." (1970-72) 2 episodes, "Chopper One" (1974), "The Rookies" (1972-74) 3 episodes, "The Waltons" (1975), "Medical Center" (1972-75) 3 episodes, "Fantasy Island" (1978), "Barnaby Jones" (1973-78) 3 episodes, "Hagen" (1980), "Charlie's Angels" (1981), "Murder, She Wrote" (1985), "Magnum, P.I." (1983-86) 2 episodes, "Disneyland" (1967-86) 3 episodes, "Simon & Simon" (1981-86) 4 episodes and "Adventures of the Book of Virtues" (1996).

- **Charles Napier** was born on April 12, 1936 in Mt. Union, Kentucky.
- He was the son of Sara Lena (nee Loafman) and Linus Pitts Napier.
- After graduating from high school in 1954 he enlisted in the United States Army and attained the rank of sergeant.

- When he finished his army service he attended Western Kentucky University and graduated in 1961 with a major in arts and a minor in physical education.
- After trying several jobs he decided to go with acting and made his uncredited debut in an episode ("Night Out of Time") of "Mannix" in 1968.
- He made his film debut in the movie "The Hanging of Jake Ellis" in 1969.
- Several more film roles followed including "The House Near the Prado" (1969), "Cherry, Harry & Raquel!" (1970), "Beyond the Valley of the Dolls" (1970), "Moonfire" (1970), "The Seven Minutes" (1971) and "Love and Kisses" (1971).
- Following this, he guest starred in a number of TV episodes including "Mission: Impossible" (1972), "The Mod Squad" (1972), "Kojak" (1975), "The Streets of San Francisco" (1975), "Baretta" (1975), "Baa Baa Black Sheep" (1976) and "Delvecchio" (1976).
- In 1976, he was cast as "Luther Sprague" in the TV series "The Oregon Trail". He appeared in 13 episodes from 1976 to 1977.
- In 1979, he had a recurring role as "Hammer" in the TV series "B.J. and the Bear". He appeared in 6 episodes from 1979 to 1981.
- Also in 1979, he voiced the character "Hulk" in the TV series "The Incredible Hulk".

- In 1982, he played the character "Maj. Harrison" in the three-part mini-series "The Blue and the Gray".
- Then in 1986, he was cast as "Wolfson Lucas" in the TV series "Outlaws". He appeared in 12 episodes from 1986 to 1987.
- In 1994, he voiced the character "Duke Phillips" in the TV series "The Critic". He voiced 23 episodes from 1994 to 1995.
- In 1997, he voiced the character "Zed" in the TV series "Men in Black: The Animated Series". He voiced 52 episodes from 1997 to 2001.
- Another series he voiced a character in was "Squidbillies". He was the "Sheriff" in 9 episodes from 2005 to 2006.
- His final acting job was in the "Archie" series. He voiced "Dr. Speltz" in 2011.
- Charles was married twice – Delores Wilson and Dee Napier. He had three children.
- In 2011, he co-wrote a book with Dante W. Renzulli Jr. titled "Square Jaw and Big Heart – The life and times of a Hollywood actor".
- Charles' other film credits include "Supervixens" (1975), "The Blues Brothers" (1980), "Wacko" (1982), "Swing Shift" (1984), "The Night Stalker" (1986), "Ernest Goes to Jail" (1990), "The Silence of the Lambs" (1991), "Loaded Weapon 1" (1993), "Philadelphia" (1993), "Silent Fury" (1994), "The Cable Guy" (1996), "Macon County Jail"

(1997), "Very Mean Mean" (2000), "The Manchurian Candidate" (2004), "Annapolis" (2006) and "One-Eyed Monster" (2008).

- His other TV credits include "The Rockford Files" (1975-77) 2 episodes, "Starsky and Hutch" (1975-78) 2 episodes, "Concrete Cowboys" (1981), "Simon & Simon" (1982), "Dallas" (1982-83) 4 episodes, "The Dukes of Hazzard" (1981-83) 2 episodes, "Street Hawk" (1985), "Guns of Paradise" (1989), "L.A. Law" (1991), "Renegade" (1993) 3 episodes, "Murder, She Wrote" (1986-95) 3 episodes, "George & Leo" (1997), "Walker, Texas Ranger" (1999), "Superman" (1997-2000) 3 episodes, "Diagnosis Murder" (2001) 2 episodes, "The Practice" (2001) 2 episodes, "God, the Devil and Bob" (2000-01)(voice) 4 episodes, "The Legend of Tarzan" (2001), "The Simpsons" (2001-05)(voice) 4 episodes, "C.S.I." (2005), "Curb Your Enthusiasm" (2007) and "Cold Case" (2008).

"The Outcasts"

Years : 1968 - 1969

Episodes : 26 (1 season)

Cast :-

Don Murray (b. 1929) - Played Earl Corey

Otis Young (b. 1932 d. 2001) - Played Jemal David

Synopsis :-
The story of a bounty hunter who teams up with a
newly released slave in the 1860's.

Trivia & Tidbits :-

"The Show"

- **"The Outcasts"** premiered on ABC on
  September 23, 1968 and last aired on May 5,
  1969.
- The show ran for one season with a total of 26
  episodes.
- The series was created by Ben Brady and Leon
  Tokatyan and produced by Screen Gems
  Television.
- The music was composed by Hugo Montenegro
  and was nominated for an Emmy Award in
  1969.

- "The Outcasts" was the first television Western with a black co-star (Otis Young).
-

"In Memoriam"

- **Otis Young** died of a stroke on October 11, 2001 (69) in Los Angeles, California.

"The Stars"

- **Don Murray** was born Donald Patrick Murray on July 31, 1929 in Hollywood, California.
- He is the only child of Dennis and Ethel Murray. His father was a Broadway dance director and stage manager and his mother a former Ziegfeld performer.
- Don attended East Rockaway High School, New York and played football as well as being a member of the track team.
- After graduating from high school he studied at the American Academy of Dramatic Arts.
- In 1951, he made his Broadway debut in the play "The Rose Tattoo". He played the character "Jack Hunter".
- Don made his TV debut in an episode ("The Taming of the Shrew") of "Studio One" in 1950.
- In 1956, he made his movie debut in the film "Bus Stop" opposite Marilyn Monroe.
- Several more film roles followed including "The Bachelor Party" (1957), "A Hatful of Rain" (1957), "From Hell to Texas" (1958), "One Foot in Hell" (1960), "Advise & Consent"

(1961), "Baby the Rain Must Fall" (1965), "The Plainsman" (1966) and "The Viking Queen" (1967).

- In 1968, he was cast as "Earl Corey" in the TV series "The Outcasts". He appeared in 26 episodes from 1968 to 1969.
- In 1977, he appeared as "Anderson" in the TV mini-series "How the West Was Won".
- Then in 1979, he was cast as "Sid Fairgate" in the TV series "Knots Landing". He appeared in 33 episodes from 1979 to 1981.
- In 1989, he played "Roger Gibbons" in 6 episodes of the TV series "A Brand New Life".
- Following this he appeared as "Bing Hammersmith" in 7 episodes of the TV series "Sons and Daughters".
- His last acting role, to date, was in the film "Island Prey" in 2005.
- Don has been married twice - Hope Lange (1956-61) and Elizabeth Johnson (1962-present). He has two children with Ms. Lange and three children with Ms. Johnson.
- He served as a volunteer overseas during the Korean War.
- At the 1957 Academy Awards he was nominated as Best Actor in a Supporting Role for "Bus Stop".
- Don has a Star on the Hollywood Walk of Fame for his contribution to Motion Pictures.
- His other film credits include "Conquest of the Planet of the Apes" (1972), "Cotter" (1973), "Deadly Hero" (1975), "Endless Love" (1981), "Peggy Sue Got Married" (1986), "Ghosts Can't Do It" (1989) and "Elvis Is Alive" (2001).

- Don's other TV credits include "Disneyland" (1972), "Police Story" (1973-75) 2 episodes, T.J. Hooker" (1986), "Hotel" (1987), "Matlock" (1987), "Murder, She Wrote" (1993) and "The Single Guy" (1996).

- **Otis Young** was born on July 4, 1932 in Providence, Rhode Island.
- At the age of 17, he joined the U.S. Marine Corps and served in the Korean War.
- After the war he enrolled in acting classes at New York University and then trained at the Neighborhood Playhouse.
- Following this he worked off-Broadway as an actor and writer.
- Otis made his TV debut in an episode ("I Before E Except After C") of "East Side/West Side" in 1963.
- He made his movie debut in the film "Murder in Mississippi" in 1965.
- In 1968, he was cast as "Jemal David" in the TV series "The Outcasts". He appeared in 26 episodes from 1968 to 1969.
- Otis was married to Barbara Young at the time of his passing. They had four children.
- He was the Communications Professor and Director of the Drama Program at Monroe Community College, New York from 1989 to 1999.
- Otis' other film credits include "Don't Just Stand There" (1968), "The Last Detail" (1973), "The Clones" (1973), "The Capture of Bigfoot" (1979), "Blood Beach" (1980) and "After Image" (2001).

- His other TV credits include "Daktari" (1966), "Daniel Boone" (1967), "The F.B.I." (1968), "Columbo" (1975), "Cannon" (1976), "The Mississippi" (1983) and "Hill Street Blues" (1985).

"Outlaws"

Years : 1960 - 1962

Episodes : 50 (2 seasons)

Cast :-

Barton MacLane (b. 1902 d. 1969) - Played Marshal Frank Caine

Don Collier (b. 1928) - Played Deputy Marshal Will Foreman

Bruce Yarnell (b. 1935 d. 1973) - Played Deputy Marshal Chalk Breeson

Synopsis :-
The story of a marshal who operated in a lawless section of the Oklahoma Territory.

Trivia & Tidbits :-

"The Show"

- **"Outlaws"** premiered on NBC on September 26, 1960 and last aired on May 10, 1962.
- The show ran for two seasons with a total of 50 episodes. The first season was shown in

black and white and the second season in color.

- The series was produced by the National Broadcasting Company (NBC).
- Filming took place in Bronson Canyon and Griffith Park, California.
- Among the cast members was the dog that appeared in the Disney film "Old Yeller" (1957).

"In Memoriam"

- **Barton MacLane** died of cancer January 1, 1969 (66) in Santa Monica, California.
- **Bruce Yarnell** died in a plane crash on November 30, 1973 (37) in California.

"The Stars"

- **Barton MacLane** was born Ernest Barton MacLane on December 25, 1902 in Columbia, South Carolina.
- He attended Wesleyan University in Connecticut where he was a member of the football team. His athletic ability lead to a small uncredited role in the film "The Quarterback" (1926).
- After graduation he attended the American Academy of Dramatic Arts.
- Barton made his Broadway debut in the play "The Trial of Mary Dugan" in 1927.
- Two more plays ("Gods of the Lightning" and "Subway Express") followed before he had

another uncredited role in the Marx Brothers film "The Cocoanuts" (1929).

- In 1931, he had his first credited role in the film "His Woman".
- In 1932, he wrote and starred in another Broadway play titled "Rendezvous".
- Several more film roles followed including "Man of the Forest" (1933), "Lone Cowboy" (1933), "G Men" (1935), "Bengal Tiger" (1936), "The Prince and the Pauper" (1937), "Prison Break" (1938), "Big Town Czar" (1939), "High Sierra" (1941), "Zane Grey's Western Union" (1941), "The Maltese Falcon" (1941), "Marine Raiders" (1944), "San Quentin" (1946), "The Treasure of the Sierra Madre" (1948) and "Kansas Pacific" (1953).
- In 1960, he was cast as "Marshal Frank Caine" in the TV series "Outlaws". He appeared in 27 episodes from 1960 to 1961.
- In 1965, he was cast as "General Peterson" in the TV series "I Dream of Jeannie". He appeared in 35 episodes from 1965 to 1969.
- Barton was married twice - Martha Stewart (1925-30) and Charlotte Wynters (1939-69). He had two children with Ms. Stewart.
- He played several musical instruments including piano, guitar and violin.
- Barton was also a published playwright and author.
- He owned a 2,000 acre cattle ranch in Madera County, California.
- Barton's other film credits include "The Glenn Miller Story" (1954), "Rails into Laramie" (1954), "Naked Gun" (1956), "Frontier Gun"

(1958), "Noose for a Gunman" (1960), "Pocketful of Miracles" (1961), "Law of the Lawless" (1964) and "Buckskin" (1968).

- His other TV credits include "Cheyenne" (1956), "Wire Service" (1957), "Circus Boy" (1957), "Tales of Wells Fargo" (1957), "Black Saddle" (1959), "Disneyland" (1959-60) 3 episodes, "Overland Trail" (1960), "Laramie" (1960-63) 4 episodes, "Perry Mason" (1959-64) 4 episodes, "Gunsmoke" (1966-67) 2 episodes and "Hondo" (1967).

- **Don Collier** was born on October 17, 1928 in Santa Monica, California.
- After graduating from high school he joined the United States Navy at the end of the Second World War.
- Following the war he attended the Hardin-Simmons University in Texas and then transferred to Brigham Young University in Utah.
- In 1948, he had an uncredited part in the film "Massacre River". This was followed by further uncredited roles in "Fort Apache" (1948) and "Davy Crockett, Indian Scout" (1950).
- In 1960, he was cast as "Deputy Marshal Will Foreman" in the TV series "Outlaws". He appeared in 49 episodes from 1960 to 1962.
- In 1967, he was cast as "Sam Butler" in the TV series "The High Chaparral". He appeared in 63 episodes from 1967 to 1971.
- In 1988, he played the part of "Adm. Russ Carton" in the TV mini-series "War and Remembrance", starring Robert Mitchum.

- Then in 1989, he was cast as "William Tompkins, Shop Keeper" in the TV series "The Young Riders". He appeared in 24 episodes from 1989 to 1992.
- His last acting role, to date, was in the film "Jake's Corner" in 2008.
- Don is married to Holly Hire and they have six children and eleven grandchildren.
- He has appeared in many commercials, the most famous being his character "Gum Fighter" for Hubba Bubba Bubble Gum.
- Don's other film credits include "Seven Ways from Sundown" (1960), "Paradise, Hawaiian Style" (1966), "El Dorado" (1966) uncredited, "The War Wagon" (1967), "The Undefeated" (1969), "The Sacketts" (1979)(TV), "The Cellar" (1989), "Tombstone" (1993), "Gunsmoke: One Man's Justice" (1994)(TV) and "Bonanza: Under Attack" (1995)(TV).
- His other TV credits include "Wide Country" (1962), "Temple Houston" (1963), "Perry Mason" (1964), "Profiles in Courage" (1965), "Wagon Train" (1965), "Branded" (1965) 3 episodes, "Death Valley Days" (1962-67) 5 episodes, "Bonanza" (1960-72) 5 episodes, "Gunsmoke" (1964-74) 2 episodes and "Legend" (1995).

- **Bruce Yarnell** was born on December 28, 1935 in Los Angeles, California.
- He graduated from Hollywood High School.
- Bruce sang on Broadway as a baritone before making his TV debut.

- In 1961, he was cast as "Deputy Marshal Chalk Breeson" in the TV series "Outlaws". He appeared in 24 episodes from 1961 to 1962.
- Bruce made his movie debut in the film "Irma la Douce" (1963), starring Jack Lemmon and Shirley MacLaine.
- He was married to Joan Patenaude.
- Bruce sang baritone roles at the San Francisco Opera from 1971 until his death in 1973.
- On Broadway he appeared in musicals including "Camelot", "The Happiest Girl in the World" and "Annie Get Your Gun".
- Bruce's other film credits include "Good Old Days" (1966)(TV), "Annie Get Your Gun" (1967)(TV) and "The Road Hustlers" (1968).
- His other TV credits include "Wide Country" (1963), "Bonanza" (1964-65) 2 episodes, "Hogan's Heroes" (1965), "Laugh-In" (1968) and "The Legend of Robin Hood" (1968).

"Overland Trail"

Years : 1960

Episodes : 17 (1 season)

Cast :-

William Bendix (b. 1906 d. 1964) - Played Frederick Thomas 'Fred' Kelly
Doug McClure (b. 1935 d. 1995) – Played Frank 'Flip' Flippen

Synopsis :-
Adventures of a stagecoach driver and his assistant.

Trivia & Tidbits :-

"The Show"

- **"Overland Trail"** premiered on NBC on February 7, 1960 and last aired on June 5, 1960.
- The show ran for one season with a total of 17 black and white episodes.
- The series was produced by Overland Stage-Bilben Productions, Stagecoach Productions and the National Broadcasting Company (NBC).

- Filming took place on the Universal Studios Backlot and Red Rock Canyon State Park, California.
- Music for the series was composed by Jeff Alexander, David Kahn and Stanley Wilson.
- The show aired opposite "Lassie" and "Dennis the Menace" on CBS and "Walt Disney Presents" and "Maverick" on ABC.

"In Memoriam"

- **William Bendix** died of lobar pneumonia on December 14, 1964 (58) in Los Angeles, California.
- **Doug McClure** died of lung cancer on February 5, 1995 (58) in Sherman Oaks, Los Angeles, California.

"The Stars"

- **William Bendix** was born on January 14, 1906 in Manhattan, New York City.
- He was the son of Oscar and Hilda (nee Carnell) Bendix.
- William graduated from Public School 5 in the Bronx and then attended Townsend Harris High School.
- As a teenager in the early 1920's he was a batboy for the New York Yankees baseball team. During this time he became friendly with the great Babe Ruth.

- After this he managed a grocery store and then joined the Federal Theatre Project.
- He next appeared in a production ("The Time of Your Life") for the Theatre Guild where he was discovered by Hal Roach and signed to a film contract.
- In 1942, he made his movie debut in the film "Woman of the Year" starring Spencer Tracy and Katharine Hepburn.
- Several more film roles followed including "Wake Island" (1942), "The Glass Key" (1942), "China" (1943), "Lifeboat" (1944), "Abroad with Two Yanks" (1944), "The Blue Dahlia" (1946), "The Time of Your Life" (1948), "The Babe Ruth Story" (1948), "The Life of Riley" (1949), "Streets of Laredo" (1949), "Detective Story" (1951) and "Submarine Command" (1951).
- In 1944, William began playing the character "Chester A. Riley" on the radio show "The Life of Riley". The show ran from January, 1944 until June, 1951.
- Then in 1953, he was cast as "Chester A. Riley in the TV series "The Life of Riley". He appeared in 217 episodes from 1953 to 1958.
- In 1960, he was cast as "Frederick Thomas 'Fred' Kelly" in the TV series "Overland Trail". He appeared in 17 episodes.

- In 1943, William was nominated for an Oscar as Best Actor in a Supporting Role for "Wake Island".
- William was married to Theresa Stefanotti from 1927 until his death in 1964. They had two daughters, Lorraine and Stephanie.
- He has two Stars on the Hollywood Walk of Fame for his contribution to radio and television.
- On the TV series "This Is Your Life" (1952) it was revealed that Bendix was a descendant of composer Felix Mendelssohn.
- Although he played working class characters in his films, he was a staunch Republican.
- His other film credits include "Blackbeard, the Pirate" (1952), "Dangerous Mission" (1954), "Black Stations" (1956), "Idol on Parade" (1956), "For Love or Money" (1963) and "Law of the Lawless" (1964).
- William's other TV credits include "Four Star Revue" (1952), "Goodyear Television Playhouse" (1956), "Wagon Train" (1958), "Riverboat" (1959), "Mister Ed" (1961), "Follow the Sun" (1962) and "Burke's Law" (1963-64) 2 episodes.

- **Doug McClure (see "Barbary Coast")**

"Pistols 'n' Petticoats"

Years : 1966 - 1967

Episodes : 26 (1 season)

Cast :-

Ann Sheridan (b. 1915 d. 1967) - Played Henrietta Hanks

Ruth McDevitt (b. 1895 d. 1976) - Played Grandma Effie Hanks

Douglas Fowley (b. 1911 d. 1998) - Played Grandpa Andrew Hanks

Gary Vinson (b. 1936 d. 1984) – Played Sheriff Harold Sikes

Carole Wells (b. 1942) – Played Lucy Hanks

Robert Lowery (b. 1913 d. 1971) – Played Buss Courtney

Synopsis :-
Stories of two hillbilly women.

Trivia & Tidbits :-

"The Show"

- **"Pistols 'n' Petticoats"** premiered on CBS on September 17, 1966 and last aired on March 11, 1967. The first episode was titled "A Crooked Line".
- The show ran for one season with a total of 26 color episodes (not including the original pilot episode).
- The series was created by George Tibbles.
- "Pistols 'n' Petticoats" was produced by Kayro/Universal Television for CBS Productions.
- The theme music was composed by Jack Elliott and George Tibbles.
- It was filmed on the Universal Backlot and Universal Studios.
- In the pilot episode Chris Noel was cast as "Henrietta's" daughter, however, due to poor audience responses, she was replaced by Carole Wells for the series.

"In Memoriam"

- **Ann Sheridan** died of esophageal cancer on January 21, 1967 (51) in Los Angeles, California.
- **Ruth McDevitt** died of natural causes on May 27, 1976 (80) in Hollywood, California.
- **Douglas Fowley** died on May 21, 1998 (86) in Woodland Hills, California.
- **Gary Vinson** committed suicide on October 15, 1984 (47) in Redondo Beach, California.

- **Robert Lowery** died of a heart attack on December 26, 1971 (58) in Hollywood, California.

"The Stars"

- **Ann Sheridan** was born Clara Lou Sheridan on February 21, 1915 in Denton, Texas.
- She was the daughter of G.W. Sheridan, an automobile mechanic, and Lula Stewart Warren Sheridan.
- Ann was involved in dramatics at Denison High School and then went to North Texas State Teachers College.
- Whilst at North Texas, she entered and won a beauty contest with the prize being a bit part in the Paramount film "Search for Beauty" (1934).
- Ann then appeared in several more films including "Come On, Marines!" (1934), "Kiss and Make-Up" (1934), "Ladies Should Listen" (1934), "Wagon Wheels" (1934) uncredited, "College Rhythm" (1934) uncredited, "Behold My Life!" (1934), "Enter Madam!" (1935), "Car 99" (1935), "The Red Blood of Courage" (1935) and "Fighting Youth" (1935).
- In 1936, she signed with Warner Bros. and appeared in the film "Black Legion" (1937).
- This was followed by many more film roles including "San Quentin" (1937), "Alcatraz Island" (1937), "Mystery House" (1938), "Cowboy from Brooklyn" (1938), "Angels with Dirty Faces" (1938), "Dodge City" (1939),

"Angels Wash Their Faces" (1939), "Castle on the Hudson" (1940), "They Drive by Night" (1940), "The Man Who Came to Dinner" (1942), "Kings Row" (1942), "George Washington Slept Here" (1942), "Shine on Harvest Moon" (1944), "Nora Prentiss" (1947), "I Was a Male War Bride" (1949), "Stella" (1950), "Steel Town" (1952) and "Take Me to Town" (1953).

- In 1953, she made her TV debut in an episode ("Malaya Incident") of "The Ford Television Theatre".
- In 1966, she was cast as "Henrietta Hanks" in the TV series "Pistols 'n' Petticoats". She appeared or was credited in 26 episodes from 1966 to 1967.
- Ann was married three times – Edward Norris (1936-38), George Brent (1942-43) and Scott McKay (1966-67).
- She was known as the "Oomph Girl".
- In 1939, she was named Max Factor's "Girl of the Year".
- In 1960, she was awarded a Star on the Hollywood Walk of Fame for her contribution to Motion Pictures.
- Ann's other film credits include "Appointment in Honduras" (1953), "Come Next Spring" (1956), "The Opposite Sex" (1956) and "Woman and the Hunter" (1957).
- Her other TV credits include "Schlitz Playhouse of Stars" (1953), "Four Star Revue" (1953), "Lux Video Theatre" (1953-57) 2 episodes, "Playhouse 90" (1957), "Pursuit" (1958), "The United States Steel Hour" (1956-60) 2

episodes, "Wagon Train" (1962) and "Another World" (1965-66).

- **Ruth McDevitt** was born Ruth Thane Shoecraft on September 13, 1895 in Coldwater, Michigan.
- After attending the American Academy of Dramatic Arts, she married and decided to devote her time to the marriage. After her husband died in 1934, she returned to her acting career.
- In 1937, Ruth made her Broadway debut in the play "Straw Hat".
- She then appeared in several more Broadway plays including "Young Couple Wanted", "Goodbye in the Night", "Mr. Big" and "Meet a Body".
- In 1949, she made her TV debut in the series "A Woman to Remember".
- In 1951, she made her film debut in the movie "The Guy Who Came Back".
- Then in 1953, she had the recurring role of "Mom Peepers" in the TV series "Mister Peepers". She appeared in 5 episodes.
- In 1966, she was cast as "Grandma Effie Hanks" in the TV series "Pistols 'n' Petticoats". She appeared in 26 episodes from 1966 to 1967.
- From 1974 to 1975, she had the recurring role of "Emily Cowles" in the TV series "Kolchak:

The Night Stalker". She appeared in 12 episodes.

- Her last acting appearance was in the TV movie "The Cheerleaders" in 1976.
- She was married to Patrick John McDevitt until his death in 1934.
- Over the years, Ruth appeared on Broadway in several more plays including "Harvey" (1944-49), "Sleepy Hollow" (1948), "The High Ground" (1951), "The Male Animal" (1952-53), "Picnic" (1953-54), "Diary of a Scoundrel" (1956), "The Best Man" (1960-61) and "Absence of a Cello" (1964-65).
- Ruth's other film credits include "Boys' Night Out" (1962), "The Birds" (1963), "Dear Heart" (1964), "The Shakiest Gun in the West" (1968), "Angel in My Pocket" (1969), "Change of Habit" (1969), "Skyway to Death" (1974)(TV), "Mame" (1974), "Mixed Company" (1974) and "Man on the Outside" (1975).
- Her other TV credits include "Studio One" (1956-57) 3 episodes, "Matinee Theatre" (1956-58) 2 episodes, "Harbormaster" (1958), "The United States Steel Hour" (1958-59) 3 episodes, "Naked City" (1961), "Dr. Kildare" (1962), "Route 66" (1964), "The Andy Griffith Show" (1968) 2 episodes, "The Debbie Reynolds Show" (1969), "Ironside" (1970), "Bewitched" (1967-70) 3 episodes, "The New Andy Griffith Show" (1971) 3 episodes, "Love,

American Style" (1970-72) 3 episodes, "Room 222" (1972) 2 episodes, "Mannix" (1969-73) 2 episodes, "The New Dick Van Dyke Show" (1973), "McCloud" (1974), "Gunsmoke" (1974), "All in the Family" (1973-75) 3 episodes, "The Streets of San Francisco" (1973-75) 2 episodes and "Medical Center" (1975).

- **Douglas Fowley** was born Daniel Vincent Fowley on May 30, 1911 in The Bronx, New York.
- When he was still young he moved to Los Angeles and studied at the Los Angeles City College.
- Douglas made his film debut in the movie "The Woman Who Dared" in 1933.
- Over the next twenty years he appeared in numerous films including "Student Tour" (1934), "Two for Tonight" (1935), "Crash Donovan" (1936), "Charlie Chan on Broadway" (1937), "Alexander's Ragtime Band" (1938), "Dodge City" (1939), "20 Mule Team" (1940), "Ellery Queen, Master Detective" (1940), "Secret of the Wastelands" (1941), "Bar 20" (1943), "Don't Fence Me In" (1945), "Undercover Maisie" (1947), "Bad Men of Tombstone" (1949), "Rider from Tucson" (1950), "Singin' in the Rain" (1952), "The Man

Behind the Gun" (1953) and "The Lone Gun" (1954).

- In 1955, he had the recurring role of "Doc Holliday" in the TV series "The Life and Legend of Wyatt Earp". He appeared in 40 episodes from 1955 to 1961.
- In 1966, he was cast as "Andrew Hanks" in the TV series "Pistols 'n' Petticoats". He appeared in 26 episodes from 1966 to 1967.
- In 1979, he was cast as "Robert Redford" in the TV series "Detective School". He appeared in 11 episodes.
- His last acting appearance was in an episode ("Graduation") of "Father Murphy" in 1982.
- Douglas was married several times and had a number of children.
- He is the father of Kim Fowley, record producer, songwriter and co-founder of the band "The Runaways". His mother was Shelby Payne.
- Douglas appeared in over 240 films and dozens of TV shows.
- His other film credits include "The Lonesome Trail" (1955), "The Broken Star" (1956), "The Badge of Marshal Brennan" (1957), "Buffalo Gun" (1961), "7 Faces of Dr. Lao" (1964), "Guns of Diablo" (1965), "From Noon Till Three" (1976) and "The White Buffalo" (1977).
- Douglas' other TV credits include "The Abbott and Costello Show" (1953), "City Detective"

(1954), "Wild Bill Hickok" (1955), "Cheyenne" (1956), "The Californians" (1958), "U.S. Marshal" (1958), "State Trooper" (1957-59) 3 episodes, "Perry Mason" (1964), "Bonanza" (1965), "Daniel Boone" (1966), "Death Valley Days" (1968), "Gunsmoke" (1973), "The Oregon Trail" (1976) and "Chips" (1979).

- **Gary Vinson** was born Robert Gary Vinson on October 22, 1936 in Los Angeles, California.
- Over his career, Gary appeared in many TV shows starting off with "The Whirlybirds" in 1957. Other shows included "Perry Mason" (1957), "Gunsmoke" (1957), "The Adventures of Ozzie and Harriet" (1958), "Maverick" (1959), "Bachelor Father" (1960), "Hawaiian Eye" (1960), "Colt .45" (1960), "Bronco" (1961), "Laramie" (1962), "77 Sunset Strip" (1962), and "Lawman" (1962).
- In 1957, he made his uncredited film debut in the movie "Fear Strikes Out".
- In 1960, he was cast as "Chris Higbee" in the TV series "The Roaring 20's". He appeared in 39 episodes from 1960 to 1962.
- In 1962, he was cast as "George Christopher" in the TV series "McHale's Navy". He appeared in 138 episodes from 1962 to 1966.
- In 1966, he was cast as "Sheriff Harold Sikes" in the TV series "Pistols 'n' Petticoats". He appeared in 26 episodes from 1966 to 1967.

- His last acting appearance was in an episode ("Chance of a Lifetime") of "Boone" in 1983.
- Gary was married twice – Paula J. Hill (1962-?) and Lavonne R. Wuertzer (1969-84).
- In 1984, whilst living in Redondo Beach, Gary committed suicide. It was rumoured that he was distraught about a possible criminal charge.
- Gary's other film credits include "Rockabilly Baby" (1957), "Yellowstone Kelly" (1959), "McHale's Navy" (1964), "McHale's Navy Joins the Air Force" (1965) and "The Munster's Revenge" (1981)(TV).
- His other TV credits include "McCloud" (1972), "Streets of San Francisco" (1973), "The Waltons" (1974), "Barnaby Jones" (1980) and "The Incredible Hulk" (1982).

- **Carole Maureen Wells** was born on August 31, 1942 in Shreveport, Louisiana.
- She began her acting career, at age 12, in TV commercials. Her first commercial was "Dial Soap".
- In 1956, she made her TV acting debut in an episode ("The Green Promise") of "Lux Video Theatre".
- Many TV guest appearances followed including "Medic" (1956), "Cavalcade of America" (1956), "Father Knows Best" (1958), "Bachelor Father" (1958) 2 episodes, "Maverick" (1959-

60) 2 episodes, "Fury" (1960), "The Donna Reed Show" (1960) and "The Many Loves of Dobie Gillis" (1960).

- Carole made her uncredited film debut in the movie "The Absent-Minded Professor" in 1961.
- In 1960, she was cast as "Edwina Brown" in the TV series "National Velvet". She appeared in 58 episodes from 1960 to 1962.
- In 1966, she was cast as "Lucy Hanks" in the TV series "Pistols 'n' Petticoats". She appeared in 26 episodes from 1966 to 1967.
- Her last acting appearance, to date, was in the film "Molly and the Ghost" in 1991.
- Carole has been married three times – Edward Laurence Doheny IV (1963-73), Walter Karabian (1977-84) and Jerry Dean Vanier (2000-present). She has two children with Mr. Doheny and two children with Mr. Karabian.
- She has spent a lot of her adult life doing charity work.
- In 2012, she authored the book "Amberella: An Action Hero Adventure".
- Carole's other film credits include "A Thunder of Drums" (1961), "Come Blow Your Horn" (1963) uncredited, "The Lively Set" (1964), "Get to Know Your Rabbit" (1972) uncredited, "The House of Seven Corpses" (1974), "Funny Lady" (1975) and "The Cheap Detective" (1978).

- Her other TV credits include "Wide Country" (1962), "Laramie" (1962), "Wagon Train" (1962-63) 2 episodes, "Leave It To Beaver" (1963), "Ben Casey" (1963) 2 episodes, "Perry Mason" (1965), "The Virginian" (1967), "The Brian Keith Show" (1973), "Switch" (1975), "McCloud" (1976) and "1st & Ten" (1989).

- **Robert Lowery** was born Robert Larkin Hanks on October 17, 1913 in Kansas City, Missouri.
- He was the son of Louis R. Hanks, a Kansas City attorney, and Leah Thompson, a concert pianist and organist.
- Bob graduated from Paseo High School in Kansas City, and was invited to sing with the Slats Randall Orchestra in the early 1930's.
- He also played baseball with the Kansas City Blues minor league baseball team.
- Bob's father died in 1935, so he and his mother packed up and moved to Hollywood.
- He enrolled in the Lila Bliss acting school and later signed a contract with 20th Century Fox in 1937.
- Bob made his uncredited film debut in the Fox movie "The Lady Escapes" in 1937.
- His first credited role was in the film "Wake Up and Live" in 1937.
- For the next twenty years he appeared in numerous films including "Life Begins in College" (1937), "Submarine Patrol" (1938),

"Mr. Moto in Danger Island" (1939), "Charlie Chan in Reno" (1939), "Charlie Chan's Murder Cruise" (1940), "The Mark of Zorro" (1940), "Revenge of the Zombies" (1943), "Dangerous Passage" (1944), "Death Valley" (1946), "The Dalton Gang" (1949), "Train to Tombstone" (1950), "The Homesteaders" (1953) and "Two-Gun Lady" (1955).

- In 1956, he was cast as "Big Tim Champion" in the TV series "Circus Boy". He appeared in 49 episodes from 1956 to 1957.
- In 1966, he was cast as "Buss Courtney" in the TV series "Pistols 'n' Petticoats". He appeared in 20 episodes from 1966 to 1967. This was his last acting role.
- Bob was married three times – Vivian Wilcox (1941-44), Rusty Farrell (1947-48) and Jean Parker (1951-71). He had one child with Ms. Parker.
- He was related on his father's side to Nancy Hanks, Abraham Lincoln's natural mother.
- Bob was the second actor to play "Batman" on screen ("Batman and Robin" – 1949).
- After he retired from acting, he had a celebrity travel cruise business with Jackie Coogan.
- He was an accomplished stage actor and appeared in productions such as "Born Yesterday" and "The Caine Mutiny".
- Bob's other film credits include "The Parson and the Outlaw" (1957), "The Rise and Fall of

Legs Diamond" (1960), "Deadly Duo" (1962), "When the Girls Take Over" (1962), "Young Guns of Texas" (1962), "McLintock!" (1963), "Stage to Thunder Rock" (1964), "Waco" (1966) and "The Ballad of Josie" (1967).

- His other TV credits include "Cowboy G-Men" (1952-53) 6 episodes, "The Gene Autry Show" (1953) 2 episodes, "Death Valley Days" (1953), "Judge Roy Bean" (1956) 3 episodes, "Casey Jones" (1958), "26 Men" (1958) 3 episodes, "The Adventures of Rin Tin Tin" (1956-58) 3 episodes, "The Texan" (1959), "Maverick" (1958-59) 2 episodes, "Disneyland" (1960), "Hotel de Paree" (1960), "Wagon Train" (1958-60) 2 episodes, "Perry Mason" (1960-61) 2 episodes, "Rawhide" (1959-62) 3 episodes, "77 Sunset Strip" (1958-62) 4 episodes, "Hawaiian Eye" (1959-62) 5 episodes and "Hazel" (1962).

"The Quest"

Years : 1976

Episodes : 15 (1 season)

Cast :-

Kurt Russell (b. 1951) - Played Morgan Beaudine

Tim Matheson (b. 1947) - Played Quentin Beaudine

Synopsis :-
Two brothers roam the West looking for their sister who was captured by Indians.

Trivia & Tidbits :-

"The Show"

- **"The Quest"** premiered on NBC on September 22, 1976 and last aired on December 29, 1976.
- The show ran for one season with a total of 15 episodes (only 11 episodes were actually aired).
- The series was created by Tracy Keenan Wynn and produced by David Gerber Productions and Columbia Pictures Television.

- "The Quest" TV series was preceded by a TV movie of the same name and starring the same actors.
- Location scenes were filmed in Arizona.

"The Stars"

- **Kurt Russell** was born Kurt Vogel Russell on March 17, 1951 in Springfield, Massachusetts.
- He is the son of Louise Julia (nee Crone), a dancer and Neil Oliver "Bing" Russell, a character actor.
- Kurt's father played "Deputy Clem Foster" in the TV series "Bonanza".
- Kurt graduated from Thousand Oaks High School in 1969.
- He made his first credited TV appearance in an episode of "The Dick Powell Show" in 1962.
- Following this, he made several guest appearances on TV shows including "Dennis the Menace" (1962), "Sam Benedict" (1963), "The Eleventh Hour" (1963) and "Our Man Higgins" (1963).
- In 1963, he was cast as "Jaimie McPheeters" in the TV series "The Travels of Jaimie McPheeters". He appeared in 26 episodes from 1963 to 1964.
- Kurt also made his film debut in 1963. He had an uncredited part in the movie "It Happened at the World's Fair", starring Elvis Presley.
- In 1974, he was cast as "Bo Larsen" in the short-lived TV series "The New Land". He appeared in 6 episodes before the show was canceled.

- Then in 1976, he was cast as "Morgan Beaudine" in the TV series "The Quest". He appeared in 15 episodes.
- Since 1977, Kurt has concentrated on his film career. He has not guest starred in a TV series since an episode ("Deadly Doubles") of "Hawaii Five-O" in 1977.
- Kurt was married to Season Hubley from 1979 to 1983. They have one son, Boston Russell.
- Since 1983, he has been the partner of actress Goldie Hawn. They also have one son, Wyatt Russell.
- In the early 1970's, Kurt played minor league baseball before damaging his rotator cuff (shoulder). The injury forced him to retire in 1973 and as a result he returned to acting.
- Kurt's father was a former baseball player (he also owned the minor league baseball team The Portland Mavericks) and his nephew, Matt Franco, was a former Atlanta Braves' first baseman.
- In the 1970's, he signed a ten year contract with the Walt Disney Company.
- In 1998, he was made a Disney Legend.
- Kurt was nominated for a Primetime Emmy Award (Outstanding Lead Actor in a Limited Series or a Special) for the TV movie "Elvis" (1979).
- He was also nominated for a Golden Globe (Best Performance by an Actor in a Supporting Role in a Motion Picture) for "Silkwood" (1983).
- Kurt is a FFA licensed private pilot.

- His other film credits include "Guns at Diablo" (1965), "Guns in the Heather" (1969), "The Computer Wore Tennis Shoes" (1969), "The Barefoot Executive" (1971), "Superdad" (1973), "The Quest" (1976)(TV), "Elvis" (1979)(TV), "Escape from New York" (1981), "Silkwood" (1983), "Swing Shift" (1984), "Big Trouble in Little China" (1986), "Tequila Sunrise" (1988), "Tango & Cash" (1989), "Backdraft" (1991), "Tombstone" (1993), "Stargate" (1994), "Escape from L.A." (1996), "Vanilla Sky" (2001), "Poseidon" (2006) and "The Art of the Steal" (2013), "The Hateful Eight" (2015) and "Deepwater Horizon" (2016).
- Kurt's other TV credits include "The Virginian" (1964-65) 2 episodes, "The Legend of Jesse James" (1966), "The Fugitive" (1964-66) 2 episodes, "The Road West" (1967), "Daniel Boone" (1965-69) 5 episodes, "Disneyland" (1967-72) 7 episodes, "Gunsmoke" (1964-74) 2 episodes and "Police Story" (1974-75) 2 episodes.

- **Tim Matheson** was born Timothy Lewis Matthieson on December 31, 1947 in Glendale, California.
- He made his TV debut as "Roddy Miller" in the TV series "Window on Main Street" (1961), starring Robert Young ("Father Knows Best").
- This was followed by guest appearances on TV shows including "Leave It To Beaver" (1962-63) 2 episodes, "My Three Sons" (1962-63) 3

episodes, "Ripcord" (1963) and "The Farmer's Daughter" (1964).

- At age 17, he provided the voice of "Jonny Quest" in the TV series of the same name.
- At the same time he also provided the voice of "Sinbad Jr." in the TV series "Sinbad Jr.".
- In 1966, he provided the voice of "Jace" in the TV series "Space Ghost". He voiced in 10 episodes.
- Then in 1967, he provided the voice of "Samson" in the TV series "Young Samson & Goliath". He voiced in 20 episodes from 1967 to 1968.
- In 1969, he was cast as "Jim Horn" in the TV series "The Virginian". He appeared in 24 episodes from 1969 to 1970.
- In 1972, he was cast as "Griff King" in the TV series "Bonanza". He appeared in 15 episodes from 1972 to 1973.
- In 1976, he was cast as "Quentin Beaudine" in the TV series "The Quest". He appeared in 15 episodes.
- Another TV series he appeared in was "Tucker's Witch". He played the character "Rick Tucker" in 12 episodes from 1982 to 1983.
- In 1988, he was cast as "Harry Stadlin" in the short-lived TV series "Just in Time". He appeared in 6 episodes.
- Another short-lived series he appeared in was "Charlie Hoover". He played the main character in 7 episodes in 1991.

- In 1997, he voiced the character "Capt. John O'Rourke" in the TV series "The Legend of Calamity Jane". The series lasted 13 episodes.
- In 2001, he played the character "Sheriff Matthew Donner" in the TV series "Wolf Lake". He appeared in 9 episodes from 2001 to 2002.
- Following this, he played "Bill Dunne" in the TV series "Breaking News" (2002). He appeared in 12 episodes.
- In 1999, he began a recurring role as "John Hoynes" in the critically acclaimed TV series "The West Wing". He appeared in 20 episodes from 1999 to 2006.
- In 2012, he provided the voice of "Brad Chiles" in the TV series "Scooby-Doo! Mystery Incorporated". He voiced the character in 13 episodes from 2012 to 2013.
- Another recurring role was the character "Larry Sizemore" in the TV series "Burn Notice". He appeared in 5 episodes from 2008 to 2013.
- In 2011, he was cast as "Dr. Brick Breeland" in the TV series "Hart of Dixie". He appeared in 55 episodes from 2011 to 2014.
- Tim has been married twice - Jennifer Leak (1968-71) and Megan Murphy Matheson (1985-2010). He has three children with Megan.
- He met his first wife, Jennifer, when they were co-starring in the film "Yours, Mine and Ours" (1968).
- Tim once owned the magazine "National Lampoon". However, he sold it in 1991 due to mounting debts.

- He is also an accomplished director. Tim has directed episodes of "Third Watch", "Ed", "The Twilight Zone", "Cold Case", "The West Wing", "Criminal Minds" and "Burn Notice". In 2009, he directed the pilot episode of "Covert Affairs".
- Tim has been nominated twice (2002 and 2003) for a Primetime Emmy. Both times as Outstanding Guest Actor in a Dramatic Series ("The West Wing").
- His other film credits include "Divorce American Style" (1967), "Magnum Force" (1973), "The Last Day" (1975)(TV), "The Quest" (1976)(TV), "The Quest : The Longest Drive" (1976)(TV), "Animal House" (1978), "1941" (1979), "To Be or Not to Be" (1983), "Fletch" (1985), "Solar Crisis" (1990), "While Justice Sleeps" (1994)(TV), "A Very Brady Sequel" (1996), "The Story of Us" (1999), "Jackie Bouvier Kennedy Onassis" (2000)(TV), "Judas" (2004)(TV), "Redline" (2007) and "Talker" (2011)(TV).
- Tim's other TV credits include "Adam-12" (1969), "Bracken's World" (1970), "Here's Lucy" (1972), "Kung Fu" (1973), "Owen Marshall, Counselor at Law" (1971-74) 4 episodes, "Rhoda" (1976), "Hawaii Five-O" (1977), "Insight" (1972-78) 6 episodes, "Fallen Angels" (1993), "The King of Queens" (2002), "Shark" (2007), "Entourage" (2008), "CSI" (2013) 2 episodes and "Tom Green Live" (2014).

"Rango"

Years : 1967

Episodes : 17 (1 season)

Cast :-

Tim Conway (b. 1933) - Played Rango

Norman Alden (b. 1924) - Played Captain Horton

Guy Marks (b. 1923 d. 1987) - Played Pink Cloud

Synopsis :-
Adventures of a bumbling Texas Ranger.

Trivia & Tidbits :-

"The Show"

- **"Rango"** premiered on ABC on January 13, 1967 and last aired on May 5, 1967.
- The show ran for one season with a total of 17 episodes.
- The series was created by R.S. Allen and Harvey Bullock and produced by Thomas/Spelling Productions and Timkel Productions.
- Filming took place at Desilu Studios, California.

- The theme song "Rango" was composed by Earl Hagen (music) and Ben Raleigh (lyrics) and performed by Frankie Laine.
- In 2002, TV Guide ranked the series No.47 on its list of "50 Worst Shows of All Time".

"In Memoriam"

- **Norman Alden** died of natural causes on July 27, 2012 (87) in Los Angeles, California.
- **Guy Marks** died on November 28, 1987 (64) in Brigantine, New Jersey.

"The Stars"

- **Tim Conway** was born Thomas Daniel Conway on December 15, 1933 in Willoughby, Ohio.
- He changed his name to "Tim" to avoid confusion with actor Tom Conway.
- Tim's father was a whip in Ireland and continued working with horses once he moved to the United States. As a child, Tim dreamed of becoming a jockey.
- He grew up in Chagrin Falls, Cleveland.
- Tim earned a degree in speech and radio from Bowling Green State University, Ohio.
- After graduation from University he joined the army for two years and then took a job answering mail for a Cleveland radio station, where he went on to become a writer in the promotional department.

- In 1956, Rose Marie, comedienne, discovered him at a local Cleveland television station and then arranged for him to audition for "The Steve Allen Show" (1956). He so impressed Allen that he ended up with a regular spot on the show.
- In 1962, he was cast as "Ensign Charles Parker" in the TV series "McHale's Navy". He appeared in 137 episodes from 1962 to 1966.
- In 1967, he was cast as "Rango" in the TV series of the same name. He appeared in 17 episodes.
- He was a cast member of "The Carol Burnett Show" from 1968 to 1975.
- Tim has been married twice. First to Mary Anne Dalton (1961-78) and currently to Charlene Fusco (1984-present). He had seven children with Ms. Dalton.
- Tim wrote and starred in the films "The Billion Dollar Hobo" (1977), "The Prize Fighter" (1979) and "Private Eyes" (1981).
- He was the voice of "Barnacle Boy" on "SpongeBob SquarePants" from 2000 to 2005.
- In 2001, Tim and Harvey Korman starred in the 25th anniversary reunion special, "The Carol Burnett Show Stoppers". The show drew 30 million viewers and became the 4th highest rated TV show of the season.
- In 2002, he and Harvey were inducted into the Academy of Television Arts and Sciences' Hall of Fame.
- In 2003, he and Harvey were featured performers on CBS's 75th Anniversary Special.
- In 2004, he was named a Disney Legend.

- In 2005, he and the rest of the cast of "The Carol Burnett Show" received TV Land's Legend Award.
- On stage, Tim played "Felix" in 182 performances of "The Odd Couple". He also wrote and starred in "Just for Laughs: A Day with Gates and Mills", which toured for 20 weeks and 130 performances.
- Tim's DVD's of "Dorf on Golf" and "Dorf Goes Fishing" have both reached platinum sales status.
- He is the co-founder of the Don MacBeth Memorial Jockey Fund to aid injured and disabled jockeys.
- In his career Tim has won six Emmy Awards ("The Carol Burnett Show" (4), "Coach" (1), "30 Rock" (1)) and one Golden Globe Award ("The Carol Burnett Show").
- Tim's other TV credits include "The New Steve Allen Show" (1961), "The Gary Moore Show" (1962), "The Danny Kaye Show" (1966-67), "The Hollywood Squares" (1967), "The Jim Nabors Hour" (1969), "Newhart" (1990), "Married With Children" (1995), "Mad About You" (1999), "Diagnosis Murder" (1999), "Yes Dear" (2001-2005) 7 episodes as "Tom Warner" and "30 Rock" (2008).
- His other film credits include "McHale's Navy" (1964), "McHale's Navy Joins the Air Force" (1965), "The World's Greatest Athlete" (1973), "The Apple Dumpling Gang" (1975), "The Shaggy DA" (1976), "The Apple Dumpling Gang Rides Again" (1979), "Cannonball Run II"

(1984) and "Garfield's Fun Fest" (2008)
(Voice).

- **Norman Alden** was born Norman Adelberg on
September 13, 1924 in Fort Worth, Texas.
- He served in the U.S. Army during the Second
World War and after his discharge attended
the Texas Christian University under the G.I.
Bill of Rights.
- It was here that he developed his acting ability
by participating in the on-campus theater.
- He made his acting debut in an episode
("Nightmare") of "Panic!" in 1957.
- Several more TV appearances followed
including "The Bob Cummings Show" (1957),
"The 20th Century-Fox Hour" (1957), "Leave It
To Beaver" (1957), "Circus Boy" (1957),
"Goodyear Theatre" (1958), "Panic!" (1957-
58) 2 episodes, "Alcoa Theatre" (1958),
"Flight" (1958) 2 episodes, "Yancy Derringer"
(1958), "Pony Express" (1959), "Mackenzie's
Raiders" (1959), "Steve Canyon" (1958-59) 2
episodes, "The Texan" (1959), "The
Adventures of Rin Tin Tin" (1958-59) 2
episodes, "Perry Mason" (1959), "Mr. Lucky"
(1959-60) 2 episodes and "The Untouchables"
(1959-60) 3 episodes.
- In 1959, he was cast in a recurring role as
"Grundy" in the TV series "Not for Hire". He
appeared in 16 episodes from 1959 to 1960.
- In 1961, he played "Johnny Ringo" in 3
episodes of "The Life and Legend of Wyatt
Earp".

- Another recurring role he had was in the TV series "Hennesey". He played the character "Seaman Pulaski" in 5 episodes from 1959 to 1962.
- In 1967, he was cast as "Captain Horton" in the TV series "Rango". He appeared in 17 episodes.
- In 1970, he played "Tom Williams" in 6 episodes of the TV series "My Three Sons".
- Then in 1973, he supplied the voice of "Aquaman" in 16 episodes of the animated TV series "Super Friends".
- Following this, he played the recurring character "Al Cassidy" in the TV series "Fay". He appeared in 5 episodes from 1975 to 1976.
- His next TV series was "Mary Hartman, Mary Hartman". In 1976, he played "Leroy Fedders" in 8 episodes.
- In 1976, he was cast as "Frank Heflin" in the TV series "Electra Woman and Dyna Girl". He appeared in 16 episodes.
- His last acting appearance was in the TV movie "Our House" in 2006.
- Norman was married to Sharon Hayden from 1966 to 1978. They had two children. He also had a long-term (over 30 years) relationship with Ms. Linda Thieben.
- He played "Lou", the mechanic, in a series of commercials for AC Delco.
- Norman's other film credits include "The Power of the Resurrection" (1958), "The Walking Target" (1960), "Portrait of a Mobster" (1961), "The Nutty Professor" (1963), "The Patsy" (1964), "Andy" (1965), "First to Fight" (1967), "The Devil's Brigade" (1968), "Tora! Tora!

Tora! : The Attack on Pearl Harbor" (1970), "Cannon" (1971)(TV), "Ben" (1972), "The Honorable Sam Houston" (1975)(TV), "I Never Promised You a Rose Garden" (1977), "Borderline" (1980), "Back to the Future" (1985), "Ed Wood" (1994), "Patch Adams" (1998) and "Detective" (2005)(TV).

- His other TV credits include "Hong Kong" (1960), "The Americans" (1961), "The Lawless Years" (1959-61) 9 episodes, "Lawman" (1961), "Bonanza" (1960-61) 2 episodes, "77 Sunset Strip" (1962) 2 episodes, "Cheyenne" (1962), "The Dakotas" (1963) 2 episodes, "Combat!" (1963-64) 2 episodes, "Family Affair" (1966), "The Andy Griffith Show" (1966-67) 2 episodes, "The Big Valley" (1967), "Iron Horse" (1967), "Lassie" (1969) 2 episodes, "The Doris Day Show" (1968-70) 2 episodes, "Hogan's Heroes" (1965-71) 2 episodes, "The Mod Squad" (1968-72) 4 episodes, "Love, American Style" (1971-73) 3 episodes, "Gunsmoke" (1967-73) 6 episodes, "The F.B.I." (1972-74) 2 episodes, "Mannix" (1970-74) 3 episodes, "Cannon" (1973-75) 2 episodes, "The Streets of San Francisco" (1972-75) 4 episodes, "Young Dan'l Boone" (1977), "The All-New Super Friends Hour" (1977)(voice), "Operation Petticoat" (1977-78) 3 episodes, "Barnaby Jones" (1974-79) 2 episodes, "Charlie's Angels" (1977-81) 3 episodes, "Falcon Crest" (1983) 3 episodes, "Matt Houston" (1983-85) 3 episodes, "Hunter" (1985-86) 3 episodes, "Murder, She Wrote" (1986-88) 2 episodes, "Valerie"

(1990), "Rugrats" (1997) and "Like Family" (2003).

- **Guy Marks** was born Mario Scarpa on October 31, 1923 in Philadelphia, Pennsylvania.
- He was one of eleven children born to Adelina and Ermelindo Scarpa, a concert clarinettist.
- After finishing school, he enlisted in the U.S. Army and served for two years. Following this he had a six year stint in the Merchant Marines.
- He started his show business career by doing impressions of W.C. Fields, Wendell Wilkie and The Ink Spots.
- Following this, he headed for New York and began working in nightclubs in New York, Atlantic City and Chicago.
- After a winning performance on "Arthur Godfrey's Talent Scouts" he secured an appearance on "The Ed Sullivan Show" (1960).
- In 1962, he was cast as "Freddy" on the TV series "The Joey Bishop Show". He appeared in 20 episodes from 1962 to 1963.
- He made his film debut in the TV movie "Munroe" in 1963.
- In 1965, he was cast as "Ed Robbins" in the TV series "The John Forsythe Show". He appeared in 29 episodes from 1965 to 1966.
- Then in 1967, he was cast as "Pink Cloud" in the TV series "Rango". He appeared in 17 episodes.
- In 1986, he played the character "Harry" in 5 episodes of the TV series "You Again?" starring Jack Klugman. This was to be his last acting appearance.

- Guy was married three times – Barbara Thomas (1952-?), Kathleen Marks (1962-1966) and Judy Marie De Salle (1971-?).
- He was better known as a stand-up comic and world-class impressionist.
- Guy guest-starred on many TV variety shows including "Hollywood Palace", "The Milton Berle Show", "The Dean Martin Show", "The Pat Boone Show" and "The Joey Bishop Show".
- In 1968, he released a "one-hit wonder" novelty song called "Loving You Has Made Me Bananas".
- Guy appeared on two "Dean Martin Celebrity Roasts" – "The Dean Martin Celebrity Roast: Michael Landon" (1975) and "The Dean Martin Celebrity Roast: George Burns" (1978).
- His other movie credits include "Fol-de-Rol" (1972)(TV), "Train Ride to Hollywood" (1975) and "Great Day" (1977)(TV).
- Guy's other TV credits include "The Dick Van Dyke Show" (1963), "Make Room for Daddy" (1963-64) 2 episodes, "My Favorite Martian" (1965), "Here's Lucy" (1969), "The Odd Couple" (1974), "McCoy" (1975) and "Police Woman" (1977-78) 2 episodes.

"The Road West"

Years : 1966-1967

Episodes : 29 (1 season)

Cast :-

Barry Sullivan (b. 1912 d. 1994) - Played Ben Pride

Andrew Prine (b. 1936) – Played Timothy Pride

Brenda Scott (b. 1943) – Played Midge Pride

Kelly Corcoran (b. 1958 d. 2002) – Played Kip Pride

Kathryn Hays (b. 1933) – Played Elizabeth Reynolds

Charles Steel (b. 1897 d. 1980) – Played Tom Pride

Glenn Corbett (b. 1933 d. 1993) – Played Chance Reynolds

Synopsis :-
Shortly after the American Civil War a family leaves Springfield, Ohio and moves west.

Trivia & Tidbits :-

"The Show"

- **"The Road West"** premiered on NBC on September 12, 1966 and last aired on May 1, 1967.
- The show ran for one season with a total of 29 episodes.
- The series was produced by Universal TV. Norman Macdonnell was the producer (creator of "Gunsmoke").
- The theme music was composed by Leonard Rosenman.
- The show aired opposite "The Andy Griffith Show" and "Family Affair" on CBS and "Felony Squad" and "Peyton Place" on ABC.
- Kraft Foods sponsored the series.

"In Memoriam"

- **Barry Sullivan** died of a respiratory ailment on June 6, 1994 (81) in Sherman Oaks, Los Angeles, California.
- **Kelly Corcoran** died on April 17, 2002 (43) in Sanger, California.
- **Charles Seel** died on April 19, 1980 (82) in Los Angeles, California.
- **Glenn Corbett** died of lung cancer on January 16, 1993 (59) in San Antonio, Texas.

"The Stars"

- **Barry Sullivan (see "The Tall Man")**

- **Andrew Prine (see "The Wide Country")**

- **Brenda Scott** was born Brenda J. Smith on March 15, 1943 in Cincinnati, Ohio,
- She made her acting debut in an episode ("The Editor's Daughter") of "Window on Main Street" (1961), starring Robert Young.
- Several more TV guest appearances followed including "Ben Casey" (1962), "The Detectives" (1962), "Shannon" (1962), "Hazel" (1962) 2 episodes, "Leave It To Beaver" (1962), "The Donna Reed Show" (1963), "Gunsmoke" (1963), "Wagon Train" (1963) 2 episodes, "Temple Houston" (1963), "My Three Sons" (1962-63) 2 episodes, "Dr. Kildare" (1962-64) 3 episodes, "Rawhide" (1964), "Bonanza" (1965), "The Long, Hot Summer" (1965) and "The Fugitive" (1964-66) 2 episodes.
- In 1966, she was cast as "Midge Pride" in the TV series "The Road West". She appeared in 29 episodes from 1966 to 1967.
- Brenda made her uncredited film debut in the movie "13 West Street" in 1962.

- She made her last acting appearance, to date, in the film short "The Problem with Fiber Optics" in 2005.
- Brenda has been married four times. On three of those occasions it was to Andrew Prine (1965-66); (1968-69) and (1973-78). She has been married to Dean Hargrove since 1979.
- Her other film credits include "The Hanged Man" (1964)(TV), "Johnny Tiger" (1966), "Journey to Shiloh" (1968), "The Savaged Land" (1969)(TV) and "Chase" (1973)(TV).
- Brenda's other TV credits include "Dragnet 1967" (1967), "Ironside" (1968) 3 episodes, "The Virginian" (1964-69) 4 episodes, "Here Come the Brides" (1969), "The Name of the Game" (1970), "Mannix" (1968-70) 2 episodes, "Cade's County" (1971), "The Mod Squad" (1969-72) 2 episodes, "Medical Center" (1971-73) 2 episodes, "Adams of Eagle Lake" (1975) 2 episodes, "Disneyland" (1979) 2 episodes and "Simon & Simon" (1983).

- **Kelly Patrick Corcoran** was born on August 7, 1958 in Los Angeles, California.
- He was the son of William 'Bill' Corcoran, a maintenance chief at M.G.M. Studios and Kathleen McKenney.

- Kelly's two older siblings Noreen ("Bachelor Father") and Kevin ("The Adventures of Spin and Marty") were also in the acting business.
- He made his uncredited acting debut in the film "The Courtship of Eddie's Father" in 1963.
- This was followed by appearances in TV series such as "Dr. Kildare" (1964), "The Baileys of Balboa" (1965), "The Adventures of Ozzie & Harriet" (1964-65) 2 episodes and "Run for Your Life" (1966).
- In 1966, he was cast as "Kip Pride" in the TV series "The Road West". He appeared in 29 episodes from 1966 to 1967.
- Kelly's other film credits include "Picture Mommy Dead" (1966) and "This Savage Land" (1969)(TV).
- His other TV credits include "The Big Valley" (1969), "Family Affair" (1970) 2 episodes and "Adam-12" (1970).

- **Kathryn Hays** was born Kay Piper on July 26, 1933 in Princeton, Illinois.
- Her first TV appearance was in an episode ("Total Eclipse") of "Hawaiian Eye" in 1962.
- Several more TV appearances followed including "Surfside 6" (1962), "Naked City" (1962), "The United States Steel Hour" (1963), "Wide Country" (1963), "Dr. Kildare" (1963), "Route 66" (1963), "The Nurses" (1964), "Mr. Novak" (1964), "Bonanza"

(1964), "The Virginian" (1965), "Branded" (1965) and "Run for Your Life" (1966).

- In 1966, she was cast as "Elizabeth Reynolds" in the TV series "The Road West". She appeared in 29 episodes from 1966 to 1967.
- In 1972, she was cast as "Kim Hughes" in the TV soap "As the World Turns". She appeared in over 1,500 episodes from 1972 to 2010.
- Kathryn has been married three times. Her second marriage was to actor Glenn Ford (1966-69). She has one child from her first marriage.
- She has appeared on the Broadway stage several times, including "Dames at Sea" with Bernadette Peters.
- Kathryn's film credits include "Ladybug Ladybug" (1963), "Ride Beyond Vengeance" (1966), "Counterpoint" (1967), "This Savage Land" (1969)(TV), "Breakout" (1970)(TV) and "Yuma" (1971)(TV).
- Her other TV credits include "The High Chaparral" (1968), "Mannix" (1968), "Here Come the Brides" (1969), "Marcus Welby, M.D." (1971), "Bearcats!" (1971), "Cade's County" (1972), "Ghost Story" (1973), "Law & Order" (1999) and "One Life to Live" (2010).

- **Charles Seel** was born on April 29, 1897 in New York City, New York.

- He was a former vaudevillian and radio star in 1929.
- Charles acted in early silent films on the east coast.
- He moved to Hollywood in 1937 and made his uncredited acting debut in the film "Comet Over Broadway" in 1938.
- Three more uncredited roles followed – "Off the Record" (1939), "Blackwell's Island" (1939) and "Here Comes Mr. Jordan" (1941).
- Charles made his TV debut in an episode ("Ghost Trails") of "Hopalong Cassidy" in 1952.
- Several more TV guest appearances followed including "Terry and the Pirates" (1952), "Four Star Playhouse" (1953-54) 2 episodes, "Lux Video Theatre" (1955), "Medic" (1955), "Highway Patrol" (1955), "Dragnet" (1956), "State Trooper" (1957), "Broken Arrow" (1957), "Suspicion" (1957) and "The Court of Last Resort" (1957).
- In 1957, he was cast in a recurring role as "Otis – Bartender" in the TV series "Tombstone Territory". He appeared in 5 episodes from 1957 to 1958.
- In 1959-60, he appeared in 3 episodes of the TV series "The Deputy". He played the part of "Dr. Miller".
- Then in 1960, he had a recurring role as "Mr. Krinkie" in the TV series "Dennis the Menace". He appeared in 9 episodes from 1960 to 1963.

- In 1966, he was cast as "Tom Pride" in the TV series "The Road West". He appeared in 29 episodes from 1966 to 1967.
- Another recurring role he had was in the TV series "Gunsmoke". His character name was "Barney Danches" and he appeared in 11 episodes from 1965 to 1972.
- His last acting appearance was in the TV movie "Dan August: Once Is Never Enough" in 1980.
- Charles' other film credits include "I Was a Teenage Frankenstein" (1957), "The Horse Soldiers" (1959) uncredited, "Pollyanna" (1960) uncredited, "Return to Peyton Place" (1961) uncredited, "The Man Who Shot Liberty Valance" (1962) uncredited, "Tammy and the Doctor" (1963), "Mr. Buddwing" (1966), "Winning" (1969) uncredited, "Duel" (1971)(TV), "Westworld" (1973) and "Airport 1975" (1974) uncredited.
- His other TV credits include "M Squad" (1958), "Cimarron City" (1958), "Bat Masterson" (1959), "Schlitz Playhouse of Stars" (1953-59) 5 episodes, "The Rifleman" (1959) 2 episodes, "Wichita Town" (1959-60) 3 episodes, "The Tall Man" (1960), "Wagon Train" (1957-60) 2 episodes, "Letter to Loretta" (1958-61) 5 episodes, "Bronco" (1961), "Death Valley Days" (1961), "77 Sunset Strip" (1961-62) 2 episodes, "Surfside 6" (1960-62) 3 episodes, "Tales of Wells Fargo" (1957-62) 2 episodes,

"Laramie" (1962), "The Dick Powell Show" (1962-63) 2 episodes, "Mr. Novak" (1963), "Destry" (1964), "The Munsters" (1965), "Lassie" (1964-65) 2 episodes, "F Troop" (1965-67) 2 episodes, "The Man from U.N.C.L.E." (1964-67) 3 episodes, "Cimarron Strip" (1967), "The Guns of Will Sonnett" (1967-69) 3 episodes, "Bonanza" (1962-69) 4 episodes, "The Virginian" (1962-69) 5 episodes, "The Mod Squad" (1972), "Adam-12" (1970-74) 3 episodes and "Marcus Welby, M.D." (1972-76) 2 episodes.

- **Glenn Corbett** was born Glenn Edwin Rothenburg on August 17, 1933 in El Monte, California.
- He was the son of a garage mechanic.
- Glenn had a stint in the United States Navy.
- He met his wife, Judy, at college and was also discovered by talent scouts from Columbia Pictures.
- Glenn made his film debut in the Columbia movie "The Crimson Kimono" in 1959.
- A number of films followed including "Man on a String" (1960), "The Mountain Road" (1960), "All the Young Men" (1960), "Homicidal" (1961) and "The Pirates of Blood River" (1962).

- In 1962, he was cast as "Wes Macauley" in the TV series "It's a Man's World". He appeared in 19 episodes from 1962 to 1963.
- In 1963, he was cast as "Linc Case" in the TV series "Route 66". He appeared in 32 episodes from 1963 to 1964.
- Then in 1966, he was cast as "Chance Reynolds" in the TV series "The Road West". He appeared in 29 episodes from 1966 to 1967.
- In 1976, he joined the cast of the daytime soap "The Doctors". He played "Jason Aldrich" from 1976 to 1981.
- In 1983, he started a recurring role as "Paul Morgan" in the TV series "Dallas". He appeared in 19 episodes from 1983 to 1990.
- His last acting appearance was in the film "Shadow Force" in 1992.
- Glenn married Judy Daniels in 1957 and they had two children, Jason and Jocelyn.
- His other film credits include "Shenandoah" (1965), "Guns in the Heather" (1969), "Chisum" (1970), "Big Jake" (1971), "Ride in a Pink Car" (1974), "Nashville Girl" (1976), "Midway" (1976) and "Stunts Unlimited" (1980)(TV).
- Glenn's other TV credits include "12 O'Clock High" (1964-65) 2 episodes, "The Virginian" (1965), "The Legend of Jesse James" (1966), "Star Trek" (1967), "Disneyland" (1969) 3

episodes, "Marcus Welby, M.D." (1971), "The F.B.I." (1968-71) 2 episodes, "Bonanza" (1965-71) 2 episodes, "Medical Center" (1971-72) 2 episodes, "The Mod Squad" (1972), "Gunsmoke" (1964-74) 3 episodes, "Police Story" (1974-76) 5 episodes, "The Rockford Files" (1979), "The Fall Guy" (1982) and "Automan" (1984).

"The Rounders"

Years : 1966 - 1967

Episodes : 17 (1 season)

Cast :-

Ron Hayes (b. 1929 d. 2004) - Played Ben Jones

Patrick Wayne (b. 1939) - Played "Howdy" Lewis

Chill Wills (b. 1902 d. 1978) - Played Jim Ed Love

Synopsis :-
Stories of two idle, woman-chasing cowboys.

Trivia & Tidbits :-

"The Show"

- **"The Rounders"** premiered on ABC on September 6, 1966 and last aired on January 3, 1967. The first episode was titled "A Horse On Jim Ed Love".
- The show ran for one season with a total of 17 color episodes.
- The program was loosely based on the 1965 film of the same name.

- "The Rounders" was created by Marion Hargrove.
- The series was produced by MGM Television and distributed by the American Broadcasting Company (ABC).
- The theme music was composed by Jeff Alexander.
- The show ran opposite "The Red Skelton Show" on CBS and the sitcom "Occasional Wife" on NBC.

"In Memoriam"

- **Ron Hayes** died of a subdural hematoma after a fall on October 1, 2004 (75) in Malibu, California.
- **Chill Wills** died of cancer on December 15, 1978 (76) in Encino, California.

"The Stars"

- **Ron Hayes** was born Ronald G. Hayes on February 26, 1929 in San Francisco, California.
- He was the son of Sam Hayes and Marion de Rode Brune. Both parents were involved in the theater and acting.
- In 1952, Ron graduated from Stanford University with a degree in foreign relations.
- He was a United States Marine during the Korean War.
- After the war, he worked for radio station KSJO in San Jose, California.

- In 1957, he moved, with his family, to Hollywood to begin an acting career.
- Ron made his TV debut in an episode ("A Case of Sudden Death") of "The Joseph Cotton Show: On Trial" in 1957.
- In 1959, he made his film debut in the movie "Gunmen from Laredo".
- During this time he guest starred on a number of TV shows including "M Squad" (1957), "Colt .45" (1958), "26 Men" (1958), "Maverick" (1958-59) 2 episodes, "Bronco" (1958-59) 3 episodes, "Cheyenne" (1957-59) 2 episodes, "Hotel de Paree" (1960), "The Texan" (1959-60) 3 episodes, "Tombstone Territory" (1959-60) 2 episodes, "Death Valley Days" (1960) 2 episodes, "Shotgun Slade" (1960), "The Rifleman" (1961), "Bat Masterson" (1960-61) 4 episodes and "Two Faces West" (1961).
- In 1961, he was cast as "Lincoln Vail" in the TV series "Everglades". He appeared in 39 episodes from 1961 to 1962.
- In 1966, he was cast as "Ben Jones" in the TV series "The Rounders". He appeared in 17 episodes from 1966 to 1967.
- Then in 1971, he was cast as "Garth Holden" in the TV series "Lassie". He appeared in 10 episodes from 1971 to 1972.
- From 1980 to 1981, he had the recurring role of "Hank Johnson" in the TV series "Dallas". He appeared in 6 episodes.
- His last acting appearance was in the TV movie "Dead Solid Perfect" in 1988.

- Ron was married twice – Joan Hayes and Betty Endicott (1966-2004). He had three children, Vanessa, Peter and Heidi, with Joan Hayes.
- He was a lifelong environmental activist and was one of the founders of "Earth Day".
- Ron's other film credits include "Face of a Fugitive" (1959), "The Mayor" (1965)(TV), "Around the World Under the Sea" (1966), "Lassie: Peace in Our Profession" (1970)(TV), "Four Against the Desert" (1977)(TV), "Zero to Sixty" (1978), "Galyon" (1980), "Death Wish 3" (1985) and "LBJ: The Early Years" (1987)(TV).
- His other TV credits include "Rawhide" (1959-62) 2 episodes, "Ripcord" (1963), "Laramie" (1960-63) 3 episodes, "The Littlest Hobo" (1964), "Wagon Train" (1960-64) 7 episodes, "Destry" (1964), "Flipper" (1965) 2 episodes, "Daktari" (1966-68) 4 episodes, "The High Chaparral" (1968-69) 2 episodes, "Bonanza" (1960-69) 6 episodes, "Gunsmoke" (1960-70) 8 episodes, "Hawaii Five-O" (1970-73) 2 episodes, "The Bionic Woman" (1976), "How the West Was Won" (1979), "Barnaby Jones" (1979) and "The A-Team" (1983).

- **Patrick Wayne** was born Patrick John Morrison on July 15, 1939 in Los Angeles, California.
- He is the son of movie star John 'Duke' Wayne and his first wife, Josephine Alicia Saenz.
- After high school he attended Loyola Marymount University and graduated in 1961.

- Patrick made his uncredited film debut in the John Wayne movie "Rio Grande" in 1950.
- He would go on to appear in another nine films with his father – "The Quiet Man" (1952) uncredited, "The Conqueror" (1956) uncredited, "The Searchers" (1956), "The Alamo" (1960), "The Comancheros" (1961), "Donovan's Reef" (1963) uncredited, "McLintock! (1963), "The Green Berets" (1968) and "Big Jake" (1971).
- In 1955, he made his TV debut in an episode ("Rookie of the Year") of "Screen Directors Playhouse".
- In 1966, he was cast as "Howdy Lewis" in the TV series "The Rounders". He appeared in 17 episodes from 1966 to 1967.
- From 1979 to 1980, he had the recurring role of "Lew Armitage" in the TV series "Shirley", starring Shirley Jones. He appeared in 4 episodes.
- His last acting appearance, to date, was in the film "Deep Cover" in 1997.
- Patrick has been married twice – Peggy Hunt (1965-78) and Misha Anderson (1999-present).
- In 1958, he won a Golden Globe Award (Most Promising Newcomer – Male) for "The Searchers" (1956).

- During the 1970's, he portrayed "Marathon John" in commercials for Mars Inc's Marathon Candy Bar.
- In 1980, he hosted "The Monte Carlo Show".
- From 1990 to 1991, he hosted the game show "Tic Tac Dough".
- In 2003, he became chairman of the John Wayne Cancer Institute after his brother, Michael, passed away.
- Patrick's other film credits include "The Sun Shines Bright" (1953), "The Long Gray Line" (1955), "Mister Roberts" (1955), "The Young Land" (1959), "Cheyenne Autumn" (1964), "Shenandoah" (1965), "An Eye for an Eye" (1966), "The Gatling Gun" (1971), "Beyond Atlantis" (1973), "Mustang Country" (1976), "Sinbad and the Eye of the Tiger" (1977), "Texas Detour" (1978), "Rustler's Rhapsody" (1985), "Young Guns" (1988) and "Her Alibi" (1989).
- His other TV credits include "Mr. Adams and Eve" (1957), "Have Gun – Will Travel" (1960), "Branded" (1965), "12 O'Clock High" (1966), "The F.B.I." (1968-72) 2 episodes, "McCloud" (1974), "Police Woman" (1974), "The Life and Times of Grizzly Adams" (1978), "Fantasy Island" (1981-83) 3 episodes, "The Love Boat" (1979-86) 6 episodes, "Murder, She Wrote" (1987), "MacGyver" (1988), "Alfred Hitchcock Presents" (1989) and "Silk Stalkings" (1997).

- **Chill Wills (see "Frontier Circus")**

"Sara"

Years : 1976

Episodes : 12 + 1 TV Movie (1 season)

Cast :-

Brenda Vaccaro (b. 1939) - Played Sara Yarnell

Brett Kramer (b. 1934 d. 2001) – Played Emmet Ferguson

Albert Stratton (b. 1937 d. 2011) – Played Martin Pope

Synopsis :-
The life of a spinster school teacher in Colorado in the 1870's.

Trivia & Tidbits :-

"The Show"

- **"Sara"** premiered on CBS on February 13, 1976 and last aired on May 7, 1976.
- The show ran for one season with a total of 12 color episodes plus 1 television movie.

- The series was created by Michael Gleason and produced by George Eckstein and Richard J. Collins.
- Lee Holdridge composed the show's theme song "Sara's Theme".
- "Sara" was based on the novel "The Revolt of Sarah Perkins" by Marian Cockrell.
- On July 30, 1976, CBS broadcast a made-for-television movie, "Territorial Men", compiled from footage shot for the weekly series.

"In Memoriam"

- **Bert Kramer** died of melanoma on June 20, 2001 (66) in Los Angeles, California.
- **Albert Stratton** died on April 26, 2011 (73) in Sarasota, Florida.

"The Stars"

- **Brenda Buell Vaccaro** was born on November 18, 1939 in Brooklyn, New York.
- She is the daughter of Italian/American parents Christine M. (nee Pavia) and Mario A. Vaccaro, a restaurateur.
- Brenda was raised in Dallas, Texas where her parents co-founded "Mario's Restaurant".
- After graduating from Jefferson High School, she returned to New York to study at the Neighborhood Playhouse.

- In 1961, she made her debut on Broadway in the play "Everybody Loves Opal". The show was short-lived.
- She made her TV debut in an episode ("The Corpse Ran Down Mulberry Street") of "Naked City" in 1961.
- Several TV appearances followed including "The Greatest Show on Earth" (1963), "The Fugitive" (1963), "The Reporter" (1964), "The Defenders" (1962-65) 3 episodes, "The Doctors and Nurses" (1965), "Vacation Playhouse" (1966) and "Coronet Blue" (1967).
- In 1969, she made her movie debut in the film "Where It's At". This was followed by a part in the Academy Award winning film "Midnight Cowboy", starring John Voight and Dustin Hoffman.
- Following this, she guest starred on many TV shows including "The F.B.I." (1969), "The Name of the Game" (1970-71) 2 episodes, "Marcus Welby, M.D." (1972), "Banacek" (1972), "The Streets of San Francisco" (1973-74) 2 episodes, "McCoy" (1975) and "Good Heavens" (1976).
- In 1976, she was cast as "Sara Yarnell" in the TV series "Sara". The show was short-lived and only lasted 12 episodes.
- In 1979, she was cast as "Det. Sgt. Kate Hudson" in the TV series "Dear Detective". The show aired for four episodes.
- Then in 1984, she was cast as "Julia Blake" in the TV series "Paper Dolls". She appeared in 13 episodes.
- From 1986 to 1989, she supplied voices in the TV series "Smurfs". She voiced 15 episodes.

- Then from 1997 to 2004, she supplied voices for "Bunny Bravo/Mama/Melissa in the TV series "Johnny Bravo". She voiced 55 episodes
- Brenda has been married four times – Martin Field (1965-70), William S. Bishop (1977-78), Charles J. Cannizzaro (1981-82) and Guy Hector (1986-present).
- Over the years, Brenda has appeared in a number of Broadway productions including "The Affair" (1962), "Children From Their Games" (1963), "Cactus Flower" (1965-68), "How Now, Dow Jones" (1967-68), "The Goodbye People" (1968), "Father's Day" (1971), "The Odd Couple" (1985-86) and "Jack's Women" (1992).
- She had Tony Award nominations for "Cactus Flower", "How Now, Dow Jones" and "The Goodbye People".
- In 1974, she won a Primetime Emmy Award for "The Shape of Things" (1973) (Best Supporting Actress in Comedy-Variety, Variety or Music).
- In 1976, she won a Golden Globe Award for "Once Is Not Enough" (1975) (Best Supporting Actress – Motion Picture). She was also nominated for an Academy Award for this part.
- Brenda's other film credits include "I Love My Wife" (1970), "Going Home" (1971), "Lily" (1974)(TV), "Airport '77" (1977), "The First Deadly Sin" (1980), "Zorro: The Gay Blade" (1981), "Supergirl" (1984), "Heart of Midnight" (1988), "Ten Little Indians" (1989), "Lethal Games" (1991), "The Mirror Has Two Faces" (1996), "You Don't Know Jack" (2010)(TV) and "Kubo and the Two Strings" (2016)(voice).

- Her other TV credits include "The Love Boat" (1984) 2 episodes, "Columbo" (1990), "The Golden Girls" (1990), "The Critic" (1994)(voice) 5 episodes, "Friends" (1995), "Touched by an Angel" (1996), "Ally McBeal" (1997), "Spawn" (1997-99)(voice) 6 episodes, "Becker" (2001) and "The War at Home" (2006).

- **Bert Kramer** was born Albert George Kohnhorst on October 10, 1934 in San Diego, California.
- He made his TV debut in an episode ("How to Kill a Toy Soldier") of "Blue Light" in 1966.
- Following this, he appeared in many TV shows including "The F.B.I." (1966-71) 4 episodes, "Mission: Impossible" (1969-70) 4 episodes, "Longstreet" (1971), "M.A.S.H." (1972), "Mannix" (1971-73) 3 episodes, "Police Story" (1974) 2 episodes, "Kojak" (1974), "The Six Million Dollar Man" (1975) and "Doctors' Hospital" (1975).
- In 1976, he was cast as "Emmet Ferguson" in the TV series "Sara". The series only lasted 12 episodes.
- He appeared in the TV mini-series "Once an Eagle" in 1976.
- In 1977, he was cast as "Mike Fitzpatrick" in the TV series "The Fitzpatricks". He appeared in 13 episodes from 1977 to 1978.

- Then in 1980, he was cast as "Alex Wheeler" in the TV series "Texas". He appeared in 27 episodes from 1980 to 1981.
- During the 1980's, he appeared in two TV soaps – "Another World" and "The Young and the Restless".
- His last acting appearance was in the film "Boys to Men" in 2001.
- Bert was married to Patricia Lynn.
- He made a number of national television commercials during the 1980's.
- Bert's other film credits include "Lady Sings the Blues" (1972), "Earthquake" (1974) uncredited, "Moment by Moment" (1978), "Bloody Birthday" (1981), "Thunder Alley" (1985), "Murder C.O.D." (1990)(TV), "Tall Tale" (1995), "Volcano" (1997) and "Between Christmas and New Year's" (2000).
- His other TV credits include "The Bionic Woman" (1976), "Westside Medical" (1977), "The Rockford Files" (1977-78) 2 episodes, "CBS Afternoon Playhouse" (1978) 5 episodes, "Little House on the Prairie" (1979), "Dynasty" (1984) 2 episodes, "Paradise" (1988), "Full House" (1989), "Matlock" (1987-91) 3 episodes, "Picket Fences" (1996), "Spy Game" (1998) and "Manhattan, AZ" (2000).

- **Albert Stratton** was born on October 23, 1937 in Cleveland, Ohio.

- He made his TV acting debut in an episode of "Love Is a Many Splendored Thing" in 1973.
- Albert made his film debut in the TV movie "The Last of the Belles" in 1974.
- In 1973, he was cast as "Paul Drake" in the TV series "The New Perry Mason". He appeared in 15 episodes from 1973 to 1974.
- In 1976, he was cast as "Martin Pope" in the TV series "Sara". The series only lasted 12 episodes.
- Also in 1976, he appeared as "Thomas Jefferson" in the TV mini-series "The Adams Chronicles". He appeared in 4 episodes.
- In 1983, he appeared as "McGeorge Bundy" in the TV mini-series "Kennedy". He appeared in 5 episodes.
- In 1989-90, he had a recurring role as "Eric Kane" in the TV soap "All My Children".
- His last acting appearance was in an episode ("Farewell, My Lovely") of "Knots Landing" in 1993.
- Albert's other film credits include "Born Beautiful" (1982)(TV), "Wedlock" (1991) and "Obsessed" (1992)(TV).
- His other TV credits include "Petrocelli" (1975), "Mannix" (1975), "Wonder Woman" (1976), "Lovers and Friends" (1977), "The Fantastic Journey" (1977), "Quantum Leap" (1991) and "Baywatch" (1991-92) 3 episodes.

"Shane"

Years : 1966

Episodes : 17 (1 season)

Cast :-

David Carradine (b. 1936 d. 2009) - Played Shane

Bert Freed (b. 1919 d. 1994) - Played Rufe Ryker

Jill Ireland (b. 1936 d. 1990) - Played Marian Starett

Tom Tully (b. 1908 d. 1982) - Played Tom Starett

Christopher Shea (b. 1958 d. 2010) - Played Joey Starett

Synopsis :-
The story of a gunfighter who works for a woman after the death of her husband.

Trivia & Tidbits :-

"The Show"

- **"Shane"** premiered on ABC on September 10, 1966 and last aired on December 31, 1966.

- The show ran for one season with a total of 17 episodes.
- "Shane" was based on a 1949 book of the same name written by Jack Schaefer.
- A film of the same name, and starring Alan Ladd, was released in 1953.
- The series was created by Herschel Daugherty and Gary Nelson and produced by Titus Productions.
- The theme music was composed by Victor Young.

"In Memoriam"

- **David Carradine** died of accidental asphyxiation on June 3, 2009 (72) in Bangkok, Thailand.
- **Bert Freed** died of a heart attack on August 2, 1994 (74) in Sechelt, British Columbia, Canada.
- **Jill Ireland** died of breast cancer on May 18, 1990 (54) in Malibu, California.
- **Tom Tully** died of cancer on April 27, 1982 (73) Newport Beach, California.
- **Christopher Shea** died of natural causes on August 19, 2010 (52) in Los Angeles, California.

"The Stars"

- **David Carradine** was born John Arthur Carradine on December 8, 1936 in Hollywood, California.
- He was the eldest son of actor John Carradine and Ardanelle McCool (his other siblings were Keith, Robert, Calista and Kansas).
- David graduated from Oakland High School in 1955 and then attended Oakland Junior College before transferring to San Francisco State College where he studied drama and music theory.
- After dropping out of college he hung around with the "beatniks" of San Francisco's North Beach and Venice, California.
- In 1960, he was inducted into the United States Army where he spent two years before being honourably discharged in 1962.
- Following his discharge from the Army he decided to try acting and made his TV debut in an episode ("Secret Document X256") of "Armstrong Circle Theatre" in 1963.
- Several more TV appearances followed including "Wagon Train" (1963), "East Side/West Side" (1963), "Arrest and Trial" (1964), "The Virginian" (1964), "The Alfred Hitchcock Hour" (1964-65) 2 episodes and "The Trials of O'Brien" (1966).
- In 1966, he was cast as "Shane" in the TV series of the same name. He appeared in 17 episodes.
- In 1972, he was cast as "Kwai Chang Caine" in the TV series "Kung Fu". He appeared in 63 episodes from 1972 to 1975.

- Then in 1985, he appeared as "Justin La Motte" in the TV mini-series "North and South".
- In 1993, he resurrected the character "Kwai Chang Caine" in the TV series "Kung Fu: The Legend Continues". He appeared in 84 episodes from 1993 to 1997.
- At the time of his death in 2009 he still had several unreleased films including "Six Days in Paradise" (2010), "Money to Burn" (2010), "True Legend" (2010), "Stretch" (2011) and "Night of the Templar" (2012).
- David changed his name from John to David after he was discharged from the Army so that he would not be confused with his father.
- He was married five times – Donna Lee Becht (1960-67), Linda Gilbert (1977-83), Gail Jensen (1988-97), Marina Anderson (1998-2001) and Annie Bierman (2004-09). David also lived with Barbara Hershey from 1969 to 1975.
- David had three children of his own from his marriages plus four step-children.
- In 1997, he was awarded a Star on the Hollywood Walk of Fame for his contribution to television.
- David appeared on Broadway in the plays "The Deputy" (1964) and "The Royal Hunt of the Sun" (1965-66).
- He was also a director of films and TV shows, including three episodes of "Kung Fu".
- David was also a musician who could play the piano, guitar and flute.

- His autobiography, "Endless Highway", was published in 1995.
- During his career David was nominated for one Emmy Award ("Kung Fu") and four Golden Globe Awards ("Kung Fu", "Bound for Glory", "North and South" and "Kill Bill: Vol.2").
- David's other film credits include "Taggart" (1964), "The Violent Ones" (1967), "Boxcar Bertha" (1972), "Cannonball!" (1976), "The Long Riders" (1980), "Behind Enemy Lines" (1986), "Open Fire" (1989), "Bird on a Wire" (1990), "Karate Cop" (1991), "Macon County Jail" (1997), "The Donor" (2001), "Kill Bill: Vol.1" (2003), "Miracle at Sage Creek" (2005) and "The Rain" (2009).
- His other TV credits include "Cimarron Strip" (1967), "Gunsmoke" (1971), "Ironside" (1968-71) 3 episodes, "The Fall Guy" (1983), "Matlock" (1987-89) 3 episodes, "The Young Riders" (1990), "Profiler" (1999), "Family Law" (2000) 3 episodes, "Alias" (2003-04) 2 episodes and "Mental" (2009).

- **Bertram "Bert" Freed** was born on November 3, 1919 in The Bronx, New York.
- He began his acting career whilst attending Penn State University.
- Following a stint in the Army during the Second World War, he made his debut on Broadway in the musical "The Day Before Spring" (1945)
- Bert made his uncredited movie debut in the film "Carnegie Hall" in 1947.

- He then made his TV debut in an episode ("Arsenic and Old Lace") of "The Ford Theatre Hour" in 1949.
- Bert then appeared in many films including "Ma and Pa Kettle Go to Town" (1950), "Halls of Montezuma" (1950), "Detective Story" (1951), "The Atomic City" (1951), "The Long, Long Trailer" (1953), "The Desperate Hours" (1955), "Paths of Glory" (1957) and "The Goddess" (1958).
- In 1966, he was cast as "Rufe Ryker" in the TV series "Shane". He appeared in 16 episodes.
- His last acting appearance was in an episode ("Are You My Mother?") of "ABC Afterschool Specials" in 1986.
- Bert was married to Nancy Lee Wurzberger from 1956 until his death in 1994. They has two children.
- He played the character "Columbo" in a live 1960 episode of the "Chevy Mystery Theatre". This was seven years before Peter Falk made the character famous.
- Bert's other film credits include "What Ever Happened to Baby Jane?" (1962), "Invitation to a Gunfighter" (1964), "Nevada Smith" (1966), "Madigan" (1968), "Hang 'Em High" (1968), "There Was a Crooked Man..." (1970), "Billy Jack" (1971), "Norma Rae" (1979) and "Charlie and the Great Balloon Chase" (1981)(TV).
- His other TV credits include "The Alcoa Hour" (1956), "The Sheriff of Cochise" (1957), "U.S. Marshal" (1959), "Laramie" (1959), "Riverboat" (1959), "M Squad" (1960), "Outlaws" (1960), "The Rifleman" (1959-61) 2

episodes, "Adventures in Paradise" (1962), "The Defenders" (1963), "Perry Mason" (1960-64) 4 episodes, "Gunsmoke" (1959-65) 2 episodes, "Ironside" (1967) 2 episodes, "Bonanza" (1960-68) 2 episodes, "The Big Valley" (1966-68) 4 episodes, "The Virginian" (1963-71) 3 episodes, "Cannon" (1972-76) 2 episodes, "The Knight Rider" (1983) and "Riptide" (1985).

- **Jill Dorothy Ireland** was born on April 24, 1936 in London, England.
- She was the daughter of a wine merchant.
- Jill started her entertainment career as a dancer and then made her movie debut in the film "No Love for Judy" in 1955.
- Several more U.K./European films followed including "Oh...Rosalinda!!" (1955), "Three Men in a Boat" (1956), "Hell Drivers" (1957), "Robbery Under Arms" (1957), "Carry on Nurse" (1959), "Jungle Street" (1960) and "So Evil, So Young" (1961).
- In the mid 1960's she moved to America with her husband, actor David McCallum.
- Jill then guest starred on a number of TV series including "Ben Casey" (1964), "The Third Man" (1964), "Voyage to the Bottom of the Sea" (1964), "My Favorite Martian" (1965) and "12 O'Clock High" (1965-66) 2 episodes.
- In 1966, she was cast as "Marian Starett" in the TV series "Shane". She appeared in 17 episodes.
- Her last acting appearance was in the film "Caught" in 1987.

- Jill was married twice - David McCallum (1957-1967) and Charles Bronson (1968-1990). In all she had five children.
- Her adopted son, Jason, with David McCallum died of a drug overdose in 1989 (six months before she died).
- In 1984, she was diagnosed with breast cancer. The disease finally claimed her life in 1990.
- In 1988, she was presented the American Cancer Society's Courage Award by President Ronald Reagan.
- In 1989, she was awarded a Star on the Hollywood Walk of Fame for her contribution to Motion Pictures.
- Jill appeared in 15 films with her second husband Charles Bronson.
- Her other film credits include "The Karate Killers" (1967), "Villa Rides" (1968) and "The Girl, the Gold Watch & Everything" (1980)(TV).
- Jill's other TV credits include "Star Trek" (1967), "The Man from U.N.C.L.E." (1964-67) 5 episodes, "Mannix" (1968), "Daniel Boone" (1969) and "Night Gallery" (1972).

- **Tom Tully** was born Thomas Kane Tulley on August 21, 1908 in Durango, Colorado.
- After a stint in the U.S. Navy, Tom decided to try acting and appeared in ten Broadway plays in the late 1930's and early 1940's.
- His first credited movie appearance was in the film "Northern Pursuit" in 1943.
- Several more film appearances followed including "Destination Tokyo" (1943), "The

Town Went Wild" (1944), "The Virginian" (1946), "The Lady in the Lake" (1947), "Killer McCoy" (1947), "A Kiss for Corliss" (1949), "Tomahawk" (1951), "Return of the Texan" (1952), "The Jazz Singer" (1952) and "The Caine Mutiny" (1954).

- Tom made his TV debut in an episode ("In This Crisis") of "Cavalcade of America" in 1952.
- In 1954, he was cast as Inspector Matt Grebb in the TV series "The Lineup" (the show was retitled "San Francisco Beat" when it was repeated). He appeared in 185 episodes from 1954 to 1959.
- In 1966, he was cast as "Tom Skarett" in the TV series "Shane". He appeared in 17 episodes.
- Tom made his final acting appearance in an episode ("The Donation") of "Temperatures Rising" in 1973.
- He was married twice - Frances McHugh (1938-53) and Ida Johnson (1954-82).
- In his days before acting, Tom worked as a junior reporter for the Denver Post in Denver.
- In 1955, he was nominated (Best Actor in a Supporting Role) for an "Oscar" for his performance in "The Caine Mutiny" (1954).
- In 1960, he was awarded a Star on the Hollywood Walk of Fame for his contribution to Motion Pictures.
- In 1969, he toured Vietnam to entertain troops. Whilst there he contracted a filarial worm which affected his health for the remainder of his life. He subsequently had one leg amputated.

- Tom's grandfather, David F. Day, was a Medal of Honor winner in the American Civil War.
- His other film credits include "Soldier of Fortune" (1955), "Ten North Frederick" (1958), "The Wackiest Ship in the Army" (1960), "The Carpetbaggers" (1964), "McHale's Navy Joins the Air Force" (1965), "Coogan's Bluff" (1968) and "Charley Varrick" (1973).
- Tom's other TV credits include "Zane Grey Theatre" (1957) 2 episodes, "Make Room for Daddy" (1953-57) 4 episodes, "Tales of Wells Fargo" (1961), "Empire" (1962), "The Untouchables" (1963), "Perry Mason" (1964) 2 episodes, "Rawhide" (1961-65) 2 episodes, "The Loner" (1965), "Bonanza" (1965-67) 2 episodes, "The Dick Van Dyke Show" (1964-66) 2 episodes, "The High Chaparral" (1969) and "The Rookies" (1972-73) 2 episodes.

- **Christopher Shea** was born on February 5, 1958 in Los Angeles, California.
- He had two younger brothers who were also actors, Eric and Stephen.
- Chris started his acting career by providing the voice of "Linus van Pelt" in a number of "Charlie Brown" TV specials – "A Charlie Brown Christmas" (1965), "Charlie Brown's All Stars" (1966), "It's the Great Pumpkin, Charlie Brown" (1966), "You're in Love, Charlie Brown" (1967) and "He's Your Dog, Charlie Brown" (1968).
- In 1966, he was cast as "Joey Starett" in the TV series "Shane". He appeared in 17 episodes.

- His final acting appearance was in an episode ("Tami Knows Best") of "Friday Night Lights" in 2008.
- Chris was married to Sara Straton until his death in 2010. They had two children, Nicea and Teal.
- His other film credits include "Firecreek" (1968) uncredited, "Smith!" (1969), "Angel in My Pocket" (1969) uncredited, "The Love God?" (1969) uncredited, "The Boy Who Stole the Elephant" (1970)(TV) and "A Little Game" (1971)(TV).
- Chris' other TV credits include "That Girl" (1966), "Bonanza" (1968), "The Invaders" (1967-68) 2 episodes, "Green Acres" (1968) 2 episodes, "Here Come the Brides" (1969), "Disneyland" (1970) 2 episodes and "The Odd Couple" (1971) 3 episodes.

"Stagecoach West"

Years : 1960 - 1961

Episodes : 38 (1 season)

Cast :-

Wayne Rogers (b. 1933 d. 2015) - Played Luke Perry

Robert Bray (b. 1917 d. 1983) - Played Simon Kane

Richard Eyer (b. 1945) - Played Davey Kane

Synopsis :-
Luke Perry and Simon Kane run a stagecoach line in the Old West.

Trivia & Tidbits :-

"The Show"

- **"Stagecoach West"** premiered on ABC on October 4, 1960 and last aired on June 27, 1961.
- The show ran for one season with a total of 38 black and white episodes.

- The series was produced by Four Star Productions and Hilgarde Productions.
- "Stagecoach West" was a spin-off of "Dick Powell's Zane Grey Theatre" (CBS).
- The show aired opposite "Thriller" (NBC) and "The Red Skelton Show" (CBS).
- The series original music was by Skip Martin.

"In Memoriam"

- **Wayne Rogers** died of pneumonia on December 31, 2015 (82) in Los Angeles, California.
- **Robert Bray** died of a heart attack on March 7, 1983 (65) in Bishop, California.

"The Stars"

- **Wayne Rogers** was born William Wayne McMillan Rogers III on April 7, 1933 in Birmingham, Alabama.
- He attended Ramsay High School in Bell Buckle, Tennessee. In 1954, he graduated from Princeton University with a history degree.
- Following his graduation from university he served in the United States Navy for three years.
- In 1959, he made his movie debut in the film "Odds Against Tomorrow".
- Wayne also made his TV debut in 1959 in an episode ("The Lonely Gun") of "Zane Grey Theatre".

- In 1960, he was cast as "Luke Perry" in the TV series "Stagecoach West". He appeared in 38 episodes from 1960 to 1961.
- In 1972, he was cast as "Trapper John McIntyre" in the hit TV series "M.A.S.H." He appeared in 73 episodes from 1972 to 1975.
- Following this, in 1976 he was cast as "Jake Axminster" in the TV series "City of Angels". The series only lasted 13 episodes.
- In 1979, he played the character "Dr. Charley Michaels" in the TV series "House Calls". He appeared in 57 episodes from 1979 to 1982.
- From 1993 to 1995 he played the recurring character "Charlie Garrett" in the TV series "Murder, She Wrote". He appeared in 5 episodes.
- His last acting appearance was in the film "Nobody Knows Anything!" in 2003.
- Wayne was married twice – Mitzi McWhorter (1960-83) and Amy Hirsh (1988-present).
- In 2005, he received a Star on the Hollywood Walk of Fame for his contribution to the television industry.
- Today, Wayne is chairman of Kleinfeld Bridal (a bridal store in New York) and also chairman of Wayne Rogers & Co., an investment strategist firm.
- Wayne has also produced a number of plays on Broadway including "Einstein and the Polar Bear" (1981), "Duet for One" (1982) and "The Odd Couple" (1985-86).
- His other film credits include "The Glory Guys" (1965), "Chamber of Horrors" (1966), "Cool Hand Luke" (1967), "Pocket Money" (1972),

"Top of the Hill" (1980)(TV), "I Dream of Jeannie...Fifteen Years Later" (1985)(TV), "Bluegrass" (1988)(TV), "The Goodbye Bird" (1993), "Ghosts of Mississippi" (1996) and "Three Days of Rain" (2002).

- Wayne's other TV credits include "Wanted: Dead or Alive" (1960), "Johnny Ringo" (1960), "Gomer Pyle, U.S.M.C." (1964), "Death Valley Days" (1965), "Gunsmoke" (1959-65) 3 episodes, "The Fugitive" (1966), "The Big Valley" (1968), "The F.B.I." (1966-71) 7 episodes, "The Larry Sanders Show" (1994) and "Diagnosis Murder" (1997).

- **Robert Bray** was born on October 23, 1917 in Kalispell, Montana.
- The family moved to Seattle, Washington where he attended Lincoln High School.
- After graduation he worked as a lumberjack and cowboy.
- He joined the United States Marine Corps in 1942 and saw action in the South Pacific during the Second World War.
- After the war he signed a contract with RKO Pictures and spent three years appearing in uncredited roles.
- His first credited part was in the film "Wild Horse Mesa" (1947), starring Tim Holt.
- Many films followed including "Western Heritage" (1948), "The Arizona Ranger" (1948), "Stagecoach Kid" (1949), "Law of the Badlands" (1951), "The Gunman" (1952), "The Marshal's Daughter" (1953), "The Yellow Tomahawk" (1954) and "Bus Stop" (1956).

- He made his first TV guest appearance in an episode ("Salted Mine") of "Racket Squad" in 1951.
- Several more TV guest appearances followed including "The Adventures of Kit Carson" (1952), "Dragnet" (1953), "Cowboy G-Men" (1952-53) 5 episodes, "Stories of the Century" (1954), "Medic" (1954-55) 3 episodes, "The Lone Ranger" (1952-55) 6 episodes, "The Life and Legend of Wyatt Earp" (1955) 3 episodes, "Frontier" (1956), "You Are There" (1955-56) 4 episodes, "State Trooper" (1957), "Studio 57" (1955-58) 4 episodes, "Cheyenne" (1958), "Maverick" (1958), "Sugarfoot" (1959), "Hotel de Paree" (1960) and "Shotgun Slade" (1960).
- In 1960, he was cast as "Simon Kane" in the TV series "Stagecoach West". He appeared in 38 episodes from 1960 to 1961.
- In 1964, he was cast as "Corey Stuart" in the TV series "Lassie". He appeared in 104 episodes from 1964 to 1968.
- After "Lassie" finished Robert retired to Bishop, California in the Sierra Nevada.
- Robert's other film credits include "My Gun Is Quick" (1957), "Never Love a Stranger" (1958), "Never So Few" (1959), "A Gathering of Eagles" (1963) and "Flight of the Cougar" (1967)(TV).
- His other TV credits include "Alfred Hitchcock Presents" (1958-61) 4 episodes, "Gunsmoke" (1963), "Laramie" (1960-63) 3 episodes, "Perry Mason" (1959-63) 3 episodes and "Temple Houston" (1963.

- **Richard Eyer** was born Richard Ross Eyer on May 6, 1945 in Santa Monica, California.
- When he was young he won "personality contests" and other competitions before he started his acting career in the early 1950's.
- Richard made his TV debut in an episode ("Huntin' for Trouble") of "The Roy Rogers Show" in 1952.
- His first credited movie appearance was in the film "Ma and Pa Kettle at Home" in 1952.
- Richard then guest starred in several TV shows including "City Detective" (1954), "Letter to Loretta" (1955), "It's a Great Life" (1955), "The 20th Century-Fox Hour" (1956), "Climax!" (1956), "Cavalcade of America" (1954-57) 3 episodes, "Whirlybirds" (1958), "Father Knows Best" (1955-58) 3 episodes, "Wanted : Dead or Alive" (1959), "Rawhide" (1959), "Gunsmoke" (1959) and "Wagon Train" (1960).
- In 1960, he was cast as "Davey Kane" in the TV series "Stagecoach West". He appeared in 38 episodes from 1960 to 1961.
- His last acting appearance, to date, was in an episode ("Encounter") of "Combat!" in 1967.
- Richard was married to Laura Lynn Seabern from 1970 to 1983. They have three children - Samantha, Benjamin and Andrew.
- After he retired from acting (at age 21) he taught elementary school in Bishop, California.
- Richard's other film credits include "The Desperate Hours" (1955), "The Kettles in the Ozarks" (1956), "Friendly Persuasion" (1956), "Bailout at 43,000" (1957), "Fort Dobbs" (1958), "The 7th Voyage of Sinbad" (1958),

"Johnny Rocco" (1958) and "Calhoun : County Agent" (1964)(TV).

- His other TV credits include "Dr. Kildare" (1962), "Arrest and Trial" (1963), "The Great Adventure" (1963), "Mr. Novak" (1964) and "Lassie" (1966).

"Stoney Burke"

Years : 1962 - 1963

Episodes : 32 (1 season)

Cast :-

Jack Lord (b. 1920 d. 1998) - Played Stoney Burke

Warren Oates (b. 1928 d. 1982) - Played Ves Painter

Bruce Dern (b. 1936) - Played E.J. Stocker

Robert Dowdell (b. 1932) - Played Cody Bristol

Synopsis :-
The story of a rodeo rider in search of the Golden Buckle award.

Trivia & Tidbits :-

"The Show"

- **"Stoney Burke"** premiered on ABC on October 1, 1962 and last aired on May 20, 1963.
- The show ran for one season with a total of 32 black and white episodes.

- The series was produced by Daystar Productions and United Artists Television.
- In 1963, the show won a Western Heritage Award for the episode titled "The Contender" (first episode).

"In Memoriam"

- **Jack Lord** died of congestive heart failure on January 21, 1998 (77) in Honolulu, Hawaii.
- **Warren Oates** died of a heart attack on April 3, 1982 (53) in Los Angeles, California.

"The Stars"

- **Jack Lord** was born John Joseph Patrick Ryan on December 30, 1920 in Brooklyn, New York.
- He was the son of Irish-American parents. Jack's father, William Lawrence Ryan, was a steamship company executive.
- Jack was educated at St. Benedict Joseph Labre School, John Adams High School and the United States Merchant Marine Academy (he graduated as an Ensign with a Third Mates License).
- He then attended New York University on a football scholarship and graduated with a degree in Fine Arts.
- During the Second World War he was stationed in Persia building bridges and then returned to the Merchant Navy where he was involved in making maritime training films.

- After the war, he trained with Sanford Meisner at the Neighborhood Playhouse and then studied at the Actors Studio.
- Jack made his movie debut in the film "Project X" in 1949.
- In 1952, he made his TV debut in an episode ("The Puzzle of Pier 90") of "The Hunter". He went under the name of Jack Ryan.
- In 1954, he appeared in the Broadway play "The Traveling Lady".
- Following this, he guest starred in a number of TV shows including "Danger" (1955), "Armstrong Circle Theatre" (1955), "The Elgin Hour" (1955), "Studio One" (1956) 2 episodes, "Lux Video Theatre" (1956) 2 episodes, "Have Gun – Will Travel" (1957), "Gunsmoke" (1957), "Playhouse 90" (1957-58) 2 episodes, "The Millionaire" (1958), "The Untouchables" (1959), "Bonanza" (1960), "Route 66" (1961), "Stagecoach West" (1961) 2 episodes, "Rawhide" (1959-61) 2 episodes and "Checkmate" (1962).
- In 1962, he was cast as "Stoney Burke" in the TV series of the same name. He appeared in 32 episodes from 1962 to 1963.
- In 1968, he was cast as "Det. Steve McGarrett" in the TV series "Hawaii Five-O". He appeared in 281 episodes from 1968 to 1980.
- His last acting appearance was in the movie "M Station: Hawaii" in 1980.
- Jack was married twice – Ann Cecily Willard (1944-1947) and Marie De Narde (1949-

1998). He had one son (died when he was 13 years old) with Ms. Willard.

- He appeared as the character "Felix Leiter" in the first "James Bond" film "Dr. No" (1962).
- Jack had four siblings. One older brother (William), two younger brothers (Robert and Thomas) and a younger sister (Josephine).
- He liked fencing, horseback riding and sailing.
- "Steve McGarrett's" catchphrase "Book him, Danno" became a part of pop culture.
- Jack's other film credits include "The Court-Martial of Billy Mitchell" (1955), "The Vagabond Kid" (1956), "God's Little Acre" (1958), "Man of the West" (1958), "Grand Hotel" (1964)(TV), "Ride to Hangman's Tree" (1967) and "The Counterfeit Killer" (1968).
- His other TV credits include "Dr. Kildare" (1964), "Wagon Train" (1965), "The Loner" (1965), "Laredo" (1966), "The F.B.I." (1966), "The Virginian" (1966), "Bob Hope Presents the Chrysler Theatre" (1965-66) 3 episodes, "The Fugitive" (1967), "Ironside" (1967) and "The High Chaparral" (1968).

- **Warren Mercer Oates** was born on July 5, 1928 in Depoy, Kentucky.
- He was the son of Bayless Earle Oates, a store owner, and Sarah Alice (nee Mercer).
- Warren attended Louisville Male High School and then enlisted in the United States Marine Corps.
- After leaving the Marine Corps he became interested in the theatre and performed in

- several plays whilst at the University of Louisville.
- Warren made his TV debut in an episode ("A Day Before Battle") of "Studio One" in 1956.
- Several more TV guest spots followed including "The United States Steel Hour" (1956), "The Big Story" (1956), "Studio One" (1957-58) 2 episodes, "Rescue 8" (1958), "The Adventures of Rin Tin Tin" (1958) and "Playhouse 90" (1958).
- Warren made his uncredited movie debut in the film "Up Periscope" in 1959.
- He then guest starred in several TV Westerns including "Black Saddle" (1959), "Buckskin" (1959), "The Rough Riders" (1959), "Trackdown" (1959) 3 episodes, "Wagon Train" (1959), "The Rebel" (1959), "Tombstone Territory" (1958-60) 3 episodes, "Hotel de Paree" (1960), "Bronco" (1960), "The Westerner" (1960), "Lawman" (1960), "Wanted: Dead or Alive" (1958-61) 4 episodes, "The Rifleman" (1958-62) 5 episodes and "Bonanza" (1962).
- In 1962, he was cast as "Ves Painter" in the TV series "Stoney Burke". He appeared in 32 episodes from 1962 to 1963.
- After this, he appeared in several major films including "Mail Order Bride" (1964), "Major Dundee" (1965), "Return of the Magnificent Seven" (1966), "In the Heat of the Night" (1967), "The Wild Bunch" (1969), "Two-Lane Blacktop" (1971), "The Hired Hand" (1971) and "Dillinger" (1973).

- His last acting appearance was in an episode ("Nothin' Short of Highway Robbery") of "Tales of the Unexpected" in 1985.
- Warren was married four times – Roberta Ellis (1957-1959), Teddy Farmer (1959-1966), Vickery Turner (1969-1974) and Judy A. Jones (1977-1982). He had three children with Ms. Farmer.
- He turned down the lead role in "Support Your Local Sheriff" (1969) to appear in "The Wild Bunch" (1969).
- Author Susan Compo wrote a biography of Warren in 2009 titled "Warren Oates: A Wild Life".
- Warren's other film credits include "Yellowstone Kelly" (1959), "The Rise and Fall of Legs Diamond" (1960), "Private Property" (1960), "Ride the High Country" (1962), "Bring Me the Head of Alfredo Garcia" (1974), "Sleeping Dogs" (1977), "1941" (1979), "Stripes" (1981), "The Border" (1982) and "Tough Enough" (1983).
- His other TV credits include "The Fugitive" (1964) 2 episodes, "Branded" (1965), "Rawhide" (1960-65) 4 episodes, "The Virginian" (1963-66) 4 episodes, "The Big Valley" (1965-66) 2 episodes, "Gunsmoke" (1958-67) 10 episodes, "Cimarron Strip" (1967) 2 episodes, "The F.B.I." (1971), "Police Story" (1978) and "The Blue and the Gray" (1982) 3 episodes.

- **Bruce MacLeish Dern** was born on June 4, 1936 in Chicago, Illinois.

- He is the son of John Dern, an attorney, and Jean Dern (nee MacLeish).
- Bruce grew up in Kenilworth, Illinois and attended the Choate School (now Choate Rosemary Hall), the New Trier Township High School, Winnetka and the University of Pennsylvania.
- He was very good at athletics in high school and continued to run competitively at university.
- After university, he moved to New York and studied acting with Lee Strasberg at the Actors Studio.
- In 1958, he made his Broadway debut in the play "The Shadow of a Gunman".
- Then in 1959, he was cast in another play titled "Sweet Bird of Youth".
- In 1960, he made his uncredited movie debut in the film "Wild River".
- A number of TV guest appearances followed including "Route 66" (1960), "Naked City" (1961) 2 episodes, "Sea Hunt" (1961), "Surfside 6" (1961), "Thriller" (1961), "Ben Casey" (1961), "The Detectives" (1961), "Ripcord" (1962) and "Cain's Hundred" (1961-62) 2 episodes.
- In 1962, he was cast as "E.J.Stocker" in the TV series "Stoney Burke". He appeared in 17 episodes from 1962 to 1963.

- Once this finished, he appeared as a guest star in several more TV shows including "The Dick Powell Show" (1962-63) 2 episodes, "The Outer Limits" (1963), "77 Sunset Strip" (1964), "Wagon Train" (1963-65) 3 episodes, "The Virginian" (1964-65) 3 episodes, "Rawhide" (1965), "Laredo" (1965), "12 O'Clock High" (1964-65) 4 episodes, "Branded" (1966), "The Loner" (1966), "The Fugitive" (1963-66) 5 episodes, "Run for Your Life" (1966-67) 3 episodes, "The Big Valley" (1966-68) 5 episodes, "Gunsmoke" (1965-69) 4 episodes and "Bonanza" (1968-70) 2 episodes.
- After this period, he concentrated on his movie career and appeared in such films as "The Rebel Rousers" (1970), "The Cowboys" (1972), "The Great Gatsby" (1974), "Posse" (1975), "Coming Home" (1978), "Tattoo" (1981), "On the Edge" (1986), "Into the Badlands" (1991)(TV), "Down Periscope" (1996), "The Haunting" (1999) and "Madison" (2005).
- In 2006, he commenced a recurring role as "Frank Harlow" in the TV series "Big Love". He appeared in 29 episodes from 2006 to 2011.
- In 2014, he was nominated for an Academy Award for his role as "Woody Grant" in the film "Nebraska" (2013).

- Bruce has been married three times – Marie Dawn Pierce (1957-1959), Diane Ladd (1960-1969) and Andrea Beckett (1969-present). He had two children with Ms. Ladd.
- His eldest daughter, Diane, drowned when she was 18 months old and his youngest daughter is the Academy Award nominated actress, Laura Dern.
- In 2010, Bruce was awarded a Star on the Hollywood Walk of Fame for his contribution to Motion Pictures.
- Bruce's grandfather, George Henry Dern, was a former Governor of Utah and President Franklin D. Roosevelt's first Secretary of War.
- His autobiography titled "Things I've Said, But Probably Shouldn't Have: An Unrepentant Memoir" was published in 2007 and co-written with Robert Crane and Christopher Fryer.
- Bruce's other film credits include "Marnie" (1964), "The Wild Angels" (1966), "The War Wagon" (1967), "Will Penny" (1967), "Hang 'Em High" (1968), "Support Your Local Sheriff!" (1969), "They Shoot Horses, Don't They?" (1969), "Django Unchained" (2012) and "Cut Back" (2014).
- His other TV credits include "The High Chaparral" (1970), "The Immortal" (1970), "Space" (1985) mini-series, "King of the Hill" (2003) and "Unicorn Plan-It" (2012-13) 2 episodes.

- **Robert Dowdell** was born on March 10, 1932 in Park Ridge, Illinois.
- He got his taste for acting whilst participating in acting at the Francis W. Parker School.
- Robert then studied at both the Wesleyan University and the University of Chicago.
- Following a stint in the U.S. Army he travelled to New York and studied with renowned acting coach Wynn Handman.
- After appearing in two plays ("Time Limit" and "The Lovers") Robert headed for Hollywood and made his TV debut in an episode ("The Neon Touch") of "Deadline" in 1959.
- Robert made his movie debut in the TV film "The Fifth Column" in 1960.
- In 1962, he was cast as "Cody Bristol" in the TV series "Stoney Burke". He appeared in 32 episodes from 1962 to 1963.
- In 1964, he was cast as "Lt. Comdr. Chip Morton" in the TV series "Voyage to the Bottom of the Sea". He appeared in 109 episodes from 1964 to 1968.
- Robert's last acting appearance, to date, was in the TV documentary series "American Masters" in 1995.
- He was married to Sheila Connolly from 1965 to 1979.
- Robert's other film credits include "Macho Callahan" (1970), "City Beneath the Sea" (1971)(TV), "Terror in the Sky" (1971)(TV),

"The Initiation" (1984), "Outrage!"
(1986)(TV), "Assassination" (1987) and "Skin
Deep" (1989).

- His other TV credits include "Surfside 6"
  (1962), "Land of the Giants" (1969), "O'Hara,
  U.S. Treasury" (1971), "The F.B.I." (1972),
  "Adam-12" (1971-72) 3 episodes, "Chips"
  (1979), "Hart to Hart" (1982), "Dynasty"
  (1985), "Capitol" (1984-86) and "Hunter"
  (1991).

"The Tall Man"

Years : 1960 - 1962

Episodes : 75 (2 seasons)

Cast :-

Barry Sullivan (b. 1912 d. 1994) - Played Pat Garrett

Clu Gulager (b. 1928) - Played William Bonney

Synopsis :-
Stories about Pat Garrett and Billy the Kid set in New Mexico in the 1870's.

Trivia & Tidbits :-

"The Show"

- **"The Tall Man"** premiered on NBC on September 10, 1960 and last aired on September 1, 1962.
- The show ran for two seasons with a total of 75 black and white episodes.
- The series was created by Samuel A. Peeples and produced by the Lincoln County Productions Company and Revue Studios.

- Filming took place on the Universal Studios Backlot.
- The series original music was by Juan Garcia Esquivel.

"In Memoriam"

- **Barry Sullivan** died of a respiratory ailment on June 6, 1994 (81) in Sherman Oaks, California.

"The Stars"

- **Barry Sullivan** was born Patrick Barry Sullivan on August 29, 1912 in New York City, New York.
- Barry made his acting debut on Broadway in the play "I Want a Policeman" (1936).
- He appeared in several more plays before landing his first credited movie role in the film "High Explosive" (1943).
- Barry then appeared in many more film roles including "Rainbow Island" (1944), "Suspense" (1946), "Bad Men of Tombstone" (1949), "The Great Gatsby" (1949), "Three Guys Named Mike" (1951) and "The Bad and the Beautiful" (1952).
- In 1953, he made his television debut in an episode ("Girl from Kansas") of "Chevron Theatre".

- In 1956, he was cast as "Ken Thurston" in the TV series "The Man Called X". He appeared in 39 episodes from 1956 to 1957.
- Following this series, he was cast as "Capt. David Scott" in the TV series "Harbormaster". He appeared in 27 episodes from 1957 to 1958.
- In 1960, he was cast as "Pat Garrett" in the TV series "The Tall Man". He appeared in 75 episodes from 1960 to 1962.
- Barry appeared in another Western series in 1966. He was cast as "Ben Pride" in the TV series "The Road West". He appeared in 29 episodes from 1966 to 1967.
- In 1976, he was cast as "Senator Paxton" in the TV mini-series "Rich Man, Poor Man - Book 11". He appeared in 7 episodes.
- His last acting role was in the film "The Last Straw" in 1987.
- Barry was married three times - Marie Brown (1937-57), Gita Hall (1958-61) and Desiree Sumara (1962-65). He had three children. Johnny and Jenny (with Ms. Brown) and Patsy (with Ms. Hall).
- Jenny was married to rock star Jim Messina (a member of the rock bands "Buffalo Springfield" and "Poco").
- Patsy was married to the great songwriter Jimmy Webb ("MacArthur Park" etc. etc. etc.). They had seven children.
- Barry's last appearance on Broadway was in the play "Too Late the Phalarope" in 1956.

- He has two Stars on the Hollywood Walk of Fame. One for television and one for Motion Pictures.
- In 1956, he was nominated for a best actor Emmy Award for an episode ("The Caine Mutiny Court-Martial") of "Ford Star Jubilee".
- His other film credits include "Strategic Air Command" (1955), "Seven Ways from Sundown" (1960), "A Gathering of Eagles" (1963), "Tell Them Willie Boy Is Here" (1969), "Cannon" (1971)(TV), "Pat Garrett & Billy the Kid" (1973), "Earthquake" (1974), "Oh, God!" (1977) and "Caravans" (1978).
- Barry's other TV credits include "Zane Grey Theatre" (1958-59) 3 episodes, "Route 66" (1963), "Perry Mason" (1965), "Bonanza" (1967), "The Virginian" (1969), "Dan August" (1971), "Harry O" (1974), "The Streets of San Francisco" (1973-76) 5 episodes and "Disneyland" (1980).

- **Clu Gulager** was born William Martin Gulager on November 16, 1928 in Holdenville, Oklahoma.
- He is the son of John Gulager, a cowboy entertainer who worked in vaudeville with song and dance man George M. Cohen.
- His nickname "Clu" was given to him by his father and is derived from the clu-clu birds that were around their home.
- Clu has Cherokee Native American ancestry.
- He made his TV debut in an episode ("Bang the Drum Slowly") of "The United States Steel Hour" in 1956.

- Clu then guest starred in several TV shows including "West Point" (1957), "Black Saddle" (1959), "Wanted: Dead or Alive" (1959), "Laramie" (1959), "The Untouchables" (1959) and "The Rebel" (1960).
- In 1960, he was cast as "Billy the Kid" in the TV series "The Tall Man". He appeared in 75 episodes from 1960 to 1962.
- In 1963, he was cast as "Sheriff Emmett Ryker" in the TV series "The Virginian". He appeared in 104 episodes from 1963 to 1968.
- Then in 1979, he was cast as "Cuda Weber" in the TV series "The Mackenzies of Paradise Cove". The show only lasted 6 episodes.
- In 1986, he was cast as "Gen. Philip Henry Sheridan" in the TV mini-series "North and South, Book 11". He appeared in 6 episodes.
- His last movie role, to date, was in the film "Piranha 3 DD" in 2012.
- Clu was married to Miriam Byrd-Nethery from 1952 until her death in 2003. They had two children, John and Tom.
- He was a marine from 1946 to 1948 and stationed at Camp Pendleton.
- Clu attended Northeastern State College, Oklahoma in the late 1940's.
- He directed a short film ("A Day With the Boys") in 1969 that was nominated for a Palme d'Or Award at the Cannes Film Festival.
- Clu's other film credits include "The Killers" (1964), "Winning" (1969), "The Last Picture Show" (1971), "McQ" (1974), "The Other Side of Midnight" (1977), "The Return of the Living

Dead" (1985), "Gunfighter" (1999) and "Feast" (2005).

- His other TV credits include "Wagon Train" (1959-64) 5 episodes, "The F.B.I." (1971) 2 episodes, "Bonanza" (1972), "Ironside" (1968-73) 3 episodes, "McCloud" (1975), "The Oregon Trail" (1977), "Falcon Crest" (1981), "Knight Rider" (1985), "Walker" (1995) and "Dr. Quinn, Medicine Woman" (1996).

"Tate"

Years : 1960

Episodes : 13 (1 season)

Cast :-

David McLean (b. 1922 d. 1995) - Played Tate

Synopsis :-
A one-armed Civil War veteran turns gunfighter.

Trivia & Tidbits :-

"The Show"

- **"Tate"** premiered on NBC on June 8, 1960 and last aired on September 14, 1960.
- The show ran for one season with a total of 13 black and white episodes.
- The series was created by Harry Julian Fink and produced by Perry Como's company Roncom Video Films, Inc.
- The pilot episode was titled "Home Town".
- Kraft Foods sponsored the series.
- The theme music was composed by William Loose.

"In Memoriam"

- **David McLean** died of lung cancer on October 12, 1995 (73) in Culver City, California.

"The Star"

- **David McLean** was born Eugene Joseph Huth on May 19, 1922 in Akron, Ohio.
- He made his uncredited acting debut in the TV movie "Captain Fathom" in 1955.
- David's first credited role was a guest appearance on the TV series "Sugarfoot" in 1957.
- In 1960, he was cast as "Tate" in the TV series of the same name. He appeared in 13 episodes before the show was canceled.
- In 1965, he was cast as "Craig Merritt" in the TV soap "Days of Our Lives". He appeared in 21 episodes from 1965 to 1966.
- David was married to Lilo Diane Haig and they had one son.
- In the 1960's, David appeared in commercials for the tobacco company Philip Morris (one of his perks was free cigarettes). He was known as "The Marlboro Man".
- His other film credits include "The Silent Call" (1961), "The Right Approach" (1961), "The Strangler" (1964), "Nevada Smith" (1966), "Kingdom of the Spiders" (1977) and "Deathsport" (1978).

- David's other TV credits include "Follow the Sun" (1961), "Perry Mason" (1963), "Laramie" (1962-63) 3 episodes, "The Virginian" (1963-65) 3 episodes, "The Guns of Will Sonnett" (1968), "Gunsmoke" (1969), "Daniel Boone" (1970), "Death Valley Days" (1963-70) 7 episodes, "Bonanza" (1969-73) 3 episodes and "The Streets of San Francisco" (1973-76) 4 episodes.

"Temple Houston"

Years : 1963 - 1964

Episodes : 26 (1 season)

Cast :-

Jeffrey Hunter (b. 1926 d. 1969) - Played Temple Houston

Jack Elam (b. 1920 d. 2003) - Played George Taggart

Synopsis :-
Stories associated with real-life circuit-riding lawyer Temple Houston.

Trivia & Tidbits :-

"The Show"

- **"Temple Houston"** premiered on NBC on September 19, 1963 and last aired on April 2, 1964.
- The show ran for one season with a total of 26 episodes.
- The character "Temple Houston" was loosely based on the circuit-riding lawyer Temple Lea Houston (son of the famous Sam Houston).

- The pilot for the series was titled "The Man from Galveston" (1963), but was never aired on television. It was released theatrically in December, 1963 and directed by William Conrad ("Cannon").
- The series was produced by Jeffrey Hunter's company Apollo Productions and Warner Bros. Television.
- The theme music was composed by Frank Comstock and Ned Washington.

"In Memoriam"

- **Jeffrey Hunter** died of a stroke on May 26, 1969 (42) in Los Angeles, California.
- **Jack Elam** died of congestive heart failure on October 20, 2003 (82) in Ashland, Oregon.

"The Stars"

- **Jeffrey Hunter** was born Henry Herman McKinnies Jr. on November 25, 1926 in New Orleans, Louisiana.
- His parents moved to Milwaukee, Wisconsin when he was four years old.
- Jeffrey graduated from Whitefish Bay High School and began acting in local theatre and radio.
- He enlisted in the U.S. Navy in 1945 and remained until a medical discharge in 1946.
- Following this he attended Northwestern University in Illinois and graduated with a bachelor's degree in 1949.

- Jeffrey then went to graduate school at the University of California, Los Angeles, where he studied radio and drama.
- In 1950, Darryl F Zanuck (20th Century-Fox head) signed him to a contract and changed his name to Jeffrey Hunter.
- He made his uncredited acting debut in the film "Julius Caesar" in 1950.
- Several movie roles followed including "Call Me Mister" (1951), "Red Skies of Montana" (1952), "Dreamboat" (1952), "Three Young Texans" (1954), "White Feather" (1955) and "The Searchers" (1956), starring John Wayne.
- Jeffrey made his TV debut in an episode ("South of the Sun") of "Climax!" in 1955.
- More movie roles followed including "The Proud Ones" (1956), "Gun for a Coward" (1957), "The True Story of Jesse James" (1957), "In Love and War" (1958), "Sergeant Rutledge" (1960), "Hell to Eternity" (1960), "King of Kings" (1961), "No Man Is an Island" (1962), "The Longest Day" (1962) and "The Man from Galveston" (1963).
- In 1963, he was cast as "Temple Houston" in the TV series of the same name. He appeared in 26 episodes from 1963 to 1964.
- His last acting appearance was in the film "¡Viva America!" (Italy) in 1969.
- Jeffrey was married three times – Barbara Rush (1950-55); Joan Bartlett (1957-67) and Emily McLaughlin (1969-until his death). He had one son with Ms. Rush and two sons with Ms. Bartlett. He also adopted Ms. Bartlett's son from a previous marriage.

- In 1960, he was awarded a Star on the Hollywood Walk of Fame for his contribution to television.
- He was cast as "Christopher Pike", captain of the USS Enterprise, in the original "Star Trek" pilot in 1964.
- Whilst he was at Northwestern University he worked as a model for commercial photographers.
- Jeffrey was good friends with actor Roger Moore ("James Bond").
- His other film credits include "Dimension 5" (1966), "A Guide for the Married Man" (1967), "Custer of the West" (1967), "The Private Navy of Sgt. O'Farrell" (1968) and "Super Colt 38" (1969).
- Jeffrey's other TV credits include "Death Valley Days" (1962), "Combat!" (1962), "The Legend of Jesse James" (1966), "Daniel Boone" (1966), "The Green Hornet" (1966), "The Monroes" (1967), "The F.B.I." (1965-68) 2 episodes and "Insight" (1967-69) 2 episodes.

- **Jack Elam** was born William Scott Elam on November 13, 1920 in Miami, Arizona.
- He was the son of Millard Elam and Alice Amelia Kirby. Jack's mother died in 1922 when he was two years old.
- Jack lost the sight in his left eye due to a boyhood accident at a Boy Scout meeting.
- He was a student at Miami High School and later at Phoenix Union High School, where he graduated in the late 1930's.

- Following this he attended Santa Monica Junior College and later worked as a bookkeeper at the Bank of America in Los Angeles.
- During the Second World War he served two years in the U.S. Navy.
- After his discharge he worked as an accountant in Hollywood. One of his clients was movie mogul Samuel Goldwyn.
- In 1944, he turned to acting and made his debut in the movie short "Trailin' West" (1944).
- Following this he appeared in a number of films including "Mystery Range" (1947), "Wild Weed" (1949), "The Sundowners" (1950), "High Lonesome" (1950), "Rawhide" (1951), "Rancho Notorious" (1952), "The Battle of Apache Pass" (1952) and "Montana Territory" (1952).
- Jack made his TV debut in an episode ("The Bouncing Bullet") of "The Files of Jeffrey Jones" in 1952.
- This was followed by a number of movie roles including "The Far Country" (1954), "Cattle Queen of Montana" (1954), "Wichita" (1955), The Man from Laramie" (1955), "Jubal" (1956), "Gunfight at the O.K. Corral" (1957), "The Comancheros" (1961) and "Pocketful of Miracles" (1961).
- In 1963, he was cast as "Deputy J.D. Smith" in the TV series "The Dakotas". He appeared in 20 episodes.
- Then again in 1963, he was cast as "George Taggart" in the TV series "Temple Houston".

He appeared in 26 episodes from 1963 to 1964.

- In 1974, he was cast as "Zack Wheeler" in the TV series "The Texas Wheelers". The show only lasted 8 episodes.
- In 1986, he was cast as "Uncle Alvin 'Bully' Stevenson" in the TV series "Easy Street". He appeared in 22 episodes from 1986 to 1987.
- His last acting appearance was in the TV movie "Bonanza: Under Attack" in 1995.
- Jack was married twice – Jean Elam (1937-61) and Margaret Jennison (1961-2003). He had two children with Jean and one child with Margaret.
- In 1994, he was inducted into the Hall of Great Western Performers at the National Cowboy and Western Heritage Museum.
- At one time Jack was the manager of the Bel Air Hotel in Los Angeles.
- Jack's other film credits include "4 for Texas" (1963), "The Rare Breed" (1966), "Firecreek" (1968), "Once Upon a Time in the West" (1968), "Support Your Local Sheriff!" (1969), "Dirty Dingus Magee" (1970), "Rio Lobo" (1970), "Support Your Local Gunfighter" (1971), "Pat Garrett & Billy the Kid" (1973), "The Apple Dumpling Gang Rides Again" (1979), "The Cannonball Run" (1981), "Cannonball Run 11" (1984), "The Giant of Thunder Mountain" (1991) and "Bonanza: The Return" (1993)(TV).
- His other TV credits include "Stories of the Century" (1954), "The Lone Ranger" (1954-55) 2 episodes, "Wagon Train" (1957), "Zorro" (1958) 3 episodes, "The Texan"

(1958-60) 3 episodes, "Zane Grey Theatre" (1957-61) 4 episodes, "Sugarfoot" (1961), "The Rifleman" (1958-61) 5 episodes, "Lawman" (1958-62) 5 episodes, "The Untouchables" (1960-62) 3 episodes, "Cheyenne" (1961-62) 3 episodes, "The Wild Wild West" (1967), "Cimarron Strip" (1968), "The Outcasts" (1969), "The Virginian" (1970), "Bonanza" (1961-70) 3 episodes, "Gunsmoke" (1959-72) 15 episodes, "Disneyland" (1969-75) 3 episodes, "Phyllis" (1975-76) 3 episodes, "Eight Is Enough" (1978-80) 2 episodes, "Father Murphy" (1981) 2 episodes, "Paradise" (1989), "Home Improvement" (1992) and "Lonesome Dove : The Series" (1994-95) 2 episodes.

"The Travels of Jaimie McPheeters"

Years : 1963 - 1964

Episodes : 26 Episodes (1 season)

Cast :-

Kurt Russell - (b. 1951) - Played Jaimie McPheeters

Dan O'Herlihy (b. 1919 d. 2005) - Played 'Doc' Sardius McPheeters

Charles Bronson (b. 1921 d. 2003) - Played Linc Murdock

Mark Allen (b. 1920 d. 2003) - Played Matt Kissel

Meg Wyllie (b. 1917 d. 2002) - Played Mrs. Kissel

Michael Whitney (b. 1931 d. 1983) - Played Coulter

Donna Anderson (b. 1939) - Played Jenny

Synopsis :-
Stories surrounding a wagon train in the 1840's.

Trivia & Tidbits :-

"The Show"

- **"The Travels of Jaimie McPheeters"** premiered on ABC on September 15, 1963 and last aired on March 15, 1964.
- The show ran for one season with a total of 26 black and white episodes.
- The series was based on the Pulitzer Prize-winning novel of the same name and written by Robert Lewis Taylor.
- The theme song was composed by Leigh Harline (music) and Jerry Winn (lyrics). The Bee Gees recorded a version of this song early in their careers.
- The series was produced by MGM Television.
- The famous singing group "The Osmonds" appeared in nine episodes as the singing sons of the "Kissel" family (they also sung the theme song).
- The show aired opposite "My Favourite Martian" and "The Ed Sullivan Show" on CBS and "Walt Disney's Wonderful World of Color" on NBC.
- In 1964, a film called "Guns of Diablo" was released with both Kurt Russell and Charles Bronson reprising their roles from "Jaimie McPheeters".

"In Memoriam"

- **Dan O'Herlihy** died of natural causes on February 17, 2005 (85) in Malibu, California.
- **Charles Bronson** died of pneumonia and Alzheimers disease on August 30, 2003 (81) in Los Angeles, California.
- **Mark Allen** died on May 21, 2003 (83) in Palos Verdes, California.
- **Meg Wyllie** died of heart failure on January 1, 2002 (84) in Glendale, California.
- **Michael Whitney** died on November 30, 1983 (52) in New York City, New York.

"The Stars"

- **Kurt Russell (see "The Quest")**

- **Daniel Peter O'Herlihy** was born on May 1, 1919 in County Wexford, Ireland.
- He was educated at Christian Brothers College in Dun Laoghaire. In 1944, he graduated from University College Dublin with a degree in Architecture.
- Dan's first acting role came in 1944 in the play "Red Roses for Me" directed by Sean O'Casey.
- He made his film debut in the U.K. movie "Hungry Hill" in 1947.
- This was followed by another U.K. film titled "Odd Man Out" (1947).
- Dan made his U.S. film debut in the movie "Macbeth" in 1948.
- Following this, he appeared in a number of films including "Larceny" (1948), "Kidnapped" (1948), "The Iroquois Trail" (1950), "Soldier's

Three" (1951), "The Highwayman" (1951) and "The Blue Veil" (1951).

- Dan made his TV debut in an episode ("The Sire de Maletroit's Door") of "Your Show Time" in 1949.
- He guest starred in a number of TV shows following this, including "The Unexpected" (1952), "Cavalcade of America" (1952-53) 2 episodes, "Stage 7" (1955), "Climax!" (1955), "Schlitz Playhouse of Stars" (1955), "Letter to Loretta" (1956), "Lux Video Theatre" (1955-56) 5 episodes, "On Trial" (1957), "Zane Grey Theatre" (1957), "General Electric Theater" (1953-59) 4 episodes, "Playhouse 90" (1957-60) 2 episodes, "The Untouchables" (1960), "Rawhide" (1960), "The Americans" (1961), "The Best of the Post" (1961) 2 episodes, "The United States Steel Hour" (1954-61) 3 episodes, "Route 66" (1962), "Adventures in Paradise" (1961-62) 2 episodes, "Bonanza" (1962), "Empire" (1962), "Combat!" (1963) and "Ben Casey" (1963).
- In 1963, he was cast as "Dr. Sardius McPheeters" in the TV series "The Travels of Jaimie McPheeters". He appeared in 26 episodes from 1963 to 1964.
- In 1966, he was cast as "Boss Will Varner" (as a replacement for Edmond O'Brien) in the TV series "The Long, Hot Summer". He appeared in 12 episodes.
- Then in 1974, he had the recurring role of "Lt. Col. Max Dodd" in the TV series "Colditz". He appeared in 5 episodes.

- In 1979, he was cast as "The Director" in the TV series "A Man Called Sloane". The series only lasted 12 episodes.
- In 1984, he had another recurring role as "Carson Marsh" in the TV series "Whiz Kids". He appeared in 5 episodes.
- In 1990-91, he played the character "Andrew Packard" in the TV series "Twin Peaks". He appeared in 6 episodes.
- His last acting appearance was in the TV movie "The Rat Pack" in 1998.
- Dan was married to Elsa Bennett from 1945 until his death in 2005. They had five children.
- In 1955, he was nominated for an Academy Award (Best Actor in a Leading Role) for his performance in the film "Adventures of Robinson Crusoe" (1954).
- Dan's other film credits include "Invasion, U.S.A." (1952), "Sword of Venus" (1953), "Bengal Brigade" (1954), "The Virgin Queen" (1955), "That Woman Opposite" (1957), "Imitation of Life" (1959), "One Foot in Hell" (1960), "Fail-Safe" (1964), "100 Rifles" (1969), "A Case for Murder" (1972), "The Quest: The Longest Drive" (1976)(TV), "MacArthur" (1977), "Mark Twain: Beneath the Laughter" (1979)(TV), "The Last Starfighter" (1984), "RoboCop" (1987), "RoboCop 2" (1990) and "Love, Cheat & Steal" (1993).
- His other TV credits include "Profiles in Courage" (1964), "The Defenders" (1965), "Dr. Kildare" (1961-65) 4 episodes, "The Road West" (1966), "The Big Valley" (1967), "The High Chaparral" (1967), "Hondo" (1967), "The Man from U.N.C.L.E." (1965-68) 4 episodes,

"Ironside" (1973), "QB VII" (1974) (mini-series), "Hawaii Five-O" (1975) "The Quest" (1976) 2 episodes, "The Bionic Woman" (1977), "Charlie's Angels" (1978), "Barnaby Jones" (1979) 2 episodes, "Nancy Astor" (1982) (mini-series), "The Secret Servant" (1984) 3 episodes, "Wildfire" (1986) 2 episodes, "L.A. Law" (1988), "The Pirates of Dark Water" (1991) (voice) 9 episodes, "Under the Hammer" (1994) and "VR" (1995).

- **Charles Bronson** was born Charles Dennis Buchinsky on November 3, 1921 in Ehrenfeld, Pennsylvania.
- He was the son of Walter Buchinsky, a Lithuanian immigrant, and Mary Valinsky, a Lithuanian- American.
- After he graduated from high school he went to work in the coal mines of Pennsylvania.
- In 1943, he enlisted in the United States Army Air Forces and served in the Pacific. He was awarded a Purple Heart for wounds received in battle.
- After the war, he worked odd jobs and then joined a theatrical group in Philadelphia.
- He then moved to New York City and shared an apartment with actor Jack Klugman ("The Odd Couple").
- In 1949, he relocated to Hollywood and enrolled in the Pasadena Playhouse.

- Charles made his TV debut in an episode ("Friend of the Family") of "Fireside Theatre" in 1949.
- He made his uncredited film debut in the movie "You're in the Navy Now" in 1951.
- This was followed by a series of movie roles including "The People Against O'Hara" (1951) uncredited, "Red Skies of Montana" (1952) uncredited, "My Six Convicts" (1952), "Pat and Mike" (1952) and "Battle Zone" (1952) uncredited.
- Charles then guest starred on a number of TV shows including "Biff Baker, U.S.A." (1952) 2 episodes, "The Red Skelton Show" (1952), "The Roy Rogers Show" (1952), "The Doctor" (1952-53) 2 episodes, "Chevron Theatre" (1953) 2 episodes, "Four Star Playhouse" (1953), "Waterfront" (1954), "The Joe Palooka Story" (1955) 2 episodes, "Treasury Men in Action" (1954-55) 3 episodes, "Crusader" (1955-56) 2 episodes, "Medic" (1954-56) 2 episodes, "Telephone Time" (1956), "The Sheriff of Cochise" (1957), "Hey, Jeannie!" (1957), "Richard Diamond, Private Eye" (1957), "Colt .45" (1957) and "Studio One" (1957) 2 episodes.
- In 1958, he was cast as "Mike Kovak" in the TV series "Man with a Camera". He appeared in 29 episodes from 1958 to 1960.

- In 1962, he had the recurring role of "Paul Moreno" in the TV series "Empire". He appeared in 13 episodes from 1962 to 1963.
- Then in 1963, he had the recurring role of "Linc Murdock" in the TV series "The Travels of Jaimie McPheeters". He appeared in 13 episodes from 1963 to 1964.
- His last three acting roles were in the TV movies "Family of Cops" (1995), "Breach of Faith: A Family of Cops II" (1997) and "Family of Cops III: Under Suspicion" (1999).
- Charles was married three times – Harriet Tendler (1949-67), Jill Ireland (1968-90) and Kim Weeks (1998-2003). He had two children with Ms. Tendler and one child with Ms. Ireland.
- In 1972, he received a Golden Globe Award (shared with Sean Connery) for World Film Favorite – Male.
- In 1980, he was awarded a Star on the Hollywood Walk of Fame for his contribution to Motion Pictures.
- Charles' other film credits include "House of Wax" (1953), "Riding Shotgun" (1954), "Apache" (1954), "Vera Cruz" (1954), "Have Camera Will Travel" (1956)(TV), "Jubal" (1956), "Showdown at Boot Hill" (1958), "Machine-Gun Kelly" (1958), "Never So Few" (1959), "The Magnificent Seven" (1960), "Kid Galahad" (1962), "The Great Escape" (1963),

"4 for Texas" (1963), "The Sandpiper" (1965), "Battle of the Bulge" (1965), "This Property Is Condemned" (1966), "The Dirty Dozen" (1967), "Villa Rides" (1968), "Once Upon a Time in the West" (1968), "Red Sun" (1971), "Valachi Papers" (1972), "Chato's Land" (1972), "The Mechanic" (1972), "Mr. Majestyk" (1974), "Death Wish" (1974), "Breakheart Pass" (1975), "Caboblanco" (1980), "Death Wish II" (1982), "Death Wish 3" (1985), "Death Wish 4: The Crackdown" (1987), "The Indian Runner" (1991), "The Sea Wolf" (1993)(TV) and "Relative Danger" (1993)(TV).

- His other TV credits include "M Squad" (1958), "Sugarfoot" (1958) 2 episodes, "The Walter Winchell File" (1958), "Gunsmoke" (1956-58) 2 episodes, "U.S. Marshal" (1959), "Playhouse 90" (1958-60) 3 episodes, "The Aquanauts" (1960), "Riverboat" (1960), "General Electric Theater" (1955-61) 3 episodes, "Laramie" (1960-61) 2 episodes, "Hennesey" (1960-61) 2 episodes, "Cain's Hundred" (1961), "Alfred Hitchcock Presents" (1956-62) 3 episodes, "Have Gun – Will Travel" (1957-63) 5 episodes, "Bonanza" (1964), "Combat!" (1965), "The Big Valley" (1965), "Rawhide" (1965), "The Legend of Jesse James" (1966), "The Fugitive" (1967), "The Virginian" (1965-67) 2 episodes and "Dundee and the Culhane" (1967).

- **Mark Allen** was born on April 16, 1920.
- He made his TV debut in an episode ("High Ground") of "Armstrong Circle Theatre" in 1952.
- This was followed by guest appearances in a number of TV shows including "Tales of Tomorrow" (1952), "Harbormaster" (1957), "Naked City" (1958), "Richard Diamond, Private Eye" (1959), "The Lawless Years" (1959) 2 episodes, "The Man from Blackhawk" (1959), "This Man Dawson" (1960), "Riverboat" (1960), "Pony Express" (1960), "Wanted: Dead or Alive" (1959-60) 3 episodes, "Gunsmoke" (1960), "Peter Gunn" (1959-61) 2 episodes, "Death Valley Days" (1961), "Leave It To Beaver" (1960-61) 2 episodes, "The Detectives" (1961) and "Empire" (1963).
- Mark made his uncredited film debut in the movie "Who Was That Lady" in 1960.
- In 1963, he had the recurring role of "Matt Kissel" in the TV series "The Travels of Jaimie McPheeters". He appeared in 19 episodes from 1963 to 1964.
- His other film credits include "The Gambler Wore a Gun" (1961), "A Thunder of Drums" (1961) uncredited, "How the West Was Won" (1962) uncredited, "Clarence, the Cross-Eyed Lion" (1965), "A Big Hand for a Little Lady"

(1966) uncredited, "Marlowe" (1969) uncredited, "The Movie Murderer" (1970)(TV), "Cotter" (1973) and "Farewell, My Lovely" (1975).

- Mark's other TV credits include "A Man Called Shenandoah" (1966), "Dark Shadows" (1966) 7 episodes, "The Fugitive" (1966-67) 2 episodes, "The Wild Wild West" (1969), "Lancer" (1969) 2 episodes, "Bearcats!" (1971), "Bonanza" (1960-73) 2 episodes, "The F.B.I." (1966-73) 6 episodes, "Mannix" (1974), "Barnaby Jones" (1974) and "Cannon" (1973-75) 3 episodes.

- **Meg Wyllie** was born Margaret Gillespie Wyllie on February 15, 1917 in Honolulu, Hawaii.
- She grew up in the Philippines where her father worked as an engineer.
- Meg attended the Brent School in Baguio, Philippines and then moved to New York City in the 1940's.
- She acted in plays at the Pasadena Playhouse and then made her TV debut in an episode ("The Teenage Crush") of "Mister Peepers" in 1952.
- Several more TV appearances followed including "The Philco Television Playhouse" (1955), "M Squad" (1958), "Have Gun – Will Travel" (1958), "Steve Canyon" (1959), "Zane Grey Theatre" (1959), "Peter Gunn" (1959-60)

2 episodes, "Sea Hunt" (1960), "77 Sunset Strip" (1960), "The New Breed" (1961), "Dr. Kildare" (1961-62) 2 episodes, "The Untouchables" (1959-62) 2 episodes, "Death Valley Days" (1959-62) 3 episodes and "It's a Man's World" (1962).

- In 1957, she appeared on the Broadway stage in the play "The First Gentleman".
- In 1963, she was cast in the recurring role of "Mrs. Kissel" in the TV series "The Travels of Jaimie McPheeters". She appeared in 18 episodes from 1963 to 1964.
- In 1994, she appeared as "Aunt Lolly Stemple" in 4 episodes of the TV series "Mad About You".
- Meg's film credits include "Flight That Disappeared" (1961), "Beauty and the Beast" (1962), "Marnie" (1964), "Movin' On" (1972)(TV), "Our Time" (1974), "Babe" (1975)(TV), "Lipstick" (1976), "Elvis" (1979)(TV), "Second Thoughts" (1983), "The Last Starfighter" (1984), "Nothing in Common" (1986), "Dragnet" (1987) and "Worth Winning" (1989).
- Her other TV credits included "My Three Sons" (1963), "Ben Casey" (1961-64) 3 episodes, "Profiles in Courage" (1964), "Wagon Train" (1959-65) 5 episodes, "A Man Called Shenandoah" (1965), "The Loner" (1966), "Perry Mason" (1962-66) 4 episodes, "The

Rounders" (1966), "Cimarron Strip" (1967), "Judd for the Defense" (1968), "Room 222" (1970), "The Virginian" (1963-70) 2 episodes, "The F.B.I." (1966-71) 2 episodes, "Alias Smith and Jones" (1971), "Gunsmoke" (1973), "The Waltons" (1973), "Cannon" (1973 2 episodes, "Barnaby Jones" (1974), "Kojak" (1975), "Emergency!" (1972-76) 2 episodes, "Angie" (1979), "Benson" (1979-82) 2 episodes, "The Paper Chase" (1984), "Star Trek" (1986), "Family Ties" (1987), "Designing Women" (1989-90) 2 episodes, "Night Court" (1985-90) 3 episodes, "The Golden Girls" (1987-91) 4 episodes, "Family Matters" (1993) and "Coach" (1994).

- **Michael Witney** was born Whitney Michael Armstrong on November 21, 1931 in Ticonderoga, New York.
- He made his acting debut in the TV series "The Travels of Jaimie McPheeters". Michael played the character "Buck Coulter" in 14 episodes from 1963 to 1964.
- Following this, he guest starred on a number of TV shows including "The Richard Boone Show" (1964) 2 episodes", "Rawhide" (1965), "Gunsmoke" (1965), "The Fugitive" (1965), "Gilligan's Island" (1965), "A Man Called Shenandoah" (1966), "Tarzan" (1966-67) 2 episodes, "Iron Horse" (1967), "Daniel Boone"

(1968), "Star Trek" (1968), "Death Valley Days" (1965-68) 2 episodes, "The F.B.I." (1969) 2 episodes, "Bonanza" (1965-71) 4 episodes, "Night Gallery" (1972) and "Cannon" (1973).

- In 1975, he was cast as "Frank Ward" in the TV series "Oil Strike North". He appeared in 12 episodes.
- Michael was married twice - Donna (Jo Jo) Collette Bailey (1956-76) and Lesley 'Twiggy' Hornby (1977-83). He had one daughter, Carly, with Ms. Hornby.
- His film credits include "The Iron Men" (1966)(TV), "The Way West" (1967), "Darling Lili" (1970), "Doc" (1971), "Head On" (1971), "The Catcher" (1972)(TV), "W" (1974) and "There Goes the Bride" (1980).
- Michael's other TV credits include "Twiggy" (1975), "Delvecchio" (1977), "Kojak" (1978), and "Charlie's Angels" (1978-81) 3 episodes.

- **Donna Anderson** was born Donna Knaflich on September 5, 1939 in Gunnison, Colorado.
- She is the daughter of Louis John Knaflich and Wenona Hanly.
- Donna made her acting debut in the film "On the Beach" in 1959.
- This was followed by a part in the film "Inherit the Wind" in 1960.

- She made her TV debut in the TV series "The Travels of Jaimie McPheeters". She appeared as "Jenny" in 13 episodes from 1963 to 1964.
- Donna's last acting appearance, to date, was in an episode ("It's a Dog's Life") of "Murder, She Wrote" in 1984.
- Her other film credits include "Sinderella and the Golden Bra" (1964) uncredited and "Deadhead Miles" (1973).
- Donna's other TV credits include "Bob Hope Presents Chrysler Theatre" (1964), "The Lieutenant" (1964), "Gunsmoke" (1964), "Ben Casey" (1965), "Little House on the Prairie" (1975), "The Incredible Hulk" (1981) and "The A-Team" (1984).

"Two Faces West"

Years : 1960 - 1961

Episodes : 39 (1 season)

Cast :-

Charles Bateman (b. 1928) - Played Dr. Rick January

Francis De Sales (b. 1912 d. 1988) - Played Sheriff Maddox

Joyce Meadows - Played Stacy

Paul Comi (b. 1932 d. 2016) - Played Deputy Johnny Evans

Synopsis :-
A western series set in Gunnison, Colorado

Trivia & Tidbits :-

"The Show"

- **"Two Faces West"** premiered in syndication on October 17, 1960 and last aired on July 31, 1961.

- The show ran for one season with a total of 39 black and white episodes.
- The series was produced by Screen Gems Television.
- The theme music was composed by Joseph Weiss.
- Filming took place at the Iverson Movie Ranch, California.
- The series premiere episode was titled "Hot Water".

"In Memoriam"

- **Francis De Sales** died on September 25, 1988 (76) in Van Nuys, California.
- **Paul Comi** died of Alzheimer's disease on August 26, 2016 (84) in Pasadena, California.

"The Stars"

- **Charles Wilbur Bateman** was born on November 19, 1930 in San Diego, California.
- He made his TV debut in an episode ("Black Fire") of "Maverick" in 1958.
- Charles made his uncredited movie debut in the 1959 film "The F.B.I. Story", starring James Stewart.
- In 1959, he was cast as "Det. George Peters" in the TV series "Manhunt". He only appeared for 13 episodes during the first season.
- In 1960, he was cast as twin brothers, "Rick and Ben January" in the TV series "Two Faces

West". He appeared in 39 episodes from 1960 to 1961.

- In the final season (1966) of the TV series "Hazel" he played the character "Fred Williams". He appeared in 9 episodes.
- From 1971 to 1973, he had a recurring role in the TV series "Cannon". He appeared as "Lt. Paul Tarcher" in 5 episodes.
- In 1984, he was cast as "C.C. Capwell" in the TV soap "Santa Barbara". He appeared in 176 episodes from 1984 to 1985.
- Charles' last acting appearances, to date, was in an episode ("Battle Fatigue") of "The Trials of Rosie O'Neill" in 1991.
- His other film credits include "How to Murder Your Wife" (1965), "Me and Benjie" (1970)(TV), "The Brotherhood of Satan" (1971), "The Poseidon Adventure" (1972) uncredited, "Interval" (1973) and "A Reason to Live" (1985)(TV).
- Charles' other TV credits include "The Silent Service" (1958), "Lawman" (1958), "Lassie" (1959), "Yancy Derringer" (1959) 2 episodes, "Rawhide" (1959), "Perry Mason" (1960-61) 2 episodes, "Hawaiian Eye" (1961-62) 2 episodes, "The Littlest Hobo" (1963-64) 2 episodes, "Bonanza" (1964-65) 2 episodes, "Death Valley Days" (1963-66) 3 episodes, "Get Smart" (1969) 2 episodes, "Ironside" (1971), "Mannix" (1971-72) 2 episodes, "The F.B.I." (1968-72) 5 episodes, "Barbary Coast" (1975), "Police Woman" (1974-75) 2 episodes, "Barnaby Jones" (1976-78) 3 episodes,

"Matlock" (1988) 2 episodes and "Dallas" (1988-91) 2 episodes.

- **Francis A. De Sales** was born on March 23, 1912 in Philadelphia, Pennsylvania.
- He made his acting debut in an episode ("Father Malachy's Miracle") of "The Ford Theatre Hour" in 1950.
- In 1952, he was cast as "Lt. Bill Weigand in the TV series "Mr. & Mrs. North". He appeared in 53 episodes from 1952 to 1954.
- Francis made his uncredited movie debut in the film "Headline Hunters" in 1955.
- Following this, he made many guest appearances on TV shows including "Topper" (1955), "Schlitz Playhouse of Stars" (1955-56) 2 episodes, "Big Town" (1956), "Navy Log" (1955-56) 2 episodes, "Crusader" (1956) 2 episodes, "The Gray Ghost" (1957), "Studio 57" (1955-57) 5 episodes, "Leave It To Beaver" (1957), "Colt .45" (1958), "Sergeant Preston of the Yukon" (1955-58) 5 episodes, "State Trooper" (1957-58) 2 episodes, "Tales of Wells Fargo" (1958), "Death Valley Days" (1959), "Sugarfoot" (1958-59) 2 episodes and "Riverboat" (1959).
- From 1959 to 1960, he had a recurring role on the TV series "The Adventures of Ozzie & Harriet". He played the character "Ralph Dobson" in 6 episodes.
- In 1960, he was cast as "Sheriff Maddox" in the TV series "Two Faces West". He appeared in 20 episodes from 1960 to 1961.
- Once this series was finished he guest starred on a number of TV shows including "Ben

Casey" (1961), "Cheyenne" (1957-61) 3 episodes, "Bronco" (1958-61) 3 episodes, "Laramie" (1961-62) 2 episodes, "Have Gun – Will Travel" (1962), "Dr. Kildare" (1962-63) 2 episodes, "The Virginian" (1962-63) 3 episodes, "Wide Country" (1963), "Hazel" (1961-64) 2 episodes, "Wagon Train" (1961-64) 2 episodes, "Perry Mason" (1958-65) 5 episodes, "Kraft Suspense Theatre" (1963-65) 4 episodes and "The Munsters" (1965).

- In 1965, he was cast as "Rusty Lincoln" in the daytime TV series "Days of Our Lives". He appeared in 9 episodes.
- His last acting appearance was in the film "Rabbit Test" in 1978.
- Francis' other film credits include "And Suddenly You Run" (1956), "The Girl He Left Behind" (1956), "Jailhouse Rock" (1957) uncredited, "Darby's Rangers" (1958) uncredited, "Apache Territory" (1958), "Face of a Fugitive" (1959), "Psycho" (1960) uncredited, "When the Clock Strikes" (1961), "The Plainsman" (1966) uncredited, "The Pigeon" (1969)(TV), "The Outfit" (1973), "The Missiles of October" (1974)(TV), "Dynasty" (1976)(TV) and "Moving Violation" (1976).
- His other TV credits include "The Wild Wild West" (1966), "Bonanza" (1962-68) 2 episodes, "The Flying Nun" (1968), "The Mod Squad" (1969-71) 2 episodes, "The F.B.I." (1966-73) 3 episodes, "Columbo" (1973), "Hec Ramsey" (1972-74) 2 episodes, "Marcus Welby, M.D." (1971-74) 3 episodes, "Cannon" (1975) and "Ellery Queen" (1975).

- **Joyce Meadows** was born Joyce Burger on April 13, 1933 in Arrowwood, Alberta, Canada.
- The family moved to Montana when she was eight years old and then onto California whilst she was still a teenager.
- Whilst at high school she performed in Shakespeare's "Romeo and Juliet" at the Little Eaglet Theatre in Sacramento, California.
- After leaving school, Joyce studied drama with Jeff Corey, Mira Rostova and Stella Adler.
- Following this, she moved to Hollywood and changed her name to Joyce Meadows.
- Joyce made her movie debut in the film "Flesh and the Spur" in 1956.
- She then guest starred in a number of TV shows including "Dr. Christian" (1956-57) 2 episodes, "Highway Patrol" (1957), "The Web" (1957), "Harbor Command" (1958), "The Restless Gun" (1958), "Tales of Wells Fargo" (1957-58) 2 episodes, "U.S. Marshal" (1958), "Tombstone Territory" (1959) 2 episodes, "The Rough Riders" (1959) 2 episodes, "Johnny Ringo" (1960) and "The Texan" (1959-60) 2 episodes.
- In 1959, she was cast as "Lynn Allen" in the TV series "The Man and the Challenge". She appeared in 5 episodes from 1959 to 1960.
- In 1960, she was cast as "Stacy" in the TV series "Two Faces West". She appeared in 18 episodes from 1960 to 1961.
- Her last acting appearance, to date, was in the video short "A Golightly Gathering" in 2009.
- Joyce has been married to Merrill Harrington since 1984.

- In 2007, she was a guest at the Western Film Fair in Charlotte, North Carolina.
- Joyce's other film credits include "The Brain from Planet Arous" (1957), "Frontier Gun" (1958), "The Girl in Lovers Lane" (1960), "Walk Tall" (1960), "Back Street" (1961), "Zebra in the Kitchen" (1965), "The Christine Jorgensen Story" (1970), "True Identity" (1991) and "Murder of Innocence" (1993)(TV).
- Her other TV credits include "Bachelor Father" (1958-60) 2 episodes, "77 Sunset Strip" (1959-60) 2 episodes, "Wanted: Dead or Alive" (1960), "Sea Hunt" (1961), "Alfred Hitchcock Presents" (1959-61) 3 episodes, "Cheyenne" (1961), "Wagon Train" (1959-61) 3 episodes, "Lawman" (1961) 2 episodes, "Maverick" (1962), "Perry Mason" (1959-65) 3 episodes, "Punky Brewster" (1987), "L.A. Law" (1991) and "Dream On" (1995).

- **Paul Domingo Comi** was born on February 11, 1932 in Boston, Massachusetts.
- In 1957, he began his professional acting career as an apprentice at the La Jolla Playhouse in California.
- Paul had a small part in the play "Career" and this led to rave reviews in the Hollywood Reporter and Variety.
- He was signed by 20th Century Fox and cast in the film "The Young Lions" (1958).
- Paul made his TV debut in an episode ("Hideout") of "M Squad" in 1958.

- Several more TV guest spots followed including "The Silent Service" (1958), "Steve Canyon" (1958), "77 Sunset Strip" (1959), "Peter Gunn" (1959), "Tombstone Territory" (1958-59) 2 episodes, "The Untouchables" (1960), "The Man and the Challenge" (1960), "Lawman" (1959-60) 2 episodes, "Adventures in Paradise" (1960-61) 2 episodes and "Checkmate" (1961).
- In 1960, he was cast as "Deputy Johnny Evans" in the TV series "Two Faces West". He appeared in 14 episodes from 1960 to 1961.
- In 1961, he was cast as "Chuck Lambert" in the TV series "Ripcord". He appeared in 14 episodes from 1961 to 1963.
- Then in 1964, he was cast as "Yo Yo" in the TV series "Rawhide". He appeared in 6 episodes from 1964 to 1965.
- Paul's last acting appearance was in the video short "Reflections on Spock" in 2004.
- He graduated from the University of Southern California in Los Angeles.
- Paul served as president and partner of Caffe D'Amore Inc., a company started by his wife. It was subsequently sold to the Kerry Group.
- His other film credits include "In Love and War" (1958), "Pork Chop Hill" (1959), "The Outsider" (1961), "Cape Fear" (1962), "Blindfold" (1965), "Lost Flight" (1970)(TV), "Conquest of the Planet of the Apes" (1972),

"The Towering Inferno" (1974), "Death Wish II" (1982) and "A Cry for Help: The Tracey Thurman Story" (1989)(TV).

- Paul's other TV credits include "Wagon Train" (1961), "The Tall Man" (1961), "Stoney Burke" (1962), "It's a Man's World" (1962-63) 2 episodes, "Ben Casey" (1962-63) 3 episodes, "Dr. Kildare" (1964), "Perry Mason" (1965), "12 O'Clock High" (1964-66) 4 episodes, "The Big Valley" (1966-67) 4 episodes, "The Fugitive" (1964-67) 3 episodes, "The Wild Wild West" (1966-67) 3 episodes, "The F.B.I." (1965-68) 4 episodes, "The Virginian" (1963-68) 8 episodes, "Mannix" (1968-69) 2 episodes, "Cannon" (1971-73) 2 episodes, "The Blue Knight" (1975), "Barnaby Jones" (1975-80) 3 episodes, "Lou Grant" (1982), "Matt Houston" (1983), "Fame" (1986), "Murder, She Wrote" (1987), "Highway to Heaven" (1986-89) 3 episodes and "Baywatch" (1995).

"The Virginian"

Years : 1962 - 1971

Episodes : 249 (9 seasons)

Cast :-

James Drury (b. 1934) - Played The Virginian

Doug McClure (b. 1935 d. 1995) - Played Trampas

Lee J. Cobb (b. 1911 d. 1976) - Played Judge Henry Garth

Roberta Shore (b. 1943) - Played Betsy Garth

Gary Clarke (b. 1936) - Played Steve Hill

Charles Bickford (b. 1891 d. 1967) - Played John Grainger

John McIntire (b. 1907 d. 1991) - Played Clay Grainger

Stewart Granger (b. 1913 d. 1993) - Played Col. Alan MacKenzie

Clu Culager (b. 1928) - Played Emmett Ryker

Randy Boone (b. 1942) - Played Randy Benton

Russell Lane (b. 1949) - Played Elizabeth Grainger

Ross Elliott (b. 1917 d. 1999) - Played Sheriff Mark Abbot

Don Quine (b. 1938) - Played Stacey Grainger

Jeanette Nolan (b. 1911 d. 1998) - Played Holly Grainger

Synopsis :-
The story of the Shiloh Ranch in Wyoming during the 1890's.

Trivia & Tidbits :-

"The Show"

- **"The Virginian"** premiered on NBC on September 19, 1962 and last aired on March 24, 1971.
- The show ran for nine seasons with a total of 249 episodes.
- "The Virginian" became television's first 90-minute Western series.
- The final year of the series was retitled "The Men From Shiloh".
- The show was the third longest running Western (behind "Gunsmoke" and "Bonanza").
- The series was loosely based on the 1902 novel of the same name by Owen Wister.

- James Drury ("The Virginian") and Doug McClure ("Trampas") were the only two characters to remain with the series for the entire run.
- "The Virginian's" horse was named "Joe D" and "Trampas'" buckskin horse was "Buck".
- In 1965, Decca Records released an album of songs by Roberta Shore ("Betsy Garth") and Randy Boone ("Randy Benton").
- The first episode of "The Virginian" was titled "The Executioners", guest starring Hugh O'Brian ("Wyatt Earp").
- The series was produced by NBC, Revue Studios and Universal TV.
- The original theme music was composed by Percy Faith. For the ninth and final season the theme music changed to a new one composed by Ennio Morricone.
- Ratings - "The Virginian" figured in the Top 30 programs for 8 of the 9 seasons it was on air - 1962/64 (No.26), 1963/64 (No.17), 1964/65 (No.22), 1965/66 (No.23), 1966/67 (No.10), 1967/68 (No.14), 1968/69 (No.17), 1969/70 (-), 1970/71 (No.18).
- Filming locations for the series included the Universal Studios Backlot, Iverson Movie Ranch, Lone Pine, Bronson Canyon and CBS Studio Center.
- Episode 30, Season 3 titled "We've Lost a Train" served as a pilot for the "Laredo" series.

"In Memoriam"

- **Doug McClure** died of lung cancer on February 5, 1995 (59) in Sherman Oaks, California.
- **Lee J. Cobb** died of a heart attack on February 11, 1976 (64) in Woodland Hills, Los Angeles, California.
- **Charles Bickford** died of a blood infection on November 9, 1967 (76) in Los Angeles, California.
- **John McIntire** died of lung cancer and emphysema on January 30, 1991 (83) in Pasadena, California.
- **Stewart Granger** died of prostate cancer on August 16, 1993 (80) in Santa Monica, California.
- **Ross Elliott** died on August 12, 1999 (82) in Los Angeles, California.
- **Jeanette Nolan** died of a stroke-related illness on June 5, 1998 (86) in Los Angeles, California.

"The Stars"

- **James Child Drury Jr.** was born on April 18, 1934 in New York City, New York.
- His father, James Drury Sr. was a Professor of Marketing at New York University.
- James' childhood was spent living in New York and on the family ranch in Oregon. This is where he developed his love of horses.
- When he was eight years old he got the acting bug after playing King Herod in a children's Christmas play.

- After finishing high school he trained as a classical actor at New York University. He was credited with 12 major Shakespeare roles.
- In 1954, he moved to Hollywood to continue his acting career.
- In 1955, he made his uncredited film debut in the movie "Blackboard Jungle".
- This was followed by a number of film roles including "Love Me or Leave Me" (1955) uncredited, "The Tender Trap" (1955), "Diane" (1956) uncredited, "Forbidden Planet" (1956), "The Last Wagon" (1956), "Love Me Tender" (1956) and "Bernadine" (1957).
- James made his TV debut in an episode ("The Grown Ones") of "Cameo Theatre" in 1955.
- He then guest starred on a number of TV shows including "Alfred Hitchcock Presents" (1958), "Playhouse 90" (1958), "Broken Arrow" (1958), "Man Without a Gun" (1958), "The Silent Service" (1958), "The Texan" (1958), "Bronco" (1958), "Zane Grey Theatre" (1958-59) 2 episodes, "Have Gun – Will Travel" (1959), "Trackdown" (1959), "Lawman" (1959) 2 episodes, "Black Saddle" (1959), "Steve Canyon" (1959) 2 episodes, "Cheyenne" (1959), "Death Valley Days" (1959), "Men Into Space" (1960), "The Rebel" (1960) 2 episodes, "Gunsmoke" (1955-61) 4 episodes, "The Rifleman" (1958-61) 2 episodes, "Stagecoach West" (1961), "Rawhide" (1959-61) 3 episodes, "Perry Mason" (1961) and "Wagon Train" (1960-62) 2 episodes.

- In 1962, he was cast as "The Virginian" in the TV series of the same name. He appeared in 243 episodes from 1962 to 1971.
- In 1974, he was cast as "Captain Spike Ryerson" in the TV series "Firehouse". The series only lasted 13 episodes.
- James has been married three times – Cristall Othoneos (Orton) (1957-64), Phyllis Mitchell (1968-79) and Carl Ann Head (1979-present). He has two children with Ms. Othoneos.
- In 1991, he was inducted into the Hall of Great Western Performers at the National Cowboy and Western Heritage Museum in Oklahoma.
- His son Timothy is a keyboardist, guitarist and vocalist and has played with "The Eagles" and British group "Whitesnake".
- James' other film credits include "Good Day for a Hanging" (1959), "The Yank" (1960)(TV), "Toby Tyler, or Ten Weeks with a Circus" (1960), "Pollyanna" (1960), "Ride the High Country" (1962), "The Young Warriors" (1966), "Breakout" (1970)(TV), "The All American Cowboy" (1985)(TV), "The Gambler Returns: The Luck of the Draw" (1991)(TV), "Maverick" (1994) uncredited and "The Virginian" (2000)(TV).
- His other TV credits include "The Red Skelton Show" (1971), "Ironside" (1971), "Alias Smith and Jones" (1971-72) 2 episodes, "The Fall Guy" (1983), "Walker" (1993) 3 episodes, "The Adventures of Brisco County Jr." (1993-94) 2 episodes and "Kung Fu: The Legend Continues" (1995-96) 2 episodes.

- **Doug McClure (see "Barbary Coast")**

- **Lee J. Cobb** was born Leo Jacoby on December 8, 1911 in The Bronx, New York.
- He was the son of Benjamin (Benzion) Jacob, a compositor for a foreign-language newspaper, and Kate Neilecht.
- He studied at New York University before traveling to Hollywood and making his uncredited film debut in the 12 episode serial "The Vanishing Shadow" (1934).
- Lee returned to New York and joined the Manhattan-based Group Theatre in 1935.
- He made his Broadway debut in the play "Crime and Punishment" in 1935.
- A series of Broadway plays followed including "Waiting for Lefty" (1935), "Till the Day I Die" (1935), "Mother" (1935), "Bitter Stream" (1936) and "Johnny Johnson" (1936-37).
- In 1937, he made his credited film debut in the movie "North of the Rio Grande".
- Several film roles followed including "Rustler's Valley" (1937), "Ali Baba Goes to Town" (1937) uncredited, "Danger on the Air" (1938), "Golden Boy" (1939), "This Thing Called Love" (1940), "Men of Boys Town" (1941), "Buckskin Frontier" (1943), "The Song of Bernadette" (1943), "Winged Victory" (1944), "Anna and the King of Siam" (1946), "Captain from Castile" (1947), "Call Northside 777" (1948) and "The Dark Past" (1948).
- Lee made his TV debut in an episode ("The Moon and Sixpence") of "Somerset Maugham TV Theatre" in 1951.

- As well as appearing in movies he guest starred on a number of TV shows including "Tales of Tomorrow" (1951), "Lights Out" (1951), "The Ford Television Theatre" (1954), "Lux Video Theatre" (1955), "Medic" (1955), "The Alcoa Hour" (1956), "Studio One" (1957) 2 episodes, "Zane Grey Theatre" (1956-58) 2 episodes, "Playhouse 90" (1957-59) 2 episodes, "The DuPont Show with June Allyson" (1961), "Naked City" (1961) and "General Electric Theater" (1960-62) 2 episodes.
- In 1962, he was cast as "Judge Henry Garth" in the TV series "The Virginian". He appeared in 108 episodes from 1962 to 1966.
- In 1970, he was cast as "Attorney David Barrett" in the TV series "The Young Lawyers". He appeared in 24 episodes from 1970 to 1971.
- His last acting appearance was in the Italian film "La legge violenta della squadra anticrimine" in 1976.
- Lee was married twice – Helen Beverly (1940-52) and Mary Brako Hirsch (1957-76). He had two children with Ms. Beverly and two children with Ms. Hirsch.
- During the Second World War he served in the First Motion Picture Unit of the United States Army Air Forces.
- Lee appeared in several other plays on Broadway including "Golden Boy" (1937-38), "Thunder Rock" (1939), "The Fifth Column" (1940), "Death of a Salesman" (1949-50) and "King Lear" (1968-69).

- He was accused, by Larry Parks, of being a communist before the House Un-American Activities Committee. He chose to be a friendly witness.
- Lee was nominated for two Academy Awards – 1955 (Best Actor in a Supporting Role – "On the Waterfront") and 1959 (Best Actor in a Supporting Role – "The Brothers Karamazov").
- In 1981, he was inducted (posthumously) into the American Theatre Hall of Fame.
- Lee's other film credits include "Sirocco" (1951), "The Fighter" (1952), "The Tall Texan" (1953), "On the Waterfront" (1954), "The Racers" (1955), "The Left Hand of God" (1955), "The Man in the Grey Flannel Suit" (1956), "12 Angry Men" (1957), "The Three Faces of Eve" (1957), "The Brothers Karamazov" (1958), "The Trap" (1959), "Exodus" (1960), "The Four Horsemen of the Apocalypse" (1962), "How the West Was Won" (1962), "Come Blow Your Horn" (1963), "Our Man Flint" (1966), "In Like Flint" (1967), "Coogan's Bluff" (1968), "Mackenna's Gold" (1969), "Lawman" (1971), "The Exocist" (1973), "Last Moments" (1974) and "That Lucky Touch" (1975).
- His other TV credits include "The Dean Martin Show" (1970), "McCloud" (1973) and "Gunsmoke" (1974).

- **Roberta Shore** was born Roberta Jymme Schourop on April 7, 1943 in Monterey Park, California.

- She was raised in San Gabriel, California and began her career at age ten singing country and western songs at supermarket openings with Tex Williams.
- Tex then asked her to join his weekly TV show from Knotts Berry Farm.
- Following this, she joined "The Pinky Lee Show" (1954), NBC's number one rated children's daily television program.
- In 1956, she made her TV acting debut in an episode ("Dirty Face") of "Jane Wyman Presents The Fireside Theatre".
- In 1958, she was cast as "Laura Rogan" in the Disney TV series "Annette". She appeared in 15 episodes.
- Roberta made her film debut in the movie "The Shaggy Dog" in 1959.
- In 1959, she played the character "Joyce" in 4 episodes of "Father Knows Best".
- In 1961, she was cast as "Henrietta 'Hank' Gogerty" in the TV series "The Bob Cummings Show". She appeared in 22 episodes from 1961 to 1962.
- Then in 1962, she was cast as "Betsy Garth" in the TV series "The Virginian". She appeared in 70 episodes from 1962 to 1965.
- Her last acting appearance, to date, was in the film short "Cipher in the Snow" in 1974.
- Roberta has been married three times – Kent Christensen, Terry C. Barber and Ron Frederickson. She has two children.
- In the 1960's she toured Australia with the Mouseketeers.

- In 1984, she worked as a disc jockey at a radio station in Salt Lake City, Utah.
- Roberta was a talented yodeller and performed on the Disney sound track album of "It's a Small World".
- She recorded albums with Rex Allen and her "Virginian" co-star Randy Boone.
- Roberta's other film credits include "Blue Denim" (1959), "A Summer Place" (1959) uncredited, "Because They're Young" (1960), "Strangers When We Meet" (1960), "The Young Savages" (1961) and "Stanley Kubrick's Lolita" (1962) uncredited.
- Her other TV credits include "Studio One" (1958), "Maverick" (1959), "The Donna Reed Show" (1959-60) 2 episodes, "The Many Loves of Dobie Gillis" (1960), "Goodyear Theatre" (1960), "Wagon Train" (1961), "Zane Grey Theatre" (1961), "Lawman" (1961), "Alcoa Premiere" (1962), "Laramie" (1962), "The Tall Man" (1962) and "The Adventures of Ozzie & Harriet (1960-62) 7 episodes.

- **Gary Clarke** was born Clarke L'Amoreaux on August 16, 1933 in Los Angeles, California.
- After graduating from high school Gary decided to pursue an acting career. He won a role in a community theater play in San Gabriel, California which led to work in a series of plays in Glendale.
- During this time, he worked as a machinist and a newspaper deliveryman.

- Gary made his TV acting debut in an episode ("A Reasonable Doubt") of "Jane Wyman presents The Fireside Theatre" in 1957.
- He made his film debut in the movie "Dragstrip Riot" in 1958.
- In 1960, he was cast as "Dick Hamilton" in the TV series "Michael Shayne". He appeared in 17 episodes from 1960 to 1961.
- In 1962, he was cast as "Steve Hill" in the TV series "The Virginian". He appeared in 63 episodes from 1962 to 1964.
- Then in 1967, he was cast as "Capt. Richards" in the TV series "Hondo". He appeared in 17 episodes.
- His last acting appearance, to date, was in the film "Parkland" in 2013.
- Gary has been married three times – Marilyn L. Knudsen (1952-?), Pat Woodell (1964-77) and Jerrene Beatty (1991-present).
- He has released a number of single records including "Tomorrow May Never Come/One Way Ticket" (RCA Victor Records) and "One Summer in A Million/ Theme From The Virginian" (Decca).
- Gary's other film credits include "How to Make a Monster" (1958), "Missile to the Moon" (1958), "Date Bait" (1960), "The Absent-Minded Professor" (1961) uncredited, "Strike Me Deadly" (1963), "Passion Street, U.S.A." (1964), "Wild Wild Winter" (1966), "Tale of the Cock" (1969), "Class of '74" (1972), "Outrage" (1973)(TV), "Tombstone" (1993), "My Son Is Innocent" (1996)(TV) and "The Paperboy" (2012).

- His other TV credits include "Sky King" (1958), "Laramie" (1961), "87th Precinct" (1961), "Wagon Train" (1962), "Bachelor Father" (1962), "The Tall Man" (1962), "Gunsmoke" (1962), "Tales of Wells Fargo" (1961-62) 2 episodes, "My Three Sons" (1968), "Then Came Bronson" (1970), "The Smith Family" (1971), "Lassie" (1972), "The Streets of San Francisco" (1972), "Cannon" (1972), "Chase" (1973), "The F.B.I." (1974), "Dynasty" (1985) 3 episodes, "The A-Team" (1986), "The Highwayman" (1988), "The Young Riders" (1990-91) 4 episodes and "Legend" (1995).

- **Charles Ambrose Bickford** was born on January 1, 1891 in Cambridge, Massachusetts.
- He was the fifth of seven children and at age nine was tried and acquitted of the attempted murder of a trolley motorman who had driven over and killed his dog.
- In his teens he travelled all over the United States working as a lumberjack, investment promoter and pest exterminator.
- During the First World War, he served as an Engineer Lieutenant in the United States Army.
- He made his Broadway debut in the play "Dark Rosaleen" in 1919.
- Several more Broadway plays followed including "Houses of Sand" (1925), "Outside Looking In" (1925), "No More Women" (1926), "Chicago" (1926-27), "The Cyclone Lover" (1928) and "Gods of the Lightning" (1928).

- Charles made his film debut in the movie "South Sea Rose" in 1929.
- Several more film roles followed including "Dynamite" (1929), "Anna Christie" (1930), "River's End" (1930), "East of Borneo" (1931), "The Squaw Man" (1931), "The Pagan Lady" (1931), "Scandal for Sale" (1932), "Vanity Street" (1932), "Song of the Eagle" (1933), "Red Wagon" (1933), "A Wicked Woman" (1934), "The Farmer Takes a Wife" (1935), "East of Java" (1935), "Pride of the Marines" (1936), "The Plainsman" (1936), "Daughter of Shanghai" (1937), "The Storm" (1938), "Of Mice and Men" (1939), "Riders of Death Valley" (1941), "Tarzan's New York Adventure" (1942), "The Song of Bernadette" (1943), "Duel in the Sun" (1946), "The Farmer's Daughter" (1947), "The Babe Ruth Story" (1948), "Johnny Belinda" (1948), "Riding High" (1950), "Jim Thorpe – All-American" (1951) and "The Last Posse" (1953).
- Charles made his TV debut in an episode ("Next Stop Bethlehem") of "The Revlon Mirror Theater" in 1953.
- In 1966, he was cast as "John Grainger" in the TV series "The Virginian". He appeared or was credited in 45 episodes from 1966 to 1968.
- His last episode of "The Virginian" was to be his last acting appearance before he passed away.
- Charles was married to Beatrice Loring from 1916 until his death in 1967. They had two children, Doris and Rex.

- He was nominated for three Academy Awards – 1944 (Best Actor in a Supporting Role – "The Song of Bernadette"), 1948 (Best Actor in a Supporting Role – "The Farmer's Daughter") and 1949 (Best Actor in a Supporting Role – "Johnny Belinda").
- Charles has two Stars on the Hollywood Walk of Fame for his contributions to Motion Pictures and Television.
- In 1965, Charles published his autobiography titled "Bulls, Balls, Bicycles & Actors".
- Charles' other film credits include "A Star Is Born" (1954), "The Court-Martial of Billy Mitchell" (1955), "Mister Cory" (1957), "The Big Country" (1958), "The Unforgiven" (1960), "Days of Wine and Roses" (1962), "Della" (1964) and "A Big Hand for the Little Lady" (1966).
- His other TV credits include "Celebrity Playhouse" (1955), "Schlitz Playhouse of Stars" (1953-56) 3 episodes, "The Ford Television Theatre" (1952-56) 3 episodes, "Climax!" (1957), "Wagon Train" (1958), "Playhouse 90" (1956-60) 7 episodes, "Checkmate" (1960), "The Americans" (1961), "Dr. Kildare" (1961), "Theatre '62" (1962), "Alcoa Premiere" (1963), "The Dick Powell Show" (1961-63) 2 episodes and "Suspense" (1964).

- **John McIntire (see "The Americans")**

- **Stewart Granger** was born James Lablache Stewart on May 6, 1913 in Kensington, London, England.
- He was the only son of Major James Stewart, OBE and Frederica Eliza Lablache.
- Stewart was educated at Epsom College and the Webber Douglas Academy of Dramatic Art.
- He spent many years in the theatre at the Hull Repertory Theatre and later at the Birmingham Repertory Theatre.
- Stewart made his uncredited U.K. film debut in the movie "The Song You Gave Me" in 1933.
- Several more British films followed including "Give Her a Ring" (1934) uncredited, "Over the Garden Wall" (1934) uncredited, "A Southern Maid" (1935) uncredited, "Under Secret Orders" (1937) uncredited, "So This Is London" (1939) and "Convoy" (1940).
- At the start of the Second World War, he enlisted in the Gordon Highlanders and then transferred to the Black Watch with a rank of second lieutenant.
- However, in 1942 he suffered from stomach ulcers and was invalided out of the army.
- Stewart resumed his British film career and appeared in movies such as "Secret Mission" (1942), "The Man in Grey" (1943), "Fanny by Gaslight" (1944), "Madonna of the Seven Moons" (1945), "Waterloo Road" (1945), "Caesar and Cleopatra" (1945), "Caravan" (1946), "Captain Boycott" (1947), "Blanche Fury" (1948), "Woman Hater" (1948) and "Adam and Evelyne" (1949).

- He made his U.S. film debut in the movie "King Solomon's Mines" in 1950.
- Stewart then appeared in a number of U.S. films including "The Light Touch" (1951), "The Wild North" (1952), "Scaramouche" (1952), "Salome" (1953), "Young Bess" (1953), "Beau Brummell" (1954), "Moonfleet" (1955), "Bhowani Junction" (1956), "Gun Glory" (1957), "Harry Black and the Tiger" (1958), "North to Alaska" (1960), "Sodom and Gomorrah" (1962), "Frontier Hellcat" (1964), "The Oil Prince" (1965), "The Last Safari" (1967) and "Any Second Now" (1969)(TV).
- In 1970, he was cast as "Col. Alan Mackenzie" in the TV series "The Virginian". He appeared or was credited in 24 episodes from 1970 to 1971.
- His last acting appearance was in an episode ("It's the Pictures That Got Small") of "Pros and Cons" in 1991.
- Stewart was married three times – Elspeth March (1938-48), Jean Simmons (1950-60) and Caroline LeCerf (1964-69). He had two children with Ms. March, one child with Ms. Simmons and one child with Ms. LeCerf.
- In 1956, he and Jean Simmons became U.S. citizens.
- In 1981, he published his autobiography titled "Sparks Fly Upward".
- Stewart appeared on the Broadway stage in the play "The Circle" in 1989-90.
- His other film credits include "The Hound of the Baskervilles" (1972)(TV), "The Wild Geese" (1978), "Hell Hunters" (1986), "A Hazard of

Hearts" (1987)(TV) and "Chameleons" (1989)(TV).

- Stewart's other TV credits include "The Fall Guy" (1983), "Murder, She Wrote" (1985), "The Love Boat" (1985) 2 episodes, "The Wizard" (1987) and "Hotel" (1983-87) 2 episodes.

- **Clu Gulager (see "The Tall Man")**

- **Randy Boone** was born Clyde Randall Boone on January 17, 1942 in Fayetteville, North Carolina.
- He is the son of Clyde Wilson Boone and Rhumel E. Boone.
- Randy is related to Daniel Boone (frontiersman), Richard Boone (actor), Pat Boone (actor/singer) and Debby Boone (actress/singer).
- He graduated from Fayetteville Senior High School and then entered North Carolina State University at Raleigh. Randy subsequently dropped out of university to pursue a musical career.
- In 1962, he made his TV acting debut as "Vern Hodges" in the TV series "It's a Man's World". He appeared in 19 episodes from 1962 to 1963.
- In 1964, he was cast as "Randy Benton" in the TV series "The Virginian". He appeared or was credited in 66 episodes from 1964 to 1966.

- Then in 1967, he was cast as "Francis Wilde" in the TV series "Cimarron Strip". He appeared in 23 episodes from 1967 to 1968.
- His last acting appearance, to date, was in the film "The Wild Pair" in 1987.
- Randy was married to Sylvia Howell until 1969 (divorced) and they have one child.
- In 2011, he was inducted into the Fayetteville Music Hall of Fame.
- Randy's other film credits include "The Hanged Man" (1964)(TV), "Country Boy" (1966), "Terminal Island" (1973), "Savages" (1974)(TV) and "Dr. Minx" (1975).
- His other TV credits include "The Alfred Hitchcock Hour" (1963), "Wagon Train" (1963) 3 episodes, "The Twilight Zone: The Original Series" (1963), "The Fugitive" (1964), "Bonanza" (1966), "Hondo" (1967) 2 episodes, "Lassie" (1973), "Gunsmoke" (1975), "The Quest" (1976) and "Highway to Heaven" (1985).

- **Sara Russell Lane** was born on March 12, 1949 in New York City, New York.
- She is the daughter of actor James Rusty Lane and actress Sara Anderson.
- Sara made her acting debut in the film "I Saw What You Did" in 1965.
- In 1966, she was cast as "Elizabeth Grainger" in the TV series "The Virginian". She appeared

or was credited in 105 episodes from 1966 to 1970.

- Sara is married to Jon Scott and they have two children.
- After she retired from acting she and her husband became owners of Havens Wine Cellars in the Napa Valley, California.
- Her other film credits are "Schoolgirls in Chains" (1973), "The Trial of Billy Jack" (1974) and "Billy Jack Goes to Washington" (1977).

- **Ross Elliott** was born Elliott Blum on June 18, 1917 in The Bronx, New York.
- He began appearing in plays whilst a teenager at both high school and summer camps.
- In 1937, he graduated from New York's City College after appearing in a number of the college's dramatic productions.
- He became a member of Orson Welles Mercury Theatre and played minor parts on Broadway in "The Shoemaker's Holiday" (1938) and "Danton's Death" (1938).
- In 1941, he joined the United States Army and spent much of his time in various touring shows.
- In 1942, he appeared in the Broadway production of "This Is the Army".
- During his stint in the army he also made his film debut in the movie "This Is the Army" (1943).
- After the war, he began his film career in movies such as "The Burning Cross" (1947), "Angel on the Amazon" (1948), "Streets of San Francisco" (1949), "Dynamite Pass" (1950),

"Cody of the Pony Express" (1950), "Chicago Calling" (1951) and "Desert of Lost Men" (1951).

- Ross made his TV debut in an episode ("Hope Chest") of "Fireside Theatre" in 1950.
- He followed this up with guest appearances on TV shows such as "Racket Squad" (1951), "Gruen Guild Playhouse" (1951-52) 2 episodes, "Sky King" (1952), "The Lone Ranger" (1952-53) 2 episodes, "I Married Joan" (1953), "The Ford Television Theatre" (1952-54) 2 episodes, "Mr. & Mrs. North" (1954), "Fireside Theatre" (1954) 2 episodes, "The Pepsi-Cola Playhouse" (1954-55) 2 episodes, "City Detective" (1953-55) 3 episodes, "I Love Lucy" (1952-55) 3 episodes, "Soldiers of Fortune" (1955) 2 episodes, "Matinee Theatre" (1955-56) 3 episodes, "Four Star Playhouse" (1954-56) 3 episodes, "Fury" (1956), "Schlitz Playhouse of Stars" (1954-56) 4 episodes, "The George Burns and Gracie Allen Show" (1954-56) 7 episodes, "The Adventures of Jim Bowie" (1956) 2 episodes, "The Gray Ghost" (1957), "Cavalcade of America" (1954-57) 4 episodes, "The People's Choice" (1957), "The Thin Man" (1957), "Broken Arrow" (1956-58) 2 episodes, "State Trooper" (1957-58) 3 episodes, "The Silent Service" (1957-58) 4 episodes, "Perry Mason" (1958) and "The Texan" (1958).
- In 1958, he had the recurring role of "Virgil Earp" in the TV series "The Life and Legend of Wyatt Earp". He appeared in 4 episodes from 1958 to 1959.

- In 1961, he had the recurring role of "Jack's TV Director" in the TV series "The Jack Benny Program". He appeared in 11 episodes from 1961 to 1964.
- In 1962, he had the recurring role of "Marty Rhodes" in the TV series "Sam Benedict". He appeared in 4 episodes from 1962 to 1963.
- Also in 1962, he was cast as "Sheriff Mark Abbott" in the TV series "The Virginian". He appeared in 61 episodes from 1962 to 1971.
- His last acting appearance was in the film "Scorpion" in 1986.
- Ross was married to Esther Susan Melling from 1954 until his death in 1999.
- He appeared on the Broadway stage in 1946 in the play "Apple of His Eye".
- Ross' other film credits include "The Beast from 20,000 Fathoms" (1953), "Tumbleweed" (1953), "Ma and Pa Kettle at Home" (1954), "African Manhunt" (1955), "D-Day the Sixth of June" (1956), "Tammy Tell Me True" (1961), "Day of the Evil Gun" (1968), "Kelly's Heroes" (1970), "Skyjacked" (1972), "The Towering Inferno" (1974), "Gable and Lombard" (1976) and "Bogie" (1980)(TV).
- His other TV credits include "M Squad" (1958-59) 2 episodes, "Richard Diamond, Private Eye" (1957-59) 3 episodes, "Pony Express" (1960), "Maverick" (1960), "Zane Grey Theatre" (1957-60) 2 episodes, "The Rebel" (1960) 2 episodes, "Letter to Loretta" (1954-61) 7 episodes, "Wanted: Dead or Alive" (1958-61) 2 episodes, "Sugarfoot" (1961), "Sea Hunt" (1960-61) 6 episodes, "Cheyenne"

(1956-61) 3 episodes, "Laramie" (1960-61) 3 episodes, "Wagon Train" (1957-62) 2 episodes, "Rawhide" (1959-62) 2 episodes, "Death Valley Days" (1959-63) 2 episodes, "Gomer Pyle U.S.M.C." (1964), "The Fugitive" (1965), "The Lucy Show" (1965), "A Man Called Shenandoah" (1966), "The Invaders" (1967-68) 3 episodes, "The Felony Squad" (1967-68) 6 episodes, "The Wild Wild West" (1968), "Lassie" (1956-69) 4 episodes, "Ironside" (1969-71) 3 episodes, "Cannon" (1972), "The F.B.I." (1966-72) 7 episodes, "Bonanza" (1961-73) 3 episodes, "The Mod Squad" (1969-73) 6 episodes, "Gunsmoke" (1960-74) 3 episodes, "Emergency!" (1973-75) 4 episodes, "Barnaby Jones" (1973-75) 4 episodes, "Wonder Woman" (1977), "The Waltons" (1980), "Dallas" (1981), "Little House on the Prairie" (1982) and "The A-Team" (1983).

- **Don Quine** was born on September 11, 1938 in Fenville, Michigan.
- He made his TV acting debut in an episode ("The Short Way Home") of "The Detectives" in 1961.
- In 1965, Don had the recurring role of "Joe Chernak" in the TV series "Peyton Place". He appeared in 16 episodes.
- In 1966, he was cast as "Stacey Grainger" in the TV series "The Virginian". He appeared in 55 episodes from 1966 to 1968.
- His last acting appearance, to date, was in the TV movie "Torch Song" in 1993.

- Don was married to author Judith Balaban.
- His other film credits are "Sullivan's Empire" (1967)(TV) and "Clayton County Line" (1978).
- Don's other TV credits include "Rawhide" (1965), "Dr. Kildare" (1965), "The Fugitive" (1964-66) 3 episodes, "12 O'Clock High" (1965-66) 2 episodes, "The F.B.I." (1966), "Insight" (1968), "Lancer" (1968), "Medical Center" (1969) and "Hawaii Five-O" (1970).

- **Jeanette Nolan (see "Dirty Sally")**

"The Westerner"

Years : 1960

Episodes : 13 (1 season)

Cast :-

Brian Keith (b. 1921 d. 1997) - Played Dave Blassingame

Synopsis :-
Stories about a wandering ranch-hand in the 1870's.

Trivia & Tidbits :-

"The Show"

- **"The Westerner"** premiered on NBC on September 30, 1960 and last aired on December 30, 1960.
- The show ran for one season with a total of 13 black and white episodes.
- The pilot for "The Westerner" appeared on CBS's "Dick Powell's Zane Grey Theatre".
- The series was created by Sam Peckinpah and produced by Four Star Productions.
- External filming took place at Vasquez Rocks Natural Area Park, California.

- The series was terminated due to low ratings.
- The show aired opposite "The Flintstones" and "Route 66".
- "Dave's" dog, "Brown", played the title role in the film "Old Yeller" (1957).
- A 1963 episode ("The Losers") of "The Dick Powell Theater" revived the characters "Dave Blassingame" and "Burgundy Smith". However, "Dave" was played by Lee Marvin and "Burgundy" played by Keenan Wynn.

"In Memoriam"
- **Brian Keith** committed suicide on June 24, 1997 (75) in Malibu, California.

"The Star"

- **Brian Keith** was born Robert Keith Jr. on November 14, 1921 in Bayonne, New Jersey.
- He was the son of actor Robert Keith and stage actress Helena Shipman.
- Brian graduated from East Rockaway High School, New York in 1939 and entered the U.S. Marine Corps in 1942. He remained in the Marines until the end of the war in 1945.
- He began his film career at the age of three in the silent movie "Pied Piper Malone" in 1924.
- Brian's first film as an adult was an uncredited part in "Knute Rockne All American" in 1940.
- In 1948, he appeared in his first Broadway play ("Mister Roberts").
- After this he guest starred in several TV series including "Tales of Tomorrow" (1952), "Eye

Witness" (1953), "Robert Montgomery Presents" (1953), "The Mask" (1954), "The Elgin Hour" (1955) and "The Adventures of Ellery Queen" (1955).

- In 1955, he was cast as "Matt Anders" in the TV series "Crusader". He appeared in 52 episodes from 1955 to 1956.
- In 1960, he was cast as "Dave Blassingame" in the TV series "The Westerner". He appeared in 13 episodes.
- Then in 1966, he was cast as "Uncle Bill Davis" in the TV series "Family Affair". He appeared in 138 episodes from 1966 to 1971.
- Another TV series followed. He was cast as "Dr. Sean Jamison" in "The Brian Keith Show". He appeared in 47 episodes from 1972 to 1974.
- In 1974, he appeared as the character "Steven 'The Fox' Halliday" in the TV series "The Zoo Gang". The show only lasted 6 episodes.
- Following this, Brian appeared in another short-lived series. He played the character "Lew Archer" (6 episodes) in the TV series "Archer" (1975).
- In 1978, he was cast as "Sheriff Axel Dumire" in the TV mini-series "James A. Michener's Centennial". He appeared in 12 episodes from 1978 to 1979.
- He then appeared in the TV mini-series "The Chisholms" (1979). He was seen in 4 episodes.
- In 1983, he was cast as "Judge Milton C. Hardcastle" in the TV series "Hardcastle and McCormick". He appeared in 67 episodes from 1983 to 1986.

- In 1987, he was cast as "Prof. Roland G. Duncan" in the TV series "Pursuit of Happiness". He appeared in 10 episodes from 1987 to 1988.
- Then in 1988, he was cast as "B.L. McCutcheon" in the TV series "Heartland". He appeared in 10 episodes.
- His final TV series was "Walter & Emily". He appeared as "Walter Collins" in 13 episodes from 1991 to 1992.
- Brian's last movie appearance was in the TV film "Rough Riders" (1997). He played the character "President William McKinley".
- He was married three times - Frances Helm (1948-54), Judith Landon (1954-69) and Victoria Young (1970-97). Brian had five children with Ms. Landon (3 adopted) and two children with Ms. Young.
- Sadly his daughter Daisy committed suicide ten weeks before Brian took his own life.
- His son Michael died in 1963.
- Brian's stepmother, Peg Entwistle, committed suicide when she jumped from the "H" of the famous Hollywood sign in 1932.
- At the time of his death, Brian was suffering from emphysema and terminal lung cancer.
- Brian has a Star on the Hollywood Walk of Fame for his contribution to television.
- He guest starred on the first episode ("The Murder of Sherlock Holmes") of "Murder, She Wrote" (1984).
- Brian appeared on the cover of TV Guide three times.

- His dog, "Brown", in the TV series "The Westerner" was the same dog that played in the film "Old Yeller" (1957).
- In 1955, Brian appeared in an endorsement campaign for Camel cigarettes.
- Brian's other film credits include "Arrowhead" (1953). "Fort Dobbs" (1958), "The Parent Trap" (1961), "Savage Sam" (1963), "The Rare Breed" (1966), "Nevada Smith" (1966), "The Russians Are Coming! The Russians Are Coming!" (1966), "The Wind and the Lion" (1975), "Hooper" (1978), "The Alamo: Thirteen Days to Glory" (1987) (TV) and "The Second Civil War" (1997) (TV).
- His other TV credits include "Wire Service" (1957), "Zane Grey Theatre" (1959), "Rawhide" (1959), "Laramie" (1959), "The Americans" (1961), "The Virginian" (1963), "Profiles in Courage" (1964), "Insight" (1960-68) 10 episodes, "Disneyland" (1959-86) 10 episodes, "Evening Shade" (1991), "The Marshal" (1995) and "Touched by an Angel" (1996).

"Whiplash"

Years : 1960 - 1961

Episodes : 34 (1 season)

Cast :-

Peter Graves (b. 1926 d. 2010) - Played
Christopher Cobb

Synopsis :-
Stories about Australia's first stagecoach line Cobb
and Co. in the 1860's.

Trivia & Tidbits :-

"The Show"

- **"Whiplash"** premiered on ITV (England) on
  September 10, 1960 and last aired on June
  10, 1961.
- The show ran for one season with a total of 34
  black and white episodes.
- The series was created by Michael Noonan and
  Michael Plant and produced by Network 7,
  Artransa Park, Associated Television (ATV),
  Hill-Hecht-Lancaster Productions and
  Incorporated Television Company (ITC).

- Filming was carried out at Artransa Park Studios, Australia.
- The theme music was composed by Edwin Astley and sung by Frank Ifield.
- The series was loosely based on the life of Freeman Cobb, who was the founder of Australia's first stagecoach line "Cobb and Co."

"In Memoriam"

- **Peter Graves** died of a heart attack on March 14, 2010 (83) in Pacific Palisades, California.

"The Star"

- **Peter Graves** was born Peter Aurness on March 18, 1926 in Minneapolis, Minnesota.
- He was the son of Rolf Cirkler Aurness, a businessman, and Ruth Duesler, a journalist. His brother was James Arness ("Gunsmoke").
- When he was 16, he was a radio announcer at WMIN in Minneapolis.
- Peter graduated from Southwest High School in 1944 and spent two years in the U.S. Air Force near the end of the Second World War.
- After the war he studied drama at the University of Minnesota and then relocated to Hollywood.
- He made his film debut in the movie "Rogue River" in 1951.

- Several movies followed including "Fort Defiance" (1951), "Red Planet Mars" (1952), "Stalag 17" (1953), "Beneath the 12-Mile Reef" (1953), "The Yellow Tomahawk" (1954), "Wichita" (1955) and "Fort Yuma" (1955).
- In 1955, he was cast as "Jim Newton" in the TV series "Fury". He appeared in 116 episodes from 1955 to 1960.
- In 1961, he was cast as "Christopher Cobb" in the Australian TV series "Whiplash". He appeared in 34 episodes.
- Then in 1965, he was cast as "Maj. Frank Whittaker" in the TV series "Court Martial". He appeared in 26 episodes from 1965 to 1966.
- In 1967, he was cast as "James Phelps" in the TV series "Mission: Impossible". He appeared in 143 episodes from 1967 to 1973.
- Peter appeared in the TV mini-series "The Winds of War" in 1983. He played "Palmer 'Fred' Kirby" in 7 episodes.
- In 1988, the "Mission: Impossible" TV series was revived and he once again played "Jim Phelps". He appeared in 35 episodes from 1988 to 1990.
- In 1997, he played the recurring character "John 'The Colonel' Camden" in the TV series "7th Heaven". He appeared in 11 episodes from 1997 to 2007.
- His last acting appearance was in the TV movie "Jack's Family Adventure" in 2010.

- Peter was married to Joan Endress from 1950 until his death in 2010. They had three daughters, Kelly, Claudia and Amanda.
- He has a Star on the Hollywood Walk of Fame for his contribution to the television industry.
- Peter directed an episode ("Which Dr.") of "Gunsmoke" in 1966. His brother was the star of the series.
- During the 1990's, he hosted the documentary series "Biography" on A&E.
- Peter's final project was narrating the computer game epic "Darkstar: The Interactive Movie" in 2010.
- He won a Golden Globe Award in 1971 for his role of "Jim Phelps" in "Mission: Impossible".
- Peter also won an Emmy Award in 1997 as host of "Biography".
- His other film credits include "Canyon River" (1956), "Death in Small Doses" (1957), "Sergeant Ryker" (1965), "Texas Across the River" (1966), "Call to Danger" (1973)(TV), "Sidecar Racers" (1975), "Flying High" (1980), "Flying High II : The Sequel" (1982) and "With You in Spirit" (2003)(TV).

- Peter's other TV credits include "Biff Baker, U.S.A." (1954), "Fireside Theatre" (1955), "Cimarron City" (1959), "Route 66" (1962), "The Virginian" (1964), "Branded" (1966), "Matt and Jenny" (1980), "Fantasy Island"

(1983), "The Love Boat" (1987) and "Cold Case" (2006).

"Whispering Smith"

Years : 1961

Episodes : 26 (1 season) (6 unaired episodes)

Cast :-

Audie Murphy (b. 1925 d. 1971) - Played Tom "Whispering" Smith

Guy Mitchell (b. 1927 d. 1999) - Played George Romack

Sam Buffington (b. 1931 d. 1960) - Played John Richards

Synopsis :-
A private detective operates in the old West.

Trivia & Tidbits :-

"The Show"

- **"Whispering Smith"** premiered on NBC on May 8, 1961 and last aired on September 18, 1961.
- The show ran for one season with a total of 26 black and white episodes (6 unaired).

- The series began filming in 1959 but due to production problems did not air until 1961.
- "Whispering Smith" was based on the 1948 movie of the same name starring Alan Ladd.
- The story for the film and TV series came from a book ("Whispering Smith") written by Frank H. Spearman in 1906.
- The theme music for the series was composed by Richard Shores.
- "Whispering Smith" aired against "The Danny Thomas Show" and "Surfside 6" on CBS.
- The series was produced by Whispering Co. and NBC and filmed at Revue Studios, Hollywood, California.

"In Memoriam"

- **Audie Murphy** died in a plane crash on May 28, 1971 (45) in Roanoke, Virginia.
- **Guy Mitchell** died after surgery on July 1, 1999 (72) in Las Vegas, Nevada.
- **Sam Buffington** died after committing suicide on May 15, 1960 (28) in Los Angeles, California.

"The Stars"

- **Audie Leon Murphy** was born on June 20, 1925 in Kingston, Texas.
- He was the son of Emmett Berry Murphy, a sharecropper, and Josie Bell Killian. Audie was the seventh of twelve children.

- Audie grew up around the towns of Farmersville, Greenville and Celeste. He attended elementary school but dropped out in the fifth grade.
- His father drifted in and out of the family's life and eventually deserted the family for good.
- Audie's mother became ill and died in 1941.
- To make ends meet, Audie worked in a radio repair shop, a general store and a garage and gas station.
- In 1942 (after his sister Corrine falsified his birth date), Audie enlisted in the Army.
- Audie spent the war years fighting in Europe and eventually became the most decorated American soldier.
- After the war, Audie was invited to Hollywood by movie star James Cagney. Cagney put him under contract and trained him in acting, voice and dance.
- Audie made his movie debut in the film "Beyond Glory" (1948). This was followed by another bit part in "Texas, Brooklyn and Heaven" (1948).
- In 1950, he signed a seven year contract with Universal Studios. His first film was "The Kid from Texas" (1950) where he played the character "Billy the Kid".
- Several more film roles followed including "Sierra" (1950), "Kansas Raiders" (playing "Jesse James")(1950), "The Red Badge of Courage" (1951), "The Cimarron Kid" (1952), "The Duel at Silver Creek" (1952), "Gunsmoke" (1953), "Ride Clear of Diablo" (1954), "Destry" (1954), "To Hell and Back"

(1955), "Night Passage" (1957) and "No Name on the Bullet" (1959).

- In 1961, he was cast as "Tom 'Whispering' Smith in the TV series "Whispering Smith". He appeared in 26 episodes.
- His last acting performance was in 1969 in the film "A Time for Dying" (again playing the character "Jesse James").
- Audie was married twice - Wanda Hendrix (1949-50) and Pamela Archer (1951-71). He had two sons, Terry and James, with Ms. Archer.
- Some of the medals Audie was presented with included The Medal of Honor, Distinguished Service Cross, Silver Star, Legion of Merit, Bronze Star, Purple Heart, French Legion of Honor and Belgium Croix de Guerre.
- Audie is buried in the Arlington National Cemetery and is the second most visited grave (President John F. Kennedy is the most visited).
- In 1949, Audie released his Second World War memoir titled "To Hell and Back".
- In 1995, Empire magazine voted him No.55 in the "100 Sexiest Stars" in film history.
- He was a member of the National Rifle Association of America (NRA) and a supporter of the Democratic Party.
- Audie has a military hospital named after him - The Audie L. Murphy Veteran's Hospital in San Antonio, Texas.
- He has a Star on the Hollywood Walk of Fame for his contribution to Motion Pictures.

- In 1996, he was inducted into the Hall of Great Western Performers at the National Cowboy and Western Heritage Museum.
- Recording artist Guy Mitchell, songwriter Scott Turner and Audie collaborated on numerous songs between 1962 and 1970 - the most successful being "Shutters and Boards" and "When the Wind Blows in Chicago".
- Audie's other film roles include "Hell Bent for Leather" (1960), "The Unforgiven" (1960), "Seven Ways from Sundown" (1960), "Bullet for a Badman" (1964), "Apache Rifles" (1964), "The Texican" (1966) and "40 Guns to Apache Pass" (1967).
- His other TV credits include "Lux Video Theatre" (1952), "Suspicion" (1957), "General Electric Theater" (1958) and "Startime" (1960).

- **Guy Mitchell** was born Albert George Cernick on February 22, 1927 in Detroit, Michigan.
- At the age of eleven he was signed by Warner Bros. Pictures to be groomed as a child star.
- He also performed on radio station KFWB in Los Angeles.
- After leaving school Guy worked as a saddlemaker.
- Following this, he was hired by Dude Martin to perform with his band in San Francisco.
- Guy served in the Navy for two years and then became a singer with Carmen Cavallaro's big band.

- After this he went to New York and made records for King Records under the name of Al Grant.
- In 1950, at the suggestion of Mitch Miller, he changed his name to Guy Mitchell.
- In 1953, he made his movie debut in the film "Those Redheads from Seattle".
- Guy had his own TV show ("The Guy Mitchell Show") from 1957 to 1958.
- In 1960, he made his TV dramatic debut in an episode ("West of Boston") of "Overland Trail".
- In 1961, he was cast as "George Romack" in the TV series "Whispering Smith". He appeared in 26 episodes.
- Guy was married three times but had no children.
- He has a Star on the Hollywood Walk of Fame for his contribution to Recording.
- Guy had nine Top 10 hits in the United States - "My Heart Cries for You" (1950-No.2), "The Roving Kind" (1950-No.4), "Sparrow in the Treetop" (1951-No.8), "My Truly, Truly Fair" (1951-No.2), "Belle Belle My Liberty Belle" (1951-No.9), "Pittsburgh Pennsylvania" (1952-No.4), "Singing the Blues" (1956-No.1), "Rock-a-Billy" (1957-No.10) and "Heartaches by the Number" (1959-No.1).
- His other film credits include "Red Garters" (1954) and "The Wild Westerners" (1962).
- Guy's other TV credits include "Thriller" (1961), "The Ann Sothern Show" (1960-61) 2 episodes, "Perry Mason" (1961), "Magic Mansion" (1966) and "Your Cheatin' Heart" (1990) 3 episodes.

- **Sam Buffington** was born on October 12, 1931 in Swansea, Massachusetts.
- He made his TV debut in an episode ("Jimmy") of "The Gray Ghost" in 1957.
- Following this, he made his movie debut in the film "Invasion of the Saucer Men" (1957).
- In 1961 (the series was actually filmed from 1959), he was cast as "John Richards" in the TV series "Whispering Smith". He appeared in 17 episodes.
- Sam's other film credits include "The Rawhide Trail" (1958), "Damn Citizen" (1958), "The Light in the Forest" (1958), "They Came to Cordura" (1959) and "Blue Denim" (1959) uncredited.
- His other TV credits include "Highway Patrol" (1957), "Cheyenne" (1957), "Tales of Wells Fargo" (1957), "Tombstone Territory" (1958), "Sugarfoot" (1958), "Perry Mason" (1959), "Black Saddle" (1959), "The Rough Riders" (1959), "Maverick" (1957-59) 5 episodes, "Laramie" (1960) and "Bourbon Street Beat" (1960).

"The Wide Country"

Years : 1962 - 1963

Episodes : 28 (1 season)

Cast :-

Earl Holliman (b. 1928) - Played Mitch Guthrie

Andrew Prine (b. 1936) - Played Andy Guthrie

Synopsis :-
Stories about life on the rodeo circuit.

Trivia & Tidbits :-

"The Show"

- **"The Wide Country"** premiered on NBC on September 20, 1962 and last aired on April 25, 1963.
- The show ran for one season with a total of 28 black and white episodes.
- The pilot for the series titled "Second Chance" aired on March 13, 1962 on the anthology series "Alcoa Premiere" on ABC.
- The series was produced by Gemini Productions.

- Filming took place at the Revue Studios, Hollywood, California.
- The theme music was composed by John Williams.
- The show aired opposite "The Adventures of Ozzie & Harriet" and "The Donna Reed Show" on ABC and "Mr Ed" and "Perry Mason" on CBS.

"The Stars"

- **Earl Holliman** was born on September 11, 1928 in Delhi, Louisiana.
- His biological father died before he was born and his biological mother gave him up for adoption at birth.
- Henry Holliman, an oil-field worker, and his wife adopted Earl and everything was fine until Henry died in 1941.
- Earl's adopted mother remarried but he didn't like his step-father very much.
- During the Second World War, Earl lied about his age and joined the U.S. Navy. When the Navy found out about his real age, he was discharged.
- Earl returned home, completed high school and then re-enlisted in the U.S. Navy. (this time legally).
- Whilst in the Navy he was stationed at Norfolk and appeared in several Norfolk Navy Theatre productions.

- After his stint in the Navy he studied at the Pasadena Playhouse and also graduated from the University of California, Los Angeles.
- Earl started his film career with three uncredited roles - "Scared Stiff" (1953), "The Girls of Pleasure Island" (1953) and "Destination Gobi" (1953).
- He followed these up with credited roles in popular films such as "East of Sumatra" (1953), "Broken Lance" (1954), "The Bridges of Toko-Ri" (1954), "Forbidden Planet" (1956), "Giant" (1956), "The Rainmaker" (1956), "Gunfight at the O.K. Corral" (1957), "Don't Go Near the Water" (1957) and "Last Train to Gun Hill" (1959).
- In 1959, he was cast as "Sundance" in the TV series "Hotel de Paree". He appeared in 32 episodes from 1959 to 1960.
- In 1962, he was cast as "Mitch Guthrie" in the TV series "The Wide Country". He appeared in 28 episodes from 1962 to 1963.
- Then in 1974, he was cast as "Sgt. Bill Crowley" in the TV series "Police Woman". He appeared in 91 episodes from 1974 to 1978.
- In 1992, he was cast as "Darden Towe" in the short-lived TV series "Delta". He appeared in 17 episodes from 1992 to 1993.
- In 1997, he was cast as "Frank Dominus" in the TV series "Night Man". He appeared in 24 episodes from 1997 to 1999.
- His last acting appearance, to date, was in the film "The Perfect Tenant" in 2000.

- In 1956, Earl won a Golden Globe Award for "Best Supporting Actor - Motion Picture" for his performance in the film "The Rainmaker".
- Earl was also nominated for a Golden Globe Award in 1992 for "Best Performance by an Actor in a Supporting Role in a Television Series". The TV series was "Delta".
- During his service time in the Navy, he spent a lot of his spare time at the Hollywood Canteen, talking to the stars who dropped by to support the servicemen and women.
- He has a Star on the Hollywood Walk of Fame for his contribution to the television industry.
- Earl operated the Fiesta Dinner Theatre for many years in San Antonio, Texas.
- He played the main character in the very first "Twilight Zone" episode to be telecast, "Where is Everybody" (1959).
- Earl's other film credits include "Summer and Smoke" (1961), "The Sons of Katie Elder" (1965), "The Power" (1968), "The Biscuit Eater" (1972), "Cry Panic" (1974)(TV), "The Solitary Man" (1979)(TV), "Gunsmoke: Return to Dodge" (1987)(TV), "Night Man" (1997)(TV) and "Bad City Blues" (1999).
- His other TV credits include "Bus Stop" (1962), "Bonanza" (1965), "The Virginian" (1965), "Custer" (1967), "Cannon" (1971), "Gunsmoke" (1973), "The F.B.I." (1966-73) 4 episodes, "The Thorn Birds" (1983), "Hotel" (1986) and "Chicken Soup for the Soul" (2000).

- **Andrew Prine** was born Andrew Lewis Prine on February 14, 1936 in Jennings, Florida.
- He graduated from Andrew Jackson High School in Miami, Florida.
- Andrew made his TV debut in an episode ("Little Charlie Don't Want a Saddle") of "The United States Steel Hour" in 1957.
- In 1959, he made his Broadway debut in the production of Thomas Wolfe's "Look Homeward, Angel".
- In 1962, he was cast as "Andy Guthrie" in the TV series "Wide Country". He appeared in 28 episodes from 1962 to 1963.
- In 1965, he had a recurring role on the TV series "Dr. Kildare". He played "Dr. Roger Helvick" in 5 episodes.
- Then in 1966, he was cast as "Timothy Pride" in the TV series "The Road West". He appeared in 29 episodes from 1966 to 1967.
- In 1978, he played "Don Costello" in the short-lived TV series "W.E.B.". He appeared in 5 episodes.
- In 1994, he played the recurring character "Wayne Donnelly" in the TV series "Weird Science". He appeared in 11 episodes from 1994 to 1998.
- His last acting appearance, to date, was in the film "Beyond the Farthest Star" in 2013.
- Andrew has been married five times (including three times to Brenda Scott). His first brief marriage was to Sharon Farrell in 1962. He then had three marriages to Brenda Scott - 1965-66, 1968-69 and 1973-78. He is

presently married to Heather Lowe (since 1986).

- He has appeared onstage in several productions including "Long Day's Journey into Night", "The Caine Mutiny" and "A Distant Bell".
- Andrew was questioned as a suspect in the November, 1963 murder of actress Karyn Kupcinet. The murder has never been solved.
- His other film credits include "Kiss Her Goodbye" (1959), "The Miracle Worker" (1962), "Texas Across the River" (1966), "Bandolero!" (1968), "Chisum" (1970), "One Little Indian" (1973), "Grizzly" (1976), "Abe Lincoln: Freedom Fighter" (1978), "Chill Factor" (1989), "Gettysburg" (1993), "Hell to Pay" (2005) and "The Lords of Salem" (2012).
- Andrew's other TV credits include "Tombstone Territory" (1960), "Have Gun - Will Travel" (1960-61) 2 episodes, "The Defenders" (1962), "Gunsmoke" (1962-63) 3 episodes, "Profiles in Courage" (1964), "The Fugitive" (1964-65) 2 episodes, "The Virginian" (1965-69) 5 episodes, "Insight" (1965-70) 4 episodes, "Disneyland" (1972), "Baretta" (1975-76) 2 episodes, "Flying High" (1979), "Matt Houston" (1984), "Dallas" (1989), "Murder, She Wrote" (1984-91) 4 episodes, "Married with Children" (1994), "Melrose Place" (1996), "C.S.I." (2005) and "Saving Grace" (2008).

"The Wild Wild West"

Years : 1965 - 1969

Episodes : 104 (4 seasons)

Cast :-

Robert Conrad (b. 1929) - Played James T. West

Ross Martin (b. 1920 d. 1981) - Played Artemus Gordon

Synopsis :-
Two Secret Service agents ride the rails in the Old West.

Trivia & Tidbits :-

"The Show"

- **"The Wild Wild West"** premiered on CBS on September 17, 1965 and last aired on April 4, 1969.
- The show ran for four seasons with a total of 104 episodes.
- The series was created by Michael Garrison and produced by Bruce Lansbury Productions, Columbia Broadcasting System (CBS) and Michael Garrison Productions.

- Season 1 was filmed in black and white whilst Seasons 2-4 were in color.
- The main theme music was written by Richard Markowitz (he previously composed the theme music for the TV series "The Rebel").
- The name of the train they travelled on was "The Wanderer".
- Agnes Moorehead won an Emmy Award for her role as "Emma Valentine" in the episode titled "The Night of the Vicious Valentine".
- The title of each episode begins with "The Night" (except for Ep.5, S1 which was just titled "Night of the Casual Killer").

"In Memoriam"

- **Ross Martin** died of a heart attack on July 3, 1981 (61) in Ramona, California.

"The Stars"

- **Robert Conrad** was born Conrad Robert Norton Falk on March 1, 1935 in Chicago, Illinois.
- He is the son of Leonard Henry Falkowski and Alice Jacqueline Hartman. Robert's father was of Polish ancestry.
- Robert graduated from Northwestern University, Illinois. Following this he worked as a milk truck driver and also sung in a Chicago cabaret.
- After being signed by Warner Bros. he made several recordings including the minor

Billboard hit song "Bye Bye Baby" (reached No.113).

- In 1958, he made his first credited appearance in the film "Thundering Jets".
- He then guest starred on several TV shows including "Bat Masterson" (1959), "Maverick" (1959), "Highway Patrol" (1959), "Lawman" (1959), "Colt .45" (1959), "Sea Hunt" (1959) 2 episodes and "Lock Up" (1959).
- In 1959, he was cast as "Tom Lopaka" in the popular TV series "Hawaiian Eye". He appeared in 116 episodes from 1959 to 1963.
- In 1965, he was cast as "James T. West" in the TV series "The Wild Wild West". He appeared in 194 episodes from 1965 to 1969.
- Then in 1971, he was cast as "Deputy D.A. Paul Ryan" in the short-lived TV series "The D.A.". He appeared in 14 episodes from 1971 to 1972.
- Following this, he appeared in another TV series "Assignment Vienna" (1972). He played the character "Jake Webster" in 8 episodes.
- In 1976, he was cast as "Maj. Greg 'Pappy' Boyington" in the TV series "Baa Baa Black Sheep". He appeared in 36 episodes from 1976 to 1978.
- In 1978, he played the character "Pasquinel" in the TV mini-series "James A. Michener's Centennial". He appeared in 12 episodes from 1978 to 1979.
- Another TV series he appeared in was "A Man Called Sloane" (1979). He played "Thomas Remington Sloane III" in 12 episodes.

- In 1995, he was cast in another short-lived TV series "High Sierra Search and Rescue". He played "Griffin 'Tooter' Campbell" in 6 episodes.
- Robert has been married twice - Joan Kenlay (1952-77) and LaVelda Fann (1977-2010). He has five children with Ms. Kenlay and three children with Ms. Fann.
- After "Hawaiian Eye" was cancelled, Robert toured with a nightclub act in Australia and Mexico.
- Robert was a Deputy Sheriff for approx. eight years in the Bear Lake area.
- He was inducted into the Hollywood Stuntmen's Hall of Fame for his work on "The Wild Wild West".
- Robert's idols are Humphrey Bogart, James Cagney and John Garfield.
- He was nominated for a Golden Globe in 1978 for his work in "Baa Baa Black Sheep".
- Robert's other film credits include "Palm Springs Weekend" (1963), "Young Dillinger" (1965), "D.A. : Murder One" (1969)(TV), "D.A. : Conspiracy to Kill" (1971)(TV), "Adventures of Nick Carter" (1972)(TV), "The Wild Wild West Revisited" (1979)(TV), "More Wild Wild West" (1980)(TV), "Coach of the Year" (1980)(TV), "Will : The Autobiography of G. Gordon Liddy" (1982)(TV), "Search and Rescue" (1994)(TV), "Jingle All the Way" (1996) and "Dead Above Ground" (2002).
- His other TV credits include "The Gallant Men" (1962), "77 Sunset Strip" (1959-62) 3 episodes as "Tom Lopaka", "Temple Houston"

(1964), "Mannix" (1969), "Mission : Impossible" (1968-72) 4 episodes, "High Mountain Rangers" (1987-88) 2 episodes, "Jesse Hawkes" (1989) 2 episodes and "Nash Bridges" (2000).

- **Ross Martin** was born Martin Rosenblatt on March 22, 1920 in Grodek, Poland.
- He graduated from City College of New York and later earned a law degree from George Washington University.
- As a young boy he learned the violin and played with the junior symphony orchestra.
- During the late 1930's and early 1940's he was one half of vaudeville comedy duo "Ross & West".
- In 1953, he made his Broadway debut in the musical "Hazel Flagg".
- Ross made his TV debut in an episode of "Inside Detective" in 1951.
- He made his movie debut in the TV film "The King's Author" in 1952.
- From 1950-54 he had a small part in the TV series "Treasury Men in Action".
- In 1959, he was cast as "Andamo" in the TV series "Mr. Lucky". He appeared in 34 episodes from 1959 to 1960.
- In 1965, he was cast as "Artemus Gordon" in the TV series "The Wild Wild West". He appeared in 104 episodes from 1965 to 1969.
- In 1978, he was one of the actors to provide his voice in the animated TV series "Jana of the Jungle".

- Again in 1978, Ross appeared in 5 episodes of "Hawaii Five-O" as the character "Tony Alika".
- His last appearance, before he passed away, was in the TV movie "I Married Wyatt Earp". The film was actually made in 1981 but not broadcast until 1983.
- Ross was married twice - Muriel Weiss (1941-65) and Olavee Grindrod (1967-81). He had one daughter with Ms. Weiss and adopted Ms. Grindrod's two children (boy and girl) when they married.
- He could speak seven languages - English, Polish, Yiddish, Russian, French, Spanish and Italian.
- In 1976, he returned to the stage as "John Adams" in a touring production of the musical "1776".
- In 1963, Ross was nominated for a Golden Globe "Best Supporting Actor" Award for his role in the film "Experiment in Terror" (1962).
- Also in 1969, he was nominated for a Primetime Emmy for his role in "The Wild Wild West".
- Ross' other film credits include "Conquest of Space" (1955), "Underwater Warrior" (1958), "Geronimo" (1962), "The Great Race" (1965), "The Sheriff" (1971)(TV), "The Return of Charlie Chan" (1973)(TV), "Skyway to Death" (1974)(TV), "The Wild Wild West Revisited" (1979)(TV) and "More Wild Wild West" (1980)(TV).
- His other TV credits include "Lights Out" (1949-51) 4 episodes, "Sheriff of Cochise" (1956), "Modern Romances" (1955-57) 6

episodes, "Gunsmoke" (1958) 2 episodes, "Peter Gunn" (1959), "Laramie" (1960), "Zorro" (1961), "Wagon Train" (1963), "Columbo" (1971), "Ironside" (1973), "Sanford and Son" (1976), "Baretta" (1977), "Disneyland" (1961-79) 4 episodes, "The Love Boat" (1980) and "Mork & Mindy" (1981).

"Wrangler"

Years : 1960

Episodes : 6 (1 season)

Cast :-

Jason Evers (b. 1922 d. 2005) - Played Pitcairn

Eli Boraks (b. 1927) - Played Cowboy Sidekick

Synopsis :-
Pitcairn travels through the West helping people.

Trivia & Tidbits :-

"The Show"

- **"Wrangler"** premiered on NBC on August 4, 1960 and last aired on September 15, 1960.
- The show ran for one season with a total of 6 black and white episodes.
- It was a summer replacement for "The Ford Show Starring Tennessee Ernie Ford", but did not enjoy high ratings.
- Wrangler was filmed at the Iverson Ranch in Chatsworth, California.

- The show was nominated for a Primetime Emmy in 1961 for Outstanding Achievement in Electronic Camerawork.

"In Memoriam"

- **Jason Evers** died of heart failure on March 13, 2005 (83) in Los Angeles, California.

"The Stars"

- **Jason Evers** was born Herbert Evers on January 2, 1922 in New York City, New York.
- He quit school and joined the Army during the Second World War.
- After the war he decided to try acting after being inspired by John Wayne and Humphrey Bogart.
- His first credited TV appearance was in an episode ("Anything But Love") of "NBC Presents" in 1949.
- In 1955, he had a bit part as "The Lieutenant" in "The Phil Silvers Show". He appeared in 8 episodes from 1955 to 1958.
- In 1960, he was cast as "Pitcairn" in the TV series "Wrangler". He appeared in 6 episodes.
- In 1963, he was cast as "Professor Joseph Howe" in the TV series "Channing". He appeared in 26 episodes from 1963 to 1964.
- Then in 1967, he was cast as "James 'Jim' Sonnett" in the TV series "The Guns of Will Sonnett". He appeared in 13 episodes from 1967 to 1969.

- His last acting appearance was in the film "Basket Case 2" in 1990.
- Jason was married twice (Shirley Ballard and Diana James) but did not have any children.
- His other film credits include "Pretty Boy Floyd" (1960), "The Brain That Wouldn't Die" (1962), "A Man Called Gannon" (1968), "The Green Berets" (1968), "Escape from the Planet of the Apes" (1971), "Claws" (1977) and "Golden Gate" (1981)(TV).
- Jason's other TV credits include "Hong Kong" (1961), "The Rebel" (1961), "Cheyenne" (1960-61) 2 episodes, "Laramie" (1961-62) 3 episodes, "Perry Mason" (1961-64) 3 episodes, "Gunsmoke" (1962-64) 3 episodes, "The Virginian" (1966), "Bonanza" (1961-67) 2 episodes, "The Big Valley" (1965-68) 2 episodes, "The Mod Squad" (1969), "The Doris Day Show" (1970), "Mission : Impossible" (1969-73) 4 episodes, "Mannix" (1968-73) 5 episodes, "Cannon" (1971-74) 4 episodes, "Happy Days" (1978) 3 episodes, "T.J. Hooker" (1984) and "Matlock" (1987).

- **Eli Boraks** was born on June 30, 1927 in The Bronx, New York.
- In the mid 1950's he studied acting in New York and appeared in many off Broadway plays.
- In 1960, he made his film debut in "The Pusher", starring Robert Lansing.
- Also in 1960, he was cast as "Cowboy Sidekick" in the TV series "Wrangler". He appeared in 6 episodes.

- Following this he appeared in many uncredited bit parts including the films "The Greatest Story Ever Told" (1965), "The Best Man" (1999), "It's a Mad, Mad, Mad, Mad World" (1963) and "Mr. Saturday Night" (1992).

"Young Dan'l Boone"

Years : 1977

Episodes : 4 (aired) 8 (filmed) (1 season)

Cast :-

Rick Moses (b. 1952) - Played Daniel Boone

Devon Ericson (b. 1952) - Played Rebecca Bryan

Ji-Tu Cumbuka (b. 1942) - Played Hawk

John Joseph Thomas (b. 1964) - Played Peter Dawes

Eloy Casados (b. 1949) - Played Tsiskwa

Synopsis :-
The exploits of Daniel Boone when he was young.

Trivia & Tidbits :-

"The Show"

- **"Young Dan'l Boone"** premiered on CBS on September 12, 1977 and last aired on October 3, 1977.

- The show ran for one season with a total of 4 episodes (aired). There were actually 8 episodes filmed.

"The Stars"

- **Rick Moses** was born Richard Cantrell Moses II on September 5, 1952 in Washington, District of Columbia.
- He is the son of Marian (nee McCargo) and Richard Moses.
- Rick grew up in Pasadena, California and showed an interest in swimming, movies and music.
- He attended boarding school at the Chadwick School in Palos Verdes, California.
- At school he participated in swimming and formed several bands with his friends.
- Rick began his acting career at age fifteen in an Equity production of "The Fifth Season" at the Santa Monica Playhouse.
- He made his TV acting debut in an episode ("The Laughing Majority") of "Room 222" in 1970.
- This was followed by an appearance in "Mission: Impossible" (1971) and "The F.B.I." (1971).
- In 1977, he was cast as "Daniel Boone" in the TV series "Young Dan'l Boone". He appeared in 4 episodes before the show was canceled.
- Following this, he appeared in the movie "Avalanche" (1978) and then had the part of

"Jefferson Smith Hutchins" in the day-time soap "General Hospital" from 1979 to 1980.

- His last acting appearance, to date, was in the TV movie "Pleasures" in 1986.
- Rick has been married twice – Johnnie Morris and Colette Benhaim. He has two sons with Ms. Morris and four sons with Ms. Benhaim.
- He studied martial arts from an early age, eventually earning his black-belt. He also worked as an instructor for Bob Ozman at his Van Nuys studio.
- Rick's passion has always been music and he has appeared in many clubs all over America.
- In 1978, 20th Century Fox record division released his LP album "Face the Music".
- In 1985, he had a hit song in Hamburg, Germany with "If I Could Just Fall in Love". It was released by Teldec Records.
- Rick released a CD in 2005 entitled "Evil and Dangerous Men".

- **Devon Ericson** was born on December 21, 1952 in Salt Lake City, Utah.
- She made her TV acting debut in an episode ("The First Day") of "The Waltons" in 1974.
- Following this, she made several more guest appearances on TV shows including "The Texas Wheelers" (1974), "The Manhunter" (1974), "ABC Afterschool Specials" (1975), "Eleanor and Franklin" (1976) 2 episodes, "Starsky and Hutch" (1976) 2 episodes, "Police Story" (1977), "The Streets of San Francisco" (1975-

77) 2 episodes and "Westside Medical "
(1977).

- In 1977, she was cast as "Rebecca Bryan" in the TV series "Young Dan'l Boone". She appeared in the 4 episodes that were aired.
- In 1979, she played "Fran Lonigan" in the TV mini-series "Studs Lonigan". She appeared in 3 episodes.
- Then in 1980, she played "Betsy O'Neal" in the TV mini-series "The Chisholms". She appeared in 5 episodes.
- Devon made her film debut in the TV movie "The Dream Makers" in 1975.
- Her last acting appearance, to date, was in an episode ("Till Death Do Us Part") of "Shades of LA" in 1991.
- Devon's other film credits include "The Runaway Barge" (1975)(TV), "Return to Macon County" (1975), "The Busters" (1978)(TV), "Baby Comes Home" (1980)(TV), "Night of the Comet" (1984) and "Houston: The Legend of Texas" (1986)(TV).
- Her other TV credits include "Three's Company" (1978), "Lou Grant" (1979), "Barnaby Jones" (1975-79) 4 episodes, "Family" (1979-80) 2 episodes, "Quincy M.E." (1981) "Magnum, P.I." (1981), "Hotel" (1984), "The Love Boat" (1984), "Airwolf" (1985) 2 episodes, "St. Elsewhere" (1986) and "Square One Television" (1987) 4 episodes.

- **Ji-Tu Cumbuka** was born on March 4, 1942 in Montgomery County, Alabama.
- He is the son of a Baptist minister.
- Ji-Tu left home and moved to New York where he had several difficult years. He then joined the United States Army.
- In the army he played football and ran track. He made All-Army in both sports.
- After he left the army he attended Texas Southern University.
- Ji-Tu then moved to California to pursue his acting dreams.
- Following this, he moved back to New York and continued his education at Columbia College, earning a bachelor of arts in theatre and a master's degree in cinematography.
- He made his acting debut in the film "Uptight" in 1968.
- Also in 1968, he made his TV debut in an episode ("To Catch a Roaring Lion") of "It Takes a Thief".
- Several more film roles followed including "Change of Habit" (1969), "Brian's Song" (1971)(TV), "Blacula" (1972), "Trader Horn" (1973), "Lost in the Stars" (1974), "The Dream Makers" (1975)(TV), "Mandingo" (1975) and "Fun with Dick and Jane" (1977).
- During this time, he also appeared in many TV shows including "Daniel Boone" (1970), "Night

Gallery" (1972), "Chase" (1974), "Toma" (1974), "Ironside" (1974) 2 episodes, "Kojak" (1973-74) 2 episodes, "Kung Fu" (1975), "Lucas Tanner" (1975), "The Streets of San Francisco" (1975), "The Rockford Files" (1976), "Roots" (1977)(mini-series) 3 episodes and "Sanford and Son" (1977).

- In 1977, he was cast as "Hawk" in the TV series "Young Dan'l Boone". He appeared in all 4 episodes that aired.
- In 1979, he was cast as "Torque" in the TV series "A Man Called Sloane". He appeared in 12 episodes.
- His last acting appearance, to date, was in an episode ("Viva Las Vegas") of "CSI: Crime Scene Investigation" in 2004.
- Ji-Tu is the author of several screenplays.
- His other film credits include "Angela" (1977), "Mandrake" (1979)(TV), "Flesh & Blood" (1979)(TV), "Bachelor Party" (1984), "Brewster's Millions" (1985), "Out of Bounds" (1986), "Outrageous Fortune" (1987), "Moving" (1988), "Harlem Nights" (1989) and "Midnight Edition" (1993).
- Ji-Tu's other TV credits include "Falcon Crest" (1984), "Riptide" (1985), "The Dukes of Hazzard" (1985), "The A-Team" (1985) 2 episodes, "MacGyver" (1986), "St. Elsewhere" (1987), "Hunter" (1986-87) 2 episodes, "Crime Story" (1988), "Matlock" (1989) 2

episodes, "Knots Landing" (1990) 2 episodes, "In the Heat of the Night" (1994) and "Walker, Texas Ranger" (1994).

- **John Joseph Thomas** was born on November 9, 1964 in Arcadia, California.
- He made his TV debut by being cast as "Peter Dawes" in the TV series "Young Dan'l Boone". He appeared in the 4 episodes that were aired.
- In 1978, he appeared in 3 episodes of "Little House on the Prairie" as the character "Spence".
- In 1979, he played "Adam Clapper" in the TV mini-series "The Seekers".
- From 1978 to 1980, he supplied the voice of "Tommy" in the anthology series "ABC Weekend Specials".
- His last acting appearance, to date, was in the film "Blood Beach" in 1980.
- Following his acting career, he became a sound editor and has worked on films such as "Little Man Tate" (1991), "Loaded Weapon 1" (1993), "Last Action Hero" (1993), "Moll Flanders" (1996), "Me, Myself & Irene" (2000), "Scary Movie 2" (2001), "Good Night, and Good Luck" (2005), "I Am Legend" (2007), "The Town" (2010), "At Middleton" (2013) and "The Hunger Games: Mockingjay – Part 2" (2015).

- **Eloy Phil Casados** was born on September 28, 1949 in Long Beach, California.
- He won "Best High School Actor" for the role of "Creon" in the play "Antigone" in the Colorado Springs city competition.
- Eloy studied art at the University of New Mexico.
- Before moving to Hollywood, he worked in front of and behind the camera on dozens of Hollywood movies shot in New Mexico.
- Eloy made his movie debut in the film "Pieces of Dreams" in 1970.
- He made his TV debut in the two-part episode ("Mustang") of "Walt Disney's Wonderful World of Color" in 1973.
- In 1977, he was cast as "Tsiskwa" in the TV series "Young Dan'l Boone". He appeared in the 4 episodes that were aired.
- From 1996 to 1998, he had a recurring role as "Sheriff Sam Coyote" in the TV series "Walker, Texas Ranger". He appeared in 4 episodes.
- From 1997 to 1999, he supplied the voice of "Enrique" in the TV series "King of the Hill".
- His last acting appearance, to date, was in the film "Primal Rage: The Legend of Oh-Mah" in 2016.
- Eloy is married and has three daughters.
- His other film credits include "Panic in Echo Park" (1977)(TV), "Ishi: The Last of His Tribe" (1978)(TV), "Freedom" (1981)(TV), "Cloak &

Dagger" (1984), "The Best of Times" (1986), "Down and Out in Beverly Hills" (1986), "The Alamo: Thirteen Days to Glory" (1987)(TV), "Blaze" (1989), "White Men Can't Jump" (1992), "Cobb" (1994), "Play It to the Bone" (1999), "Hollywood Homicide" (2003), "Frost/Nixon" (2008), "Bridesmaids" (2011) and "McFarland, USA" (2015).

- Eloy's other TV credits include "Family" (1976) 2 episodes, "Police Story" (1976-78) 2 episodes, "Knight Rider" (1986), "Hill Street Blues" (1985-86) 2 episodes, "Equal Justice" (1990), "Northern Exposure" (1991), "Human Target" (1992) 2 episodes, "Murphy Brown" (1996), "Nash Bridges" (1997), "NYPD Blue" (2001), "CSI: Crime Scene Investigation" (2007), "Up All Night" (2011), "Shameless" (2014) 3 episodes and "Castle" (2014).

"Young Maverick"

Years : 1979

Episodes : 8 (1 season)

Cast :-

Charles Frank (b. 1947) - Played Ben Maverick

Susan Blanchard (b. 1948) - Played Nell McGarrahan

John Dehner (b. 1915 d. 1992) - Played Marshal Edge Troy

Synopsis :-
The story of Ben Maverick, son of Beau Maverick (Brett's cousin).

Trivia & Tidbits :-

"The Show"

- **"Young Maverick"** premiered on CBS on November 28, 1979 and last aired on January 30, 1980.
- The show ran for one season with a total of 8 episodes.

" In Memoriam"

- **John Dehner** died of emphysema and diabetes on February 4, 1992 (76) in Santa Barbara, California.

"The Stars"

- **Charles R. Frank** was born on April 17, 1947 in Olympia, Washington.
- He graduated from Middlebury College, Vermont in 1969.
- In 1970, he made his TV debut as "Dr. Jeff Martin" in the TV series "All My Children". He would appear in the series, off and on, until 1995.
- Charles made his uncredited movie debut in the film "The Anderson Tapes" in 1971.
- Several more TV guest appearances followed including "Three for the Road" (1975), Police Woman" (1976), "Barney Miller" (1976), "Laverne & Shirley" (1976) 2 episodes, "Hawaii Five-O" (1977), "Barnaby Jones" (1976-77) 2 episodes, "MASH" (1976-78) 2 episodes and "The Chisholms" (1979) 3 episodes.
- In 1979, he was cast as "Ben Maverick" in the TV series "Young Maverick". He appeared in 8 episodes from 1979 to 1980.
- In 1982, he was cast as "Stanley Beek" in the TV series "Filthy Rich". He appeared in 15 episodes from 1982 to 1983.
- Then in 1983, he was cast as "Lt. Cmdr. Jack Warren" in the TV series "Emerald Point

N.A.S.". He appeared in 22 episodes from 1983 to 1984.

- In 1988, he appeared as "Senator Peter Ryder" in 7 episodes of the TV series "Falcon Crest".
- His last appearance, to date, was in an episode ("Dead and Gone, Honey") of "Spy Game" in 1997.
- Charles has been married to fellow actor, Susan Blanchard, since 1977. They have one daughter.
- His other film credits include "The Silence" (1975)(TV), "Panache" (1976)(TV), "Riding High" (1977)(TV), "Annie Flynn" (1978)(TV), "The One and Only" (1978), "The New Maverick" (1978)(TV), "The Right Stuff" (1983), "Christmas Dove" (1986)(TV), "LBJ : The Early Years" (1987)(TV), "Changes" (1991)(TV) and "Devil's Food" (1996)(TV).
- Charles' other TV credits include "The Love Boat" (1977-85) 4 episodes, "Hotel" (1984-86) 2 episodes, "L.A. Law" (1988) 3 episodes, "Paradise" (1989) 2 episodes, "Dallas" (1991), "Midnight Caller" (1991) 2 episodes, "Life Goes On" (1990-92) 4 episodes, "Reasonable Doubts" (1992-93) 4 episodes and "Walker" (1995).

- **Susan Blanchard** was born on December 11, 1948 in the U.S.A.
- In 1971, she made her TV debut as "Mary Kinnecott Martin" in the TV series "All My Children". She would appear in the series until 1975.

- Susan made her TV movie debut in the film "How to Succeed in Business Without Really Trying" in 1975.
- In 1976, she was cast as "Tina Kelly" in the short-lived series "Mr. T and Tina". The series lasted 6 episodes.
- In 1979, she was cast as "Nell McGarrahan" in the TV series "Young Maverick". She appeared in 8 episodes from 1979 to 1980.
- Her last acting appearance, to date, was in the TV short "Adventures in Babysitting" in 1989.
- Susan has been married to fellow actor, Charles Frank, since 1977. They have one daughter.
- She was the spokesperson for "No Nonsense" (a brand of pantyhose) from 1978 to 1982.
- Susan's other film credits include "The President's Mistress" (1978)(TV), "The New Maverick" (1978)(TV), "She's in the Army Now" (1981)(TV), "The Prince of Darkness" (1987), "Russkies" (1987) and "They Live" (1988).
- Her other TV credits include "Beacon Hill" (1975), "MASH" (1977), "Police Woman" (1975-78) 2 episodes, "Magnum, P.I." (1983), "The Love Boat" (1978-84) 2 episodes, "Falcon Crest" (1984) 2 episodes and "Webster" (1988).

- **John Dehner** was born John Forkum on November 23, 1915 in Staten Island, New York.
- After leaving school he worked as an animator for Walt Disney Studios.

- He then became a radio disc jockey and eventually played "Paladin" in the radio series "Have Gun – Will Travel".
- John made his uncredited acting debut in the film "The Reluctant Dragon" in 1941.
- Several more uncredited roles followed including "Tarzan's Desert Mystery" (1943), "Thirty Seconds Over Tokyo" (1944), "Hollywood Canteen" (1944), "Christmas in Connecticut" (1945) and "State Fair" (1945).
- In 1946, he made his first credited appearance in the film "The Undercover Woman".
- He then appeared in many films including "The Last Crooked Mile" (1946), "Out California Way" (1946), "Blonde Savage" (1947), "Riders of the Pony Express" (1949), "Bandits of El Dorado" (1949), "Dynamite Pass" (1950), "Al Jennings of Oklahoma" (1951), "The Texas Rangers" (1951) and "Ten Tall Men" (1951).
- John made his TV debut in an episode ("The Dead General Story") of "Dangerous Assignment" in 1952.
- Following this, he guest starred in many TV shows including "Fireside Theatre" (1952-53) 2 episodes, "The Adventures of Kit Carson" (1953), "Stories of the Century" (1954), "Four Star Playhouse" (1954-55) 3 episodes, "The Millionaire" (1955), "Adventures of the Falcon" (1956), "Frontier" (1956) 2 episodes, "Cheyenne" (1957), "Have Gun – Will Travel"

(1957), "Zorro" (1958), "Cimarron City" (1958), "Wagon Train" (1957-58) 2 episodes, "The Restless Gun" (1958-59) 3 episodes, "Wanted : Dead or Alive" (1959) 3 episodes, "The Texan" (1960), "Black Saddle" (1959-60) 2 episodes, "The Alaskans" (1959-60) 4 episodes, "Zane Grey Theatre" (1957-60) 4 episodes, "The Westerner" (1960) 3 episodes, "The Rifleman" (1959-61) 4 episodes, "Stagecoach West" (1961) 3 episodes and "Tales of Wells Fargo" (1959-61) 4 episodes.

- In 1960, he was cast as "Duke Williams" in the TV series "The Roaring 20's". He appeared in 27 episodes from 1960 to 1962.
- In 1964, he was cast as "Commodore Cecil Wyntoon" in the TV series "The Bailey's of Balboa". He appeared in 26 episodes from 1964 to 1965.
- Then in 1971, he was cast as "Cyril Bennett" in the TV series "The Doris Day Show". He appeared in 48 episodes from 1971 to 1973.
- In 1973, he was cast as "Dr. Charles Cleveland Claver" in the TV series "Temperatures Rising". He appeared in13 episodes from 1973 to 1974.
- In 1977, he appeared in another short-lived TV series. He played "Barrett Fears" in 9 episodes of "Big Hawaii".

- Then in 1979, he was cast as "Marshal Edge Troy" in the TV series "Young Maverick". He appeared in 8 episodes from 1979 to 1980.
- In 1980, he played "Lt. Joseph Broggi" in the TV series "Enos". He appeared in 18 episodes from 1980 to 1981.
- John appeared in another TV series in 1983. He played "Hadden Marshall" in 8 episodes of "Bare Essence".
- His last acting appearance was in the 1988 TV mini-series "War and Remembrance". He played the character "Adm. Ernest King".
- John was married twice – Roma Leonore Meyers (1941-1970) and Evelyn Severance (1973-1992). He had two children with Ms. Meyers.
- Between 1941 and 1988, John appeared in over 260 films and television programs.
- His other film credits include "Scaramouche" (1952), "Southwest Passage" (1954), "Carousel" (1956), "The Iron Sheriff" (1957), "The Left Handed Gun" (1958), "The Chapman Report" (1962), "Youngblood Hawke" (1964), "Tiger by the Tail" (1970), "Dirty Dingus Magee" (1970), "Support Your Local Gunfighter" (1971), "The Missiles of October" (1974)(TV), "Guardian of the Wilderness" (1976), "The Boys from Brazil"(1978), "Bare Essence" (1982)(TV) and "The Right Stuff" (1983).

- John's other TV credits include "Lawman" (1962), "Hawaiian Eye" (1962), "Maverick" (1958-62) 5 episodes, "Bronco" (1959-62) 3 episodes, "77 Sunset Strip" (1960-63) 5 episodes, "Bonanza" (1960-64) 2 episodes, "Rawhide" (1960-64) 5 episodes, "Branded" (1965), "The Wild Wild West" (1965-66) 2 episodes, "The Road West" (1966), "Gunsmoke" (1955-68) 12 episodes, "Judd for the Defense" (1967-69) 3 episodes, "The Virginian" (1963-69) 7 episodes, "Petrocelli" (1975), "Barbary Coast" (1975), "How the West Was Won" (1976-77) 4 episodes, "Disneyland" (1955-86) 7 episodes and "The Colbys" (1986-87) 4 episodes.

Acknowledgments :-

1. Halliwell's Television Companion by Leslie Halliwell with Philip Pueser (1982)

2. Cult TV - The Essential Critical Guide by Jon E. Lewis & Penny Stempel (1993)

3. Whatever became of - Ninth Series by Richard Lamparski (1985)

4. Whatever became of - Eleventh Series by Richard Lamparski (1989)

5. A Pictorial History of Television by Irving Settel and William Laas (1969)

6. The Disney Studio Story by Richard Holliss and Brian Sibley (1988)

7. IMDb at http://www.imdb.com/

8. Wikipedia - The Free Encyclopedia at http://www.en.wikipedia.org/

9. TV Guide at http://www.tvguide.com/

The End

Made in the USA
Middletown, DE
16 June 2021